NEED FOR CHANGE

Towards the New International Economic Order

Other Titles of Interest

BALASSA, B.
Policy Reform in Developing Countries

COLE, S.
Global Models and the International Economic Order

FOXLEY, A. *et al.*
Redistributive Effects of Government Programmes: The Chilean Case

FRANKO, L. G. and SEIBER, M. J.
Developing Country Debt

MENON, B. P.
Global Dialogue

SAUVANT, K.
Changing Priorities on the International Agenda

SKOROV, G. E.
Science, Technology and Economic Growth in the Developing Countries

UNECE
Factors of Growth and Investment Policies

A Related Journal

WORLD DEVELOPMENT*
The multidisciplinary international journal devoted to the study and promotion of world development

Chairman of the Editorial Board:
Dr. Paul Streeten, The World Bank, Washington

*Free specimen copy available on request

NEED FOR CHANGE

Towards the New International Economic Order

by

GAMANI COREA

SECRETARY-GENERAL OF THE UNITED NATIONS
CONFERENCE ON TRADE AND DEVELOPMENT (UNCTAD)

A SELECTION FROM MAJOR SPEECHES
AND REPORTS WITH AN INTRODUCTION

PERGAMON PRESS

OXFORD · NEW YORK · TORONTO · SYDNEY · PARIS · FRANKFURT

U.K.	Pergamon Press Ltd., Headington Hill Hall, Oxford OX3 0BW, England
U.S.A.	Pergamon Press Inc., Maxwell House, Fairview Park, Elmsford, New York 10523, U.S.A.
CANADA	Pergamon of Canada, Suite 104, 150 Consumers Road, Willowdale, Ontario M2J 1P9, Canada
AUSTRALIA	Pergamon Press (Aust.) Pty. Ltd., P.O. Box 544, Potts Point, N.S.W. 2011, Australia
FRANCE	Pergamon Press SARL, 24 rue des Ecoles, 75240 Paris, Cedex 05, France
FEDERAL REPUBLIC OF GERMANY	Pergamon Press GmbH, 6242 Kronberg/Taunus, Hammerweg 6, Federal Republic of Germany

First edition 1980

British Library Cataloguing in Publication Data
Corea, Gamani
Need for change.
1. International economic relations
I. Title
382.1'08   HF1411   80-40800

ISBN 0-08-026095-0

Printed and bound in Great Britain by
A. Wheaton & Co. Ltd, Exeter

THIS VOLUME IS DEDICATED TO THE MEMORY
OF MY MOTHER, MRS FREDA COREA

CONTENTS

INTRODUCTION

The present volume represents a selection of speeches given during the period 1974 to early 1980. One of the problems in making a selection is that invariably the speeches given on any occasion tend to cover the broad platform of UNCTAD taken as a whole. Although this results in an element of repetition in respect of the issues dealt with, there are over time significant shifts in emphasis which reflect the way these issues have evolved in the context of multilateral negotiation and discussion. It is for this reason that the speeches, though not arranged strictly in chronological order, are grouped in terms of broad phases or periods in the development of UNCTAD's work. In most cases they are transcripts from oral presentations and are reproduced more or less as delivered.

Since the text of this volume was presented for publication, there have been several positive developments in UNCTAD which need to be brought to the attention of readers. Much of the discussion in this volume refers to certain major negotiating processes undertaken by UNCTAD and to the experience gained in the course of these negotiations. It is certainly satisfying to be able to say now that some of these negotiations have been brought to a successful conclusion. In October 1979, as mentioned in the *Overview* to follow, a new international commodity agreement on rubber was successfully negotiated. In March 1980 it proved possible to adopt by consensus an agreement on multilaterally agreed equitable rules and principles to govern restrictive business practices. This was one of the issues included in the Programme of Action for a New International Economic Order and the final result was achieved through a negotiating process which covered a period of over three years.

In May 1980 the negotiation on international multimodal transport was successfully completed with the adoption, once again by consensus, of the text of a Convention on the subject. Whilst the rules and principles on restrictive business practices will take the form of guidelines to be embodied in a resolution of the General Assembly that will provide for an intergovernmental mechanism within UNCTAD to monitor progress, the Convention on multimodal transport will be a legally binding instrument which will come into force following ratification by governments. The negotiations on the Convention spanned a period of nearly seven years. Like the rules and principles it would apply to all member states of UNCTAD. Taken together with the earlier Convention on liner conferences, also a legally binding instrument, the new Convention represents an important contribution made through UNCTAD in the area of the regulation of international shipping.

In June 1980 the negotiations on the Common Fund for Commodities were also brought to a successful conclusion with the unanimous adoption of the Articles of

Agreement of the Fund. This result undoubtedly represents a major success for UNCTAD. The Common Fund was perhaps the most prominent issue under negotiation in the context of the north–south dialogue. The Fund has been described as the key element of the Integrated Programme for Commodities and the final agreement on its establishment represents a decisive breakthrough in the implementation of the Programme. The Common Fund will be a new international institution in the area of world commodity trade. It aims at a universal membership and incorporates a voting pattern with a much stronger voice for the developing countries than in any other international financial institution. Through its so-called "First Account", the Fund will be capable of financing up to two-thirds of the stocking needs of commodities in the Integrated Programme once these commodities become the subject of international agreements—stocking needs whose costs have been estimated at an eventual total of about $6 billion. The "Second Account" of the Fund represents a further significant innovation since this will constitute a source of finance for programmes in the field of commodity development other than schemes for price stabilization through buffer stocks. Through its responsibility for coordination and co-financing, the Common Fund could help mobilize resources from other financial institutions as well and thereby provide a commodity focus to international assistance and lending. The Common Fund will come into being after ratification by at least 90 member states. As an interim measure a preparatory commission of 28 members will be set up in UNCTAD to prepare the ground for the decisions of the first governing council. The commission will be serviced by a special unit to be set up by the Secretariat of UNCTAD. The Common Fund itself once established will take the form of a specialised agency of the United Nations. These recent successes are also significant from another point of view. They confirm the negotiating capacity of the United Nations system and particularly of UNCTAD. In many of my speeches I had stressed the need to make UNCTAD a forum not only for discussion and debate but also for negotiations. The agreements on restrictive business practices, multimodal transport, and the Common Fund were not resolutions or declarations: they constitute complex instruments of a legal or at least quasi-legal character. The difficulties of conducting negotiations of this kind within UNCTAD with its membership of over 160 countries were, of course, evident at all stages, but the fact that they were successfully concluded shows that the negotiating process is capable of producing results and that the group system in UNCTAD where the developing countries, the OECD countries, the Socialist countries of Eastern Europe, and China speak through selected spokesmen is a valuable instrument, particularly in the absence of formalized procedures for negotiation in small groups. It is to be hoped that the results already achieved in UNCTAD will serve as an encouragement for future efforts, not only within UNCTAD but within the United Nations system in general, particularly in the context of the forthcoming round of global negotiations that the General Assembly intends to launch in 1981. With the completion of some of the major negotiations entrusted to it, UNCTAD has now to turn to the future. Inevitably UNCTAD's preoccupations in the time ahead will be determined by the unfolding crisis in the international economy. It is now becoming clearer than ever that there needs to be a concentration of attention on basic issues. UNCTAD must of course continue with its efforts to build further on the integrated programme for commodities and to turn its attention not only to the stabilization of markets, but also to other aspects of the commodity problem, particularly the participation of developing countries in the marketing, distribution and processing of their products. But it has to do much more than this.

UNCTAD has to intensify its efforts in these areas that are of critical importance to the restructuring of the international economic framework. It has to address itself to the question of the international framework of trade, for it is by no means clear that the trading framework as presently constituted, severely undermined as it has been by events, will be able to accommodate future processes of change, particularly the growing industrialization of the countries of the Third World. Parallel to this is the need for a monetary system that will facilitate the smooth working of the international economy and is more responsive to the requirements of developing countries. Whilst the specifics of monetary reform would be the subject of negotiations in the International Monetary Fund, UNCTAD can make a valuable contribution to progress in this area because it is uniquely constituted to deal with the problems of interdependence of issues in the areas of money, trade and development. The third critical area is that of economic cooperation amongst the developing countries themselves, for it is becoming increasingly evident that these countries must look to themselves in finding at least part of the solution to the problems that face them in the current context. Each of these issues was prominent on the agenda for UNCTAD V and in each case the decisions of the conference to provide a basis for actions that could lead to major negotiating processes in the future.

The crisis facing developing countries has at no time been more critical than at present. In the face of unparalleled payment deficits most developing countries are already being constrained to curtail their development efforts and to slow down the rates of growth of their economies. At the same time, the developed countries see their own problems of recession and inflation as restraining their capacity for international cooperation in development. Yet this very crisis makes imperative the need for action. There is a particular need for actions which would help developing countries meet their immediate needs for external finance. But the problems can hardly be overcome by short-term measures and emergency actions alone. They are a reflection of a deeper malaise in the international economy, a reflection of the changes that have undermined the systems of trade, money, and finance that were established at an earlier time. These issues cannot therefore be evaded, however difficult might be their ultimate solution.

In August this year the General Assembly of the United Nations meets to adopt an international development strategy for the 1980s, and to launch a round of global negotiations which would encompass in an interrelated way the problems of energy, raw materials and food, money and finance, trade and development. Whatever the precise agenda and the organizational structure of the global negotiations, it is evident that this is a process to which UNCTAD, with its experience and expertise, must make a maximum contribution. Success in these negotiations could pave the way to the changes so urgently needed in the interests of the international community as a whole.

The Brandt Commission has strongly underlined not only the urgency of the current crisis and the need for basic changes in international economic relations, but also the strong interest that the developed countries themselves have in such solutions. Clearly an awareness of such convergence of interest is one of the essential ingredients for success in future negotiating processes. But together with this there is a need also for an increasing mobilization on the part of the developing countries themselves of their capacity to act, to cooperate with each other, and to exercise a strong and effective presence at the negotiating table itself.

A number of persons have helped with the preparation of this volume, but I must specially acknowledge the assistance I received from Susan P Joekes, a Research Officer at the Institute of Development Studies at the University of Sussex, England, in the selection and grouping of the material and in preparing the index; and also from Ramses Nassif, for his constant encouragement and assistance, Susan Trachsel and Alan Lamond in the many other tasks involved in making this volume ready for publication.

August 1980   GAMANI COREA

PART I

An Overview [1]

I

I see the six years during which I have been associated with UNCTAD as falling into three broad phases. The first phase was that from the commencement of my tenure of office in 1974 until the Nairobi Conference. That was a period in which we were trying to give a new image to UNCTAD, to obtain recognition for UNCTAD not only as a forum in which one would debate major issues in the field of development and international relations, but also as one in which specific results could be obtained through a process of negotiation.

The second phase, which started after the Nairobi Conference (May–June 1976) and extended up to the Manila Conference and which in a sense has yet to be completed, was one in which UNCTAD succeeded in gaining recognition as a negotiating forum and in which the negotiating process itself began to unfold. In that period there were a great many experiences, a great many lessons, and I thought that it would be useful to try to reflect on these and to draw some broad conclusions which could be relevant for the future. The third phase, which began before the second phase had really ended, was the one which led up to the Manila Conference in May 1979, in which UNCTAD was seeking to go beyond the mandates it had obtained in Nairobi and to extend the negotiating process to a wider range of issues which are relevant to the concept of a New International Economic Order.

This third phase is, of course, in an initial stage, and I believe that it will dominate the scene in UNCTAD for the next two or three years. But I would like in the course of this discussion to comment on each of these three phases in order to provide the background against which the specific activities of UNCTAD were being fashioned.

Since its very inception, UNCTAD has been at the centre of what I call "the great debate on development and the international framework for development". It was in UNCTAD that the North/South dialogue, as it is being called now, may be said to have actually begun in 1964 with the first session of the Conference. It was at that session that the Group of 77 developing countries came to be established. That session was the occasion on which the developing countries expressed their own unity by forming themselves into a single coherent group, backing a single platform and giving expression to their demands in a united way. At the time when UNCTAD was first established there was, of course, a broad thrust which was in itself novel in that period. Under the leadership of Raúl Prebisch, UNCTAD sought to draw attention to the inadequacy of the existing international framework as a support for the development process in the Third World.

---

[1]An adaptation of three talks given at the Marga Institute, Colombo, in December 1979/80.

1

One of the main themes of Dr. Prebisch during that period was the need for what he called "a new trade policy for development", because he felt that the existing framework of international trade, dominated primarily by market forces, guided by structures which had been established in the interests of the leading industrial powers, was not particularly conducive to the needs of the developing countries.

The first report of Dr. Prebisch to UNCTAD was entitled in fact, *Towards a New Trade Policy for Development*. In the period since then, I think that UNCTAD came to be seen as being primarily a forum in which the developing countries gave expression to their problems and their demands, a forum in which they sought to apply a degree of pressure on the international community to gain recognition of these problems and of the need for solutions. But it was not seen particularly as a forum in which hard decisions were taken, a forum in which concrete business was done, a forum in which specific agreements and arrangements were brought about through a negotiating process. It is true that there have been exceptions. UNCTAD in the early days was responsible, through a negotiating process, for establishing what has now come to be known as the Generalized System of Preferences. This has been recognized as one of the major achievements of UNCTAD in the earlier period. UNCTAD was also responsible for initiating negotiations on a number of commodities and for the establishment of at least one new commodity agreement—that for cocoa. UNCTAD in its early period also initiated negotiations seeking to establish a convention on a code of conduct for liner conferences, which is now on the way to being ratified. It served, too, as the forum for the negotiation of the Charter on the Economic Rights and Duties of States. But apart from those exceptions, the main image of UNCTAD was primarily one of a debating house.

Even in that period, the reactions of the various component parts of the international community to UNCTAD differed. The developed countries—I do not think that this would be an exaggeration—initially viewed UNCTAD with a degree of hostility, with a degree of suspicion, because they felt that UNCTAD was becoming a means of applying pressure on the industrialized countries in order to make a never-ending series of concessions to the developing countries. Later this attitude of suspicion, and even hostility, underwent a change, and I think that in the later part of the first phase of UNCTAD's existence there was a certain degree of tolerance of UNCTAD as an organization which functioned as a safety valve in which the developing countries could give expression to their problems and preoccupations, but still not as a forum in which concrete agreements were to be negotiated. The developed countries saw this latter function as being primarily the responsibility of other organs in the international set-up, particularly the monetary organs established at Bretton Woods— the International Monetary Fund and the World Bank—and the trade organization embodied in GATT. In the view of the developed countries, therefore, UNCTAD was primarily looked upon as perhaps a necessary nuisance, but not as an organization to be taken seriously as a negotiating instrument.

The developing countries, of course, from the very beginning had a very close attachment, a loyalty, to UNCTAD. They felt that it was in a way the only organization in which they were able to win a certain degree of recognition of their problems, the only organization in which there was a secretariat with a decidedly development orientation, a secretariat which, if it was biased, was biased in the direction of being sensitive to the problems of the Third World and to the problems of development. But even the developing countries did not regard UNCTAD as a strong and potent instrument for bringing about specific changes in the prevailing international system. They felt that, whilst UNCTAD served to create a climate of opinion, they had to go elsewhere in order to arrive at particular agreements and arrangements, particularly the Bretton Woods institutions and GATT.

This situation was, of course, in a sense harmful to UNCTAD from a long-term point of view. There was beginning to emerge a discernible tendency for the developing countries themselves to question the efficacy of UNCTAD as a place in which serious business could be done. There was a feeling among the developing countries that, whilst UNCTAD might serve a broad purpose as a debating house, they should not look to it as an instrument in which they could actually gain acceptance of their demands. I remember very vividly the head of government of one of the leading developing countries telling me: "You know, we have a complaint to make against UNCTAD." I asked what that complaint was. He said, "Well, nothing happens in UNCTAD", to which I could reply only that UNCTAD was an intergovernmental organization and that the responsibility for the results was not with the organization but with the Member States of the organization. But I did feel at the time when I took office at UNCTAD that there was a need, if UNCTAD was to retain its credibility as an institution in the international arena, to transform its image somewhat into that of a forum whose purpose was not only debate and discussion but also the attainment of concrete results. I felt, of course, that UNCTAD should at no stage lose its image of being a generator of new ideas. That was a valuable function of UNCTAD which it needed to continue to perform in the new phase. But I felt that one needed to add a new dimension at the same time which would transform UNCTAD as a forum in which one merely passed broad resolutions and formulated goals and objectives into one in which more complex, more concrete, more specific agreements could be initiated, negotiated, and agreed upon.

At the time when I joined UNCTAD—it was the beginning of April 1974—by coincidence there took place the sixth special session of the General Assembly. In fact, one day after I had assumed office in Geneva I had to proceed to New York to attend that session of the General Assembly. The sixth special session had been convened at the request and on the initiative of the Government of Algeria and its President, Houari Boumedienne, as a response to the problems that were seen to have arisen out of the action of the oil-producing countries in late 1973 in quadrupling the price of oil. There was little doubt that that action had very far-reaching effects and appeared as a new element in the entire economic scene. The developed countries at the time, and particularly the Government of France, had proposed the convening by the United Nations of a session of the General Assembly specifically on the issue of energy. But the oil-producing countries, led by Algeria, which was at that time the Chairman of the Non-aligned Group, countered this move by asserting that the problem of energy could not be discussed in isolation because they felt that the session would then become an occasion on which pressures would be unilaterally placed on the oil-producing countries. If energy was to be discussed it should be discussed in a broader context together with a number of other crucial issues of concern to the developing countries.

So the sixth special session of the General Assembly turned out to be not a session devoted to the energy issue but to the broader subject of raw materials and development, the energy issue being part of the wider canvas. I believe that in many ways the session was a watershed in the evolution of the whole process of international economic relations and had enormous significance for the evolution of UNCTAD as an instrument of the international community in the arena of international economic relations. There were two main developments which provided the backdrop to the convening of the special session. I mentioned one of these—the action of the OPEC countries in respect of the price of oil. But there was another development, perhaps less dramatic but not less traumatic, which also contributed to the feeling of the need for basic reforms in the prevailing framework of international relations, and this was the breakdown taking place in the prevailing framework of international monetary relations and also in the framework of the world system of economic growth and international trade in the early seventies.

Many changes began to take place, which had the effect of undermining some of the pillars on which the entire structure of international economic relations, drawn up at the time of the Second World War, was predicated.

One was the abandonment of the convertibility of the dollar unilaterally by the United States in the early seventies. This was followed by the abandonment of the system of fixed exchange rates, which was one of the basic tenets of the monetary system established at Bretton Woods and incorporated into the Articles of Agreement of the International Monetary Fund. At the same time the developed countries were beginning to experience for the first time a process of mild recession accompanied by rising inflation, the beginnings of what has now come to be called "stagflation" becoming evident in the early seventies.

These developments were already at that time beginning to call into question the premises on which the international development strategy for the seventies, for the Second United Nations Development Decade, had been established. When the strategy for the Second Development Decade was formulated there was an implicit assumption that the processes of growth and expansion, which were experienced by the industrialized countries in the whole post-war period in the fifties and in the sixties, would continue unabated into the seventies; there was an implicit assumption that the developed countries would continue to grow at 5 or 6 per cent or more a year; that world trade and trade among the industrialized countries in particular would continue to expand at a rapid rate; and that the wheels of the world economy would continue to function smoothly as they had done before.

Consequently the main thrust of the strategy was to try to see how the developing countries might extract a share of these benefits through such processes as resource transfers by aid and other means. Aid targets which industrialized countries were supposed to adhere to were given a very prominent place in the strategy for the seventies. In other words, the strategy for the seventies did not question the prevailing framework. It assumed that this framework would continue to flourish and expand, and that the main need was to try to get a better benefit for the developing countries from it. But the events of the early seventies, to which I have referred, began to call into question the very basic premiss on which this strategy was predicated. Already, in 1974, when the sixth special session of the General Assembly convened, it was quite evident that the goals and targets set for the Second Development Decade were not likely to be achieved. Developing countries were showing signs of falling back in performance, aid targets were not being adhered to, and in many ways it was evident that this strategy was going off course and that a series of crises were beginning to develop which called for new approaches and new orientations.

At the same time as these developments were taking place, came the action of the OPEC countries in regard to the price of oil. I am sure you will recollect that at the time the OPEC countries decided to increase the price of oil to something like four times above the then prevailing level, there was, contrary to expectation, a broad sentiment of understanding, sympathy, and support on the part of the rest of the developing countries for this action of the oil producers. It was felt by the developing countries, although they themselves as importers of oil were liable to pay the higher prices, that for the first time a group of such countries was able to exhibit a capacity for action through the mobilization of their own strength.

The developed countries had shown an enormous reluctance to expand their aid to reach the 0.7 per cent target set by the General Assembly as the norm for official resource transfers. Aid flows at that time were less than $10 billion, and achieving the 0.7 per cent target would not have resulted in a massive transfer of resources from the developed to the developing countries. Nevertheless, there was a great reluctance on the part of the developed countries to implement even that modest goal. But then the OPEC countries, by one stroke of the pen as it were, succeeded in achieving financial transfers from the industrialized countries to the oil-producing countries of something like $60 or $70 billion. I think that this act had a very dramatic impact on the developing countries themselves, for they saw in it the beginnings of a process by which the countries of the Third World would be able to exert a degree of leverage in the international economic scene.

I can think of no parallel except the kind of situation which one reads about as having arisen at the time of the first Russo-Japanese war when the defeat of the Russian navy by the Japanese resulted in a surge of confidence throughout Asia and was one of the sparks which lit the subsequent nationalist revival in what was then a situation of very strong imperial control over the countries of Asia. This is, of course, a somewhat far-fetched parallel, but there was something akin to that in the way in which the developing countries reacted to the action of the oil-producing countries.

For that reason, and despite the efforts to stigmatize the action of the OPEC countries as being the main factor responsible for the convulsions in the world economic scene, the developing countries maintained their unity and refused to be separated from the oil-producing countries. One of the lessons of the sixth special session was that the action of the OPEC countries was seen to be accepted in a sense by the other developing countries, which at the same time maintained their common front with the OPEC countries as the Group of 77.

Against this background it was not surprising that the main themes of the sixth special session—which came to be incorporated in what has been called the Declaration and Programme of Action on the Establishment of a New International Economic Order—encompassed two basic strands, each of which reflected the developments to which I have referred. These two strands were, on the one hand, the insistence on what has now come to be called "structural change" as being a necessary ingredient in the evolution of international economic relations, and, on the other, the concept of "collective self-reliance".

These are the two threads which run through the whole concept of a New International Economic Order—one, the need to bring about basic fundamental changes in the existing mechanisms and relationships which govern international economic relations, and the other, the need for the developing countries to mobilize their own strengths through the exercise of their collective bargaining power in terms of what has been called collective self-reliance.

I think the New International Economic Order and its concepts differ fundamentally from the strategy for the seventies, which had been formulated and adopted only two or three years earlier, because of this new flavour, this emphasis on structural change. The old strategy was predicated on the continuance of the earlier framework. The New International Economic Order set it as an imperative that this framework needed to be changed, not only because the developing countries required these changes but because the international economy and the international community as a whole needed new responses to cope with the new challenges that were arising.

In this context it appeared that there was a new responsibility, indeed a new opportunity, a new challenge, for UNCTAD itself as an organization which was at the centre of the development issue. It was UNCTAD more than any other part of the international institutional system which dealt with the basic problems affecting the framework of international economic relations, and with the new emphasis on effecting basic changes in the prevailing framework it was natural for UNCTAD to respond to this challenge by seeking to translate some of these broader goals incorporated in the New International Economic Order into specific changes and specific arrangements through a negotiating process; and in that wider context it is also not surprising that, of all the key issues of relevance to a New International Economic Order, particular attention came to be paid to the problem of raw materials and commodities. After all, the sixth special session itself was a session dedicated to the subject of raw materials and development. It had been inspired by the action of a group of developing countries in respect of one particular raw material, and it was therefore natural that the developing countries as a whole saw in the need for structural change the need to give particular emphasis to restructuring the framework which had hitherto governed their trade and their international relations in the field of primary products and commodities.

In terms of the specific issues enumerated in the Declaration and Programme of Action for a New International Economic Order, one would find nothing that was specially new, except for the general flavour which I mentioned earlier. In essence, the specifics of the New International Economic Order were a reiteration of many of the issues which had earlier been on the UNCTAD agenda, a listing of these issues, and a call for progress in respect of them. But in respect of the commodity issue there was a new element because for the first time the Declaration and Programme of Action for a

New International Economic Order not only underlined the problem of commodities, but also emphasized the need for what was called "an integrated approach" to the commodity problem.

In my own address to the General Assembly on the occasion of the special session, I tried to highlight the importance of taking action in the arena of commodities because I felt that this was one of the weakest elements in the prevailing economies of developing countries. The commodity sector of the economies of developing countries was very much a heritage of their past history.

Although these countries had reached the phase of political independence, the phase of decolonization, many of the salient features of their economies continued to reflect the earlier historical pattern—a pattern of dependence, a pattern of dominance, a pattern of relationships reflecting an earlier period; and if one talked about a New International Economic Order, it seemed to me very logical that one ought to try to change with a high degree of priority the essential character of a major sector of the economies of developing countries, which was in a way the very embodiment of the earlier economic order.

For that reason, the commodity issue began to acquire a new, important, and growing significance. Of course, there was to a certain degree excessive expectation, in regard to the way in which the lesson of oil could be applied in dealing with other products. There was a vague sentiment, not made particularly articulate, that what the oil producers succeeded in doing in the case of petroleum could also be achieved by the other developing countries in respect of the other commodities of which they were the producers. There was not perhaps a sufficient recognition of the special conditions which governed the market for oil—the fact that it was an essential material, the fact that it was in short supply, the fact that it was already enjoying an upward price movement, the fact that the producers of oil were few in number and easily capable of being organized. But despite that, there was a feeling that the action of the oil-producing countries had some moral, had some lessons for other developing countries should they be able to organize themselves and acquire a degree of collective control over the supply of the commodities they produced.

The developed countries also were, for a different set of reasons, somewhat more receptive to the treatment of the commodity issue as a priority item in the international agenda. On the one hand, they themselves had always subscribed to the principle at least of stabilizing commodity markets; even the Havana Charter drawn up in the aftermath of the Second World War gave considerable emphasis to the need for the stabilization of commodity markets by means of international commodity agreements. But even more, the developed countries were mindful of the inflationary consequences of rising commodity prices for their own economies. They felt that by subscribing to an international regime which imparted stability to commodity markets they would succeed in avoiding some of the harsher consequences of the inflationary spiral in the prices of commodities which they had experienced from time to time and which fuelled the wage–price spiral in their own economies.

Accordingly, they were beginning to see in the commodity issue elements of self-interest which made it possible for them also to look somewhat more positively at initiatives in this field. Moreover at the back of the minds of the developed countries there was perhaps the fear that, the failure to treat the commodity question would be a further invitation, a further stimulus, for the developing countries to attempt to deal with the commodity problem *ex parte*, unilaterally, outside a framework of international co-operation and understanding, and that was a process that they did not wish to encourage, having experienced at first hand the results of what the oil producers were able to do.

For all these reasons, it happened to be opportune to bring the commodity question to the forefront of international attention as part of the process of giving concrete form to the goals and objectives of the New International Economic Order. UNCTAD did not have any specific mandate to launch new initiatives on the commodity issue. But given our earlier interest in commodities, given my own perception of the importance of the commodity problem to a developing country, with my own experience of Sri Lanka fresh in mind, it came somewhat naturally for me to lend my own support and devote my efforts to the treatment of the commodity issue as one of high priority.

Shortly after the sixth special session, therefore, the secretariat of UNCTAD presented to the Trade and Development Board a set of proposals which came to be described as the Integrated Programme for Commodities. I think it is true to say that this was the first effort, by an international organization to respond to the broad concepts of the New International Economic Order, by presenting some concrete proposals for action. The Integrated Programme for Commodities came to dominate, not only the activities of UNCTAD, but also the whole international negotiating process in the period between the sixth special session and the present time; and I mention here some of the elements which lay behind the concepts of the Integrated Programme for Commodities as it was presented to governments by the secretariat of UNCTAD.

There were two basic themes which in a sense were new, not in terms of concepts but in terms of emphasis. One of these themes was the insistence in the whole programme on the idea of an integrated approach to the commodity issue. In the earlier period we had had a great deal of experience of the effort to deal with individual commodities on a piecemeal, case-by-case basis.

At UNCTAD III at Santiago in 1972, UNCTAD was in fact given a mandate to initiate what were called "intensive consultations" on as many as fourteen commodities of interest to developing countries. These consultations were organized by UNCTAD in the period after Santiago, but without exception they failed to produce any results whatsoever. In virtually every case there was a long and protracted discussion of the complexities facing each individual commodity, and these complexities stood in the way of finding solutions. In the event, the process of intensive consultations on individual products petered out, resulting in a great deal of frustration, a great deal of dissatisfaction, a great deal of demoralization, and very little in the way of concrete results.

For that reason, with this experience behind us, we felt the need for a new approach which did not deny the importance of dealing with the specific problems of individual commodities on a case-by-case basis, but which would at the same time present the commodity issue as a single problem with many common facets, with many common interests, in which all the developing countries as major producers of commodities had a stake, irrespective of the particular products in which they were interested. We thought, therefore, that if a new effort was to succeed in dealing with the commodity problem, it was important to break away from the fragmented approach of the past and to treat the commodity problem within a common framework of principles, goals, objectives, and instruments in which a number of commodities were treated more or less as part of a single programme of action.

This is why the word "integrated" assumes such an important place in the title of the commodity programme presented. It was an effort to present the commodity problem as a single complex problem affecting the economies of developing countries whose dimensions went beyond the specific trading problems of particular commodities which had earlier dominated the individual consultations on particular products.

The second major theme underlying the commodity programme was the emphasis given to the need for international intervention in markets to prevent the periodic collapse of commodity prices in the free market. This had been very much a part of the experience of virtually all developing countries. They found that the development plans that they formulated were invariably disrupted by unforeseen cycles in the prices of the commodities on which they were dependent, leading to the need to dismantle their plans or in one way or another to recast them and to scale down their dimensions. We felt that there was a particular need to provide at least a safety net, a floor, for the downward movement in commodity prices so that developing countries could be given an assurance of at least minimum protection in respect of prices on which they could predicate their development plans.

It had been the experience in the past that in virtually all the commodity negotiations there was a failure to reach agreement on international action to support prices because of an unwillingness on the part of the consumer countries to provide financing for this act of international market intervention. The principle of establishing commodity stocks in periods of downward movements in commodity prices has for long been an element in economic theory regarding ways and means of dealing with commodity fluctuations. But whenever a specific commodity agreement came to be negotiated, it proved to be extremely difficult, virtually impossible, to incorporate provisions for stocking because of what seemed to be the intractable problem of providing finance. For that reason, even the few commodity agreements which were in existence either made no provision whatsoever for stocking and relied entirely on export restraints and export quotas as a means of regulating supplies, with all the burdens they impose on developing producer countries, or provided for minimal stocks to be virtually financed entirely by the producing countries themselves. The producing countries, not being in possession of vast financial resources, were not able for that reason to incorporate major stocking provisions in commodity agreements.

Consequently, from the very outset of our thinking on a new approach for dealing with the commodity problem there was emphasis on finding some solution to what appeared to be one of the major bottlenecks which had blocked the negotiation of adequate commodity arrangements in the earlier period. Of course, a number of options were available in respect of the way in which finance could be provided in order to support commodity markets in periods of falling prices. In the 1940s, Lord

Keynes himself had proposed, as one of a triad of institutions to regulate the post-war economy, the establishment of a commodity organization. He proposed, for short-term needs, an international financial institution which eventually came into being as the International Monetary Fund; he proposed a financing institution for long-term development and reconstruction, which came into being as the International Bank for Reconstruction and Development—the World Bank; but he also proposed a third instrument which was to be a commodity organization whose function would be to intervene in commodity markets in order to give stability to commodity prices.

This third proposal by Lord Keynes did not win acceptance, and in the series of institutional developments after the war no provision was made for any organization to deal with commodities. But given the reluctance, indeed a certain hostility, on the part of the major consuming countries—and on that of some of the developing countries also—to the idea of establishing an international organization with powers to intervene in commodity markets over which their ability to exercise an adequate degree of control was unsure, it seemed to us to be not feasible to return to a proposal on those lines, even though it would have represented quite a significant contribution to dealing with the commodity problems.

Hence, in the UNCTAD secretariat we did not feel that it would be practicable to propose the establishment of a comprehensive commodity organization with wide powers to deal directly in the commodities in which developing countries were interested. We felt, however, that there was a good prospect of gaining acceptance for the establishment of a financing institution which would not directly intervene in commodity markets, but which would provide finance to commodity bodies and other agencies which were authorized to deal in commodity markets and over which the main producers and consumers of commodities were able to exercise a degree of control. That is why the proposal for a Common Financing Fund was evolved for commodities whose objective was to mobilize adequate resources for commodity organizations, either those already in existence or those to be brought into being, whose function would be to intervene in commodity markets. The Secretariat felt that by establishing such a Common Fund we would be introducing a new institution into the world commodity economy which would serve not only as a source of finance in a passive sense, but also in a more active sense as a catalyst in furthering the establishment of commodity agreements. It was felt that if we succeeded in creating such an institution endowed with adequate resources, its very existence would help to break the deadlock impeding movement towards commodity agreements. We felt that the commodity stocking needs for the products of interest to developing countries were substantial. We estimated that if most of the commodities produced by developing countries and suited for stocking were to be made the subject of commodity agreements incorporating provisions for market intervention, something like a total of $6 billion would be needed in order to finance the stocking operations.

Accordingly, the secretariat prepared the outlines of a financial institution which would be capable of mobilizing and making available a sum of up to $6 billion to meet the needs of market intervention for the products of importance to developing countries. It was thought at that time that such a financial institution, being inherently profitable because it would be making monies available at times of low prices and moving them at times of high prices, could be conceived of and operated on commercial terms. It was also considered that such an organization would prove attractive as an alternative outlet for the investment of some of the surplus funds of developing countries, particularly the oil-producing countries, which were being lodged in the existing financial institutions of the West because of the need for security and the need for an adequate rate of return.

It was, felt that if the oil-producing countries were able to see not only the economic advantages but also the political advantages to them of underwriting an institution whose purpose was to give strength and support to the commodity economies of the developing countries, this in itself would reinforce the links between the oil-producing countries and the other developing countries.

This Common Fund, therefore, was conceived as a new kind of institution by which resources for stocking would be mobilized not only from the capital markets of the world, not only from the industrialized countries, but also from the developing countries, and particularly the oil-producing countries. The corollary to this concept was that we would also be creating a financial institution with a voting pattern and a pattern of decision-making different from anything known before.

As is well known, the existing financial institutions have a decision-making pattern in which voting is weighted in terms of subscriptions and in which subscriptions are very heavily oriented or geared towards the major industrialized countries. The developing countries have for that reason only a minor voice in the affairs of these institutions—the International Monetary Fund and the International Bank for Reconstruction and Development in particular. Thus it was felt that creating a Common Fund would be a new departure inasmuch as it would be creating for the first time a financial institution in which the developing countries would have, if not a preponderant voice, at least a decisive voice, depending on the extent to which the developing countries themselves would be able to subscribe to the capital and the resources of this new institution.

For that reason alone, in a political sense as much as in an economic and financial sense, the Common Fund concept was seen to be a reflection of the new strivings of the developing countries in search of a New International Economic Order.

Of course, one has to be mindful of the limitations inherent in the concept of the Integrated Programme for Commodities. I myself did not see the Integrated Programme for Commodities, even if implemented substantially, as being the resting point for commodity policy. I did not see it as providing the final and total answer to the commodity problem; I saw it rather as an important, even decisive, phase in the evolution of the commodity problem designed to give greater strength and stability to the developing countries as producers of major commodities; and it seems to me very important that this should be understood.

Nor did I see the emphasis on the commodity issue as being in any way an alternative to the need for the developing countries to pursue relentlessly the goal of economic transformation through industrialization. I felt, on the contrary, that the objective of imparting strength to the commodity sectors should be essentially to strengthen the base on which this process of transformation could proceed. After all, for most developing countries commodities continue to be the chief source of revenues.

If this base is weakened or continues to languish, the capacity of these countries to go ahead with the transformation process is to that extent weakened and diminished. The greater the success in strengthening the commodity base of the developing countries, in strengthening their revenues and strengthening their resources, the greater will be their capacity to proceed towards the goal of industrialization. Accordingly, I saw the thrust towards the Integrated Programme for Commodities as a means of helping the developing countries to achieve this goal.

I should also like to emphasize that, although the objectives of the Integrated Programme have been presented in terms of imparting strength and stability to commodity markets, it is not my view, and it is not in any way implicit in the concepts of the Integrated Programme, that the main problem of commodities is that of stabilizing prices as distinct from that of raising them.

I think we are all very mindful of the fact that developing countries face two problems in respect of their primary products. One is that their commodities are sensitive and vulnerable to crises and disruptive fluctuations with recurrent booms and slumps, and the other is that the long-term trend facing many of their commodities continues to be weak. In the long run the developing countries need not only to stabilize prices but also to organize their commodity production and marketing in such a way that the long-term price trend is upwards. But one could not, through the medium of an international commodity agreement, try to realize the goal of generating an upward movement in commodity prices whilst at the same time gaining universal consensus on the need for market regulation. The consuming countries are able to participate in commodity arrangements insofar as these are designed to bring stability to commodity markets because they themselves feel that they do not benefit by fluctuating and unstable commodity prices. But naturally they cannot as consumers be asked to be a willing party to a process whose objective was to raise the long-term trend of commodity prices.

It is, of course, a matter for debate as to whether commodity agreements, even though their objective is stabilization, have not in one way or another also contributed to strengthening the long-term trend of prices. Consumer countries have always suspected that commodity agreements act in that way through innumerable influences and in an intangible manner. That is part of the reason why they have been reluctant to enter into commodity agreements. They feel that by establishing a floor to prices these agreements—even though their objective has been to give stability to markets—create a market atmosphere which imparts strength to commodity prices and encourages an upward trend. It is perhaps not—though some may argue that it is—a coincidence that those four or five commodities which have been the subjects of commodity agreements in the past are also those commodities which are today exhibiting powerful upward trends. It is difficult, of course, to discern with any great accuracy the relationship between commodity agreements and the long-term market trend of prices. But I think it is right to say that there is in many quarters a suspicion that, if commodity agreements influence at all the market trend, it is in a positive upward direction.

There is another element of relevance to the case for commodity agreements as compared with other approaches. Sometimes it has been asked why it is necessary for developing countries to enter into international commodity agreements with consumers in order to strengthen their commodity markets when they might be able to realize their goals through unilateral action as producers acting on their own. This precisely is what the oil producers have done. Of course, if the developing producer countries do have the capacity, do have the organizational strength to act on their own, it is valid to ask: Do they indeed need international commodity agreements? My own view is perhaps that they would not in such a situation need agreements. But the fact is that the developing countries, as producers—in the case of a large number of products—have up to now not shown sufficient ability, to organize themselves for unilateral action or even to unite for the purpose of taking joint action with consumers. Our experience of commodity negotiations has been that producers, far from being able to "go it alone", have had great difficulties even in establishing a common position *vis-à-vis* consumers at these negotiations.

For that reason, I am inclined to view this whole thrust towards international commodity agreements as a necessary phase in the evolution of the commodity economies of developing countries. Perhaps in time, when developing countries are accustomed to coming together, they might be able to develop the instruments for action by themselves; but that time has not come yet. I feel the organization of commodity negotiations and preparatory exercises is serving the necessary purpose of bringing the producers of commodities together for the first time. Often it is in a commodity meeting convened by UNCTAD that the producers of the product in question are first able to meet together in order to face the consumers. Perhaps this process will evolve over time and a stage may be reached in the future in which developing countries will dispense with the idea of producer–consumer agreements. Certainly at this juncture I do not see that it is a realistic alternative for developing countries, except perhaps in the case of some products in scarce supply, particularly non-renewable resources, to follow the unilateral path.

One of the issues which arose in the debate on commodity questions at the time of the sixth special session was that of the indexation of commodity prices, and I have often been asked by developing countries why it is that the Integrated Programme for Commodities did not put the indexation issue very high up on its list of priorities. The developing countries demanded that the export prices of their products should be indexed to the prices of the manufactured products which they import, since the latter prices have been moving relentlessly upwards as a result of inflation. However, while indexation is a valid goal it cannot be implemented merely through the adoption of resolutions. The price of tea cannot be indexed by the adoption of a resolution in UNCTAD or elsewhere to the effect that the price of tea should be indexed. To do this it is necessary to control the market for tea, and to establish the mechanisms by which its price could be regulated. The oil producers are able to index—in fact they have been indirectly indexing—the price of petroleum because they are in control of the market for petroleum. But the producers of tea and cocoa and rubber do not yet control their markets, and until the instruments for regulating markets exist there is no way of implementing the objective of indexation. Once there is a commodity agreement, of course, it would be possible to include in its price provisions something akin to an indexation process; in fact in the Integrated Programme the international community recognized for the first time the need to revise the prices set in commodity agreements periodically in the light of developments, taking into account not only changes in costs of production and other factors but also changes in the prices of imported goods.

These have been some of the main conceptual elements of the Integrated Programme for Commodities. Once it had been presented in the UNCTAD forum, the Programme did, of course, encounter a great deal of resistance. The developed countries were uncertain as to its implications. They felt that in some way or other the Integrated Programme would be the thin end of a wedge, that it would launch a process whose ultimate goals would be difficult to predict, and for that reason they were hesitant from the very commencement, not so much about the principle of commodity stabilization as about the idea of an integrated approach to commodities and about the idea of a Common Fund.

For example, in 1975, when the General Assembly of the United Nations held a seventh special session which adopted a resolution on development and international economic co-operation, the developing countries failed to obtain even the mention in it of a Common Fund as a basic element of an Integrated Programme for Commodities. After protracted negotiations the developed countries agreed to some wording which referred to the need for "adequate financing facilities", but not to the specific need for a single institution called a Common Fund. It was from that point onwards after the seventh special session, that in UNCTAD and elsewhere we put the emphasis specifically on the Common Fund; we described it in fact as the "integrating element of the Integrated Programme" and as a very necessary basis for the whole approach of the Programme. And it was in the period between the seventh special session and UNCTAD IV in Nairobi that the Common Fund concept gradually came to be given greater emphasis by the Group of 77 itself.

A decisive element in that process before the Nairobi Conference was the meeting of the developing countries in Manila as the Group of 77 when President Marcos, on behalf of the Government of the Philippines, announced a contribution of $50 million to the Common Fund. This is clearly a milestone in the history of the Common Fund because up to that point the Common Fund was just a vague hope; it was an aspiration; there was no confidence even on the part of the developing countries that it would become a reality. But by the decision of the Government of the Philippines to provide hard financial resources in the no small amount of $50 million, the concept of the Common Fund assumed a certain concreteness.

From then onwards it was no longer a hazy wish but a fairly concrete proposal with a serious promise of finance. But notwithstanding that, the Nairobi Conference proved to be a very difficult event from the point of view of gaining acceptance of the Common Fund. This is not the occasion to narrate the history of UNCTAD IV in Nairobi, but it is worth noting that the Conference virtually came to a breakdown on the last days, and it was only at the closing meetings of the Conference, as a result of a great deal of pressure by the developing countries, that the developed countries agreed to initiate a negotiating process in which the possibility of establishing a Common Fund could be considered. Even this agreement they made subject to very strong reservations, making clear that it was in no way a commitment even in principle to the concept of the Common Fund. But what happened essentially at Nairobi was that the broad concept of an Integrated Programme came to be accepted and its realization became the subject of a negotiating process.

In the period since Nairobi UNCTAD has been involved not so much in gaining acceptance of broad principles and broad concepts as in trying to implement these concepts through a very hard-headed negotiating process. I do not want to give the impression that UNCTAD IV and even the period prior to it was dominated exclusively by the commodity issue. Although commodities loomed large at Nairobi, there were other issues on the agenda and on some of these negotiating processes came to be launched. But for various reasons it was on commodities that the focus fell more sharply.

This is not the place on which to evaluate the results of the Nairobi Conference. When that Conference concluded, there was as usual a reaction of disappointment on the part of the developing countries. They had wanted a firmer endorsement, in fact an immediate implementation of the Common Fund and of the Integrated Programme and action on all the other items on the agenda, and their spokesmen tended for tactical as much as for substantive reasons to describe the Nairobi Conference as a failure. But I think it is part of the negotiating experience of bodies like UNCTAD that this kind of reaction must be expected. I once said that it is usual for us to see all our failures described as being total and all our successes as being partial. This experience happens because if a negotiation does not end in agreement, it is pronounced a failure, whereas if an agreement is reached it is as a result of a compromise and is therefore depicted as being only a partial success. I said immediately after the Conference that the real test would be whether, as a result of the negotiating processes started in Nairobi, we would eventually have an Integrated Programme with a series of commodity agreements and would see the Common Fund established; and whether we would make progress on all the other items which were to become the subject of negotiations after the Nairobi Conference. These negotiating processes greatly absorbed the energies of the organization in the post-Nairobi period.

II

I want now to dwell on the experience of the negotiating process since Nairobi, and particularly to consider the lessons to be drawn from the vast concentration of UNCTAD as an organization on that endeavour in the years since then.

As we have seen, the Nairobi Conference may in retrospect have said to have served a major purpose. It was a launching pad for an extensive negotiating process quite unparalleled in the history of UNCTAD. The Conference did not take any definitive decisions which could be described as solutions to particular problems, but it did initiate this process of negotiation. The negotiating exercises launched at Nairobi were, of course, primarily concerned with the area of commodities; but the focus was not exclusively on the commodity issue. Perhaps less noticed at the time were other decisions taken at Nairobi for starting negotiating processes and new actions in other areas as well.

It was at Nairobi that UNCTAD was given a mandate to initiate negotiations leading to the adoption of a code of conduct on the transfer of technology to the adoption of equitable rules and principles governing restrictive business practices; it was the same Conference which provided action programmes in the area of least-developed countries, in the area of trade between countries with different economic and social systems, in the area of economic co-operation among developing countries, and also in the area of the external debt problems of developing countries. Taken together, all these decisions of Nairobi ushered in a new phase in the activities of UNCTAD.

I need hardly emphasize that there is a vast difference between an intergovernmental meeting or conference whose end result is merely a resolution—a broad exhortation couched sometimes in the form of a statement of principles, sometimes in the form of a declaration, even a programme of action—and a negotiating process the final product of which is not a resolution or a declaration or a programme of action, but a complex instrument, sometimes of a legally binding character. It may be a commodity agreement which after ratification has legal force; it may be the setting up of a new institution such as the Common Fund with a constitution and articles of agreement of its own; it may be a code of conduct which, even if it is not legally binding, has the quality of an instrument expressed in legal terms; it may be a set of rules and principles to regulate restrictive business practices, also expressed in an elaborate, comprehensive, well-articulated, and precise manner.

Because of this difference in the end result, therefore a negotiating process differs very much from a purely deliberating process.

Since the Nairobi Conference, as a result of the broad mandates given to UNCTAD, we have witnessed a veritable transformation in the workload of UNCTAD, even in the character of UNCTAD. There has been an impressive escalation in the schedule of activities, in the number of meetings, convened under the auspices of UNCTAD, not only month after month but week after week, day after day. When I first joined UNCTAD we had something like fourty-four weeks of meetings on the calendar of the organization. In 1978 and 1979 we have had to cope with something like 140–160 weeks of meetings in UNCTAD. In fact in 1979, up to the beginning of December, UNCTAD had to service with full conference facilities—interpretation, documentation and so on—over 3000 half days of meetings of intergovernmental bodies. And as you can imagine, this new phenomenon, unprecedented as it was, had a far-reaching impact on the workstyle of the secretariat and on the activities of the representatives of governments themselves, whether stationed in Geneva or coming to Geneva for these meetings.

Whilst we have been engaged in this process ever since Nairobi, we have still to see the culmination of the negotiating exercises which followed the Nairobi Conference. We have doubtless made a great deal of progress on each and every one of the negotiating issues entrusted to UNCTAD. There has been progress in regard to the establishment of a Common Fund. We have had a consensus on the basic character of the Fund; but we have still to see the Fund established because we have still to complete the process of getting agreement on the Articles of Agreement.

Similarly, we have made immense progress on the negotiations on a code of conduct for the transfer of technology. The great bulk of the code has now been accepted but there are still certain outstanding issues. This is also true of our efforts to intro-duce principles and guidelines to regulate restrictive business practices.[1] We were able to complete one commodity agreement starting from scratch after Nairobi, and that is the agreement on rubber; for the first time a new commodity not previously covered by an international understanding in the post-war period was made the subject of a consensus. But in other areas in respect of other products, progress has been faltering. We have even failed to accomplish the renegotiation of some agreements which had earlier been in existence. This is true of cocoa; it is also true of wheat.

But despite the progress that has been made, the tempo of such progress has been undoubtedly slow, and this had led to a feeling of disappointment, even of frustration, on the part of governments, particularly governments of the developing countries. Time and time again spokesmen for the developing countries have complained of the paucity of results, the inability to bring issues to a conclusion, and this complaint has been reflected in the media, which have tended to highlight the failures, the negative aspects, and perhaps to give too little recognition to the complexities of the process and to the need for patience in regard to the attainment of final goals. But despite the analyses that one can present of the factors that have retarded progress, the fact is that there is a deep sentiment of disappointment, disillusionment and frustration on the part of the developing countries, and this became manifest at the Manila Conference in a chorus of complaint about the paucity of progress, and particularly about the lack of political will, as they described it, on the part of developed countries to respond to the agenda of the international dialogue on development issues.

While it is understandable that there should be this expression of disappointment and impatience, I think at the same time it is important to put these issues in perspec-tive and not to allow this disappointment and impatience to lead to a sense of defeatism, which would result in the abandonment of the quest for results. Although it is useful politically and tactically for the developing countries to complain, and to complain loudly, they must not allow themselves to become convinced of the futility of the efforts to reorder international economic relations, and they must not undermine the efficacy and the credibility of the institutions and the forums in which these efforts are being undertaken.

Whilst developing countries give expression to their discontent, they should at the same time be cautious in not allowing this expression to be interpreted as an opting out of the negotiating process itself and out of the institutions which are the instru-ments for such a negotiating process. My personal view is that all the mandates given to UNCTAD at Nairobi will be successfully acomplished in time and that we have come close to the point of reaching final results. I believe that eventually we shall have a Common Fund; I believe that we shall have a code of conduct on the transfer of technology; that we shall have more commodity agreements; that we shall have an understanding on the rules and principles regarding restrictive business practices; and I believe that in time we shall also succeed in discharging another mandate which was

---

[1] In April 1980 agreement was reached in UNCATD on a multilaterally accepted equitable rules and principles for the regulation of restricting business practices.

given to us which relates to the establishment of a convention in respect of multi-modal transport.

Accordingly, I am positive about the prospect for eventual success, though fully aware of the hurdles that still remain to be overcome and the difficulties in the way, and of the fact that it might take some time before final success is achieved. And I would like to impress on the developing countries the need for a feeling of confidence in this regard because there is a tendency for their discontent to lead to impatience and also for the results of a negotiating process, which inevitably involves adjustment and compromise, to give rise to a certain disenchantment with the end result itself. The final outcome of a multilateral negotiation is bound to fall short of the initial demands presented by the developing countries in their pristine form, sometimes as a starting point, sometimes for tactical reasons; one has to expect that final results are not going to measure up in full to the initial goals, expectations and proposals presented by the developing countries.

But whilst there is this prospect of ultimate success, a great deal needs to be done from now onwards, not only to ensure that the negotiations already commenced may be brought to a satisfactory conclusion, but also to ensure that the even more important negotiations that lie ahead will be tackled successfully. For this reason there are a number of changes which the various players or actors in the process of multilateral negotiations must make if this process is to gain in efficacy and effectiveness in the period to come.

Let us take a look at the main actors in this multilateral negotiating process; first of all, the Group of 77. There is a prime need for the Group of 77 to transform itself from being a pressure group, as it has been up to now, into an effective negotiating team. In the early phase of the consideration of multilateral issues it was adequate for the Group to act as a pressure group, but in the present phase its members have to be effective as participants in a complex negotiating exercise. For this, the requirements are very different. It is easy for the Group of 77 to establish their unity in pursuit of broad goals and objectives; it is easy for them to unite in order to ask for better prices for commodities, for higher levels of aid, for an easing of the debt burden, and so on. But it is less easy for the Group of 77 to sustain this unity when it comes to implementing these goals, when it comes to agreeing on mechanisms or modalities by which these objectives could be realized. Then the conflict of interests within the Group comes into play.

The Group of 77 needs to learn how to reconcile in the negotiating process the different interests within the Group itself, how to accommodate the different emphases placed by different components of the Group, how to make sure that the platform of the Group taken as a whole has something in it of interest to each and every one of the subgroups which compose the wider membership of the Group of 77. It is unlikely that there would be an equal stake for each and every developing country in each and every one of the issues on the agenda of the negotiations. Some countries may have a greater interest in commodities; others may wish to emphasize trade in manufactures; the interest of some countries in the issue of the transfer of technology is greater than the interest of others, and so on. But if the Group of 77 is to maintain its unity, then it will have to manage somehow to keep a broad platform, which is of interest to the

Group as a whole and also within each issue, to accommodate the various interests of its differentiated membership.

If the developing countries are to succeed in the negotiating process in the future, it is imperative that they maintain this unity because the unity of the developing countries is by and large the most potent and the strongest instrument at their disposal. There are a number of factors which could undermine the capacity of the developing countries to act as a single unit. I have on other occasions identified six of them; there may be more.

There is the potential division among developing countries between the oil-producing countries and the non-oil-producing countries. There is also the potential division between the more advanced developing countries, the more industrialized, and the less-advanced or least-developed countries. The development experience of these groups and the point, which each has attained in the development process, is different, and these differences could be used to undermine the unity of the Group as a whole. There is a third possibility. The developing countries could find their unity weakened by the clash of regional geographical interests. It is possible to pit the Latin American continent against the African continent, the African continent against the Asian continent and so on. Then, again, it is possible that the play of institutional interests—the question of UNCTAD versus the GATT versus the IMF versus the World Bank; the question of the Geneva group versus the New York group, and so on—may also operate as a divisive force. Then, again, there are the bilateral relationships between developing countries taken individually and developed countries taken individually. We do not know to what extent these bilateral linkages are utilized in the process of pressure that arises in the multilateral context. But it would be naive to assume that they are not utilized. There is also the political spectrum within the Group of 77. There are conservative States at one extreme and very radical States at the other, and these differences can be likewise a source of friction which, if not taken into account, could tend to weaken the negotiating stance of the developing countries.

On all these counts, therefore, there is a new challenge which faces the developing countries and which they have to master and respond to, and this calls for a number of responses on the part of these countries themselves. It calls for a greater degree of expertise on the part of the representatives of the developing countries at negotiating conferences. Up to now the developing countries have relied on the international secretariats for this expertise, on UNCTAD and on other bodies. But there is a limit to the abilities of the international secretariats to respond to these needs. In my view, the developing countries would benefit by the establishment of their own secretariat; I believe that there would be no conflict between the role of UNCTAD as an institutional hammer, so to speak, for the solution of development problems, and the need for the developing countries to receive assistance from their own organs for tactical and substantive purposes.

UNCTAD can present issues, it can analyse issues, but it cannot help developing countries in their negotiating tactics. I do not subscribe to the view that UNCTAD should be neutral with regard to development issues. While it cannot, of course, be partisan in supporting individual country interests, it has to push as hard as it can on the development issue, for that is the rationale of UNCTAD, that is its *raison d'être.*

I have often quoted Dr. Prebisch as saying that UNCTAD could no more be neutral about underdevelopment than WHO, for example, could be neutral about malaria. Both are scourges which have to be eradicated, and there has to be a total commitment to their eradication. But this does not mean that UNCTAD as an organization can do the work of the Group of 77 when it comes to formulating and identifying positions in a negotiating process. The developing countries need to acquire this expertise not only through their representatives in Geneva but also through the contribution of expertise from the capitals.

I find that there is a contrast between the way the developing countries organize themselves for international negotiations and the way in which the developed countries do so. The developed countries invariably bring experts from the capitals to handle a specific negotiation. The developing countries leave this to their representatives in Geneva, to their Permanent Missions in Geneva, sometimes buttressed by a few people from the capitals. The representatives of the developing countries in Geneva have a very wide margin of latitude in the negotiating process. It is very seldom that they are subject to strict instructions from their capitals, and although this situation might have advantages it also means that the commitment of the capitals to these negotiating exercises is not as great as it ought to be if success is to be achieved.

I want to emphasize this issue of commitment because it has been mentioned by the representatives of the developed countries themselves. They have often indicated to me that, whilst spokesmen for developing countries have been eloquent, even insistent in their pronouncements in international forums, including UNCTAD and the General Assembly on the various goals of a New International Economic Order and the various goals of UNCTAD, the Common Fund, the Integrated Programme for Commodities and so on, a comparable commitment to these issues is not always seen to exist in their capitals. Often they tell me that when their ministers visit the capitals of developing countries, having been briefed in advance about the importance which these countries attach to multilateral issues and the objectives of the new order, these ministers come back saying that they have found no echo whatsoever of this commitment from the senior officials and their counterparts whom they met. In fact, they say that they have found relative innocence concerning these issues. They take this to mean that discussion in the forum of the General Assembly and of UNCTAD about the goals of the new order is a kind of political game engaged in by the diplomats and the Foreign Office representatives of developing countries which, as individual States, attach relatively small priority to these goals.

Of course, this must to some extent be a misunderstanding. It arises partly because developing countries in their contacts with the developed countries at the bilateral level assume that they have to give priority to their bilateral interests and that the international goals are something which they stress collectively, in the relevant international forums. They somehow feel that it is not for them to advocate the broad platform of the Third World as a whole in the course of their bilateral dealings, although this does not mean lack of endorsement of these goals. Perhaps also the developing countries do not have adequate mechanisms for keeping their decision-making authorities regularly informed of what is happening in multilateral forums.

I once ventured the thought that, given the multiplication of international events and the incessant calls for developing countries to be represented at these events, to participate in them, and to take positions, there may well be a need for developing countries to appoint within their own cabinets, or at least at a very high level, a minister or senior official who would be really responsible for multilateral economic events. This official would not replace the sectoral ministers but complement them, accompany them and maintain an element of continuity in the position of developing countries on the international scene. Such a minister or senior official could receive ministers and officials from other countries and express to them the developing countries' interest in these multilateral issues.

But, above all, the developing countries must not only acquire a greater deal of expertise and commitment, but must also mobilize and apply much greater pressure on the developed countries if they are to gain recognition of their needs. You will notice that it is not difficult for a developed country to take a negative or a hard line on an international issue without jeopardizing its bilateral relationships with any developing country. If a developed country says "no" to the Common Fund, or to the Integrated Programme for Commodities, or to the code of conduct on the transfer of technology, or to the negotiations on restrictive business practices, and so on, this attitude would not in any way damage its relations with any individual developing country. These go on as before. Such attitudes might be more difficult to maintain, however, if developing countries utilized not only their multilateral opportunities but also their bilateral contacts with individual developed countries to make these countries aware of the importance which developing countries attach to these multilateral goals.

There have been a few examples where the use of such bilateral contacts have proved useful. In the evolution of the negotiations on the Common Fund, the members of the Association of South-East Asian Nations (ASEAN) used the occasion of their bilateral discussions with the United States, Japan and the European Economic Community in order to emphasize the high priority which the ASEAN countries attached to the Common Fund and the Integrated Programme. This expression of emphasis in a bilateral context went a long way towards making the leading developed countries aware of the practical importance which developing countries attach to the multilateral goals.

Another example was the initiative taken by the Prime Minister of Jamaica, Mr. Norman Manley, in calling a meeting of a small group of Heads of State, in which, again, the importance of the Common Fund was underlined by him and a few of his colleagues from developing countries. I was told that this meeting had a very profound effect on some Heads of State from Western countries who until then had not appreciated the importance and the priority which developing countries attached to these goals.

Hence it seems to me that in the period to come there is a very urgent need for the developing countries to mobilize their capacity to apply pressure. If they do apply this pressure, if 160 or more developing countries each used their embassies and other channels to make known to each of the developed countries their commitment to these goals, I find it hard to believe that this would not affect the attitudes and approaches of the developed countries. The developing countries underestimate their collective power; they have a much bigger presence on the international economic and political scene than they imagine. But this power is not yet adequately mobilized, it is not yet adequately harnessed to the furthering of the global process of negotiations.

I consider, therefore, that if there is one major lesson to be drawn from our experience of the negotiating process, it is that the group of developing countries has to undergo this transformation from being essentially a pressure group into being a serious negotiating unit. This transformation calls for expertise, for commitment, for organization, and even for the commitment of financial resources on the part of developing countries themselves in support of their objectives. I once said to a gathering of developing countries that they should not recognize failures; they should only recognize weaknesses. If they have failed to achieve results, the failure is a reflection of their own weakness in mobilizing themselves and in exercising the pressure that they need to impart to achieve results.

Certain responsibilities are incumbent also on the other actors in the negotiating exercise. The developed countries themselves have tended up to now to approach international negotiations in a somewhat minimalist frame of mind. They have not seen the various objectives as reflecting their own felt needs. They see them as objectives put forward by the developing countries in order to satisfy the requirements of this group of countries, and as calling for concessions on the part of the developed countries. The developed countries see these initiatives as being, in one way or another, attempts—and they are such—to change the *status quo*, and for that reason they are defensive and cautious because it is they who have to make the changes. They see themselves as the givers rather than the receivers in this negotiating process; and for that very reason it is the developed countries that come to negotiations with a much greater degree of preparedness and with a much greater degree of sophistication than the developing countries. And this very process within the developed countries of preparing for negotiations contributes to slowing down the progress in negotiations.

When the representatives of a developed country come to a negotiating conference, they come with a position fairly well thought out which has previously had to be cleared by a number of decision-making entities within the developed countries themselves—the foreign ministries, the treasuries and economic ministries, the sectoral ministries, and so on—and with a brief that has been broadly endorsed by their responsible authorities. They also have, furthermore, to co-ordinate positions with other developed countries. The developed countries do not thus have that degree of flexibility that would enable them to change their brief at the negotiating table itself; and that is why often, when an issue proves to be intractable, there is no way of making progress at the negotiation itself; instead it becomes necessary to adjourn the conference and to resume later when governments have had time to consult among themselves and to rethink their positions.

It is also important to appreciate that, whilst we talk of the developed countries, even the OECD countries, as a single group, they themselves are made up of a spectrum. There are the bigger powers, which by and large have tended to take a more cautious or even more hard-line attitude in international negotiations, and the smaller countries, which have tended to be somewhat more forthcoming, to be more responsive. At Nairobi, for the first time, a new group was formed within the OECD countries calling themselves "the group of like-minded countries", made up of the Scandinavian countries, the Netherlands, Belgium, Austria, Canada, Ireland and others, and this group has since then been meeting from time to time and been trying to play the role of a bridge between the larger industrialized countries and the developing countries. One must not assume, therefore, that the developed countries are a monolithic group. They themselves are to some extent differentiated, and they, too, have the task of adopting a common position for the negotiations, and, of course, because they have to adopt a common position and a common stance. In the end the developed countries often have to conform to the lowest common denominator, to adopt as a common position that stance which would command support from the developed countries as a whole, although this does not mean that individual developed countries would not be prepared to go further in making accommodations and responses to the issues on the agenda for a negotiation.

In the period ahead two factors could play a role of decisive importance in changing the responsiveness of the developed countries to the negotiations. One of these I have already referred to, and that is the application of a greater degree of pressure by the developing countries, not as an exercise in supplication or persuasion, but as an exercise in the application of leverage. But besides that, I also feel that a decisive factor would be a greater awareness on the part of the developed countries in the future of their own interest in the reordering of the international framework of economic relations. They would have to see the New International Economic Order not as a one-way street, not as involving any loss and transfer to others of the gains that they have achieved, but rather as a new set of relationships without which the global economy itself can hardly survive or function smoothly in the future.

The developed countries, now more than before, are beginning to sense that they have a stake in the acceleration of the progress of the Third World, that if there is stagnation in the developing countries, the resulting turmoil and turbulence will affect the whole fabric of international political relations. They may now begin to see that the developing countries' growth and prosperity could be part of the solution to the world's economic ills rather than, as they have tended to see it up to now, part of the problems facing them in a difficult situation.

Until now developed countries have looked upon responses to Third World demands as constituting an additional burden in an already difficult situation of recession, unemployment, inflation and so on. But they should realize that responding to Third World demands could ultimately accelerate and give strength to a recovery process in the global economy; that if the developing countries were to succeed in attaining high rates of growth, the functioning of the world economy as a whole would be bound to receive a stimulus. And if the developed countries are sensitive to each of these strands—the mounting pressure from developing countries over time and the convergence of interest in a reordering of international economic relations—then the prospects for success in the future would be greater than before.

I also wish to make an observation about the role of the socialist countries of Eastern Europe. The socialist countries have been supportive of developing countries in the earlier phase of UNCTAD when the emphasis was on the formulation of goals and objectives. But in a negotiating phase, for the socialist countries as much as for any other group, the play of national interests comes to the fore and the socialist countries have themselves to give some thought as to how to identify their own interest in responding positively to the specific issues under negotiation in UNCTAD and elsewhere.

There is, of course, an enormous potential in regard to future trade and other linkages between the socialist countries and the developing countries. Socialist countries are in the process of transforming their own economies; their own internal trade is growing very fast; their trade with the developing countries has been expanding at a faster rate than the trade of developing countries with the rest of the world. But the base is still low, it is still minimal. Here again one has to search for new approaches, new orientations, and to provide a new framework within which this wider goal could be attained. But the socialist countries interests are not confined to improving their trade and other relationships with the developing countries. They see UNCTAD as a forum for dealing with the universality of problems within its field including their trade with the Western countries. I certainly feel that it is within UNCTAD's mandate to be responsive to this view. In fact it is my impression that in the early stages of UNCTAD the socialist countries supported the broad platform of the developing countries in the expectation that the latter would in turn be supportive of the goals of the socialist countries. They may have the feeling that this expectation has not been adequately realized.

Then, again, the negotiating exercise calls for responses on the part of the international organizations themselves and of the secretariats of these organizations, in particular UNCTAD. UNCTAD was established in the earlier period to be the centre of the great debate on development. As a consequence the secretariat of UNCTAD was structured to service debates rather than to service negotiations. The operating style of UNCTAD has been to convene meetings because an intergovernmental body has requested them, and to prepare documentation which highlights the issues of relevance to each particular meeting and serves as an aid to the debate and to the formulation of resolutions.

Up to now the secretariat of UNCTAD has not been structured to service a negotiating process, to support the taking of complex decisions rather than the passing of broad resolutions. If UNCTAD is to perform this function in the future, the secretariat itself would need to undergo a veritable transformation. I feel that the secretariat of UNCTAD needs to have much greater contact with capitals. For example, if we want to contribute to the conclusion of an agreement on a commodity, let us say copper, in my view the best way of doing that is not to convene meeting after meeting on copper and prepare for each one a background paper outlining the history of past efforts to deal with copper. The best way to establish an agreement on copper would be for the secretariat of UNCTAD to maintain close relationships with the major producers and consumers of copper, to assess their views and their approaches, to try to form a bridge between the various groups, to try to contribute to the maturing of the decision-making process, and then, when the point has been reached at which an agreement is in prospect, to convene the meeting with a much greater chance of success than before.

As we are presently constituted we do not operate in that way because we would then need to have at our disposal more high-level people whom we could send to capitals, who have access to ministers and senior officials, and who have diplomatic and political skill, as well as people with an adequate technical background. I feel, therefore, that there is a need for UNCTAD as an organization also to adapt itself and recast its own character to meet the needs of negotiation.

Then there is one major issue which comes up incessantly when one talks of negotiations within the United Nations. People ask: Is it really possible, is it really practical, for the United Nations or any part of the United Nations such as UNCTAD to be a really effective instrument for negotiations? Is it possible for anything serious, anything complex, anything concrete, to be negotiated by over 160 countries meeting together, each country being supported by delegations of five or ten persons? When UNCTAD calls a conference on any issue we use a room holding 400, 500 or 600 people. Can a conference of such a size conduct a negotiating process?

To this I have two answers. One is that we have no alternative. If we are to enter into international negotiations, if we are to restructure the international economic order, then we have to see this as a universal process which needs the involvement and the commitment of all Member States. If we fail to do that, we would be sowing the seeds of future conflict and of future tensions. So there is no question that these issues have to be negotiated within the United Nations. The question is how the United Nations can succeed in resolving the conflict between the vast size of its membership and the needs of a disciplined negotiation.

We must not forget that a smaller size would not in itself ensure success. You will recollect that sometime in 1975 a smaller-sized negotiation was launched called the "Conference on International Economic Co-operation" or the "Paris Conference" on North/South issues which was confined to a limited number of countries—I think nineteen developing countries and about eight developed countries. It was felt that this small size would be conducive to progress. But the Paris Conference did not, any more than other UN bodies, succeed in making headway on North/South issues. In retrospect, the Paris Conference is seen to have been a conference which failed to achieve its objectives. The reason was that though it was not handicapped by size it failed because of substantive factors—the difficulty of reconciling the conflict of interests between the developed countries, oil-producing countries and the other developing countries. Size should not prevent the United Nations from serving as the main forum of negotiations. But it will have to innovate in this new phase and design instruments which would make the representative character of the UN compatible with the needs of a negotiating process.

I must not leave the impression, however, that an UNCTAD negotiation is a bedlam in which 160 countries or more all try to make individual contributions to a final solution. In UNCTAD we work through groups. We have the Group of 77, which adopts a common position and chooses a single spokesman; we have the group of developed countries of the OECD, which we call the B Group and which organizes itself and performs in a similar way; we have the socialist countries of Eastern Europe, called the D Group, which also participate in negotiations through a single spokesman; and we have China. So informally, if not formally and constitutionally, we have improvised negotiating mechanisms which have managed to reconcile the need for representativeness with the demand for small groups.

But these improvisations are still informal, and it is true to say that from a constitutional point of view we have yet to devise mechanisms which provide a guarantee of success. Anyone who has attended an UNCTAD conference will have seen that the closing days are a virtual nightmare. One is never sure before the conclusion whether or not there will be success, whether or not even the Conference will end on a successful note. Invariably a great deal of time is lost in the initial preparations, in the selection of chairmen and office bearers, in the formulation of positions, in the making of statements, while the concrete negotiations, in which a process of give and take is needed, are delayed until little time remains. As a result night sessions are not uncommon; in fact they are the rule in UNCTAD in the closing stages of a conference. And all along one is never sure whether the compromises thrashed out between the small team of negotiators representing their respective groups will gain the endorsement of the groups as a whole. Sometimes the groups have rejected and denounced the arrangements reached by their representatives in a smaller group, and this has resulted in an atmosphere of crisis and the need to suspend the conference from time to time and make a fresh effort. So there is much to be done on the organizational front too.

We have now reached a stage where the calendar of events is so crowded that there are serious risks in adjourning a conference when more time is needed to settle outstanding issues. It may not be possible to accommodate a resumed session of a negotiating conference for another 8, 9, or 10 months, and that means that a period of time is lost, not for substantive reasons but for logistical reasons; and when that conference resumes 10 months later it is found that while some outstanding issues have been resolved there are still some others remaining, and hence a further resumption becomes necessary. The conference, therefore, has to be reconvened after another interval of 8 or 10 months. Before one knows what has happened, a year or two will have elapsed without the conference being finally concluded. In the meantime a great deal of frustration has been created; developing countries proclaim failure, and there is an undermining of confidence.

It is one thing to delay results for substantive reasons; it is quite unacceptable that results should be delayed for logistical reasons, and I am afraid that this is what is happening now in UNCTAD. If, therefore, we are going to enter into a new phase after the accomplishment of the Nairobi negotiations, all these problems will have to be addressed and solutions will have to be found for the future.

III

I have already referred to three phases in the recent experience of UNCTAD which I wished to comment upon. The first was the period leading up to the Nairobi Conference when UNCTAD was striving to obtain a mandate for a negotiating process. The second phase was that following the Nairobi Conference when, having received a mandate for negotiations, UNCTAD became immersed in the process of negotiations itself, and I have just offered some observations and reflections on our experience in that process.

The third phase is that which commenced, perhaps, with the preparation of UNC-TAD V in Manila in which the main thrust was to extend the negotiating process to even more basic areas of the international economy than were covered by the Nairobi mandates, and obviously this third phase is far from having reached its termination. Indeed, it is only beginning, and in one way or another the principal themes which dominated this phase at Manila will remain relevant in the period ahead, particularly in the decade of the eighties. I want here to reflect on the basic themes that are now relevant, and also to give some thought as to how they might evolve in the period ahead.

The Manila Conference, UNCTAD V, was held three years after UNCTAD IV, as against the customary four-year interval. This did not signify a permanent change of the previous four-year cycle to a three-year one—it was a decision specific to UNC-TAD V, and I think that the principal reason behind it was the desire on the part of the developing countries to remove the UNCTAD meetings from the American election year in which they had been falling ever since UNCTAD I. The United States, as a leader of the group of developed countries, always pointed out that an election year was a difficult period in which to take up new positions and to come up with new orientations. The developing countries thought that, by modifying the cycle, that particular reason for a lack of responsiveness on the part of the developed group would be removed. But the result of that decision was that we had to prepare for UNCTAD V in a situation in which the main negotiations launched at UNCTAD IV had not been completed, and for that reason it was very difficult to focus on a single issue as a dominant theme for the Conference in the way that the commodity issue had been the dominant theme for UNCTAD IV. The commodity programme was under negotiation and so were other programmes in the field of technology, restrictive business practices and so on. Furthermore, in the field of trade and tariffs the multilateral trade negotiations under the auspices of GATT were still going on and it was very difficult to make that issue—the issue of the trading structure—the particular focus of UNCTAD V.

Given that constellation of factors, there was little choice but to structure UNC-TAD V as a wide-ranging type of conference in which a whole series of issues would be brought before the international community for discussion and debate. In effect, what UNCTAD V was trying to do was to set a scenario whose relevance would really extend beyond the period of the Conference. All that seemed possible at Manila, even before the event, was to gain some kind of endorsement on the part of the international community for extending the negotiating process launched at Nairobi into other even more fundamental areas, and to treat these negotiating processes as part of an interrelated whole based on the main concept of the need for structural change in the world economy. It was for that reason that this issue of structural change came to be the dominant strand of the Manila agenda.

The agenda touched, of course, on the traditional UNCTAD items—commodities, money and finance, trade in manufactures, technology, shipping, least-developed countries, economic co-operation among developing countries and so on. But the main thrust under each heading was the need for some new basic orientations going beyond what had been on the agenda for discussion in the past. What is more, these basic orientations relevant to each subject were treated as interrelated elements which, taken together, would result in bringing about major changes in the whole structure of international economic relations, particularly relations between developed and developing countries. In fact, structural change was not only the theme of each agenda item; it was also the subject of a separate agenda item which was intended to provide a conceptual frame for the Conference and in the context of which the international community was invited to confirm its conviction that structural changes were needed and to set up a mechanism for keeping issues in this field under review, particularly issues arising out of the interdependence of problems in the field of trade, money, and development.

I do not want to embark upon a lengthy evaluation of UNCTAD V having done this on several other occasions before the Economic and Social Council and elsewhere. Basically, my reaction to the results of UNCTAD V was to regard them as a somewhat mixed bag. Quite clearly, UNCTAD V had a very negative image in the media and also it evoked a great deal of disappointment on the part of the developing countries. Understandably, they felt frustrated because the basic themes of UNCTAD V did not gain the kind of recognition for which they had hoped. Partly they were also themselves not clear as to what it was that UNCTAD V was seeking to do, and their inability to point to specific concrete results and say that this or that was achieved at Manila contributed to this feeling of restiveness and dissatisfaction.

Whilst that reaction is understandable, I think that one has to take into account, in making any overall evaluation of UNCTAD V, that in certain areas UNCTAD V did produce positive conclusions even though in other areas it failed to do so. It is true to say that in one way or another, UNCTAD V provided mandates for negotiating processes in at least three key areas—that of commodities, protectionism, and structural adjustment and monetary reform. In other areas, such as technology, economic co-operation among developing countries and least-developed countries, it provided mandates for new action programmes and work programmes for UNCTAD and the international community. In still other areas it did not yield any decisions whatsoever.

However, in one way or another the agenda of UNCTAD will continue to be the agenda for the so-called North/South dialogue in the period to come. And now the General Assembly of the United Nations has taken a unanimous decision to launch a new round of global consultations within the UN forum, taking into account energy, trade and development, raw materials, food and a number of other central subjects. I believe that these negotiations, which are meant to be of an interrelated and well-structured character, will inevitably have to turn to the issues which were first put on the agenda at UNCTAD V. I believe, therefore, that from that point of view UNCTAD V was a watershed. It was to be seen not so much as an isolated event but as forming part of a process, and this process will gain in relevance and in momentum in the period to come.

I have been asking myself what form this agenda for the eighties is going to take, particularly in the light of the experience of the Manila Conference. The global negotiations that are to take place will need to be different from the so-called North/South dialogue which took place under the auspices of the Government of France in Paris in 1975 and 1976. That was a meeting of a selected number of countries; there were nineteen developing countries invited, after consultations, by the Government of France and eight developed countries from the OECD group meeting together. They were not representative of the developing countries as a group. The socialist countries and China were not participants in that negotiation. It has been recognized that one should not attempt to negotiate basic issues in a small selected group, and that the new round of negotiations should be brought firmly within the forum of the UN.

I feel that the Paris negotiations, partly because of its character, was not well structured. The nineteen developing countries were very conscious of the fact that, although they had been invited individually, they were still part of the Group of 77 and were therefore hesitant to take initiatives and positions which would have departed from the earlier expressed positions of the Group. The result was that at Paris the developing countries placed on the agenda for negotiation a whole list of demands that had earlier been formulated by the Group of 77 mostly at a series of meetings set up to prepare for the Nairobi Conference. There was no selectivity and no structuring of the agenda in terms of linkages and interrelationships. Not surprisingly, therefore, the Paris Conference failed to achieve results simply because the agenda was too vast and that the developing countries did not feel they were in a position to negotiate away any of the basic positions taken up by the Group of 77 on earlier occasions. The developed countries in turn were disappointed because they did not find a scenario in which the energy problem—their primary interest—could become the subject of a global deal.

There is now a general feeling that the new round of negotiations should not only be universal but should in one way or another be better structured and made more selective. The specific structure of these negotiations and the way in which the issues should be handled would be the responsibility of the Committee of the Whole of the General Assembly, and the final decision on the structure of the Conference and on the launching of the global negotiations is to be taken in August 1980 when the General Assembly meets in special session.

With respect to the structure of the negotiations there is now active discussion going on as to whether this new round of global negotiations should be centralized and held primarily in New York under the auspices of the General Assembly, with other parts of the United Nations like UNCTAD being called to give support through documentation and so on; or whether it should be decentralized, with the General Assembly keeping for itself an overall monitoring and surveillance role but leaving it to the individual organizations—UNCTAD, GATT, the IMF, UNIDO and so on—to carry on the negotiating process, coming to the General Assembly from time to time to report on results and to receive stimulus and impetus, and particularly to break any deadlocks that might arise.

There has been no decision yet as to whether the Conference would be primarily a centralized one or a decentralized one. But all groups have been saying that they would not want the global negotiation to undermine the negotiations going on in UNCTAD and elsewhere, and it has been written into the resolution that the global round will not in any way do this but would rather reinforce and draw upon these current negotiations. It remains to be seen how this is going to be done and whether in fact the global sound can avoid jeopardizing these negotiations by giving an excuse to governments—bureaucracies being what they are—to postpone decisions because some major process is under way. But I believe that in one way or another the scenario for the eighties will have to encompass a number of key issues, and I should like to touch upon some of these as I see them.

I mentioned in the first part of this introduction that in a basic sense it would appear that we have already seen the end of one epoch and the beginning of another. The framework of international economic relations, which was set up after the end of the Second World War and which has evolved in the three decades that have elapsed since then, will certainly not endure in the period ahead. Many developments have taken place which have undermined some of the cornerstones of this earlier framework. Now we have to think in terms of a new scenario, and as we approach the eighties we cannot be blind to the fact that the overriding note that has to be struck is one of concern about the numerous crises that have been manifesting themselves in recent years and which seem likely to continue into the eighties and in a sense to dominate them.

I think that the very existence of crises calls for basic responses and structural changes, but it is very important to realize that we enter upon the eighties with a number of anxieties and concerns on many fronts. Although UNCTAD has not been directly involved in this, the prospect for economic development in the eighties will be inextricably linked with the way in which the international political situation is going to evolve in the period ahead, and this is an issue on which one would hesitate to make any kind of predictions. But certainly if the arms race is going to continue, if vast resources—reportedly $400 billion a year—are going to be devoted not only to the production of armaments but also to a growing world trade in armaments, then to that extent the resolution of fundamental issues of development will be more difficult.

Although in the narrower context of international economic discussions one does not talk about this background of rising international tensions and armaments, in one way or another I feel that this is going to be of fundamental importance. The world food situation is also going to be a major element that will colour the way in which the eighties can be viewed. If the international community does not deal with the many threats that seem to be posed on the food front, then all the efforts at restructuring other aspects of the international economy might be thwarted by overriding crises brought on by food shortages and famine in important areas of the Third World. Accordingly disarmament and food will be important issues for the eighties, as a backdrop, so to speak, to the other structural issues arising in specific economic processes and negotiations.

In the context of these economic processes I can see at least four major issues or themes which will be important in the eighties. Three of these were on the agenda at Manila, and the other has received increasing emphasis since then. The one which was not taken up in depth at Manila, but which was very much in the background, is the issue of energy. By now it is quite clear that any global consultation or negotiation aiming at a settlement of overriding issues between developed and developing countries cannot ignore the energy issue; in fact the oil-producing countries themselves have agreed to the inclusion of energy as one of the basic themes of the forthcoming North/South negotiations.

It is still not clear how energy will be treated. Of course the oil-producing countries have been very insistent that the question of the pricing of petroleum should not be the subject of an international discussion because they regard pricing as falling within their own competence and they would not want to yield the power of decision making in regard to the pricing of oil. But there are other facets of the energy issue which can become the subject of international negotiation and which, I am sure, the oil-producing countries themselves would want to see discussed because they are issues causing concern to the oil producers themselves.

For example, for the oil-producing countries the problem of energy is partly one of how to sustain the real value of their earnings in the face of an incessant process of inflation in the world at large. One reason for the periodic adjustment of the price of oil is simply that the price of oil has failed to keep pace with inflation in the price of imports of manufactures and other goods purchased by the oil-producing countries. They have insisted that by their recent price actions they have essentially served to sustain the real value of the price of oil in the face of world inflation. The oil price increases of 1973 were eroded in real terms by this inflationary process, and in their subsequent actions the OPEC countries have tried to recapture ground that had been lost.

The energy issue for the OPEC countries is also a question of how to safeguard the real value of their financial reserves in the face of the depreciation of the values of the major currencies in which they have been holding their reserves, particularly the dollar. The oil-producing countries have found that, whilst they have been extracting their scarce resources, which left in the ground would have a growing value in the future, and converting these into financial assets, the value of these assets themselves has been declining because of the regular depreciation in the dollar and other currencies in which they are denominated. For the oil-producing countries, therefore, a solution to the energy problem must include, amongst other things, a solution to the problem of inflation in the world economy and to the problem of the continuing depreciation in the value of major reserve currencies. For these countries it is a question of the ability of the financial system to guarantee the real value of their financial assets and to provide secure and remunerative outlets for their surpluses. But in addition, and even more fundamental for these countries, is the problem of the conservation of their natural resources. These are being depleted at a rate much in excess of that needed to satisfy their own import requirements for the purpose of meeting what has been up to now an unregulated expansion in global demand reflecting most of all the consumption patterns of the industrialized countries. A better balance between demand and supply is of vital importance to the oil-producing countries.

For the developed industrialized countries the energy issue, apart from the issue of price, is very much a problem of security of supplies of the energy that they need for the smooth functioning of their economies. The developed countries have been saying that they have found the uncertainty of supplies a disruptive element and have pointed to the intemittent, irregular way in which prices have been fixed, as another cause of disruption. For the industrialized countries, therefore, the energy problem is the problem of how to bring some order into the energy market, how to obtain some assurance of supplies, how to make sure that price trends follow a smooth and regular pattern.

It is also the problem of how a very fundamental point—the consumption patterns of these very countries—could be altered, for quite clearly there is no future for the present patterns or trends of consumption. So when one talks about solving the energy issue one has to reflect very seriously about the future pattern of supply and demand for energy, bearing in mind the very real scarcity of this non-renewable resource. The stability of capital and money markets arising out of the need of the oil-producing countries for investment outlets is also a matter of concern to the industrialized countries.

For the non-oil-producing developing countries the energy problem is partly a problem of how they themselves can sustain their development in the context of rising energy prices, a problem of how they could be helped to develop their own sources of energy, how they could be helped in their own search for alternative sources and substitutes, and how they could be cushioned in some measure against the balance-of-payments effects of the energy crisis. The fact is that the present dimensions of the payments gaps of developing countries are radically different from those that prevailed at the time when the Bretton Woods facilities were first designed and that the developing countries have inadequate access to accommodation to meet the new situation facing them. Some developing countries have had access to commercial markets in which they have been able to borrow on commercial terms, a process which has led to an escalation in their external indebtedness. However, other developing countries, notably the poorest among them, have not had access even to that source of funds. They have had to respond to the current crisis by curtailing their imports and by dampening the tempo of their development programmes.

Quite clearly, the energy problem for the developing countries is also one of how to obtain supplies in a situation of scarcity, of how to cushion themselves against the price impact of these supplies, either by assistance or rebates or by access to financial accommodation on a scale commensurate with the size of the problems, and of how they themselves could be helped by the international community to develop their indigenous energy resources in order to provide some assurance against the shortages that seem inevitably in prospect for the future.

As I have shown, the energy issue has a number of dimensions and for that reason I feel that the oil-producing countries have been right to insist that the problem cannot be dealt with in isolation; it has to be taken up in connection with a number of other issues. Most of these other issues pertain to the way in which the world monetary and financial system could evolve in the light of all the new dimensions in the energy field. In fact, what has been described as an energy crisis is really a crisis of a monetary and financial system unable to adapt itself to the changed situation in the energy field. The price of oil is likely to continue its upward course until it equals the cost of alternative sources of energy. The basic facts of supply and demand point to this and there is no use wishing that price trends were otherwise. The real challenge is how to cope with and adjust to the facts of the situation.

This brings me to the second of the major areas which must inevitably be the subject of debate and discussion in the eighties, and that is the whole question of the future evolution of the world monetary and financial system. There is no doubt that the system as set up in Bretton Woods after the end of the Second World War has fallen apart. We cannot say today that there is anything that has the coherence and the consistency of what could be described as a system. We have responded to all the crises as an international community by *ad hoc* improvisations and adaptations, rather than by a recasting of the system as a whole; and increasingly today it is becoming evident that the improvisations, the move to flexible exchange rates and so on, are an inadequate answer to the basic problems and the basic crises of the international monetary system.

Sooner or later there will have to be a new attempt on the part of the international community to recast the monetary system, and the important thing here is to make sure that in this process the developing countries are able to gain recognition of their own needs. The old monetary system was designed virtually without their participation. There is a danger that the industrialized countries, faced with a crisis, may again rearrange the monetary system to respond to their own problems, and drag in the developing countries as passive partners in a new system without giving them the opportunity of participating in its restructuring.

That is why I have been saying time and time again that the developing countries must get involved in the exercise of restructuring the monetary system in order to ensure that their own demands are met. Conventionally, when one talks of the reform of the international monetary system, one talks about the need for setting up a new instrument of international liquidity, the special drawing right, to replace the dollar; one talks about restoring a degree of stability in the international exchange markets; one talks about having a symmetrical process of adjustment between the industrialized countries in surplus and the industrialized countries in deficit and so on. I think that these are necessary ingredients of a reform of the monetary system.

But for the developing countries the emphasis must surely be somewhat different. For them the emphasis has to be on the inadequacy of the accommodation which the present system provides for meeting their needs; for them no reform of the monetary system would be adequate, however effective it might be in terms of a new exchange regime and adjustment process, unless at the same time it afforded to the developing countries a way out of the terrible dilemma involved in having to choose between increasing their indebtedness or curtailing their development programme and their development imports in the light of world economic events. A new system has to provide for a radically enhanced system of financial accommodation on terms and conditions appropriate to those of the developing countries.

That is why we in UNCTAD have recently made a number of critical studies of the present IMF system. We have recognized the valuable efforts which the IMF has been making in recent years to augment its existing facilities, but we have pointed out that the very philosophy underlying these facilities is inadequate to the needs of the developing countries. We have felt that developing countries in the present juncture need not only short-term facilities, such as those which the IMF provides today, but also facilities of a medium- to long-term character, because their financial crisis is closely linked to their need to participate in and to engender a development process—which is not a short-term process. We have therefore suggested that some thought should be given to the establishment of a new medium-term facility, within the IMF or outside the IMF, which would supplement the very meagre short-term facilities that are now available.

We have also drawn attention to the adjustment process and to the conditionality which the Fund has been imposing on developing countries seeking recourse to its resources; we have pointed out that often developing countries have been asked to respond to crises caused by external factors by a process of internal contraction. This is not a logical response because the origins of the difficulties are not internal. We have therefore argued for a new look at the Fund's conditionality and particularly at the need to link the adjustment process in developing countries to the adequacy of resources helping them to sustain their development, for it makes no sense in the name of monetary soundness to respond to a disturbed external situation by internal contraction at the expense of development. Such a perverse response would simply postpone the problems of development for the future. This, then, is a major area to which new thinking needs to be given in the context of a new dialogue on the restructuring of relations.

There is a third area, and that concerns the system of world trade itself. We can no longer assume implicitly that the world trading system as it has evolved since the end of the Second World War will continue unaltered in the period ahead in the face of all the crises and difficulties that have arisen. Despite variations and aberrations, the trading system established at the end of the Second World War and embodied in GATT was based on the principle of free trade, the principle of an open and non-discriminatory trading system, with the concept of the most-favoured nation having a dominant place. This principle, however, has been undermined by a number of developments. For example, the setting up of the European Economic Community, creating a free-trade area among nine major industrialized countries, reduces the relevance of the principle of most-favoured-nation treatment since the trade concessions which these countries have granted to each other have not been extended to their GATT partners. Furthermore the growth of economic co-operation among developing countries and the establishment of the generalized system of preferences have been deviations from the original concept of an open trading system.

Moreover as a consequence of the recession, we have seen the emergence of protectionism in the industrialized countries themselves, which has made further inroads into the system as we have known it. It is my feeling—and I have voiced this opinion on many occasions—that it would be wrong to see the protectionist trend in the industrialized countries as being primarily a temporary cyclical phenomenon linked to the current difficulties of recession and unemployment. I feel, that these difficulties are not temporary and cyclical but somewhat more deeply grounded. I believe that in the long run, irrespective of the economic cycle in the industrialized countries, there is going to be pressure for protectionism simply because of the threat posed to the industrialized countries by the growing industrialization of the Third World. Since the developing countries are in a process of economic transformation in the course of which they seek to acquire the very capacities which the industrialized countries already have, any attempt on the part of the developing countries to seek outlets for their new productive capacities is going to encounter competition with existing capacities in the industrialized countries.

This process of competition from developing countries seeking to displace a capacity established in the industrialized countries is going to be one of the phenomena of the future. It started with textiles and leather goods, but it is not going to be confined to these areas. Increasingly, it is already beginning to extend to other areas—to shipbuilding, to electronics, to the manufacture of automobiles and so on. Whatever capacities developing countries set up, the industrialized countries are going to be under pressure within their own societies to avoid the disruptions caused by free trade and open competition by imposing more and more protectionist barriers.

In the long run the industrialized countries themselves would, of course, benefit by a division of labour in which trade is transacted on the basis of comparative advantage; they would benefit if they could themselves restructure their economies by replacing the old-established capacities which are now being acquired by the developing countries by new capacities in areas where they have an advantage in dynamism and know-how, particularly the areas based on new technologies. But the fact is that, unless the industrialized countries show adaptability, unless they themselves pursue conscious policies in this direction, social and political pressures may push them into the opposite policy of trying to preserve their old industries by the establishment of protectionism and so on.

It is in this sense that the resolution passed at Manila on protectionism and structural change is of fundamental importance, for it hinges on the way in which the world trading system is going to evolve. I think that one cannot be content with the present GATT rules. There is a need to recast them and to take account of all the developments that have occurred since they were formulated. The need for the developing countries to give preferences to each other and possibly have a most-favoured-nation system of their own, the need to incorporate formally the system of preferences granted to them by industrialized countries into the body of rules, the need to provide for conscious policies of structural adjustment in the industrialized countries, the need to provide for codes whereby a problem caused by competition would be dealt with, not unilaterally but through a system of multilateral consultation and so on—all these are part of the requirements of the time which are not provided for in the present body of GATT rules. So again I think that there is a major challenge here to which a response needs to be given in the eighties.

I also consider that there is going to be a need for another major development, which this time will be not a North/South but rather a South/South linkage. One of the major themes of the future will have to be the complete transformation of the very meagre linkages which developing countries have with each other today. The developing countries are still oriented towards the former metropolitan powers; their economies are geared to those of these powers. The developing countries' links, exchanges, and relations with each other—not only in the field of trade but in the fields of transport, communications, and cultural exchange—are all minimal, and I believe that in any reordering of the international framework there has to be a vast departure from this historical situation. I think at the same time there can be a new set of linkages, whose potential for the future has still to be explored, between developing countries and socialist countries.

I believe, therefore, that in this area, too, there is going to be the need for a great deal of negotiation, partly between developing countries and socialist countries, but mostly amongst the developing countries themselves.

The developing countries have endorsed the principle of mutual economic co-operation; they have endorsed the principle of collective self-reliance. But here, too, they have to move from the general to the specific; they have to implement, they have to concretize some of the broader themes which have been identified as belonging to the area of economic co-operation among developing countries and make them part of the reality of our times. At Arusha, the developing countries identified some prospects; they even specified certain priorities; notably the establishment of a preferential trading system amongst themselves, joint ventures and multinational enterprises of developing countries which would have sufficient presence in the international scene; and systems of co-operation among State trading enterprises, particularly systems for the pooling of imports. They have also identified a host of other possibilities. But none of these has yet been given flesh and blood, so to speak, on a significant scale; none of them has been brought to the stage of implementation and concretization, and this again is one of the overriding challenges for the future.

Most of these issues would have to be part of the global negotiation, however it is structured; and I personally feel that, although there is a strong drive to keep the energy issue and related immediate financial problems separate from other questions there is merit in linking the energy issue to some of the wider issues because any leverage developing countries may have is in respect of energy. It seems to me natural that they should try to use this leverage in order to achieve a better result in the area of the restructuring of the monetary system and the trading system and so on. This does not mean that the urgent financial problems arising out of the energy situation would not have to be discussed as matters of great importance, but I think in the longer run a solution of the energy problem would have to be linked to a more basic restructuring of these major components of the world economic system.

In my view there are for the developing countries, or rather the international community as a whole, two basic conditions for success in future negotiations. On the one hand the developing countries would have to organize themselves better in order to gain results. On the other hand, the developed countries would have to see that they themselves have a stake in the restructuring of the world economy, not only because these new structures would be responsive to their own problems but because they themselves and the world economy could benefit by a transformation in the Third World. If the idea that Third World development could contribute to a healthy world economy was to meet with understanding and acceptance, this would augur well for success in the period ahead.

I have just one last thought to put forward, and that is my conception of the way in which international institutions, and particularly UNCTAD, could respond to the many challenges that this unfolding scenario would present. UNCTAD, of course, has a somewhat ambiguous mandate. It was set up in 1964 partly because both the developing countries and the socialist countries felt that the existing international institutions did not give them a sufficient presence or a sufficient voice. From that point of view UNCTAD's mandate is wide ranging. It covers the whole field of trade and development, but at the same time no specific subjects have been made the special responsibility of UNCTAD.

If one looks at each of the issues that UNCTAD is dealing with, one finds that there are other parts of the international system exercising a responsibility in regard to those very issues. In the case of commodities, the Food and Agriculture Organization has responsibilities; in the field of trade in manufactures, so does GATT and UNIDO; as regards technology, the World Intellectual Property Organization, UNESCO and UNIDO have certain functions; money and finance are within the competence of the Bretton Woods institutions, the International Monetary Fund, and the World Bank; shipping is the concern of the Intergovernmental Maritime Consultative Organization as well as of UNCTAD. Economic co-operation among developing countries is a subject that also closely concerns the regional economic commisions. In fact, I once said that insurance was the only subject in which UNCTAD seemed to be the sole master and in which there were no competitiors so far! To judge by experience, therefore, if UNCTAD initiates proposals in any of these fields which fall within its wide mandate, this raises anxieties and concerns in other bodies which feel that, in one way or another, their area of responsibility is being trespassed upon. Clearly this kind of conflict could be exploited for the purpose of minimizing results.

Consequently, I consider that in one way or another the international community and the developing countries in particular will have to give more specific endorsement to the role of UNCTAD as a forum for negotiations. At Manila we succeeded in obtaining some wording in a resolution, saying that UNCTAD was a principal instrument of the General Assembly in the area of trade and development and so on. But this was primarily language for the moment; it will not mean very much until there is a specific overhaul of the institutional system and a specific allocation of responsibilities.

It is possible that in the process of recasting the world trading system a new comprehensive trade organization might emerge. This objective is as old as the Havana Conference, in the post-war period, where there was talk of establishing an international trade organization. Such an organization never came into being. The socialist countries of Eastern Europe have consistently supported the idea of establishing one and it has been suggested that UNCTAD and the GATT might eventually merge into a comprehensive trade organization. Although this kind of institutional evolution is still not on the agenda for action, I suspect that in the eighties the need may arise for putting it there.

I have been saying in many of my speeches that perhaps sometime in the eighties there might be the need for a world economic conference, by which I did not mean the global negotiations that are now planned but a conference on the lines of the Havana Conference of the post-war period, in which the recasting of the world economic framework could be accomplished more comprehensively. The results of the global negotiations might prove to be building-blocks toward that end.

The fact is that the rules and principles drawn up at an earlier time need now to be restated and recast. A number of developments that have since taken place have to be incorporated in a new statement of these rules and principles. I have not proposed specific action by governments on this because I feel that there will have to be a period of reflection on the idea before concrete proposals could be put to governments. But I do feel that in the eighties there will need to be a restatement and reformulation of what have been called the "rules of the game". i.e. the rules and principles which guide the conduct of international economic relations. The revised rules must reflect a new framework which will take into account the needs of the developing countries and of the socialist countries as much as those of the other industrialized countries whose needs have so far determined the institutional framework of international economic relations.

PART II

The Post-War International Economic System in Crisis

Part II presents a diagnosis of the weaknesses besetting the world economic system from the point of view of the developing countries. It serves essentially as a prelude to Part III, in which the large number of specific proposals put forward by the secretariat of UNCTAD as suitable curative measures are set out and explained. First, then, the disruptions in the world economy in the period since 1974 and the failures and shortcomings of the post-war international economic system are described with respect to the situation and prospects of the developing countries. The opening speech, which was the first delivered by Mr. Corea in his capacity as Secretary-General, in April 1974, describes the world situation in the immediate aftermath of the breakdown of the Bretton Woods monetary system in 1971, the emergence of high rates of inflation in the industrialized countries and the end of the era of unduly cheap energy. The subsequent speeches examine the complex and deepening nature of the difficulties. No fundamental changes have been made to the system, which has managed to accommodate to stresses and strains only by a series of limited, *ad hoc* measures. These have brought no hope that prospects for the international economy have improved, while there is every sign that the former expectation of sustained growth in the economies of the industrialized countries is weakened and that the situation of many individual developing countries is actually getting worse, and would not improve even if the richer countries were to recover the former pattern of growth.

Ad hoc Committee of the Sixth
Special Session of the General Assembly

15 April 1974

I feel privileged indeed to be asked to address this Committee of the General Assembly so shortly after assuming my new duties in the footsteps of my distinguished predecessors. My intention is only to offer some introductory remarks which I hope will serve as background material and help the Committee in its task. I shall be making available a somewhat longer note on some of the issues before the special session.

Mr. Chairman, even before the recent increase in the price of oil and other commodities the world economy was subject to severe stresses and strains. Already the international monetary system had been shaken, whilst inflation had been growing rapidly from year to year. Even more important, the international economic system has failed, over the past two decades and beyond, to transmit adequately to the developing countries the remarkable expansion that has taken place in the developed countries. At the heart of this failure lies the unfavourable trend in the terms of trade of the developing countries. By 1972, the terms of trade of the non-oil-exporting developing countries had deteriorated by about 15 per cent compared with the mid 1950s. This is equivalent to a loss in 1972 alone of around $10 billion—more than 20 per cent of these countries' exports, and an amount significantly in excess of the total of official development assistance from the developed market economy countries in that same year. The year 1973 witnessed an up-turn in commodity prices, but despite this, the terms of trade of these countries remain less favourable than the position two decades ago.

It is now amply evident therefore that recent increases in the prices of essential imports have created immediate payments difficulties for a large number of countries, both developed and developing.

As far as the developed market economy countries are concerned, it is true that the increased payments on account of oil imports represent only a small proportion of their gross national product. But these countries nevertheless do face problems in the field of external payments, and it is important that appropriate solutions be found for them. Without such solutions they may well resort to such measures as the competitive depreciation of their currencies, the imposition of trade restrictions, as well as other actions of a contractionary nature.

For developing countries, the problem is more fundamental and more serious—especially since the existing international machinery is largely inadequate for their needs. In recent years all developing countries have experienced a sharp and continued increase in the price of their essential imports. The prices of manufactured goods have been increasing year after year in the wake of the inflationary processes generated in the industrialized countries. But the price increases have by no means been confined to manufactured goods. Food prices—for example, rice, sugar, and wheat—have risen to dramatic heights. The recent increase in the price of oil is but one in this series of price increases. Between 1972 and 1973 price increases for manufactured goods added $4.5 billion to the import bill of the oil-importing developing countries. The higher price of food and other primary products other than fuels added another $5 billion. The total increase for these two categories of $9.5 billion is larger than the probable increase in the net cost of petroleum imports to this group of countries in 1974—estimated at around $7.5 billion to $8 billion.

It is true that those developing countries which have benefited from the recent increases in the prices of commodities have been able in varying degrees to cushion themselves against the impact of the increases in prices of their imports. But we cannot afford to be complacent on this score. Apart from the case of oil and certain other non-renewable resources, where the price situation may remain strong, there is little to ensure that the newly experienced upsurge in the field of commodity prices will endure. There has been no change in basic mechanisms, no new arrangements to secure this result. On the contrary, the commodity boom is in large part a reflection of forces which may well prove to be short-lived. It is a reflection, for example, of high rates of overall growth in the industrialized countries in recent years, of shortfalls in crops on account of climatic factors, and also perhaps of speculation in commodities as a hedge against inflation and currency depreciation. These forces may not sustain commodity prices in the period ahead. In fact, there are already signs of a slackening in the tempo of expansion in the developed countries.

It is also important to remember that the main beneficiaries of the commodity boom have been developed countries. For the developed market economy countries, the increase in export earnings attributable to primary products other than petroleum was, in 1973, $29 billion—nearly three times as high as the corresponding increase of $11 billion in the commodity exports of the developing countries.

No less important is the fact that there are many developing countries—including some of the largest and poorest—which have not benefited appreciably from this recent improvement in commodity prices. The commodity boom has bypassed such products as bananas, citrus fruits, iron ore, jute, tea and tungsten, with severe consequences for the countries that are heavily dependent upon them. For these countries the increases in import prices have occurred in a situation in which they were already weakened by depleted external reserves, high debt service burdens and markedly reduced imports. They have little margin left for a further downward adjustment of their imports and face the threat not merely of a slackening of growth and development, but of dislocation in even the normal working of their economies and a serious deterioration in levels of food consumption that are already low.

In this situation it is not necessary to underline the compelling need for solutions.

There is a particular need in the current context for action on at least two fronts. The first of these relates to the measures or the mechanisms which could be taken or be set up to help the developing countries meet the problems caused by the mounting import bills which they have to face. This is indeed a new element in the network of financial mechanisms that has hitherto been discussed. Up to now we have been accustomed to discussing the need for compensatory arrangements to help countries meet shortfalls in their export earnings. In the present situation the need is also for arrangements to help countries to cope with an increase in their import outlays.

The possibilities on this score are numerous. These can include bilateral arrangements related to the trade flows of particular commodities such as oil and certain foodstuffs. Such arrangements could include dual price systems, rebates, loans or deferred payments. But since such bilateral arrangements may meet only a part of the problem, there would also be a need for a more general multilateral approach. Here, again, a variety of arrangements are possible. Much can be done within the existing machinery of the IMF, the World Bank, the Regional Banks and other lending institutions by raising the volume of disbursements, by softening their terms and by accelerating their pace. The proposed new IMF oil facility could, provided it is properly structured, be of value to oil-importing countries. But besides this, there is a need for further international initiatives that would specifically benefit the developing countries. There is indeed a need, as has been suggested in several statements made in the plenary, to create one or more new facilities of an emergency character—facilities that would serve to provide rapid balance-of-payments relief to developing countries in need—relief that should be provided in the form of grants or soft loans. It is indeed encouraging to note the intention of oil exporters, themselves developing countries, to assist in this process.

It may well be the case that the balance-of-payments problem of the developing countries in the present situation would eventually be attacked through more than one type of arrangement or facility. But whatever the solutions finally agreed, it is important to ensure that at least three basic conditions are satisfied by them when taken together. The first of these is of course that the amount of relief provided broadly matches up to the magnitude of the problem and that its scale is large enough to be meaningful. It is also important to ensure that the assistance is of a kind that would not create serious problems in the future for the recipient countries by adding to debt service burdens that are already heavy. In other words, the terms on which relief is granted are of crucial importance. It should be remembered that the need for relief to cover the high costs of imports is likely to remain for some time. Lastly, and no less important is the need to ensure that the arrangements are adequate in terms of timing, since for many countries the problem is an immediate one.

It is also important when providing assistance to ensure that financing criteria are established that take account of not only the increased cost of essential imports, but also of such other elements as the growth in export earnings of individual developing countries, their net monetary reserves and their foreign indebtedness. Furthermore, it will only be natural to expect that contributions to the new facilities would be made by those developed countries and oil-exporting countries which are in a position to do so.

The case for emergency financial support applies also to the need to increase the flow of official development assistance, and in the case of certain developing countries, for agreements to reschedule and when appropriate to even write off their debt service burdens. Indeed, action on these lines would provide support for the bilateral and multilateral efforts needed to extend short-term financial support to developing countries.

A new factor of a longer-term character that must be taken into account is the accumulation of external assets by some oil-exporting countries. It should be noted that these assets are derived from the depletion of finite resources and must be invested in a manner consistent with the interests of future generations in oil-producing countries. Special efforts should be made by the entire international community to devise new techniques for lending to channel part of these funds, directly or indirectly, into developing countries.

But action to provide financial assistance to developing countries is only one side of the coin. The problem of rising import payments cannot be met by emergency support alone. The more basic solution would be to enable countries to cope with this problem through higher export earnings. This would encompass both earnings from the export of manufactures as well as of commodities and calls for action in a number of areas where hitherto the political will has been lacking. But in the context of this special session on raw materials, I would like to dwell in particular on the problems of commodities and primary products.

Primary products still account for by far the greater part of the exports of the developing countries. The problems in this area remain a major element of weakness in the international economic system. Up to now, despite many declarations on the importance of strengthening and stabilizing commodity prices, there has been little effective action on the part of the international community. Commodity agreements have been few in number and not all those that have been established are functioning well or are supported by all. In short, action taken by the international community in this field so far has clearly failed to produce adequate results.

The time is surely opportune therefore for giving a new impetus to action in this field, and it is encouraging to note the new awareness of the need for action shown at the special session on the part of the developed and the developing countries alike. There are, after all, new elements in the present situation which warrant such an initiative. There is now, perhaps more than ever before, a greater awareness of the convergence of interests of both the producing and consuming countries. The consuming countries are concerned more perhaps than in the past with the need for assured supplies of several products and for an orderly price situation. Producers are concerned with the need for strengthened earnings and assured markets. Both are concerned with the problem of the depletion of non-renewable resources and with their rational exploitation.

Out of this special session on raw materials there must surely emerge a new concentration of political attention and a new thrust for an action programme in the field of raw materials and commodities. Past approaches have proved inadequate partly because they suffered from a lack of political will and partly because they looked to mechanism and instruments that were too narrow in scope. It would be the task of the international community in the period ahead to work out the elements of a new strategy for commodities. The new approach would need to be more comprehensive in scope than in the past. Whilst there would be a continuing need for instituting arrangements for specific commodities, these could be established in the context of a wider framework of principles and approaches which are firmly secured by a political will on the part of the international community to secure results.

A broader approach to the commodity problem can also encompass, where appropriate, arrangements for buffer stocks which are based on not one, but several commodities supported, for example, by a central fund. The new approach, even in the case of a single commodity, should also be more multidimensional than in the past. It would need to include not only the traditional stabilization function based on export quotas and buffer stocks, but also make provision for other features as well. These could include measures in the field of marketing, distribution and promotion; the greater use of long-term contracts, both bilateral and multilateral; the assurance of adequate supplies, the linking of prices of commodities to the prices of manufactured goods and the greater co-ordination of policies by the producing countries with a view to stabilizing and improving their earnings. Finance for diversification and for new investments and for processing of these products in the producing countries could also be elements of a multidimensional approach. Furthermore, to the extent that these arrangements do not suffice to improve prices and earnings, or the commodities concerned are not amenable to buffer stock and export quota measures, there would also be scope for arrangements for compensatory financing, both of a short- and long-term character, to help meet unforeseen shortfalls. Indeed, had a system of compensatory financing of a proper kind been in existence—a system aimed at safeguarding development plans against disruptive and adverse changes in the terms of trade—some current problems might well have been considerably ameliorated.

The institution of financial arrangements to help meet the payments problems of developing countries and a new thrust in the field of commodity policy are amongst the initiatives that could emerge in the context of the present discussion. But they will not suffice by themselves. For example, the world food problem requires priority attention. Arrangements for closer co-operation among governments in the field of transfer of technology and greater control by developing countries over the use of their natural resources are needed. The activities of multinational corporations will have to be harnessed and made consistent with the development objectives of developing countries. The development of international economic relations on a just and equitable basis need to be embodied in the Charter of Economic Rights and Duties of States. These issues and several others mentioned in my note may form part of a comprehensive restructuring of the international trade, monetary and financial systems.

This special session provides a new opportunity to set in motion the actions needed to bring about the changes that must be made in the international economic order. The goal must be a new dynamic equilibrium; a system that would be stable and viable and which will tap the full growth potential of all member countries— developed market economy countries, socialist countries and developing countries; a system that will utilize the interdependence of economies to generate additional benefits for all; a new partnership based on mutual respect.

Trade and Development Board

10 March 1975

The present special session of the Board has the advantage of being held early in the year, the advantage of being able, for this reason, to contribute to and influence the deliberations to come. The session is devoted to three closely related issues: the mid-term review and appraisal of the International Development Strategy, the implementation of the Declaration and the Programme of Action for the Establishment of a New International Economic Order, and the efficacy of the UN system for dealing with the basic issues of development. These issues will be the concern of the General Assembly later this year, both at its seventh special session and at its thirtieth regular session. It is the hope and expectation of all, I am sure, that out of these events will emerge a better understanding of the development problem, a new commitment to the development objective and an identification of new directions to be pursued.

What can we say on the substantive issues which pertain to the International Development Strategy? If we begin by reflecting on the first five years of the Second Development Decade and of the Strategy, what observations could we make? There are doubtless several, but a few basic ones come to mind.

The first is that rapid expansion and rising prosperity in the developed countries, as witnessed in the initial period of the decade and even earlier, do not spontaneously and readily percolate to the developing countries—at least not on a comparable scale. It is true that, at the time of the biennial review, we found some satisfaction in the fact that the growth rate of the developing countries taken as a whole was on average around the 6 per cent target set for the Decade. But, even then, it was evident that the average concealed an unsatisfactory pattern of distribution in which the poorest and the most populous countries fared relatively badly. The mechanisms of transmission of the process of growth and prosperity appear to be as weak internationally as they are nationally. There is no assurance that the increasing affluence of the rich will always lift up the poor.

The second observation concerns the instruments of development co-operation. Although there are other elements in the development co-operation policy of the industrialized countries—the generalized system of preferences is an example—development aid has been one of its main pillars. But here the picture has been one of relative failure. Despite good performances by some countries, there have in general been substantial shortfalls in respect of the targets in this field. The Chairman of the Development Assistance Committee of OECD has, in his recent report, pointed to the paradox that, although during the ten years 1963–73 the member countries of OECD experienced marked expansion and prosperity—with their total product increasing by

as much as two-thirds and their per capita product by 50 per cent in real terms—
official development assistance actually declined—also in real terms—by some 7 per
cent. This is surely a reflection that something is wrong with the aid instrument for
development co-operation as we have known it, a reflection of some underlying
malaise whose roots go deeper than the difficulties and problems of the developed
countries. The experience we have had points, I believe, to the need to set the role of
assistance within a broader framework of measures to meet the external resource
needs of developing countries and to explore new and more assured mechanisms for
financial resource transfers.

The third observation we need to make is that now, at the mid-point in the Decade,
we have moved into a phase of multiple crises, a phase in which rapid expansion in
the developed countries is not in prospect. We have entered a phase of economic
slowdown, occurring in a setting of continued inflation, increasing payments problems
and major changes in price relationships. The crisis has enveloped the developing
countries as well. Many of them face a desperate situation where, instead of growth
and development, there is a feverish struggle to avert a breakdown. But the problems
caused by high prices for food, fuel, machinery, equipment, fertilizers and other imports and those caused by falling prices for commodity exports, lie atop more deep-
seated tensions, reflecting the processes of demographic, political, social and economic
change, reflecting the expectations and aspirations of growing numbers of young
people entering the work force in search of employment. These are, indeed, massive
problems, which pose a serious challenge even in the most favourable external environment.

What conclusions can we draw from all this that are of relevance to the Strategy
during the remaining part of the Decade? Our experience of the first five years points
to but one basic conclusion: that there is an absolutely urgent—I would say
imperative—need to get development moving again, and to get it moving on a new
course. There are both internal and external dimensions to this problem, national as
well as international aspects. Internally, in the developing countries, there is a need for
new strategies, new styles of development that are more responsive to the human
condition—strategies that combine economic growth and the transformation of productive capacity with employment creation, better income distribution, better health
and nutrition, better education and better resource use and conservation. Above all,
the developing countries need to greatly intensify their efforts to raise domestic food
production. All this is a responsibility which the developing countries themselves must
bear; it is a test of the strength of will and of the sincerity of purpose of their
governments.

But, as UNCTAD has repeatedly emphasized, the success of their efforts will be
thwarted in the absence of a suitable international framework. Such a framework has
now to be fashioned in the context of a new global situation—one which is not
predicated entirely on exceptionally high growth rates in the developed countries,
although quite clearly the avoidance of dislocation and disruptions in these countries
is essential for a smoothly functioning global economy. It has to be fashioned in the
context of a global situation where the countries of the Third World have acquired a
new awareness of themselves and of their capacity for action; a global situation where

there is a growing concern with problems of resource utilization; one in which important changes in political relationships have taken place, resulting from a relaxation of international tensions that could enable the socialist countries to strengthen their presence and participation in the global economy.

Report to UNCTAD IV

May 1976

On 1st May 1974 the General Assembly adopted a Declaration and a Programme of Action on the Establishment of a New International Economic Order.[1] This was indeed a momentous event, for it summed up in one gesture the dissatisfaction of the countries of the Third World with the prevailing system of economic relations and their conviction that a solution of their problems needed more than peripheral changes or adjustments to this system. The Charter of Economic Rights and Duties of States adopted by the General Assembly some months later[2] lent support to the concept of the need for a changed order.

The fourth session of the United Nations Conference on Trade and Development takes place in the aftermath of these events, as well as of the subsequent seventh special session of the General Assembly. For this reason, it would be only logical to see the fourth session of the Conference as an occasion for implementing, or for starting to bring into being, the essential elements of a "new order". However, the very need for a new order is still not universally accepted or even understood. It is true that the need for continuous changes and improvements is seldom contested, but these are not always viewed in the context of any one need for a basic restructuring of international economic relations. To many, the "new order" remains a rhetorical phrase—a source of needless controversy and vexation that would only stand in the way of more pragmatic approaches.

Nevertheless it is essential that the issues before the Conference be viewed in a wider perspective. Without such a perspective, the need for action will appear less urgent and inevitably the kind of action taken will prove inadequate. A major crisis of development is engulfing the three continents of Latin America, Africa and Asia—a crisis that is reflected in the inability of the developing countries to cope not only with their economic but also with their political and social problems, a crisis that is not, all the same, sufficiently understood in its true dimensions by the developed countries. The problem is not merely that of the growing gap between the developed and the developing countries, although this is in itself of serious consequence to the prospect

---

[1] General Assembly resolutions 3201(S-VI) and 3202(S-VI).
[2] General Assembly resolution 3281(XXIX) of 12 December 1974.

for global peace and stability. It is also that the pace of development and transformation in the developing countries is falling hopelessly short of the needs—let alone the aspirations—of their populations.

The problem cannot be understood in purely static terms, i.e. as a problem of large numbers of people continuing to live in a traditional setting of poverty and destitution whose condition calls for a humanitarian response. It is also a problem that needs to be seen in its dynamic context—in the context of the incessant processes of demographic, social and political change which are unfolding within the societies of these countries. These are processes that involve growing numbers of young people, imbued with new expectations and aspirations, and becoming increasingly impatient with the very fabric of their own societies. The governments and leaders of the developing countries face the task of coping with this groundswell from below. Theirs is a task of enormous magnitude, calling for the most resolute and dedicated of efforts on their part. But the fulfilment of this task will prove futile if the international framework in which they find themselves continues to frustrate rather than to aid, to undermine rather than to support, the best of their efforts. As the present report seeks to demonstrate, the international framework was just not adequate for the needs of development even when it served to foster a remarkable expansion in global trade and production. It is even less adequate in the conditions of today, when so many of its basic elements have been deeply undermined.

The need for change in the international framework is not confined to the developing countries. Many facets of the economic order as it has prevailed up to now are in need of modification, even from the viewpoint of the developed countries. The international monetary system established at the end of the Second World War, predicated as it was on fixed parities and the covertibility of currencies into gold, has collapsed, bringing in its train unstable exchange rates and disequilibrating movements of capital. Despite some interim arrangements, the task of establishing a new system has yet to be accomplished. Likewise, the "energy crisis" has demolished the premiss of cheap energy, which was until recently an important ingredient of the prosperity and the economic growth of the developed countries. At the same time, the environmental issue has called into question prevailing assumptions regarding the availability and use of natural resources, with serious implication for the continuation of patterns of development that were founded on their wanton exploitation. Furthermore, the ability of the developed countries to combine full employment with relative monetary and price stability has been seriously undermined, giving rise to processes of inflation, and more recently of recession, which have had a disruptive effect on the entire global system.

The need for changes in the existing order is also obvious from the point of view of the socialist countries. Their participation in world trade and other international exchanges was seriously circumscribed by a host of constraints, as much political as economic. During the post-war period they succeeded in attaining impressive rates of economic expansion under a planned system of development. Yet this expansion by and large betokened a process of relatively self-contained growth—of collective self-reliance, in fact—under conditions which cut these countries off from the mainstream of the world economy. The removal of the constraints that impede the fuller participation of these countries in world trade is one of the requisites of a New Economic Order. The very fact of the growing expansion and diversification of their productive potential provides new opportunities for beneficial exchanges, both with the developed market-economy countries and with the developing countries. A new order must provide for the full utilization of these opportunities so as to enable the socialist countries of Eastern Europe and of the Third World to enter more fully into the mainstream of world trade and development.

From the standpoint of the developing countries, the need for a change in the present international economic order rests on factors that differ fundamentally from those just described in the case of the developed market-economy countries and the socialist countries of Eastern Europe. For the developing countries the compelling need for a new order is not based on the consideration that the prevailing order is no longer working well, but on the more fundamental premiss that it did not satisfy their needs even when it was working at its best. The changes called for are not simply those that will rectify the shortcomings which now handicap the economies of the developed countries—changes that will help only towards a better functioning of the present system. The changes must be more far-reaching and bear upon the very mechanisms that weakened, or impeded, the growth and expansion of the developing countries—mechanisms that have contributed to a widening, rather than a narrowing, of global inequality.

The facts on this score are indeed dramatic. Over the quarter of a century from the end of the Second World War to the early 1970s, the prevailing order brought unprecedented expansion and prosperity to the developed market-economy countries: there was a phenomenal rise in their productive capacity, in their real incomes and in their levels of consumption. Over the same period, however, the experience of the developing countries provides a disquieting contrast. Taking the twenty years from 1952 to 1972, the total gross product of the developed market economies rose from $1250 billion to about $3070 billion, in terms of 1973 prices, the increment alone ($1810 billion) being $3\frac{1}{2}$ times the aggregate gross product of the developing countries in 1972 ($520 billion).

In terms of per capita real income, the contrast is even greater. Real income in the developed market-economy countries rose by $2000 per head of population (again, valued at 1973 prices) from 1952 to 1972, to a figure of almost $4000 in the latter year. The corresponding real per capita income for the developing countries in 1972 was about $300, the increase since 1952 being only $125. Thus, the increment in per capita real income over this period in the developed market economies amounted to 16 times the increment in per capita real income of the developing countries during the same period.

As a result of these uneven developments, the global income inequality gap has widened even further. Today, the developed market-economy countries, with 20 per cent of world population, enjoy about two-thirds of total world income. By contrast, the developing countries—excluding China—with almost 50 per cent of world population, receive only one-eighth of world income. Within the latter total, the poorest developing countries, with some 30 per cent of world population, have only 3 per cent of world income; their average per capita income, of approximately $120, is only about one-fifth of that for all other developing countries, and only about 3 per cent of the average per capita income in the developed market-economy countries.

Taking the post-war period as a whole, the increments in *per capita* real income have proved to be merely marginal in a considerable number of developing countries, and totally inadequate for making any significant impact on the urgent economic and social problems that confront these countries. More often than not, the benefits of growth, such as they were, did not percolate to the mass of the population, but resulted rather in a widening of existing social disparities and a heightening of internal political tensions. Though these are, in some respects, matters for which the developing countries are themselves answerable, they cannot be entirely divorced from the manifold ways in which the domestic systems in these countries are linked to the International Economic Order.

The widening of the economic gap between developed and developing countries over the past twenty years or more, as indicated by the real income figures, can also be traced more concretely in terms of the consumption of basic foods, clothing, housing and essential services such as health care and education. In many of these elements making up the individual's standard of living, it would seem that only marginal progress has been made in a great many developing countries. Moreover, the underlying problems of hunger and malnutrition, even famine, of unemployment and under-employment, of rural poverty and urban degradation, are even more pressing today than they were a quarter of a century ago at the beginning of the phase of rapid economic expansion in the developed countries.

The fact that the developing countries did not share adequately in the prosperity of the developed countries when the latter were experiencing remarkably rapid expansion indicates the existence of basic weaknesses in the mechanisms that link the economies of the two groups of countries. These mechanisms have evolved from the historical relationship between the developing and the developed countries, a relationship in which the developing countries were essentially providers of primary commodities in exchange for the supply of investment capital, technological know-how and manufactured goods from the developed countries. Though the character of this relationship has been undergoing much change, particularly with the progress of industrialization in many Third World countries, it still dominates the structure of economic relations between the developed and developing countries.

The weaknesses of this structure, the inadequacy of the mechanisms by which growth in the developed centres is transmitted to the Third World, are manifested in each of the major areas of economic relations between developed and developing countries—in the trade in commodities and manufactures, in the transfer of technology and in the provision of financial resources through the international monetary and financial system.

A major feature of trade over the post-war period has been the relative lag in the growth of international trade in primary commodities compared with world trade as a whole. From the mid-1950s to the early 1970s world trade in primary commodities (other than petroleum) rose by some 4.5 per cent a year, as against 7.5 per cent for world trade as a whole. In value terms, the discrepancy was even greater; a growth of 5 per cent a year for primary commodities (again, excluding petroleum), as against 8.5

per cent for total trade. The weakness in the commodity sector of world trade reflects in part the relatively slow expansion of demand in developed countries for the food and industrial materials traditionally produced in the developing countries. One important factor here has been the protectionist policies of developed countries. But the persistent weakness in the markets for the commodity exports of developing countries cannot be attributed solely to the slow growth of demand. In addition, the relationships between the buyers of primary commodities—often transnational corporations of developed market-economy countries—and the sellers in developing countries were frequently not conducive to the strengthening of the underlying trend in commodity prices. In many commodity markets the buyers were concentrated and well organized, while the sellers were numerous, widely dispersed and poorly organized. Although the international community has accepted in principle the need for an effective system of commodity market stabilization that would provide adequate returns to producers in developing countries, very little has so far been done to achieve this objective.

Several important constraints have also operated to limit the market potential for the manufactured exports of developing countries. Both tariff and non-tariff barriers have been major impediments to the manufactured exports of developing countries, particularly in those labour-intensive products in which these countries have a cost advantage. The introduction in recent years of "voluntary" export restraints in effect represents an extension of the prevailing system of quantitative regulation of manufactured imports on the part of developed market-economy countries.

Constraints on trade arising from barriers to market access in developed countries have generally been compounded by constraints on the supply side in the developing countries. These constraints derived in part from the policies and practices of the developing countries themselves, which often were not directed to the encouragement of the export of manufactures. But they reflect, also, limitations arising from restrictive business practices of transnational corporations, particularly restrictions on exports of manufactures produced under licence in developing countries and restrictive conditions attached to the use of modern technology transferred by these corporations. Moreover, developing countries face an increasing foreign-exchange burden resulting from the acquisition of technology. The annual foreign-exchange cost to these countries, both direct and indirect, of the acquisition of foreign technology may now be in the range of $3 billion to $5 billion, constituting a heavy burden on scarce foreign exchange resources. At the same time, the rapid expansion of the international market in skills has fostered a reverse transfer of technology through the loss of trained manpower from the developing countries.

The inadequacy of the prevailing mechanisms linking developing countries to the main industrial centres of economic growth is reflected also in the field of financial flows. The rapid economic expansion in the developed market-economy countries was not accompanied by a commensurate surge of private investment in the developing countries, as had been the experience of an earlier era. At the same time, the post-war era witnessed the emergence of a new instrument—official development assistance—for the transfer of resources to developing countries. Yet it is one of the ironies of this period that growing prosperity in the developed market-economy countries was accompanied by a decline in the flow of development assistance in real terms. Not only was the aid target not achieved by these countries as a group; there was in fact a retrogression from the target on the part of major donor countries. Over the decade from 1964 to 1974, the real value of official development assistance from the developed market-economy countries (in terms of purchasing power over imports from the latter countries) declined by about 3 per cent. This is in sharp contrast to the expansion, of over 50 per cent, which occurred in the aggregate real product of the developed market-economy countries over the same decade. This period has also witnessed a vast expansion in world expenditure on armaments which, by 1974, totalled almost $250 billion annually; a reduction of 5 per cent in this expenditure would free resources equivalent to the existing level of official aid to developing countries from all sources.

One result of the inadequacy of official development assistance was that many developing countries were forced to borrow on commerical markets, or resort to suppliers' credits, at high interest rates and with relatively short maturities. This, in turn, contributed to a sharp increase in the external indebtedness of the developing countries, from $9 billion at the end of 1956 to $90 billion (for the non-oil-exporting developing countries) at the end of 1972.

At the same time, the international monetary system served to distribute directly the vast accretion in international liquidity that took place over this period almost exclusively to the developed market-economy countries. Of the total world increase in official external reserves from 1952 to 1972 of $108 billion, about two-thirds, or $70 billion, accrued to the developed market-economy countries. More recently, the value of the reserves of those countries was further augmented by the abolition of the official price of gold. An upward revaluation of the official gold stocks of developed market-economy countries members of the Group of Ten by, say, a threefold increase in the price of gold (which would still leave the gold price below the current market level) would raise their combined reserves by about $60 billion, whereas the corresponding increase for the non-oil-exporting developing countries would be only some $5 billion. It is evident that, had a similar increase in total monetary reserves been brought about instead by SDR allocations, the shift in the distribution of reserves at the expense of developing countries could have been avoided.

The inadequacy of the various mechanisms which linked the fortunes of the developing countries to the developed countries in a largely bipolar relationship was not offset to any significant extent during this period by compensating expansions of the economic exchanges of developing countries among themselves and with the socialist countries. While trade between developing countries and the socialist countries of Eastern Europe increased at a rapid rate over the past decade, the magnitude of these exchanges remains relatively small—only some 4 per cent of the total trade of developing countries. Likewise, the developing countries did not succeed in increasing their mutual trade as a proportion of their total trade; indeed, this proportion declined to 20 per cent in the early 1970s from 26 per cent two decades earlier.

Over this period, however, there emerged a powerful new force, in the form of the transnational corporations which—in the absence of countervailing developments— only served to intensify the dependence of the developing countries on the main industrial centres. These corporations embody an unprecedented concentration of financial power, technological know-how and productive capacity, which has enabled them to occupy a dominant position not only in the trade of developing countries but also in world trade in general. The estimated share of the transnational corporations in world trade exceeds one-half, and may be as high as two-thirds; their share in the total exports (excluding oil) of developing countries is of the order of 40 per cent.

The several limitations that characterize the workings of the prevailing order in respect of the developing countries, as outlined above, would by themselves justify the need for change, for a new set of international economic relationships. However, these limitations manifested themselves during a period in which the prevailing order was functioning relatively well from the point of view of the developed countries. The more recent period has seen the system itself in deep crisis. It has received such severe shocks as to call into question its ability to continue as before and to satisfy the needs of even the developed countries. Some of the events that have jolted the system since the beginning of the 1970s have already been referred to: the disruption of the international monetary system and the violent shifts in payments positions that accompanied it; the onset of severe inflationary pressures; the quadrupling of oil prices; and the advent of a recession more deep-seated and prolonged than any since the 1930s. All these, and other developments, have challenged the validity of major facets of the prevailing framework in the developed countries themselves.

For many developing countries, the impact of the crisis in the system has been disastrous. It is true that the developing countries exporting oil have seen a dramatic improvement in their terms of trade and a consequent increase in the financial resources available to them. Yet even for them, the change in fortunes must be set in the perspective of their need for the transformation and improvement of their own societies, of the rising prices they have to pay for imports, and of the quality of the investment outlets available to them to offset the depletion of their natural resources. The situation for many of the non-oil-exporting countries, however, is catastrophic. They are faced with a combination of rising prices for their essential imports—food, manufactures and fuel—and falling prices for their commodity exports, sparked off by the recession in the industrialized world. These countries are experiencing payments problems of such huge dimensions as to threaten the very foundation of their societies.

The overall payments deficit of the non-oil-exporting developing countries with the rest of the world was of the order of $12 billion in 1973. Since then, it escalated to about $45 billion in 1975, and can be expected to remain in the region of $35 billion to $40 billion in the years immediately ahead. These deficits are not based on levels of imports that allow high rates of economic growth. Rather, they reflect import requirements that are vital for a modest and minimal rate of expansion.

This new shift in the pattern of external payments against the non-oil-exporting developing countries raises serious questions concerning the implications of its continuance. If the deficits are not bridged in one way or another, import levels must fall disastrously, disrupting the normal functioning of the economies of these countries and making nonsense of even the limited goals and objectives of the Second United Nations Development Decade. It must not be forgotten that these countries contain the bulk of the population of the Thirld World.

There should be no presumption that these problems would be solved automatically by the recovery of the industrialized countries from the present recession. The process of recovery in these countries has itself been halting and weak. In any case, as part experience has shown, even a strong upswing in the industrialized countries, helpful as it would be, may not be accompanied by a sufficiently strong revival of the trade and export earnings of the developing countries. Moreover, the recovery of the industrialized countries does not hold out any promise of relief in respect of one of the key factors that have contributed to the present predicament of the developing countries— the incessant upward movement in the prices of their imports. On the contrary, there is a danger that a revival of activity in the industrialized countries will reinforce and give new momentum to the inflationary process.

The immediate response of the international community to the new problems facing the developing countries has, not unnaturally, been to provide financial assistance on an emergency basis, although the volume of such assistance has fallen quite short of needs. But the financing of the massive payments deficits of the developing countries, even if successfully accomplished, must inevitably be a short-term answer to the problem. It cannot constitute a permanent solution. Such financing implies nothing less than a further and indefinite escalation of the external indebtedness of these countries, a problem which is already severe enough. To meet what does not appear to be just a fleeting and temporary shift in payments patterns by continued emergency assistance alone would amount to little more than turning the countries affected into recipients of indefinite relief. It has been usual—even before the current drop in export earnings—to depict the problems of the "most seriously affected" countries as being caused by rising import prices. But higher import prices are only one side of the coin. The rise in prices of food, fuel, fertilizers and manufactures in recent years has been worldwide. The reason why some countries have been more affected than others is simply that the increase in their import bill was not matched by an offsetting increase in their export earnings. If the prices of their imports are to remain high in the future, these countries must at all costs increase their export earnings if they are to escape the trap of mounting indebtedness. Yet, there is little to suggest that this will occur spontaneously within the present order of things. Basic changes are called for that will alter existing structures and establish a new and better framework to govern the trade and external receipts of the developing countries.

Extract from *New Directions and New Structures for Trade and Development*

Report to UNCTAD V

May 1979

The particular significance of the Manila Conference is the linking of all the issues on the agenda into a wider framework. The actions of the Conference on each issue could result in structural changes in the relevant areas; but the actions of the Conference when taken together could contribute towards the restructuring of the global economy. It is for this reason that the theme of structural change can be said to be the binding thread of the agenda.

There is, of course, no identity of views on the meaning of structural change or even on the need for it. Several interpretations and formulations are possible and it is difficult to do more than discuss some aspects of the issue, particularly those that are relevant to the international dimensions of the development process. For the developing countries the emphasis on the need for structural change springs largely from two considerations. Firstly, a conviction that, in the present situation, an adequate tempo of development in these countries cannot be attained as a mere byproduct of the recovery of the industrialized countries and a return by them to previous patterns of growth—even if such a path were possible. The development process was not assisted at all adequately in previous periods when the economies of the industrialized countries experienced unprecedented expansion and prosperity. It is unlikely to be so assisted in the future. Secondly, there is the further conviction that the development process cannot be assisted adequately by aid or voluntary resource transfers alone from the developed to the developing countries, even if the volume of such flows were to be vastly enhanced. The development of the countries of the Third World requires changes of a more fundamental character—changes in prevailing mechanisms, systems and relationships—because it is precisely the deficiencies in this realm that help to perpetuate underdevelopment. This is why basic changes or reforms are seen to be needed in the prevailing structure of world trade in commodities, in the conditions that have determined the present share of developing countries in the global distribution of industry, in the prevailing international framework in the field of money and finance, and in existing patterns of trade.

The end result of the process of structural change would, in this context, be three-fold. The process would lead to changes in present patterns that govern the distribution of global production and trade with a transformation particularly of the share at present of developing countries in world industry and in trade in industrial products. It would lead also to better control by the developing countries over their own natural resources and to a strengthening of their participation in decision-making processes in the realm of international economic affairs—involving changes in their present relationships with transnational corporations and their voice in international financial institutions. Finally, the process of structural change would both require, and result in, a continued evolution in the rules and principles that govern international economic relationships so that they always remain relevant to the demands of a changing world.

There are also a number of aspects to the theme of structural change viewed from the vantage point of the developed countries. One of these relates to the need for basic changes in prevailing mechanisms, practices, policies and institutions within these countries in order to help them overcome problems of unemployment and recession and to facilitate a dynamic process of technological change and adaptation. The debate on structural change in this context can embrace such issues as adjustment assistance, energy conservation, environmental protection, patterns of consumption and so on. The present crisis facing the developed countries is not simply of a cyclical character. Some of the problems they face are so deep-seated that their solution appears to require changes of a structural character.

More directly related to the international dimension of the theme of structural change, however, are two other aspects. The first of these concerns the interest which the developed countries themselves have in basic reforms in existing mechanisms and systems in the international arena. Such an interest could be seen to exist in respect of the responses called for on each of the major issues facing the Manila Conference. The developed countries no less than the developing could benefit from the better functioning of commodity markets and the reduction of extreme fluctuations. They have a basic long-term interest in the avoidance of a restrictive trading system. No less important, they have a vital stake in a soundly structured monetary and financial system which would provide a protection against the disruptions and dislocations of recent times.

The other aspect concerns the benefits that could accrue to the developed countries as a result of structural changes that promote development in the Third World. The developing countries are coming to occupy a place of increasing importance in the economies of the developed countries. There is already a wide awareness of their importance as sources of supply of essential materials. But what is also significant, if less widely recognized, is their importance as markets for the products of the developed countries. Around 40 per cent of US exports of manufactured goods are to developing countries and a similar proportion obtained with respect to Japan and the European Economic Community taken as a whole. For particular sectors of industrial production in the developed countries the degree of dependence is much greater. The significance of this is that policies and measures that promote development in the Third World could stimulate recovery and expansion in the developed countries themselves. In the context of the idle capacity which presently exists in the capital goods sector of the developed countries, the impact of additional demand from the developing countries could be considerable.

Too often development aid and other measures that respond to developing country needs are resisted on the grounds that they impose additional burdens on the developed countries which already find themselves in a difficult situation. But the argument is faulty. Measures to stimulate expansion in developing countries should, on the contrary, form an important part of the policies of developed countries aimed at recovery and balance in their own economies. They should also form an integral and vital part of international policies aimed at improving the global economy not only in the long term but also in the more immediate context.

The need for structural change has recently been recognized and underlined in pronouncements by gatherings of the leaders of industrial countries at the highest levels. There is some debate in these countries whether government policy should facilitate such changes or actively promote them by conscious measures towards that end. Whatever the relative merits of the different sides to the debate, in would seem that in the absence of conscious policies to bring about structural changes, particularly in the area of industry, there is a danger that prevailing and inappropriate patterns will come to be reinforced by contrary policies of a protectionist nature. The danger, in other words, is that if structural change is not consciously fostered, it is likely to be consciously impeded.

The themes pertaining to structural change have been discussed here in terms largely of the developing countries, on the one hand, and the developed market economy countries, on the other. The concept, however, is vitally significant for the socialist countries of Eastern Europe as well. Many of the international mechanisms which impede trade and expansion in the developing countries—limitations to market access, finance, etc.—also impose limitations on the opportunities available to the socialist countries of Eastern Europe. But there is also another dimension of particular relevance in these countries. The restructuring of international economic relations must provide for the fullest development of the potential for trade and other exchanges made possible by the economic growth of the socialist countries of Eastern Europe. This could benefit all groups of countries, but it is particularly relevant to trade between these countries and the developing countries.

Agenda item 8 before the Conference draws attention also to the interdependence of issues in the field of money, trade and development. Such interdependence is of course of relevance to the pursuit of long-term structural change. But more immediately, it is of vital importance to the formulation of policies, whether national or global, to deal with the pressing problems that afflict the international economy. The fact of interdependence is of course well recognized. What is less easy is to ensure that sufficient account is taken of it in the formulation of policy. To some extent the developed market-economy countries already have mechanisms—the summit meetings which consider economic issues and other arrangements—that could partially at least respond to this need. What is sorely lacking at present is a particular mechanism which could take into account the interests and concerns of the developing countries and of the socialist countries of Eastern Europe in the consideration of interdependence and the formulation of policies. Whilst the theme of interdependence is central to UNCTAD's very mandate, there has been no adequate arrangement so far to deal with this. This is one of the important issues on which the Manila Conference needs to act. By establishing an appropriate mechanism in UNCTAD, the Conference could make both a major and an urgent contribution not only on the institutional scale but also to the evolution of international policy.

Item 8 of the agenda also makes particular reference to the need for further evolution in the rules and principles that have hitherto governed international economic relations. This is a subject of the most fundamental importance. The basic framework of rules and principles now in existence was essentially formulated in the period immediately following the end of the Second World War and embodied in such instruments as the General Agreement on Tariffs and Trade, which was a by-product of the negotiations at the Havana Conference and the agreement on an international monetary system negotiated at Bretton Woods. At this time neither the developing countries nor the socialist countries of Eastern Europe brought to bear a strong presence in international economic negotiations, and it is not surprising that their particular needs were barely, if at all, taken into the reckoning. Whilst these needs may, to some extent, have been accommodated in actions taken subsequently, such actions have largely taken the form of exceptions, waivers or qualifications to the prevailing body of rules rather than a recasting of this body of rules itself.

It is relevant to ask whether the time has not now arrived to examine the need for a recasting of earlier doctrine and the body of rules that reflect it. Despite the *ad hoc* measures to accommodate developing countries, these countries do not find the existing framework adequately responsive to their requirements. This is implicit in the expression they have given for the need for a New International Economic Order. What is more, the existing framework itself has been so severely undermined that it has lost much of its coherence as a system and is proving inadequate to meet even the requirements of the industrialized countries. Whilst some of the basic features of the international monetary system were destroyed as far back as 1971, only interim arrangements and *ad hoc* improvisations have been put in its place. No less significant are the increasingly severe strains placed upon the international trading system by the emergence of tendencies that contradict the fundamental principles of the system as embodied in the General Agreement on Tariffs and Trade itself.

There are already in existence components that should be taken into account and incorporated in any recasting of the body of rules and principles. Most of these embody international agreements or international policy instruments that have emerged over the years since the original body of rules and principles was adopted. Yet they have arisen separately, sometimes as responses to particular needs, and remain outside the main body of doctrine itself. They include the concepts inherent in the Declaration on the Establishment of a New International Economic Order, the principles reflected in the Charter on the Economic Rights and Duties of States, the commitment to the regulation of international trade in commodities as reflected in the Integrated Programme for Commodities, the principles recognized in the generalized system of preferences, the principles reflected in the several international codes of conduct that have been negotiated or are in process of being negotiated in respect of shipping, the transfer of technology, restrictive business practices and transnational corporations. There are also other developments deeply relevant to the continuing validity and effectiveness of the old system but which were not adequately foreseen in the earlier period. There has been the major thrust towards integration on the part of the industrialized countries of Europe with principles and modalities relevant to this process. There is also the emerging trend towards co-operation, even integration, amongst developing countries at various levels. During the post-war period, the socialist countries of Eastern Europe too have participated significantly in world trade using modalities and mechanisms appropriate to their economic systems.

As mentioned, all these developments, though forming part of internationally accepted principles or practices, remain for the most part outside the basic framework of rules and principles drawn up at an earlier period. There is a growing need therefore for a recasting of the rules and principles so as to make them more relevant to the realities of our time. Such a revised framework would be responsive to the requirements of all groups of countries, the developing countries and the socialist countries of Eastern Europe, as much as the developed market-economy countries.

It might be suggested that the process of recasting the rules and principles should be a major undertaking for a new international gathering some time in the 1980s, a gathering analogous to the earlier Havana Conference and working over a period of time. The end result of such an effort might be a new international economic convention. The Conference at Manila, whilst it cannot, of course, assume the role of such a gathering, could give attention to the relevant issues and consider how the process leading up to such a result might best be initiated.

The agenda for the fifth session also refers to the contribution that UNCTAD must make to the international strategy for the Third Development Decade and to the special session of the General Assembly which is to address itself to this subject in 1980. The Conference could do so in two ways. First, by the very decisions of the Conference itself on each of the agenda items. These decisions should provide the orientation and direction of international policy for the period ahead in the relevant areas. They would therefore be directly relevant to the content of an international strategy for development. But in addition, the Conference might also take specific steps to establish appropriate arrangements to prepare the further contribution which UNCTAD could make to the formulation of the strategy. This parallels the experience in connection with the strategy for the Second Development Decade, when the Trade and Development Board did make a similar contribution which proved to be a major influence on the ultimate formulation of the strategy itself by the General Assembly. A process on similar lines could be set in motion by the Conference at Manila.

Extract from *Restructuring the International
Economic Framework*

PART III

Restructuring the International Framework

This section includes two statements of the full UNCTAD programme (that of May 1975 being much more detailed than that of July 1974) and brief descriptions of the early history of the organization and the nature of its early achievements. The emergence of the emphasis on commodities within an integrated programme as the main priority in the period up to the fourth session of the Conference in Nairobi in May 1976 is evident almost from the beginning; the secretariat was authorized by the Trade and Development Board in the autumn of 1974 to prepare specific proposals, as described in the second speech below.

APRIL 1974 TO MAY 1976: SEEKING A
MANDATE TO NEGOTIATE

United Nations Economic and
Social Council

9 July 1974

This present session is one of more than ordinary significance. Occurring as it does in the aftermath of the sixth special session of the General Assembly, it has naturally to be concerned with action—action to implement and to follow up the decisions of the General Assembly.

The Declaration on the Establishment of a New International Economic Order, and the Programme of Action—and also the draft Charter of the Economic Rights and Duties of States—are essentially a reflection of, and a response to, the vast changes that are taking place in the international community and particularly in the Third World. The changes are occurring at both the national and the international levels and in a sense they parallel each other. Within the nations of the Third World there is a growing pressure from the wider masses of the people to become more active participants in their own societies and to put an end to positions of marginality. In the international arena too there is a similar quest for accommodation and participation. The countries of the Third World are no longer content to remain on the periphery of the world economy. The socialist countries are no longer in a state of isolation. On the part of all there is an insistence to play a new role, not only in the decision-making process, but in the very systems that determine the tempo and the direction of world events.

It would be readily apparent that both in the national and the international arenas these changes call for adjustment and accommodation from those who are already priviledged and well established. I do not wish to underestimate the difficulties in the way of such adaptation. More often than not, in the case of the developed countries, adaptation has to take place in a context of complex internal problems. But surely, failure to understand these changes and to anticipate the responses needed can only result in frustration, tension and conflict.

In the field of international economic relations there are at least four areas in which a process of structural accommodation and of adjustment are vitally needed. The first of these concerns the field of trade in primary products. The old pattern of commodity trade reflects the historical imperatives of an earlier period. But these patterns still persist. The developing countries still depend on primary commodities for the bulk of their external trade and on forms of organization carried over from the past. They still obtain little more than a subsistence wage for the workers engaged in the production of these goods. This order must surely change in the period ahead—for it is not consistent with the direction of change, with the growing presence of the Third World in the global economy.

Up to now, the tendency has been to see the commodity problem as being largely a problem of instability, and stabilization programmes have been the goal of international policy. But the problem is surely deeper than one of cyclical ups and downs. It is a problem of how to modernize and rationalize the whole field of commodity production and trade so as to give to its participants, and particularly the workers, an adequate and a rising standard of living. This is why there is now an urgent need for a new approach to the commodity problem—one that certainly encompasses stabilization, but also one that reaches beyond it to the problems of marketing, processing, investment and financing.

The new approach to commodities should not be seen as one that aims at exorbitant and unreal prices that exploit the consumer. Fears have often been expressed about the possibility of producer cartels engaged in aggressive price fixing. But it is important to remember that there is already today in many markets a high degree of concentration on the side of the buyers and that competition is seldom equal. Collaboration amongst producers can provide a countervailing pressure, an offset, to this unequal contest. The outcome can well be a more equitable price rather than a monopolistic price and a better organization of markets.

As mentioned elsewhere, the new approach to commodities would need in many cases to extend beyond the commodity agreements that have been envisaged in the past. They would need to utilize an array of instruments additional to mere export regulation. There would be scope, for example, as the situation demands, for multi-commodity buffer stocks, for the overhauling of marketing systems, for long-term contracts both bilateral and multilateral, for programmes of diversification and processing and, to the extent that these measures prove to be inadequate, for schemes of compensatory financing.

There are several considerations that are pertinent to the commodity problem of today. Many products have not even shared in the recent boom in commodity prices. For those that have there is now the possibility of a down-turn in prices. These prices were largely a by-product of forces of a short-term or ephermeral character. In fact, there is now already a decline in some of these prices reflecting, amongst other things, a slackening in the tempo of expansion in the developed countries. Unless timely action is taken, even those countries that are dependent on such primary products whose prices had risen could experience serious difficulties in the period ahead.

A second consideration concerns the inflationary process that is under way in the industrialized countries. This is a new and important element in the situation, for it could mean a steady erosion of the purchasing power of the exports of the developing countries. There are today no "built-in" mechanisms to safeguard the terms of trade of primary producing countries in the face of this inflationary process, and the establishment of such safeguards should therefore be a part of the new approach to commodities.

There are, thirdly, the demands that arise out of the world food situation. To the extent that part of the remedial measures to deal with this problem call for programmes of stock-building and price stabilization, these too could form an integral part of a new policy on commodities.

Lastly, there is the concern on the part of consumers over supplies—both their adequacy and their regularity. The objective of an orderly situation in this field can also form part of a new commodity approach and could provide a strong basis for a convergence of interests between producers and consumers. Schemes of self-sufficiency and withdrawal from markets on the part of industrialized countries are surely costly alternatives to a rational policy on commodities based on international co-operation.

The second potential area of change that concerns an evolving world economy relates to the strengthening of relationships amongst the developing countries themselves. In the long run, the new economic order will surely not continue to intensify the largely "bi-polar" relationships that now prevail between the Third World and the developed countries. Trade between the developing and the developed countries admittedly needs to be strengthened and transformed. But in the period ahead we should also expect new relationships between the countries of the Third World themselves as their consumption expands and their capacities to produce grow. Indeed, the evolution of these relationships is an important aspect of the concept of collective self-reliance. The scope of these relationships could well extend beyond the limits of regional co-operation schemes. There could be trading and other exchanges over a much wider canvass. But these may require a new framework of institutions and of facilities which could provide a fruitful field for action.

The wider relationships could, of course, extend beyond the field of trade alone. For the first time, for example, the oil-exporting countries of the Third World are in possession of substantial financial resources that need secure and attractive investment outlets. For the present, such outlets are largely available only in the developed countries. But it is possible to envisage the establishment, through conscious action, of investment outlets in the Third World itself which go beyond the concept of aid and emergency assistance and which provide the security and the returns that are needed. The financing of commodity stocks is a possibility in this realm to which I have referred on another occasion, but doubtless there are others as well. The investment of these new resources in the developing countries could indeed result in a new pattern of trade in which the deficits of the industrialized countries with oil-exporting countries could be matched by surpluses in the trade of the former with the rest of the Third World.

As mentioned before, the establishment of new relationships amongst the developing countries should not weaken the urgent need for the expansion of trade with the developed countries. Both the scale and the pattern of this trade needs to be transformed with a growing emphasis on the export of manufactures and of processed primary products from the developing countries. These issues should naturally loom large in the multilateral trade negotiations that are due to commence.

The third area of change and evolution concerns technology. Technological change is central to the transformation of the countries of the Third World. There is today an immense storehouse of technological knowledge. But the developing countries need to have access to such knowledge and to acquire it, to adapt it, to add to it and to utilize it. But today these countries face considerable handicaps in the acquisition of technology. The whole field of the transfer of technology is riddled with restrictive practices, high costs and unequal relationships. In fact, the market for technology is highly concentrated and highly imperfect. According to some estimates made by UNCTAD, the direct cost alone of technological transfer to the developing countries was around $1.5 billion in 1968—an amount equal to around three-fifths of the annual flow of direct private foreign investment including reinvestment. The figure is projected to reach as much as $9 billion, at 1968 prices, by the end of the seventies of the targets of the Second Development Decade are to be reached. The indirect costs in all this are even higher.

This is a field that is likely to grow in importance in the period ahead and in which most useful work can still be done. UNCTAD has already been deeply involved in this area and has addressed itself to such activities as a revision of the national and international patent system and the establishment of an international code of conduct on the transfer of technology. Although the issue of the transfer of technology and of restrictive business practices extends beyond the subject of transnational corporations, it is closely related to it as well; and I hope that UNCTAD's work in this field would be of continued value in the context of any new arrangements for dealing with the subject of transnational corporations.

The fourth major area I wish to refer to concerns that of money and of finance. It is gratifying to note that the growing participation of the developing countries in the decision-making process pertaining to the reform of the international monetary system—a participation that has for long been urged in the UNCTAD forum—has already led to some positive developments of value to the developing countries. But much work remains to be done in this field. There is still a need to secure final agreement on the establishment of a "link" between the creation of SDRs and additional development assistance. Moreover, major reforms in the international monetary system have still to be agreed upon. It is important to ensure that these reforms are not introduced in a piecemeal fashion, that they lead to a universal system and that at all times the fullest attention is given to the requirements of the developing countries in the international monetary order.

The problem of external indebtedness is another major concern at the present time. Indeed, the current economic crisis has aggravated the external debt problems of a number of developing countries and for them at least remedial measures have become a matter of the greatest urgency. The whole question of possible new approaches to the debt issue is now under active consideration by a group of governmental experts convened under UNCTAD auspices. Development assistance too will doubtless undergo changes both in concepts and in mechanisms in the period ahead.

In the meantime, there has arisen the problem of emergency assistance for countries that are now facing acute difficulties. As required by the Special Programme adopted by the General Assembly, UNCTAD has been collaborating with Dr. Prebisch and his colleagues in the emergency operation that is being conducted under the auspices of the United Nations.

UNCTAD has for long been concerned with many aspects of the broad areas I have referred to. The Programme of Action adopted by the General Assembly has given a new impetus and a sense of direction to UNCTAD's work. I need hardly say that UNCTAD will, as requested by the General Assembly, play its full part in implementing those parts of the Programme that fall within its field of responsibility. Several parts of the Programme reinforce and strengthen objectives with which UNCTAD has been already concerned. Others include fresh elements on which new work needs to be done. The implications of the Programme of Action or UNCTAD will be the subject of consideration at the forthcoming session next month of the Trade and Development Board.

Special attention will be given, amongst others, to such issues—dealt with in the Programme—as an integrated approach to commodities, the strengthening of UNCTAD's activities—including the data gathering and monitoring activities—in the field of following the development of international trade in raw materials; the indexation of the prices of primary products to the prices of manufactures; the code of conduct on the transfer of technology; and the general issue of interdependence between problems and policies in such fields as money, trade and development.

United Nations Economic and Social Council

November 1974

I am very pleased to be here this morning to be able to present to the resumed session of the Economic and Social Council the report of the Trade and Development Board of UNCTAD which held its fourteenth session from 20 August to 13 September this year.

The fourteenth session of the Trade and Development Board took place in the aftermath of the special session of the General Assembly. It was the first occasion in which the continuing machinery of UNCTAD was able to address itself to the declaration of the Programme of Action on the establishment of an International Economic Order. For that very reason, I believe that the fourteenth session was a particularly significant one. The session was also the first occasion in which the Board was able to address itself to the preparations for the fourth conference of UNCTAD which is due to take place in 1976, and when some preparatory decisions connected with the fourth UNCTAD Conference were taken.

In addition to what may be called its traditional preoccupations, the Trade and Development Board at its fourteenth session was also concerned with a number of new initiatives, some of which received a particular impetus from the special session of the General Assembly. These new initiatives related primarily to the field of commodities, to the field of co-operation among developing countries and also to some developments in the field of money and finance.

I had in my own presentation to the Trade and Development Board stressed the importance of the commodity issue in the new international situation which we are all facing. I pointed to the urgency of the problem, the need to take remedial measures, the inadequacy of past approaches and the urgency of formulating new approaches and of turning to new instruments in order to deal with the commodity problem. And in response to these issues, the Trade and Development Board adopted a comprehensive resolution on the subject of commodities.

The resolution itself basically falls into three parts. The second part of the resolution deals with the subject of an integrated approach to commodities. In my own presentation to the Board I urged that it would be important to approach the commodity issue from a more comprehensive point of view than had been the custom in the past. There was a need to get away from the somewhat narrow confines of the single commodity-by-commodity approach, although when one is dealing with commodities and setting up specific arrangements it is necessary to deal with individual commodities. But such an approach could be prefaced by a wider view where the commodity problem was looked at as a whole and where in some cases commodities could be considered not individually but in groups. In that connection, a number of proposals were made for the possible use of new instruments for dealing with the commodity situation. Instruments such as multiple commodity buffer stock financed through a Common Fund, instruments such as the use of multilateral contracting over medium- and long-term periods for the supply of commodities at assured prices, instruments such as indexation, to ensure that the prices of commodities kept pace with the price of manufactured products, and also such instruments as compensatory financing as a residual mechanism to provide countries dependent on the production of primary products with an assured source of income even in periods when the prices of these products take a downward turn. I was asked in that resolution to elaborate upon these various mechanisms, to concretize them, and to come with specific proposals relating to their use for the Committee on Commodities, which is due to convene in February next year. I think that the mandate that I have been given in this field is a very significant one which enables UNCTAD to devote a good deal of attention to the commodity problem, which is crying out for action in the present situation. I made it very clear—and I think that this was well understood by the Board—that this emphasis on primary products and commodities and raw materials would in no way detract from the priority given to the other aspect of the trade of developing countries, and that is the trade in manufactured goods. The action in the field of commodities is intended to strengthen and supplement the work that UNCTAD has already been doing in the field of the various trade problems of developing countries, particularly those pertaining to the trade of manufactures.

International Seminar of the International Youth and Student Movement for the United Nations (ISMUN)

26 September 1974

It would be true to say that for quite some time now, well before the initiative relating to a New International Economic Order was taken, the United Nations served a purpose as being a focal point for bringing about an international awareness of the problems of development. Even way back in the sixties, perhaps even in the fifties, the United Nations, through numerous international conferences, through the work of its secretariat, of its regional commissions and so on, did serve to bring to international attention the problems of development and of developing countries. The United Nations engaged in programmes of technical assistance—I know this for myself because, having worked in a national context in Sri Lanka, I was very much aware of the way in which the UN Agencies interested themselves in various aspects of the development of that country, and I think that this experience was common to many developing countries, even as far back as the fifties or the sixties.

But I think, all the same, it would be true to say that it was somewhere in the beginning of the mid-sixties, particularly with the formation of UNCTAD, that attention came to be focused on the international dimensions of the development process as against the purely national dimensions, and the work of the United Nations began then to bring within its ambit not only advice and assistance to developing countries and the policies they need to pursue internally, but also to focus attention on the international framework within which the development process takes place. I think that the creation of UNCTAD was a manifestation of the conviction of the international community, and particularly of the developing countries, that if development is to proceed apace effectively, rapidly and smoothly, there must be an international framework which is conducive to that process. So the main themes of UNCTAD I were in a sense the need to pay attention to these international dimensions, the need to improve the prospects of the developing countries for trade to enable them to sustain a level of imports commensurate with the requirements of their development plans, the need to ensure that they would be possessed of the resources with which to pay for these imports either through a strengthening of their exports or through additional resource transfers in the form of aid and other mechanisms. So UNCTAD I perhaps was the high-water mark in this process of bringing about a greater understanding and awareness of the international dimension.

But even after UNCTAD I, and right through the early years of the seventies, I think the main thrust of the international community's efforts in the field of development and its international aspect was to acclerate the transfer of resources. The main thrust, notwithstanding UNCTAD's critique of the inadequacies of the trade system, was to bring about greater resource flows through aid, sometimes on commercial terms, but mostly on concessional terms; and the implicit premise underlying this approach was that the international economy was working statisfactorily, that it was engendering adequate growth in the main centres of economic activity, and what was needed was that a part of this growth should be channelled to help the development process. In other words, the main need was to make sure the developing countries were able to share in a growing, expanding, prospering world economy. And if you look at the language of the strategies of development, particularly the more comprehensive exposition for the Second Development Decade, you find there this undertone, not stated explicitly, but rather implicitly, that the world economy was assumed to face a bright future, that the main industrialized centres are likely to continue expansion, and that what is needed is to make sure that some part of these benefits are directed to and channelled to developing countries. Since then, of course, there have been many basic changes which fundamentally called into question, even undermined, the premisses on which this earlier thinking was based.

Trade and Development Board on the Occasion of the Tenth Anniversary of UNCTAD

28 August 1974

In reflecting upon the past, we would doubtless acknowledge the successes of UNC-TAD as well as its failures. The successes have indeed been considerable. It is quite right to draw attention to what UNCTAD has been able to do in such fields as the generalized scheme of preferences, commodity agreements for sugar and cocoa, shipping and technology, and monetary affairs—particularly in relation to the participation of the developing countries in negotiations. In enumerating these achievements, we should not also overlook the part played by UNCTAD in contributing to the concepts of the International Development Strategy. But, even more significant than these specific achievements has been the general influence which UNCTAD has wielded. It has, after all, been the prime forum in which the issue of development—the issue more particularly of the international framework for development—has been kept under constant review. It is true to say that UNCTAD's impact, UNCTAD's influence extends beyond its own forum, its record goes beyond its specific achievements. UNCTAD has profoundly influenced attitudes and decisions, and even actions, in virtually every forum that has concerned itself with the development question. This in itself is an immense, a formidable, contribution.

But, despite these achievements it would, I believe, be true to say that UNCTAD has yet to realize what it first set out to realize—to achieve what its first Secretary-General called a "new trade policy for development". UNCTAD strove to establish an international framework which is conducive to the development objective and, towards this end, to bring about a basic restructuring of international economic relations. This goal has yet to be achieved. It is perhaps this failure which accounts, in a large part, for the frustration and perhaps the disappointment which is sometimes expressed about UNCTAD's achievements. But when we reflect on this and appraise and evaluate UNCTAD and the role it has played, we need to remember that UNC-TAD's goals have been particularly ambitious and far-reaching. It is inevitable for this reason that UNCTAD would be evaluated, and its performance measured, by the yardstick of its own ambitions. UNCTAD has not been content to pursue merely marginal, peripheral, adaptations of the international economic system. It has reached out for greater and more fundamental objectives.

Institute of Foreign Trade, Moscow

20 May 1975

I want in the course of my remarks to say something about the problems with which UNCTAD is concerning itself at the present juncture and, in particular, the issues that are evolving in connection with the fourth session of the Conference on Trade and Development, which is to take place one year from now in the month of May 1976 in the City of Nairobi.

Last year UNCTAD celebrated its tenth anniversary. It was an occasion to take stock, to look at the past, to evaluate what it is that UNCTAD has been able to achieve, to identify the areas in which its achievement had fallen short of expectations and, perhaps, to take a look at the future and chart a course for the period ahead. I think it was the common understanding that over the last ten years UNCTAD has had several achievements to its credit. It has served as a representative, universal forum for the discussion of problems of trade and development, problems that are central to the world community. It has also a number of specific achievements to its credit—the establishment of the generalized system of preferences, the adoption of targets for economic assistance, the adoption of the Charter of Economic Rights and Duties of States, the adoption of the Code of Conduct for Liner Conferences, the negotiation and conclusion of the International Cocoa Agreement and many other things.

But at the same time UNCTAD did not achieve some of its broader goals, partly because it was ambitious in the pursuit of these goals. UNCTAD has not been an organization content to pursue minor peripheral changes in the world system. It has aimed at a basic reorientation of international economic relations. If one asked whether there has been today such a basic reorientation, then in many respects we would still have to answer that the task remains to be done. So it is necessary in the period ahead for the pressure to be continued and for UNCTAD to continue to serve as the forum in which the quest for a New Economic Order is pursued, a forum in which specific agreements are negotiated and conclusions arrived at.

In the period ahead, the background will be different from that of ten years ago. We live in a changed situation which in many ways has brought to the surface new problems and new difficulties. Yet it is a situation which also contains a number of positive elements which give some ground for optimism regarding the possibilities for the future. The international political climate has I believe cooled by comparison with that of ten years ago. The developing countries are experiencing an increasing process of awakening and self-assertion or self-awareness. Their voice is gaining in strength. The position of the socialist countries is stronger than ever before in the world economic and political system. These are changes which hold out the promise of a better prospect for the future. We have to be mindful of the dangers, we have to grapple with them, but we have also to grasp the opportunities that we see and build on the positive and constructive elements in the world economic situation.

Now as I was saying, the first opportunity that lies before us for making a significant change, for bringing about a breakthrough in international economic relations, is perhaps the fourth session of the Conference on Trade and Development next year. This session will, of course, be preceded by a number of very crucial and strategic meetings to be held under the auspices of the United Nations—the seventh special session of the General Assembly, the regular session this year devoted to the appraisal of the international strategy for development—these are major occasions and major events. But I believe that these conferences and meetings can do no more than provide a momentum or political thrust to issues which can only be taken up for resolution and solution in detail at a meeting such as the fourth session of the Conference on Trade and Development. So I see this fourth session as coming at the climax of a series of meetings, and as an opportunity to give flesh and blood to some of the general themes and issues that might be developed and adopted in the course of the next twelve months.

The agenda for the fourth session of the Conference has not yet been adopted. It will be adopted in August this year, when the Trade and Development Board meets for its fifteenth regular session. But because the international situation is so changeable, so fluid, we have made provision for the Board to convene again later in the year, should the need arise, to take account of the decisions and developments at the seventh special session of the General Assembly and to modify the provisional agenda that it will have adopted. But although the agenda itself has not been adopted, some of the major themes of the fourth sessions of the Conference are already beginning to take shape and perhaps it might be of interest to you if I were broadly to indicate on this occasion what some of these issues might be.

I think that one can already discern that the whole question of bringing about a new element of strength to the trading situation of the developing countries is likely to loom large at the session. Up to now, too much of the policy of development co-operation, of the Western countries in particular, has been predicated on the concept of aid, on the concept of the transfer of resources from rich to poor countries, from developed to developing countries. And too little attention has been given to the other, perhaps more important, element in the international economic relationship—that of trade. There was of course this old slogan "trade not aid". But although lip-service has been paid to it, in reality the preference of the developed countries of the West has been to use the aid mechanism in preference to the trade mechanism. The reason for that of course is not difficult to understand—giving aid involved less of an interference with the established mechanisms and institutions of international economic relationships than new initiatives and new arrangements in the field of trade. When the developing countries applied pressure for an improved situation, the Western countries found it easier to respond by gestures in the field of aid rather than by bringing about basic changes in the trading mechanism. Now I think that this situation does need to change. If the trading situation of the developing countries continues to be weak, continues to be vulnerable to all the forces of disturbance in the world economy, then no matter what you do by way of aid is likely to be inadequate; it is likely to be undermined; it is likely to be thwarted by adverse developments on the economic front. I think that there is now an urgent need, a crying need, for new solutions and new arrangements in the field of the trade of developing countries because it is through trade that the developing countries still acquire the greater part of their external resources. If that front is weak, then all other attempts at assistance will in turn be inadequate.

When one looks at the trade problem of the developing countries, one naturally has to look first at the problem of trade in commodities, the problem of trade in primary products, in raw materials, because this is the major source of external earnings and of exports for developing countries. Even if you were to leave out oil, the commodity exports of developing countries account for something like 60 per cent of their total earnings of foreign exchange. So when one talks about the need for new solutions on the trade front, one must inevitably look for new solutions in the field of trade in commodities.

For the last thirty years, almost ever since the end of the Second World War, a good deal of lip-service has been paid to the problem of stabilizing primary product prices —in many international forums it has been a very popular subject of discussion and debate. But actual action, concrete arrangements have been very few and far between. Over the whole of the last thirty years there have only been five or six commodity agreements in operation, and even those are not all working satisfactorily. In the whole period of UNCTAD's existence, the whole of the ten-year period, there has been only one new commodity agreement successfully negotiated, and that is the International Cocoa Agreement. And that Agreement took seventeen years before it became a reality. So there is a need to take a look at past approaches, which have clearly proved to be inadequate, to try to see what new approaches are possible, what new ways of tackling the commodity problem are available to us and to try to see to what extent these new approaches could be incorporated in new international initiatives.

It was with this thought in mind that the secretariat of UNCTAD presented to its Board last August, following the sixth special session of the General Assembly and the Programme of Action on the Establishment of a New International Economic Order, what is now called an Integrated Programme for Commodities. The objective there is to look at the problem of commodities, not in terms of individual products, not on a piece-meal basis, not on a commodity-by-commodity basis, but as a problem which is common to the whole sector of the economies of the developing countries—the primary producing sector. It is a problem which many commodities share in common whose resolution needs a political thrust not devoted to one particular commodity or another but to the problem of primary products in general. Within the framework of such a comprehensive approach one has to find specific solutions for individual commodities. Well, with this background in mind, the integrated programme for commodities presented an approach which is based on five basic elements, none of which are new in themselves, but which taken together constitute, I believe, a whole new approach to the commodity problem. I do not want on this occasion to take up your time by elaborating at great length on the details of the integrated programme for commodities, but I might perhaps mention to you what the five basic elements of this programme are. The first is a proposal to establish a series of international stocks covering a wide range of commodities. Such stocks do not exist today except for the provision made for them in the case of one or two commodity agreements, such as those on tin and cocoa. But we believe that much could be done to stabilize commodity markets if there was an international policy dealing with stocks of commodities which could be utilized to stabilize prices when they come down or even when they reach excessively high levels.

The second element is a proposal for a common financing fund which would make financial resources available for stocking operations—a fund to which the managers of international buffer stocks could resort if they require resources to undertake their operations. We hope that this fund would be financed by producer countries, by consumer countries, and by other investors, including international institutions, but more particularly by investors such as the oil-producing countries, which are in search of outlets for their surplus resources. We can think of no better way in which the oil-producing countries can contribute to the solution of the problems of the developing countries than by supporting the proposal to establish stocks of commodities and by contributing to its financing.

The third element in the programme is a proposal for a series of long-term commitments—medium- to long-term commitments—arrived at multilaterally between buyers and sellers and embracing promises to purchase and sell commodities within agreed price ranges.

The fourth element is intended to take care of those cases which may not be adequately covered by the other mechanisms, and that is a proposal for compensatory financing to enable countries whose export earnings decline to obtain some resources which would enable them to keep their development plans going at the levels anticipated.

The fifth and final element of the programme is for a new attack on the problem of processing primary products because one cannot look at the commodity economy of developing countries in static terms. We have to look to its dynamic transformation and this can take place only through the progressive processing of commodities within the territories of the primary producing countries. The commodity sector of the developing countries is still based on old historical relationships, relationships that evolved in the period of the colonial past. In many sectors in ownership, in degrees of processing, in methods of marketing and distribution, in the degree of control they have over the sale of the products, the relationships established in the past continue. There is a need to overhaul this structure and to revise radically the basis on which the commodity economy of the developing countries has been established up to now.

Well, the whole problem of the trade in commodities I think is likely to loom very large in the context of the fourth session of the Conference on Trade and Development. The proposals that I have mentioned have already been discussed by the Committee on Commodities of UNCTAD and so far there has been a good response. I am happy to say that the socialist countries have broadly endorsed the general approach although they have not committed themselves, and no country has committed itself—

not even among the developing countries—to any of the details. But negotiations are going on and it is my expectation that this would become an important issue at the fourth session.

The question of trade in manufactures is also going to be important, but this problem is now figuring in the multilateral trade negotiations that are being undertaken under the auspices of GATT. We in UNCTAD believe that we must continue to keep this question of the trade in manufactures under active review. We cannot assume that this problem will be automatically solved by the multilateral trade negotiations. There is a need to review progress in this field, to continue to apply pressure to bring about a better situation, and also to widen the approach that we ourselves have adopted to this issue in the past in the way of looking at the other elements of the industrialization process of developing countries, which go beyond the need for improved access to markets. So in the secretariat of UNCTAD there is now beginning a new process of thinking which is aimed at a more comprehensive approach to the problem of the trade in manufactures.

Another major area of UNCTAD's concerns which would come up at the fourth session is that connected with problems in the field of money and finance. As you are well aware, the so-called international monetary system established at Bretton Woods has all but broken down. No new international monetary system has yet been established in its place. A series of temporary *ad hoc* improvisations now prevail to regulate international monetary affairs. There is a need in the future to build anew, to establish and create an international monetary system which serves the need of the whole international community, a monetary system which is universal in regard to the participation of member countries, which looks after the needs of the whole international community, the socialist countries as much as the developed countries of the West, the developing countries as much as the countries which are now participants in the international monetary system. So although the thinking in this field is still in an embryonic stage, I am sure that the question of the future evolution of the international monetary system would figure in the discussions at the fourth session of the Conference.

In the field of finance, of course, the perpetual problem of the transfer of resources from the industrialized countries to the developing countries would continue to figure. Even more significant in that context is the question of the external debt problems of developing countries, which have always been important, but which in the last year or two have assumed particularly large and frightening dimensions. I think that the question of how this problem of the external debt of developing countries can be resolved, how new principles could be established to guide the renegotiation of debts, what institutional mechanism should be set up to facilitate this process, would become of some importance in the context of the consideration of financial issues.

With regard to aid, there is a growing feeling that there is a need to establish more automatic, more dependable mechanisms for transferring resources rather than this concept of voluntary aid which is so dependent on the budgetary processes of the rich countries and particularly the Western countries. There have been several proposals for development of more automatic mechanisms but many of these are for the distant future. The establishment of a so-called "link" between the creation of special drawing rights, new international liquidity, and finance for development has been one such proposal. It has been supported, I believe, by the socialist countries in the Expert Group on International Monetary Issues, in which I myself had the privilege of participating some years back. But there are other ideas as well. There are thoughts of imposing some kind of a tax or levy on the use of non-renewable resources and to make these proceeds available for the financing of development. There has been discussion of how to utilize resources from the common property rights of mankind, the sea-bed and the ocean floor, for the benefit of all mankind and in particular for assistance to development. But these are ideas which are not going to be coming up for decision making at the fourth session of the Conference, but which are on the agenda for intellectual, conceptual, activity in the period ahead.

And then there is another theme which I believe would be of great importance at the fourth session of the Conference, and that is the whole question of the geographical direction of trade, particularly the trade of the developing countries. Up to now the whole focus, the whole emphasis in respect of the pressure which developing countries have applied in international forums has been in regard to their trade with the developed countries of the West with whom they have had historical relationships. It has been a bipolar concept—a North/South concept—seeking a further intensification, a strengthening of this trade. But far too little attention has been given to the possibilities of trade and other relationships between the developing countries and the socialist countries, and among the developing countries themselves. The trade of the developing countries with the socialist countries has, as you know, been growing much faster than the general trade of the developing countries with the rest of the world or with the Western countries. Trade between developing and socialist countries has, if I may say so, been the one dynamic element in the trade picture of the developing countries. This process must continue. But we have to ask ourselves whether it will continue spontaneously, whether there is nothing we need do to foster it, whether we could continue to rely on the development of bilateral agreements, or whether we could help to give this a further push by developing new mechanisms, new institutions and new modalities. This is one item, one subject, to which we in UNCTAD have been giving attention—the search for new ways of strengthening and facilitating the trade and other relationships between the developing countries and the socialist countries. We have a division in UNCTAD, headed by Mr. M. Pankine, who is the Director, which has been specially devoted to this problem and has already come up with new thoughts in this field. One such thought which I may bring to your attention is the possibility of developing tripartite, trilateral, triangular relationships between the developing countries and the socialist countries and the developed countries of the West. This may be a new modality added to those which already exist. But I think that we need to give a good deal of our own thinking to how this issue can be developed further. There is a need in this area for new thoughts and new ideas and this is a challenge which faces all of us. I would like to invite all of you present here to participate in the thinking process in the search for new avenues and new modalities.

But apart from this there is the question of economic co-operation amongst the developing countries themselves. Today there are very few exchanges among the countries of the Third World. I do not think that in the period ahead this will continue. I just cannot conceive of a situation in which the developing countries have industrialized, in which they have transformed their productive capacities, and in which they are continuing to unload all their exports and surplus products in the markets of the Western countries. There would be a growing potential for interchanges among themselves and we have to ask what are the obstacles to the exploitation of this potential today, and what other facilities we can suggest or provide to speed it along, to enhance it in the future. New thoughts and new ideas are already coming up—one of these relates to the possibility of setting up a preferential trading arrangement for the developing countries of the Third World. Another relates to the possibility of establishing a payments arrangement. Still another relates to mechanisms and modalities for helping to bring about the investment of the surplus resources of oil-producing countries, which are themselves members of the Third World, within the Third World itself, as opposed to their being directed exclusively to the capital markets of the West. There are questions to which answers have to be found, for which mechanisms have to be designed and instruments forged. This is an area which UNCTAD is considering and which I am sure will loom large at the fourth session of the Conference.

Apart from these substantive themes, there is the question on the institutional side—What is going to be the future of UNCTAD itself? How would UNCTAD—which has served up to now as a representative universal forum for the discussion of various matters in the field of trade and development—serve better the needs of its members—not only in relation to the problems of the developing countries but in relation to all the problems which face the Member States? The question of a comprehensive or international trade organization has been on the agenda of UNCTAD ever since its inception. But there has been up to now very little progress towards the realization of an international trade organization. Well, at the last meeting of the Trade and Development Board in March, I myself in a paper and report I presented revived this issue and asked the question whether in the changed conditions of our time we must not give fresh thought to the feasibility of an international trade organization. The situation now has many new elements in it. I mentioned some of these earlier—the changed political situation, the greater presence of the socialist countries in the world trading system, the greater need of developing countries for rules and regulations and institutions which facilitate their own objectives. The question is whether in this new situation the time is not right to ask ourselves again whether we should not strive for the establishment of an international trade organization, one which does not exist today. GATT is dealing with one segment of international trade and it is not a universal representative forum. The Soviet Union is not, as you know, a member of GATT. UNCTAD is universal but its powers are limited. So there is a need in a way to combine the decision making, regulatory authority of bodies like GATT with the comprehensive coverage of a body like UNCTAD into a new viable and dynamic institution in the field of international trade.

Well, the socialist countries have always been supporter of the idea of an international trade organization. Many developing countries have also been supporters, but I am glad to be able to say that in February this year at their meeting in Dakar in the Senegal, the developing countries as a whole adopted the idea of an international trade organization as one of the objectives that they would unitedly pursue. This is a new element in the situation. The developed countries of the West have still taken up the position that they are not ready for a change. But I think that the pressure will continue. Although I do not myself expect that at the fourth session of the Conference on Trade and Development there would be a decision to create an international trade organization, I hope that the process of thinking in that field would have advanced and the readiness to reach that goal would be greater than it has been in the past. In the meantime, we have to ask ourselves how we can strengthen UNCTAD as an institution, not just for debate, not just as a forum for discussion, but as an organ in which concrete specific business is done. This I think is the major challenge of UNCTAD in the future. It has now to change its character without losing its earlier role as a generator of new ideas. It must also serve as a body in which specific, hard negotiations take place.

Well, I have covered, I think, some of the themes which would figure at the fourth session of the Conference. It remains for me only to bring to your attention the proposals that we have made to change the structure of the session. We hope that this fourth session will be more business-like than its predecessors. Of course it is a large conference—UNCTAD has a larger membership than the United Nations itself. We are, I think, the biggest international organization and, inevitably, a session of the Conference is a very large affair with hundreds of delegates. But we have to see how in such a large multilateral forum we can succeed in bringing about creative results. I think the only way to do this is to intensify the preparation that goes on for it so that everything is not left until the session itself. To help the decision-making process we have suggested three basic changes in the structure of the session. First, we have suggested—and when I say suggested I might add that all these suggestions have now been accepted by the Board—we have proposed that the session itself should be shorter. The first session lasted three or four months in Geneva, the second lasted two months, and the third seven weeks. We have decided that the fourth session will be of no more than four weeks' duration. We hope this would be sufficient to take the decisions that would make the session a success. We have also provided for a selective agenda. Instead of allowing the session to range over every possible issue, mixing up the important with the less important, the mature issues with the less mature issues, we feel that it would be helpful if we could single out some major themes where a breakthrough is possible and try to concentrate on getting results on those. We have also suggested that the fourth session be preceded by a negotiating session to be held at Geneva about five or six weeks before the Nairobi meeting and that, at that session, the resolutions which would be presented for decision at Nairobi would already be presented. There would then be an opportunity for delegations to have an initial exchange of views on these, to break for a period of five or six weeks, go back to their capitals, reflect on their positions and come to Nairobi better prepared to take part in the process of conciliation, compromise and negotiation.

We hope that these innovations would contribute to a more successful meeting. By themselves, of course, they would not suffice, but if they could be accompanied by a good deal of preparatory work between now and the fourth session of the Conference, then I believe that we have an opportunity of making a better success of that session. That is why before I came into this hall, in the course of the discussions I had with your Director and many of your colleagues, I invited the institutions and institutes concerned with problems of foreign trade, international economic relations and development, to devote part of their time, part of their programme, maybe to discussions, maybe to seminars, maybe to meetings, or maybe to commissioning papers on issues that are likely to assume importance at the fourth session of the Conference on Trade and Development—issues which are of significance to international economic relations. If this were done, I think there would be a greater chance of getting new thoughts, new initiatives, new ideas, of exposing the policy-makers at the official level, to the academic and the intellectual people, for them to come together and to discuss these new initiatives which may then take the form of positions of governments at the fourth session itself. I am trying to organize a similar process in other countries, in the Western countries and in the developing countries, and I would very much like to see such a process launched in the socialist countries so that we can use the period between now and the fourth session for heightened conceptual activity, which would promote a greater degree of success.

Trade and Development Board

8 March 1976

I think that distinguished delegates will agree that this occasion is indeed a special one since it represents an innovation, or experiment, that is directly connected with the fourth session of the Conference itself. When the Board decided to convene this seventh special session prior to the Nairobi meeting, it had in mind the notion of a pre-Conference negotiating session at which the issues, and indeed the proposals, to be taken up in Nairobi would be discussed in advance. The whole objective was to help make the Nairobi Conference itself a decisive event, an occasion for arriving at concrete results, for reaching agreements on specific issues. Other changes have also been introduced with the same objective in view: the shorter duration of the Conference proper, the briefer and more selective provisional agenda which the Board itself has adopted and, I should add, the revised structure of the Nairobi Conference, where there would be, in addition to the plenary, but one Committee of the Whole which would from the very commencement embark upon the process of consultation and negotiation.

I do not need to underline the fact that there is and has been for some time a great deal of expectation and anticipation regarding the Nairobi Conference. It is looked upon as an occasion when the international community can take a decisive forward step in the wide-ranging field of trade and development and, indeed, in the field of relations between the developing countries and the rest of the world. For almost two years now the issue of development and of international co-operation for development has been the subject of intense discussion and debate. The Declaration and the Programme of Action on the Establishment of a New International Economic Order, the Charter of Economic Rights and Duties of States—both of them adopted in 1974—pointed to the urgent and compelling need for new orientations. In 1975 the General Assembly at its seventh special session brought about a remarkable consensus on the need to elaborate upon and further negotiate virtually all the key issues in the field of development. It is logical that the Nairobi Conference should now play its natural role in this sequence of events. In fact, the General Assembly itself has referred some of the key issues to Nairobi for decision. The Conference has to respond to the task before it, to seek agreement on the issues before it. It has indeed to be the first major manifestation of the willingness on the part of the international community to move from the general to the specific, and to give a real content to the broad goals and policies that have for so long been enunciated.

I believe that success in Nairobi will be possible only if governments see in the Conference a major political opportunity to be grasped—an opportunity to bring about a genuine breakthrough in the field of international economic relations, in the field of development and co-operation for development. No amount of exchanges, or discussions or consultations of a technical character alone, will suffice to bring about positive results if the political dimension is ignored. The problem of development is, after all, a political issue. It is a major political issue of our time and it will increase in importance in the period ahead. If the opportunity afforded by the Nairobi Conference is not grasped, there must surely be a major setback in international relations.

The issues to be taken up in Nairobi have been chosen with care. They have been placed on the agenda for the Conference by universal agreement, not only because they are important but also because there is a conviction that real progress is possible in respect of each of them. I do not propose to expand at length on the substance of the several issues before the Conference. I have done so on many previous occasions and you yourself, Mr. President, have touched upon them in the course of your address. But, in my view, a successful Conference must result in progress, must be productive of real attainments, on two fronts. On the one hand, it must produce agreements for early, even immediate, action to deal with a group of problems which have now gained critical dimensions. On the other hand, the Conference must in a number of key areas launch new initiatives and new efforts whose impact would be of a far-reaching importance over a longer period. It is true that each of the issues on the agenda for Nairobi has elements which belong to both these categories, but in my view action that might be taken at Nairobi on such subjects as commodities, the debt problem facing developing countries and the financing of their critical external payments needs could have, and would indeed need to have, a particularly early impact. Such actions could result in the establishment of a set of supportive measures to help developing countries face up to and overcome their current crisis. In the realm of commodities, Nairobi must take a decision—I hope fervently that it is a positive decision—on the integrated programme for commodities, particularly on such essential elements of the programme as the proposal for the establishment of stocks and for a common financing fund. It must take a decision on what should be done quite early on the debt question, as it affects the most seriously affected countries as well as others facing short-term debt problems. It must also, at the same time, pronounce on approaches towards overcoming the immediate financing problems faced by a very large number of developing countries.

SECTION 2

JUNE 1976 TO MAY 1979: EXERCISING
THE MANDATE

At Nairobi there was acceptance of the Integrated Programme in Commodities, and a mandate was obtained for the secretariat to organize negotiations on commodities under the Programme as well as on other subjects (technology transfer and restrictive business practices) with the aim of eventually obtaining international agreements generally of the character of legal instruments. In this section the terms of reference of this series of negotiations set at Nairobi are described, as well as the particular disappointments of the Conference. The subsequent difficult and halting progress of the negotiations themselves is the main theme of the speeches in the middle part of this section, illustrated sometimes explicitly, sometimes rather more between the lines; the process came to a dramatic climax in March 1979 when agreement was at last reached on the basic elements of a Common Fund. A subsidiary theme of this period, which is examined in detail in Part IV, Section 3, below, was the securing of improvements in the terms of aid flows and thus with the situation of external indebtedness of some developing countries. The section ends with some discussion of the business to be dealt with at the fifth session of the Conference at Manila in May 1979, and, finally, with part of the Secretary-General's Report to the Conference. The Report contains a wide ranging survey of the progress to date and of the nature of the changes to the international system which must be made if it is adequately to support the legitimate development aspirations of the countries of the Third World.

United Nations Economic and Social Council

21 July 1976

I feel privileged to be here with you this morning and to have the opportunity of sharing my thoughts on the outcome of the fourth session of UNCTAD in Nairobi, which ended over one month ago now. You will appreciate, of course, that the evaluation or assessment of such an event would lend itself to a variety of views and interpretations and what I have to say must necessarily reflect the assessment of the Conference from the vantage point of the UNCTAD secretariat.

The evaluation of UNCTAD IV depends to no small extent on the yardstick one uses to assess the results—and quite clearly several measures of performance are possible. One can evaluate the results of Nairobi on the basis of the Manila Declaration and Programme of Action of the Group of 77. One can judge the results in terms of the positions taken by the developed countries prior to Nairobi, although these were not embodied in a single formulation. One can assess the outcome of the Conference in terms of the proposals made by the UNCTAD secretariat itself, which were not identical to those made in the Manila document. Again, one can compare the results with one's prior expectations of what was possible, taking account of all the forces at work at the Conference. I believe myself that, useful as assessments by these several yardsticks might be, the essential criterion by which to judge the usefulness of UNCTAD IV is whether and to what extent it has made a difference to the prospects for international economic relations which prevailed prior to the Conference. Has UNCTAD IV brought us to a new stage from which we can proceed, or has it left us very much where we were before the Conference? I believe myself that, if one were to make a considered response to this question, then on the whole, despite the shortfalls and weaknesses that were evident at various points, one could arrive at a positive and constructive conclusion regarding the outcome of the session.

I shall elaborate on this assessment in the course of my further observations. Before doing that, however, I wish to mention some aspects of the Nairobi Conference which were of broad relevance to the substantive conclusions themselves. Certain political developments were evident at Nairobi and one has to take those into account in an assessment of the Conference. There were also lessons to be learned regarding the organization of a meeting of that character, from which we could also benefit by a moment's reflection.

On the political side, two major features struck me very forcibly. The first was the desire which was manifested at Nairobi by the developed countries to make a success of the Conference. This willingness was possibly in greater evidence than in the past, and I believe there are two basic reasons for this. Firstly, on a more general level, there is now in 1976 on the part of the world community, and the developed countries in particular, a greater awareness of and a greater sensitivity to the importance of the development issue as a factor in international relations. Secondly, and more specifically, UNCTAD IV took place in the aftermath of the seventh special session of the General Assembly, when a relatively good atmosphere was established in respect of negotiations between developed and developing countries. There was a desire in Nairobi not only to preserve that atmosphere but also to enhance and strengthen it to the extent possible. UNCTAD IV also took place more or less midway in the course of the North/South dialogue in Paris, and there was, I think, a sensitivity to the interrelationship between these two events—a feeling that a negative conclusion in Nairobi could have adverse effects on the continuation of the dialogue in Paris, and conversely that a positive and beneficial result in Nairobi could not but contribute to the discussions at the Conference on International Economic Co-operation. It may be remarked, too, that at Nairobi there was not a single view but a spectrum of views among the developed market-economy countries in regard to a number of areas, particularly that of commodities. This range of positions and attitudes was reflected in the results of Nairobi.

The other important phenomenon on the political side pertained to the Group of 77. I feel that at Nairobi, for the first time, the developing countries were able to exhibit cohesiveness in respect of matters that went beyond the general and to adopt a unified negotiating position on a number of specific concrete issues. In doing so, they were able to reconcile the inevitable divergences that might have been expected to exist amongst themselves. This was no mean achievement and I think attention should be drawn to it in the context of a political evaluation of events in Nairobi. What is more, the Group of 77 showed a capacity not only to maintain a united front in presenting their demands, but also to back up their demands with a willingness to commit their own resources towards the achievement of some of the major objectives they had in mind. This was so in particular in the case of the Common Fund for Commodities, when one developing country after the other—including countries members of OPEC—sought the podium of the Conference to make announcements of financial support for the Common Fund, sometimes expressed in quantitative terms. I think that this exhibition of the willingness and capacity of developing countries to back up their demands by their own contributions played a significant part in helping to bring about the final result in Nairobi in the realm of commodities.

On the organizational side, the fourth session of UNCTAD was structured differently from previous sessions. We scheduled a shorter meeting than before. We introduced a device of a pre-Conference Board session. The Board adopted a more selective agenda for the Conference, and dispensed with debates in committees, leaving only the plenary to involve itself in a general debate. We tried to present shorter and more pointed documents for the Conference. I think by and large these organizational innovations proved to be successful; they paid off. I think too that there are a number of lessons to be learned—a number of pointers to the way in which future organizational arrangements could be improved still further. But, by and large, my own judgement of the results of the innovations we made is a positive one. They helped in one way or another to enhance the effectiveness of UNCTAD. UNCTAD IV, I think, was able to show that it was possible for a large forum, representing virtually the whole international community, to achieve results of a specific and concrete character, despite the large numbers of participants.

One feature which made a crucial contribution to this outcome, especially in the area of commodities, was the presence, particularly at the concluding stage of the negotiations, of a number of ministers from both developed and developing countries. Indeed, one of our objectives in planning a shorter meeting had been precisely to make it possible for high-level representatives to be present in Nairobi during a greater part of the Conference. This did materialize and I think that we can conclude that it made a contribution to the success of the event.

On the substantive side, as I said before, there are a number of opinions that are possible. Prior to the Nairobi meeting, I myself had stated on several occasions that I saw the outcome of UNCTAD IV in terms of results of two broad fronts. On the one hand, I saw Nairobi as an occasion on which issues of a somewhat long-term and fundamental character could be taken up and on which foundations could be built for the future. There were a number of issues falling under the various agenda items which were amenable to this type of action.

On the other hand, there was the other category of issues where we expected results of a more operational, perhaps even a more immediate character. So we sought for this dual outcome of Nairobi—making a contribution on each of these fronts—and I would like to assess the results of the Conference in terms of the extent to which this dual objective was fulfilled.

Now, in regard to the issues where I felt that the decisions of UNCTAD IV could be relatively more operational, the key areas were commodities, the external debt problem of developing countries and institutional reform—the latter because I felt that there was an urgent and immediate need to adapt the machinery of UNCTAD to the phase of negotiations that lies ahead.

Commodities, as you know, was very much a focus of the Nairobi meeting. I think a very great part of the attention of UNCTAD IV was devoted to the issue of commodities. That issue loomed large over the Nairobi Conference. But what can we say about the decisions adopted in that area? For our part, we, in the secretariat, expected two major results from Nairobi in the realm of commodities. We sought, in the first place, to obtain a broad endorsement of a new integrated approach to dealing with the commodity problem, as a framework within which future activities in the area of commodities could take place. We had called this approach the Integrated Programme for Commodities. We also sought, as a second prong of action, agreement on a series of operational steps to be followed in pursuit of that programme. If you look at the results of the Conference in terms of these two objectives, I think you will conclude that, by and large, these objectives were achieved in Nairobi.

We did obtain in Nairobi, by consensus, an endorsement of the Integrated Programme for Commodities, including the objectives and mechanisms that are an essential part of that Programme. In the provisions of the resolution on the Integrated Programme there are many innovations and many advances that have not previously been recorded in any decision by the international community on the commodity issue. Thus, I believe that a new framework has been established within which the commodity problem can be dealt with in the future. I see this as a major step forward.

On the operational side, UNCTAD IV took two main decisions. The first was to launch a series of negotiations on a number of individual products of particular interest to developing countries. Eighteen products were mentioned specifically in the Nairobi resolution, reflecting the list of products embodied in the Manila Programme of Action of the Group of 77. UNCTAD has been authorized to convene, over the next eighteen months to two years, a series of meetings—some of them preparatory, others of a more advanced character—in respect of these commodities, with a view to arriving at commodity agreements where this proves to be possible. The important point to note is that these negotiations on individual commodities would not be fragmented in a number of isolated meetings; they would be part of a single exercise. These commodity negotiations are to be convened by UNCTAD, within a specific time frame, and they are to be monitored by special machinery to be set up within UNCTAD. So I believe that the exercise that is about to be launched will be basically different from anything that has gone on before in the area of commodities. This change is not by itself a guarantee of success, but it certainly does add an element which was missing in past commodity negotiations and was partly responsible for their lack of success.

The second main operational decision was to convene, not later than March 1977, a negotiating conference on the Common Financing Fund. The Group of 77, in its Manila Programme of Action, had called for a decision in Nairobi to establish the Fund. In the secretariat's own proposals, we had suggested that a decision be taken endorsing the fund in principle and calling for negotiations regarding its modalities and its details. In fact, no decision was taken at Nairobi to establish a Common Fund, nor did the language of the Conference resolution include a statement of universal acceptance of the principle of a Common Fund. But despite this shortcoming, there was a universal endorsement that governments should embark upon a negotiation on the Common Fund. It is to be a negotiation, not a study or a consultation—because we have been carrying out that kind of study or consultation for the last eighteen months. I presume naturally that in agreeing to the concept of a negotiation governments do have the intention of participating in it in good faith. They would not agree to a negotiation if the basic idea was itself anathema to them. So, I do hope that out of the meetings that lead up to the negotiation on the Common Fund it will be possible to bring about the establishment of the Fund itself.

We have always, in the secretariat, stressed the central importance of the common financing fund to the whole Integrated Programme for Commodities. For that reason, we look forward to the successful conclusion of these negotiations. We are very much encouraged by the fact that at Nairobi there was ample evidence of support for the establishment of the Fund on the part of a large number of countries, including not only the group of developing countries but also a number of developed countries. I believe that, if the Fund continues to receive this support and also to win new adherents in the period ahead, then we could look forward to its early establishment as a sound and constructive element of the Integrated Programme for Commodities.

As a result of these decisions taken in Nairobi on commodities, we have embarked upon a major negotiating process, a major negotiating phase, that should occupy the energies of the international community—and that of UNCTAD—over the next eighteen months to two years. It is vitally important that the Member States of UNCTAD appreciate the significance of this great challenge. Through these negotiations, we have a real opportunity of restructuring many aspects of world trade in commodities, and thereby of bringing about changes of basic significance to the New International Economic Order. I believe therefore that it is of the utmost importance that Member States should view this negotiating exercise as one of their major preoccupations in the months to come.

There are a number of ingredients which are essential if we are to make a success of this enormous endeavour. First of all, it is vitally important that the negotiations on commodities manifest the new political will to act in this area which I believe is beginning to be shown. Now, more than at any time in the past years, there is an awareness on the part of the developed countries of the importance of the commodity problem—of the need to take some kind of remedial action. If this awareness is translated into a firm commitment on the part of the participating countries to bring about concrete results, then we would be injecting an element which has perhaps been missing in past commodity negotiations and which would certainly augur well for the success of the future ones. The other important requirement for success is that the developing countries should see these negotiations as an intensive exercise calling for a great deal of concentration, organization and negotiating skill. In the commodity negotiations, they would be dealing with specifics, issues which are technically difficult, but which for this very reason call for a large measure of political resolution and organization, an overriding will to reconcile differences and present coherent positions. I believe that, if the participants demonstrate these prerequisites, we have a good chance of making real progress in the negotiations that lie ahead.

I am becoming increasingly convinced that these negotiations would be a test—perhaps the final test—of the whole concept of consumer-producer co-operation in the realm of commodities. If the negotiations were to prove unsuccessful, the international community would draw new conclusions about the validity of that concept. For this reason alone, no matter what the outcome of the negotiations is, I feel the world situation in the area of commodity policy will not remain the same after the negotiations as it was before. So the ultimate verdict on UNCTAD IV in the realm of commodities lies in the future. If the negotiations succeed in restructuring world commodity trade, bringing to it greater strength and stability, then in retrospect UNCTAD IV would be not just a successful conference but perhaps a major historic event. If they fail, the significance of UNCTAD IV would to that extent be reduced.

In respect of the other issues, I will not take up a great deal of the time of this Committee by spelling out at length the results achieved in Nairobi but I wish to touch upon each of them as briefly as I can.

The major problem of the external debt of developing countries was, as I said earlier, one in respect of which we had hoped for some operational results from Nairobi. Quite frankly, I was disappointed by the resolution adopted with regard to this issue. We had hoped for two kinds of action on the debt problem. Firstly, we sought some concrete action to help relieve the immediate debt problems of a large number of developing countries. To this end, we had proposed some specific measures, such as a moratorium on the official debts of the most seriously affected countries and the refinancing of the commercial debts of the middle-income developing countries. Secondly, we had also hoped to lay the foundations of an international policy on the debt question through the medium of a world conference—a conference which might have been an occasion for establishing a framework of principles and guidelines within which individual debt problems could be considered.

These objectives were not quite attained in Nairobi. The resolution did not embody any specific commitment regarding the action to be taken to relieve the immediate debt problems of the developing countries. What it did contain was a commitment on the part of the creditor countries to respond quickly and constructively, with a sense of urgency, to individual requests for debt relief from developing countries in difficulties, and it now remains to be seen to what extent this commitment is acted upon on the period ahead. The Conference also decided that appropriate existing international forums would work on the question of identifying common elements in dealing with individual cases of debt relief—which, to my mind, marks the beginning of an approach to establishing guidelines for dealing with policy issues in the field of debt.

But, most significant, the Nairobi resolution requires the Trade and Development Board, at a ministerial session to be held next year, to review the action taken in the field of debt, not only action to relieve immediate problems, but also action towards building up a policy framework. With that end in view, the resolution asks the secretariat of UNCTAD to convene a preparatory meeting of an intergovernmental group of experts. So it would be wrong to say that in the field of debt there was no movement at all in Nairobi. There has been some movement; but it has fallen short of expectations. UNCTAD shall continue to watch over and contribute to developments in this field, and I am sure that next year's ministerial session of the Trade and Development Board will pay specific attention to this problem from the point of view of both the objectives that I have indicated.

Now, in regard to several other issues that came up in Nairobi, we were seeking as I said before to establish foundations for the future, to sow some seeds which would bear fruit in the period ahead. I think that, broadly speaking, this aim was attained at Nairobi. On each of the agenda items, decisions were taken which contain the basic elements of a framework for dealing with these problems in a much more comprehensive and interrelated manner than before.

In the area of trade in manufactures and semi-manufactures, UNCTAD IV adopted a resolution spelling out what has been called "a set of interrelated and mutually supporting measures" to deal with the problems of developing countries. We had asked for a comprehensive programme of action in this field and, although the title of the resolution did not use those words, the resolution itself included a number of elements which we had thought should form part of a more comprehensive attack on the problem of trade in manufactures—an attack which looks beyond the question of access to markets alone and encompasses other dimensions of the problems, particularly questions of supply. That resolution endorsed the continued improvement of the generalized system of preferences and the extension of its duration. It endorsed the concept of industrial co-operation; and it endorsed the idea of working out a set of guidelines on restrictive business practices. In another resolution, the conference asked UNCTAD to pay special attention to the activities of transnational corporations in all areas pertaining to the trade of developing countries in the field of manufactures and semi-manufactures. So we do have in this area a considerable basis on which to build in the future.

In the realm of the transfer of technology, UNCTAD IV was able to make considerable advances. I think it is recognized that this was an area in which the Conference proved to be particularly successful. Three issues arose here: the question of a code of conduct on the transfer of technology; the question of the revision of the industrial property system; and, perhaps most important of all in my view, the question of building up the technological capability of the developing countries. UNCTAD IV took positive decisions on each of these three counts. It set the stage for work on the drafting and adoption of a code of conduct. We have accordingly scheduled one drafting session in the remainder of 1976 and three next year, to be followed by a conference to be convened by the General Assembly for the adoption of the code. On the vexed question whether the code should be a legally binding instrument or an optional one, there was a compromise for the present, and the drafters of the code have been authorized to include provisions in the draft which range from the mandatory to the optional.

With regard to the revision of the industrial property system, the prominent role of UNCTAD in contributing to the ongoing work is recognized and is to continue. But most significant is the new emphasis given to building up the technological capability of the developing countries themselves, and to the need for establishing, both internationally and nationally, an appropriate institutional framework for this purpose. To this end, the resolution envisages the creation of national, regional and subregional centres for the development and transfer of technology and also centres with respect to particular sectors of economic activity. It also calls on UNCTAD to provide an advisory service to developing countries on the transfer of technology. It is indeed remarkable how this issue of the transfer of technology, which barely attracted attention ten or fifteen years ago, now looms so prominently as a feature of the whole development process and as an aspect of international co-operation for development. I think it will be recognized that UNCTAD itself has played no small part in helping to bring about this metamorphosis.

In regard to co-operation amongst the developing countries, there have again been some new departures which the Nairobi Conference was able to highlight. For some time now, particularly since the sixth special session of the Assembly, co-operation among developing countries has been assuming increasing importance as a manifestation of the broader concept of collective self-reliance. At Manila, the developing countries themselves were able to spell out in broad terms the essence, the content, of what might be a policy of mutual co-operation. What UNCTAD IV was asked to do was express and confirm support for such a policy of co-operation among developing countries—support to be given by other members of the international community and by the international organizations themselves. The resolution adopted in Nairobi achieves precisely that aim. It calls for support by the international community for the co-operative efforts of the developing countries at certain key strategic points, and it endorses the role which international organizations can play in channeling this support. UNCTAD itself has been given a number of tasks in this field and it was decided to add to the intergovernmental machinery of UNCTAD a new committee to consider measures of support and assistance for co-operation among developing countries. As you know, the Group of 77 are convening a conference on this subject in Mexico City in September. A reference to this was included in the Nairobi decisions, and a preparatory meeting for the Mexico Conference is now under way here in Geneva.

With respect to trade among countries having different economic and social systems, I think the significant feature of UNCTAD IV was the awareness that was shown of the potential that exists in this field and of the need to exploit this potential through new mechanisms and new modalities. Here again the Conference resolution identifies in somewhat concrete terms a number of specific points at which the potential for an expansion of trade and other relationships is greatest, and it authorizes UNCTAD to pursue these points with greater vigour and more resources at its command than it has done before. We have been authorized to convene meetings of expert groups and to consult with the member countries of the Council for Mutual Economic Assistance and the CMEA secretariat in pursuit of a number of initiatives which up to now have not been pursued with the fullness of scope that this resolution envisages. I think that here again the ground has been prepared for a heightening of activity.

The special problems of the least-developed among the developing countries, the land-locked developing countries and the developing island countries constituted a separate item on the UNCTAD IV agenda. Here we were seeking a broader international consensus on the need to deal with the problems of these categories of countries, and specific measures to help solve them. The resolution on these issues does broadly aim at each of these goals. It has given to UNCTAD a series of new tasks which would help the countries in these categories to cope with some of their problems. For example, we have been asked to convene a meeting of institutions dealing with multilateral and bilateral financial and technical assistance, together with the least-developed countries, to look into ways and means by which the flow of resources to these countries can be enhanced and made more effective. The problems of these groups of countries are coming increasingly to be focused within UNCTAD, and we look forward to adapting our own organization to meeting the tasks that have been given to us in this area.

In all the areas that I have mentioned, one important point to take note of is the awareness of the importance of technical assistance in achieving the objectives of UNCTAD and of the role that UNCTAD can play in providing such assistance. If you look at the several resolutions that have come out of Nairobi, you find a significant new commitment to providing technical assistance—greater perhaps than ever before. This is true, for example, in the areas of the transfer of technology, co-operation among developing countries, trade among countries having different economic and social systems, the problems of the least-developed countries and so on, and this is in itself one of the important results of the Nairobi Conference to which attention needs to be drawn.

I must mention that there was one substantive area where—although much of the negotiations are undertaken in other bodies—we were hoping that UNCTAD IV would make a contribution of a long-term character but where it was virtually totally silent. That was the area of money and finance other than debt. There were three issues in this area on which no decisions were taken. These pertained to the payments problems of the developing countries in the present critical situation; to the long-term transfer of resources; and to the reform of the international monetary system. On all three issues, draft resolutions were presented by the Group of 77 and by Group B and the decision of Nairobi was that these drafts would be forwarded to the Trade and Development Board for consideration at its sixteenth session. The Conference itself was not able to focus on these issues and take decisions. I think this is an important and regrettable shortcoming, because the issues themselves are of basic importance. For one reason or another, questions of shortage of time, and concentration on other issues rebounded to the disadvantage of these issues and all I can say now is that I hope the Trade and Development Board at its sixteenth session in October will make amends for these omissions at Nairobi.

Those broadly were the substantive results of Nairobi. But there was one further area in which I think UNCTAD IV adopted a significant decision and that pertains to the institutional question. We were hoping that Nairobi would endorse the concept of a new and more effective UNCTAD serving as the arm of the United Nations for negotiations in the field of trade and development. I think that, broadly speaking, the institutional resolution adopted at Nairobi fulfils this expectation. It clearly sees the potential of UNCTAD as an instrument for negotiation, in addition to servicing as an instrument for the generation of new ideas. It recognizes the role that UNCTAD can play in reviewing the interdependence of issues in the fields of trade, money and finance. It provides for the reform and reorganization of the intergovernmental machinery of UNCTAD, for opening the membership of the Trade and Development Board to all UNCTAD members and for the Board to hold regular minsterial sessions. As far as the secretariat is concerned, the Conference has requested me to enter into consultations with the Secretary-General of the United Nations in regard to both the level of resources available to UNCTAD and the flexibility that we have in the exercise and use of these resources. So I believe that the institutional resolution is an important step forward, of a very positive and constructive character, which can lay its imprint on the institutional nature of UNCTAD. Of course, the reform of UNCTAD has to be seen in the broader context of the restructuring of the UN system and I think that the Nairobi resolution has made a contribution to this restructuring exercise in so far as the future role of UNCTAD is concerned.

There is a further observation, however, that I would like to make. I believe myself that the institutional future of UNCTAD will be determined not only by the institutional resolution to which I have just referred but also by the resolutions on the substantive issues. The resolutions on commodities, on the transfer of technology and on each of the other subjects I have mentioned, will have far-reaching effects on the character of UNCTAD. I envisage that as a result of these resolutions UNCTAD will evolve as a forum in which specific issues are, increasingly, brought up for negotiation and for decision. In this way, UNCTAD would serve as the instrument of the General Assembly for giving body and content to several elements of the new international economic order. The commodity exercise is but one of these, and in the future there would be others. So I think I can say, with a certain degree of confidence, that UNCTAD after Nairobi will not remain the organization that it was before. In one way or another, it will be deeply influenced by the decisions that were taken at Nairobi. I believe that the transformation of UNCTAD will be in the direction of making it a more effective, a more useful component of the UN system, and from that point of view, too, I believe that the decisions of Nairobi were of far-reaching importance.

These, then, are my own responses to the action that has been taken in Nairobi. I have stressed the positive aspects as best I can, and drawn attention to the areas in which we have had disappointments and shortfalls. Even when I stress the positive aspects, I do not want to generate any sense of complacency. There are enormous difficulties and challenges that lie ahead, and the value of UNCTAD IV will depend on the way in which the international community responds to these challenges.

Sri Lankan Association for the Advancement of Science

21 August 1976*

I should like to present some very broad reactions of mine after the Conference at Nairobi in the light of what we in the UNCTAD secretariat were hoping to get out of the Conference. Now I think that in the area of issues where we were aiming at results of a long-term character, I think it would be true to say that by and large the Conference produced the broad objectives which we were pursuing. Take, for example, the area of the developing countries trade in manufactures. This has always been a central concern of UNCTAD and it is of vital concern to the developing countries because it is very intimately linked up with their efforts at industrialization. But many of the immediate issues pertaining to this trade of developing countries in manufactures is now under active negotiation under the forum of the GATT, under the multilateral trade negotiations, and it was not possible within the forum of UNCTAD to duplicate these negotiations on these same issues as long as those negotiations were underway. So at Nairobi what we tried to do was look beyond the concerns of GATT, which was concerned very largely with the question of access to the markets of the West, and try to get endorsement for a strategy relating to the trade of developing countries in manufactures which is of a more comprehensive character, which takes account of the problems on the supply side, which links up with the question of technological transformation. Well, this I think we succeeded in getting in Nairobi. There was a very good resolution on the question of interrelated measures in the field of trade in manufactures although for some specific reason the word "comprehensive strategy" was not adopted in the final resolution.

Then again take the question of trade between countries with different economic and social systems. We tried in Nairobi to point to the potential which the development of the socialist countries presents for the growth prospects of the developing countries. We felt that the linkages between the socialist countries and the developing countries have still to be exploited and developed to the full and we called for a number of new initiatives all of which, more or less, were endorsed at Nairobi. We introduced a whole new programme to deal with the problems of specific categories of countries which are specially disadvantaged—least-developed countries (there are twenty-five of them), the land-locked countries, and also what is now called the island developing countries, whose membership I must say has yet to be clearly defined. But for these groups too there was an endorsement of an extensive new programme of assistance and action which could be built on in the future.

---

* Also broadcast by CBC on 13 September 1976.

Most important in the field of co-operation amongst developing countries we had a recognition of the growing significance of this, not just as an isolated attempt of a few countries trying to co-operate with each other, but as a central part of any global strategy for development—an element which cannot but grow in the future.

So in all these fields I think it is true to say that we laid good foundations. Now when it comes to the category of issues where the results were of a more operational character, the central issue was the commodity question. This dominated the Nairobi Conference. It was very much the focus of attention of everybody there. At Nairobi we sought to gain endorsement for an Integrated Programme of Commodities and for a negotiating schedule. I think it is true to say that we succeeded on both these fronts. The Nairobi resolution was a consensus resolution which adopted the Integrated Programme and its objectives and its mechanisms and gave me, as the Secretary-General of UNCTAD, a mandate to call a parallel set of negotiations both on individual commodities and on the establishment of what was called a Common Fund for the financing of stocks. This was a very dramatic issue, it nearly brought about the breakdown of the Nairobi Conference, but at the closing stages of the Conference we did succeed in bringing about a positive result by way of the consensus resolution.

The result, of course, did fall short of what the developing countries had set out in Manila. They wanted a decision, for example, to establish a Common Fund. We in the secretariat suggested that there be an acceptance in principle of the idea of a Common Fund and an endorsement of a negotiating conference to work out its details. At Nairobi we got neither a decision nor a universal endorsement in principle, but we did get agreement to a negotiating conference which would be held not later than March next year. This is going to be a negotiating conference, it is not going to be an occasion to study issues, and I believe that if countries come to a negotiating conference they will do so in good faith and would not attend or participate if the whole idea was offensive to them. In order to persuade some of the developed countries to agree on the concept of the negotiation we had to indicate to them that they would not be committing themselves to anything until the outcome of the negotiations themselves were clarified. So that was the basis on which it was agreed to call a negotiating conference. But I am myself hopeful that at this negotiating conference the Common Fund itself would be established because already at Nairobi it became clear that there was overwhelming support for it not only from all the developing countries but from a large number of developed countries as well. In fact, although no country voted against the commodity resolution or abstained from voting, the United States, Germany and the United Kingdom in their explanatory statements did make certain qualifications which indicated that they still have some uncertainties regarding how the Common Fund would function and were therefore not in a position there and then at Nairobi to commit themselves fully to it. But at the same time there was a declaration by sixteen developed countries of the OECD Group which came out unreservedly in support of the Integrated Programme and the Common Fund. So for the first time in an UNCTAD meeting I think there was a significant division within the ranks of the Western countries, with some of the countries which had hesitations on the Fund standing somewhat apart from a large number of other countries, mostly the smaller countries of Europe, the Scandinavian countries, the Netherlands and such countries as Spain, Portugal, Greece and so on, which found they were able to go along with the Fund, and I think that this division is of some political interest and perhaps also of some political significance for the future.

So I feel that in the area of commodities we have achieved our basic goal of building a framework within which to progress in the future. The whole field of commodities is a complex one. We are not out to obtain resolutions and declarations and so on, we are out to restructure commodity markets and this cannot clearly be brought about at a single conference by a single decision. It has to be a process of evolution, a process of negotiation, and what is needed is a sound effective framework for the negotiation of this issue. I have received a mandate as a result of that resolution on commodities to convene a series of negotiating meetings preceded by preparatory meetings on something like eighteen products of interest to developing countries. These are not going to be fragmented isolated commodity conferences as has been the case in the past. They are going to be part of a single exercise. They are to be convened by UNCTAD and not by a variety of miscellaneous commodity bodies which have their centres in the different capitals of the world. They are going to be subject to some overall monitoring or surveillance by machinery to be created in UNCTAD for that purpose. So what we have now is a great departure from anything that existed before. We are able for the first time to bring the future work on commodities within the umbrella of a single programme, a single overall approach. This in itself is not of course a guarantee of success, but I think that the absence of such an overall approach was one of the factors responsible in the past for the failure of commodity negotiations and this has been rectified in the Nairobi meeting.

Similarly, I have a mandate to call a negotiating conference on the common financing fund and if this Conference were to lead to positive results then we can look to the establishment of the Common Financing Fund. The Fund in my view is central to the whole integrated programme. It is a financing institution but I do not see it as only a financial device. I see it as an institution which will play a catalytic role in bringing about commodity agreements, an institution which would be able to act as a stimulus to reaching agreements on individual products by making available finances needed for intervention in markets when the prices of these products fall or rise too high. I believe that an Integrated Programme without the Common Fund will cease in fact to be an Integrated Programme and I think it is the insistence of UNCTAD on the Common Financing Fund much against the resistances of the developed countries, which succeeded in bringing the Common Fund to the centrepiece of the Nairobi Conference and in bringing about the mobilization of support from developing countries for the Fund. One of the most impressive features of the Nairobi meeting was towards the latter stages when, one after another, the developing countries sought the podium, not to make general speeches, or general statements, but to make a brief, succinct but very effective announcement that their government has instructed their delegation not just to support the Common Fund but to pledge resources for that Fund. Some countries actually made these pledges in quantitative terms. Virtually all the OPEC countries pledged support for the Fund. The key to the establishment of the Common Fund of course is the support of the oil-producing countries. If the oil-producing countries are willing to make their resources available, not as aid, not as charity, but as an investment which would give them in turn a good and sound return, if the oil-producing countries are able to do that then I am confident that nothing could stop the establishment of the Common Fund, and it was a matter of great encouragement to me to see in Nairobi that these countries in succession took the opportunity to make very firm statements indicating their support.

On the question of the external indebtedness of the developing countries we made some specific suggestions to governments for action in Nairobi. We suggested that for the most seriously affected countries—that is a category which excludes some of the oil-producing countries—that there be a write-off or moratorium of their past official debts, in other words, a write-off of repayments that they are making on account of aid that they had received in the past. Their situation called for such a write-off. For the middle-income developing countries whose debts were of a commercial character we suggested some kind of refinancing. And we also supported a proposal to have a global conference of creditors and debtors in order to work out a broad framework of international policy for the future treatment of the debt problem. We got none of these results. What we did get instead was a somewhat moderately worded resolution in which the developed countries pledged themselves to act constructively and positively and with a sense of urgency to any request by individual debtor countries for relief. And also an agreement to set up some exercises in international forums to work out what might be called some common elements of a global debt policy. But what the resolution did do, and what in my view gives it some positive content despite its limited character, is that it did mandate UNCTAD at next year's meeting of the UNCTAD Board at the ministerial level to review all action that has been taken in the field of debt, whether by way of relief to individual countries or by way of working out a set of guidelines and criteria in order to make sure that this resolution has not and is not a dead letter. And since we have received that mandate we do intend in UNCTAD to keep pursuing the issue of debt and to keep it in as sharp focus as possible. So the lack of results on that front is not being interpreted by me at any rate as a reason to relax the concentration on this issue. On the contrary, I see it as a challenge which justifies the intensification of our efforts.

Other resolutions in the field of money and finance were not acted upon at all in Nairobi because of a want of time and these have been referred to the UNCTAD Board which meets in October this year.

I have been asking myself why it is that progress in the field of debt and other monetary issues was so limited. I believe myself that there are several reasons. One of course is that the problems are very delicate and very complex, but another reason is that the developing countries themselves were not in a position to exert too much pressure on the debt issue, not in a position to exert too much leverage. Countries did feel, not unnaturally, that any identification of individual countries with serious debt problems might jeopardize their chances of securing future flows of credits, because if creditors and banks felt that countries were in a critical situation they would use this as a reason to retract and draw back, and this would in one way or another jeopardize these countries. So although the countries felt that there was a problem I had a feeling that it was not easy for them to raise their voices very loud in support of remedial measures. A further reason, of course, was the logistics of the Conference where so much time was taken up in the late stages by the commodity issue and where, consequently too little time was left for the resolution of the debt problem.

One issue in Nairobi came out very well, and that is the issue of the transfer of technology. There we have had an endorsement for a major programme on three fronts. One to draw up a code of conduct on the transfer of technology, the other to contribute to the revision of the industrial property system, which is the patent system, and the third to set about a major process to help developing countries enhance their own technological capacity, their own technological independence. There is now approval for the setting up of a number of regional, interregional, and subregional centres for the transfer of technology.

Well, these broadly were the highlights of the Nairobi meeting and as I said there are both achievements and shortcomings to point to in any overall assessment of the results of Nairobi. But I feel that now the main need is to look to the period ahead, and for the participating countries and particularly the developing countries to organize and mobilize themselves for the task that lies ahead. I have been mandated, as I indicated, to call a series of meetings on individual products within a single frame. I have been mandated to call the meeting for the Common Fund. It is very easy for UNCTAD as an international organization to send out notices to governments announcing the meeting and inviting delegations to be present in Geneva; perhaps it is just as easy for governments to ask themselves who they should send to these meetings just in order to respond to the request to be represented. But I am quite sure that if participants come to these meetings without any prior preparation, without any attempt to co-ordinate positions, without any attempt to reconcile conflicts of interest amongst themselves as developing countries, for example, then these negotiations are not going to be productive of results. The question of commodity negotiations are extemely difficult. There are a host of technical complexities and anybody who is not too enthusiastic about restructuring commodity markets has a golden opportunity to play on these technical complexities and to call for more studies and more data and more information and to allow this thing to drift on for an indefinite period of time. We have had this experience over the past thirty years. The Cocoa Conference, which finally ended up in a successful agreement in 1972, took seventeen years of meetings and conferences before it reached that result, and I am afraid that in the absence of adequate preparation we run the risk of a repetition of this kind of past experience.

That is why in the aftermath of Nairobi my main message to the Member States of UNCTAD and to the developing countries in particular is that they should recognize the importance of this negotiating phase that lies ahead. It is not a parallel to other international conferences where the outcome is a resolution or a declaration or a programme of action. The outcome we are seeking is the restructuring of individual commodity markets, and this is an entirely different type of exercise to what is required in a normal UN meeting. So there does have to be organization, there does have to be expertise, there have to be negotiating skills, and if the governments of the developing countries in particular do not see this phase as one which should be one of their major preoccupations over the next eighteen months to two years, then I am afraid that these negotiations themselves would not be creative of the results we are seeking to attain. But if, on the other hand, they mobilize themselves for this task, then

I believe that they have, for the first time, a unique opportunity to bring about basic, meaningful and fundamental changes in at least one major sector of their economies—the commodity sector. I have been making this plea because I think it cannot be repeated too often. I have noticed that in the case of the eighteen products on which we are going to meet, the consumer countries would be the same for virtually all of them, and will have ample opportunity to adopt common positions and to share experiences in dealing with each and every one of them. This is not true of the producer delegations. The producer countries coming to a meeting on tin, for example, would not necessarily be the same as the producer countries that would come to a meeting on coffee or cocoa or hard fibres. So there have to be some conscious efforts to share experiences and to build up positions which would enhance the negotiating strength of the producing countries. I believe that this one of the challenges that the developing countries would have to face before they confront the consumers at these negotiations. I do not believe that there is much of a chance for commodity negotiations to succeed, for there to be agreements between consumers and producers, if there is not, in the first place, agreement amongst the producers themselves. So I believe that this is one of the imperatives for success.

In the last analysis I would venture to say that the real test of the efficacy of Nairobi lies in the future. If these negotiations succeed then in retrospect Nairobi would be not just a successful conference but a truly historic event. If these negotiations do not succeed then the importance of Nairobi would to that extent be reduced. But come what may, whether there would be success or whether there would be failure, I believe that the world would not be the same after these negotiations as it was before. What is being now put to the test is the whole concept of producer–consumer co-operation in the commodity arena. If the UNCTAD programme were to succeed then, in one way or another, this concept would gain reinforcement. It would gain endorsement. If the negotiations were to fail then I am sure that the producer countries, despite the limitations, whatever the weaknesses they have, would be forced to ask themselves whether this whole idea of producer–consumer co-operation is the true answer to the commodity problem. So I think that whatever happens at the end of the eighteen months the whole commodity question would assume immensely different dimensions from what it has assumed up to now.

Trade and Development Board

25 April 1977

At the time when the Board last met in special session, in 1975, the thrust was inevitably towards the attempt to implement, to give some concrete content to, the issues which had then been only recently enunciated in the Programme of Action for the NIEO. There were several events in prospect which afforded the opportunity for concretization. The seventh special session of the General Assembly had been scheduled. UNCTAD IV was looming on the horizon and so was the start of the Paris dialogue on international economic co-operation. These events were seen as affording the opportunity for implementing policies that were derived from the concept of the need for structural change, from the concept of a New International Economic Order.

Some of these events have since taken place and have been concluded, others are still underway, as is the case with the Paris dialogue; but I think that, after two years, we could reflect for a moment on what conclusions we might draw out of this experience, out of two years of endeavour in implementing some of the basic essentials of the new order. I shall not attempt an exhaustive appraisal; but in general, I think that we can all agree that we are still not in a position to draw any great satisfaction from the experience of the last two years.

I do not wish to be wholly negative in any appraisal; I believe there have been some positive developments and, in that sense, the record is indeed a somewhat mixed one. In recent years we have had, for example, the establishment of the International Fund for Agricultural Development—that is a noteworthy step. We have seen some extension of the facilities of the International Monetary Fund to help countries meet their balance of payments problems and some expansion in the resources available to the International Bank for Reconstruction and Development. We have witnessed—and this has been a new phenomenon—the emergence of the OPEC countries as major donors of assistance to developing countries. These have all been positive developments, and there have been others.

Within UNCTAD itself there have been a number of developments. We have continued to move forward in the formulation of new approaches, in the enunciation of new themes. There was the resolution of the Nairobi Conference on the Integrated Programme for Commodities, which has been described as a watershed, and also the decisions of the Conference in a number of other areas. In this sense, I think it would be true to say that some valuable foundations have been laid, foundations upon which we can build in the future.

But if we were to assess these positive results, in terms of at least two yardsticks, then I think our conclusions would need to be somewhat tempered, and modest. If we were to measure what has been done by the yardstick of what was needed to be done, in the context of the scale of the problems facing developing countries, then I think we would have to conclude that the performance has fallen markedly short of needs. But, even more significantly, if we were to measure the positive achievements by the yardstick of whether or not they constitute a significant breakthrough in the field of development co-operation, then again I believe that we have to conclude that such a breakthrough has not yet been achieved—such a breakthrough has still to come.

There are several key areas where positive, concrete, adequate and satisfactory results have still to be achieved despite these last two years of concentrated endeavours in a series of negotiations, conferences, deliberations and discussions. One of these major areas is that of commodities. The Nairobi Conference did take a major step forward in this realm. It did so by establishing an extensive framework for the development and pursuit of the commodity question in terms of some new approaches, embodying new principles, mechanisms and objectives. But as I said on several occasions, the real test of the efficacy of the Nairobi resolution would depend on the outcome of the negotiations themselves. These negotiations have still to be concluded, but I do not think that we can take great comfort from the experience that we have gained in the exercises which have so far been launched. We have been carrying out parallel discussions and negotiations on individual products, as well as on a common fund. Each of these are essential elements of the Integrated Programme. But in neither case can we claim to have registered any decisive steps forward.

The Conference on the Common Fund that was concluded in the early days of this month did not result in such a decisive result. There were several reasons for this and I would not say that I have been totally discouraged by the prospect for the future. I think that there is a prospect of success. But the fact is that, when the Negotiating Conference concluded, governments were not in a position to translate whatever forward movement they have made within their own councils into any type of concrete decision. I think that there was evidence of such forward movement and this should not be neglected. But it now appears that the time was not ripe in March to take the negotiating process as far as I, for one, would like to have seen it go.

So we do need to concentrate on the tasks that lie ahead. The negotiating process in the realm of commodities is by no means over. We have to focus our attention now on the need to secure results in the months to come. I believe that there is now, more than ever before, a high awareness of the importance of the commodity issue. I would even go so far as to say that there is perhaps now a willingness to see established some kind of a new regime to help strengthen and stabilize commodity markets. But there are still many issues that are unresolved in respect of the character and content of that regime. And it is towards the task of resolving those issues that we have to devote our attention in the period ahead. This is a challenge to which all parties need to respond—individual governments, various groups of countries who get together to negotiate in UNCTAD, as well as the secretariat itself. I believe that there is still a great deal of anticipation about the ultimate outcome of the commodity issue. As a result of the inconclusive meeting in March, the world at large is watching us, watching UNCTAD and all the forums where this issue is being taken up to see to what extent any impasse which may have arisen could be broken. I have said before—and I would like to say again—that in my view no overall package of measures to deal with the development issue, to deal with the question of North/South relations, could really be considered complete and comprehensive if it ignored or excluded the commodity question. This issue must need to figure prominently in any eventual set of measures taken in response to the development problem.

The commodity question is but one of the areas in which a breakthrough is needed and has not so far taken place. There are other areas as well. A second area is that of the external debt problems of developing countries. This was an issue on which we had hoped to make considerable progress in Nairobi, and on which the results of Nairobi fell somewhat short of expectations. But the issue still remains prominent on the agenda for international discussion and debate. It will be taken up, I believe, at the Paris Conference on International Economic Co-operation and would also be amongst the subjects on the agenda of the ministerial session of the Trade and Development Board which is scheduled to take place some time this year. I believe that in the area of debt we need to register results on at least two broad fronts—we need action to bring about relief for critical debt problems, and we need to establish some kind of international framework within which the international community's responses to the debt problem might be contained. At present, there is no overall framework of policy which could provide the kind of guidance for dealing with critical issues in the realm of debt.

A third area, in which the recent period has seen no significant breakthrough is that of the transfer of real resources to developing countries. Despite the progress that I referred to in augmenting the flow of resources to developing countries at certain critical points, the fact is that the developed countries are still falling short of compliance with the targets that have been adopted for resource transfers. This has been one of the disappointments of the Second Development Decade. The need to achieve these targets, and to renew the commitment towards attaining them, still remains as important as ever.

There is perhaps also a fourth area in which, despite expectations, there has still not been the progress that was anticipated some years ago. I refer to the multilateral trade negotiations, which were launched as far back as 1973, but which have still to be brought to a successful conclusion. I would say that in the period, to come effective progress in this area would need to be included on the checklist of tasks to be accomplished.

And then I would add to these problem areas a fifth—that of international monetary reform. The issue of monetary reform was very prominent on the agenda for international action some four or five years ago. A number of innovative ideas were expressed as to the ways in which the international monetary system might be adapted and adjusted, but I think it is true to say that this quest for reform has since come to be stalled. It has been, in one way or another, overtaken by events in the monetary field, and the search for a lasting reform of the system has given way to a somewhat improvised pragmatic approach, which was perhaps needed in response to the immediate problems of the time but which, all the same, does not dispense with the need for more fundamental and long-lasting solutions.

I have listed five areas in which some kind of breakthrough is needed in the period ahead. There may well be others. But I think that it would be true to say that we would need, in UNCTAD and in other fora, to concentrate a great deal of attention on these five areas at least in the coming months. In this year alone, we have a number of opportunities to carry forward the quest for solutions. In UNCTAD we have scheduled a number of important meetings on our calendar. The Paris Conference is due to meet in ministerial session at the end of May. The General Assembly itself will be meeting, possibly in resumed session, but at any rate in regular session in the latter part of this year. And then there is the forum of the GATT where the multilateral trade negotiations are in progress. I do not say that by the end of 1977 we could expect to see this whole process of negotiation completed in each of these areas. But I believe that it would be fair to expect that some solid foundations would be laid in the course of this very critical year.

These are some very general observations of mine in regard to the experience of the recent past in the implementation of the International Development Strategy and in respect of the several efforts at negotiation that have gone by. As the Second Development Decade is now in its last years, I believe that it would be useful for the international community to draw on the experience of this decade in formulating its approaches for a strategy for the next decade. We ourselves, in the document that we have presented to you, have outlined some of our preliminary thoughts on what might be some of the ingredients of a new development strategy. In doing so, we hope to sow some seeds which might perhaps, in the months to come, bear fruit in the form of the enunciation of new policies and new approaches.

We have put forward the view that the strategy for a third development decade might be different from that adopted for the second and be built upon three pillars if I may call them that. The first of these pillars would be national development strategies, because after all the development process is at the core a process which must unfold at the national level and it would be natural and important that a development strategy should pay attention to the policies and approaches that need to be adopted at that level. In recent times, there has been a great deal of self-searching, a great deal of criticism, about the relevance of the policies that have been adopted nationally in pursuit of development goals. There has been much new thinking concerning the kinds of strategies and the styles of development that would need to be pursued by the developing countries if they are to make a reality of their quest for development. The shortcomings of past approaches have been highlighted, and prescriptions have been made as to the ways in which these shortcomings might be corrected.

A good deal has been said in recent times about the importance of basic needs strategies, or orienting development plans and policies towards a frontal attack on critical social and economic problems, of bringing about a better distribution of income, creating more egalitarian societies and meeting the goals of social justice. I am sure that these and allied themes would be reflected in any new development strategy. But I would like to put before you a thought which I have had for a long time with regard to this whole concept of basic needs strategies. I feel it is important to ensure that, whilst one endorses the need for strategies of these kinds, these strategies must not be interpreted as amounting merely to programmes of social welfare and income distribution. They have to be inextricably linked to the need for transforming the economic capabilities of the developing countries. Basic needs strategies are not an alternative to this process of economic and technological transformation. They call not for a negation of growth but rather for a reorientation of growth in the direction of patterns which have a direct impact on urgent social problems. I think that this aspect of the link between meeting basic needs and economic transformation would need to be somewhat carefully spelled out in any formulations of internal strategies that may be made in the context of the preparations for a third development decade.

The second pillar on which a new strategy would need to be based and very closely linked to the first, is that of the international framework within which these national development strategies are to operate. I do not believe that the emphasis on basic needs strategies and on national styles of development should detract from the crucial importance of creating an international environment which is conducive to the development process within the national framework. I believe that it is one of the cornerstones of a successful development policy that we do succeed in establishing an international framework which lends support and assistance to the efforts of developing countries to solve their problems at the national level.

Here again, in the realm of international policies, there has been new thinking, new emphases. In the past there was a significant amount of emphasis placed on such measures as resource transfers, aid, balance of payments support and debt relief—measures which, whilst being crucially urgent and important in themselves, do not involve changes of a structural character in existing systems. In the new thinking concerning the future evolution of the international framework, there is a strong emphasis placed, as I said earlier, on the need for structural changes, changes that would supplement the need for resource transfers, debt relief and so on. This emphasis is reflected in the quest for a new international economic order and this is what gives meaning to what we in UNCTAD are trying to do in such realms as commodities, transfer of technology, co-operation amongst developing countries, new directions and orientations of trade with the socialist countries and so on. In all these areas we are trying to establish an international framework which is different from what prevailed in the past in regard to a large number of relationships, mechanisms and systems. I think, therefore, that the underscoring of the need for structural change should play a more prominent part in any formulation of a development strategy than it has done up to now.

I would say that there is a third pillar of the strategy that needs to be built, and that is the pillar of what has been called co-operation amongst developing countries, or collective self-reliance. This is a theme that has gained enormously in significance and momentum since the formulation of the Strategy for the Second Development Decade. It is, as I said before, a corner-stone of the new international economic order. In 1976 alone it was the subject of concentrated attention on three major occasions—the third Ministerial Meeting of the Group of 77 in Manila, the Summit Meeting of the Non-aligned Movement in Colombo and the Conference on Economic Co-operation among Developing Countries in Mexico City. As a result of these endeavours, a new emphasis has been given to the whole concept of collective self-reliance and much has been done to impart flesh and blood to that concept in terms of its multiple dimensions, and a number of areas for further work have been identified. The content of this concept needs to be strengthened and elaborated upon still more, and this is a task to which I believe UNCTAD can make a contribution, particularly through its Committee on Economic Co-operation among developing countries. So I consider that in any formulation of a Strategy for the Third Development Decade, this aspect of co-operation amongst the developing countries in all its manifold aspects would need to assume a very prominent role.

I believe that these preliminary thoughts of ours regarding what might be included in a Strategy for a New Development Decade might be of some use to the various bodies within the UN system which are about to be engaged in their first attempts towards the formulation of such a strategy. But the strategy itself, once formulated, would need to be translated into somewhat operational forms. It would need to be the case not only in terms of policies, but in terms of specific targets, quantified where this is possible. I believe that the international community is now moving into a new phase in respect of the development issue. It is moving away from the phase in which the main emphasis was on the formulation of broad goals and objectives which were desirable in themselves, towards a phase of intense, concentrated negotiations through which it is sought to translate these goals and objectives into concrete actions.

I believe that the international community, and the United Nations in particular, would need to respond to the tasks inherent in this new phase, on the threshold of which we now appear to be standing. We shall need to translate the goals and objectives of the new strategy not only into quantified targets but also into programmes of negotiations, so that the processes by which these targets would be achieved could be spelled out concretely. The UN machinery will need to demonstrate new responses to make these complex negotiating tasks successful. There would also need to be a new degree of preparation and of commitment on the part of governments, both individually and in groups. The developing countries in particular would need to exhibit—more than they have done in the past—their own capacity for action, their own ability to mobilize resources and to take steps towards the achievement of the aims which they themselves have contributed to set. I think that if these conditions are satisfied then the character of the Strategy for the Third Development Decade might well be different from that of its predecessor. It would be more action-oriented, more operational in terms of its broad formulation than has been the strategy in the past.

I will not dwell further on these themes. I am sure that delegations, in the course of the days to come, will have much to say regarding their own thinking on these issues and their own responses. The Trade and Development Board has in the past made an important and crucial contribution not only to the review and appraisal of the international development strategy but also to the formulation of the strategy itself. In this way, it has been of help to the Economic and Social Council and to the General Assembly. I have no doubt that the Board will once again make a useful contribution of this occasion and that its deliberations will serve to provide some very valuable and concrete inputs to the work of the other bodies that will be dealing with the task of review and appraisal. I hope, in this connection, that the documents that the secretariat has provided will be of some assistance but I should like to stress that it is the views of the Member governments, and of the Board as a whole, that are crucial in this respect.

Asian Theological Conference*

14 January 1979

The processes started at UNCTAD IV in Nairobi have still to be completed. In the matter of individual commodity agreements, the Common Fund, the code of technology, the issue of restrictive business practices, in all these and other issues we have had a number of preparatory meetings; in some cases these had matured up to the point of negotiating conferences attended by plenipotentiaries, but unfortunately in none of these cases has it been possible up to now to bring the issue to a final conclusion. We have still to tie up the Common Fund, we have still to bring about successful commodity agreements on such products as rubber, wheat, tea, copper and so on. We have still to have accepted a code of conduct on the transfer of technology, we have still to have completed our work on acceptable rules and guidelines to govern restrictive business practices. All our efforts to bring these to a successful conclusion through negotiating conferences were in a sense frustrated because the conferences, although they made rapid progress, were not able to take that final step which was needed for the ultimate consensus. So what has happened is that each of these negotiating conferences has had to be suspended or adjourned with decisions to reconvene again in order to complete the work that has been started. So as we now prepare for UNCTAD V in Manila in May this year, we have to reconvene before that date a number of these conferences which were not able to accomplish their work in 1978 and the period before. Within the next few months UNCTAD has to reconvene the Common Fund meeting, it has to reconvene the Negotiating Conference on Rubber, it has to convene the Negotiating Conference on the Wheat Agreement, to convene a renegotiation of the Cocoa Agreement, to reconvene the Negotiating Conference on a Code of Conduct for the Transfer of Technology, to convene a Negotiating Conference on an Agreement for Olive Oil, to convene a preparatory meeting on restrictive business practices, and it has to convene a preparatory meeting on an international convention for multimodal transport. So you can see that in the weeks to come between now and May, which is not so far away, UNCTAD will indeed be a hive of activity in which an attempt would be made to make progress before the Manila meeting. And I think that it is proper to try to make this effort to make progress because much of the flavour of Manila in my view would depend on the way in which the pre-Manila issues turn out in the period ahead. If we do succeed in

---

* (Extract)

making progress, not necessarily in completing all these issues in all detail but in having a significant breakthrough in respect of a number of them, then we can go to Manila in a positive mood, with a background of achievement and use the occasion of Manila to look forward rather than to look backwards. But if, on the other hand, these issues were to continue to remain in deadlock, to continue to be in a state of impasse, then inevitably it would influence the atmosphere of Manila and then Manila would turn out to be an event, in my view, of recrimination, of frustration, of accusation, So I hope very much that the positive scenario would prevail for Manila and that the Manila Conference would convene in a background of substantial achievement in the subjects that would come up before that date.

The agenda for UNCTAD V is somewhat in contrast to the agenda for UNCTAD IV. For the Nairobi meeting one or two items, particularly the commodity problem, dominated the agenda. There was a very sharp focus on this and all the energy of the Conference was directed to getting a result in that area. For the Manila meeting, there is no single issue as far as I can see which would command that same kind of attention as the commodity issue did at Nairobi, partly because there is no single issue which has been exposed sufficiently to a pre-Conference preparatory process as the commodity issue had been exposed prior to Nairobi. The result is that the agenda for UNCTAD V is somewhat wide ranging, and being wide ranging I think it implies that the Manila meeting would be an opportunity, not so much to take decisions on this particular issue or that, but rather to provide orientations for the whole of the eighties. The Manila meeting could in that sense be a launching pad for new policies, new directions, for the international community which can help influence the world scene right through the decades of the Eighties.

But although the agenda for Manila is wide ranging, I should say, nevertheless, that there are some issues which stand out in very strong and sharp and clear contours in the context of the agenda as a whole. I think that it would be true to say that no matter how you look at it the Manila meeting would be addressed to the major problems that are today of concern to the international community and to the developing countries in the field of economic relations. First of all, if one were to travel around developing countries as I tend to do from time to time, one comes up against certain concerns which in a way are common to most of the Member States of UNCTAD. One of these concerns is the continuing phenomena of developing countries being vulnerable not only to fluctuating but also sometimes to declining terms of trade. Most developing countries have had a persistent experience of the fact that the relative prices fetched by their products have tended to move unfavourably, exhibiting not only very sharp and disruptive movements up and down from time to time, but also movements of a more long-term pervasive character in a downward direction. I think that this problem of the prices fetched by the exports of developing countries relative to the prices that they have to pay for their imports has for long been a major concern of the developing countries and continues to be a concern of these countries in the current context. And it is therefore natural that on the agenda for Manila this issue would loom very prominently. The basic thrust of the developing countries as an answer to this problem has been the Integrated Programme for Commodities which, as I said, was launched already in Nairobi. But up to now the focus under the aegis of this programme has been on bringing about individual agreements for particular products and also on setting up a common institution—the Common Fund. I believe that in Manila, in addition to taking stock of the progress achieved in these areas, there would be a new turning of attention to other aspects of the commodity problem, particularly the participation of the developing countries in the marketing of commodities, in the processing of commodities, in the transportation of these commodities. These are as important facets of the commodity problem as that of the instability of prices. And I think that it is somewhat natural that at Manila some new focus would have to be given to this aspect of the commodity problem.

A second concern of developing countries in the current context relates to their experience in the field of exporting manufactured goods. To the extent that developing countries have succeeded in transforming their productive capacity, breaking away from the dependence on raw material production, commodity production, and to the extent that they have embarked upon a process of industrialization, they have acquired a capacity to produce and to export manufactured goods. But increasingly these countries have found that their efforts to find markets for these goods are thwarted and frustrated by a new tendency in the developed countries to erect protective barriers to keep out such exports. Most of the developed countries are committed to a philosophy of liberal and open markets, but in the context of the current recession facing them, in the context of the new upsurge of industrial capacity in a number of developing countries, the Western countries have fallen back upon defensive mechanisms and have begun to undermine the basic principles of their own philosophy of open markets and to have recourse to devices of a protectionist and restrictive character. I think that this is not a temporary problem; I do not think it is a problem that would disappear with a mere return of the economies of the industrialized countries to a path of recovery; I think, on the contrary, that it is going to be a persistent and long-term problem because in the course of time more and more developing countries would be acquiring the capacity to produce industrial goods and more and more of them would be seeking outlets; and if the developed countries do have to accommodate this surplus capacity of the developing countries they have the problem of how to reconcile this with the fact that within their own boundaries there already exists capacity of a similar kind. I believe that the question of how the international community would deal with this protectionist issue would be a very important theme of the Manila Conference. I think that there is an opportunity at Manila to get agreement on a course of action which has both short-term and long-term dimensions. In the short term I think there is a need to discipline the protectionist process that is now going on. If some measures of protection are inevitable in the current context let us at least ensure that these measures are taken in an orderly, disciplined, way; with a degree of consultation; with a commitment to their being temporary rather than, as at present, being at the discretion of individual countries. And in the longer term, of course, the solution lies in the direction of the restructuring of the economies of the developed countries in a way that would also suit their own interests. For although the developed countries have problems of unemployment arising from competition from developing countries, these problems occur in the very sectors of the economies of the industrialized countries which are inefficient, which are weak, which are in need of renewal and the injection of a new dynamism. And I think that to the extent that the developed countries are able to move away from products which are now provided more competitively by developing countries and into industries where their own background of technological skill and possession of capital is dominant, the more would the interests of these countries be served. So I think that there is in principle a convergence of interest here in the global restructuring of industry. But translating this into practice comes up against a host of political and social problems in the developed countries, particularly the problem of the displacement of labour in the traditional industry. So one should not be too complacent about the complexity of the issue, but I think that the basic lines on which a solution could be found are clear enough.

A third concern of developing countries in the current context, apart from that of commodities and the question of access to markets for their manufactured goods, is their feeling of deprivation in respect of the facilities available to them in the financial field to cope with the crises and deficits in their balance of payments that they have begun to experience in increasing measure in recent times. In the last few years developing countries taken as a whole have begun to experience a very big gap between their import payments and their export receipts. To the extent that they have not been able to find financing for this gap they have had to cut down their imports, and this has meant that they have had in many cases to restrict their development plans, their plans for investment, their imports of raw materials and so on, and this has slowed down and dampened the tempo of their development. To the extent that they have been able to find financing such financing has not always been on the terms suited to them. They have had to go to the commercial banks for short-term financing at very heavy rates of interest, and as a result of that the total external debt of developing countries has been increasing by leaps and bounds and today it has really reached an astronomical figure. The fact is that the financial facilities that are now available to the developing countries were designed in the Bretton Woods institutions at a time when the needs of the developing countries were not really prominent amongst the concerns of the architects of these institutions. They were designed at a period just after the Second World War when neither the developing countries, nor for that matter the socialist countries, had much of a presence on the international scene. It is not surprising that the kind of facility and the kind of accommodation made available has proved to be inadequate to the current needs at least of the developing countries, and I think that at the Manila Conference one has an opportunity to take a look at this whole cluster of problems in the field of money and finance with a view to making sure that there is an adequate and consistent framework of mechanisms in the area of international financial co-operation and the transfer of resources from the capital surplus to the capital deficit countries.

I think a fourth issue that will come up at Manila, and which is also of concern to developing countries, is that related to ways and means of reducing the present excessive dependence they have on the economies of the former metropolitan powers. Despite over one, two, three decades now of independence in the political sense, the economies of most of the developing countries are still very heavily oriented towards the former colonial or metropolitan powers. Their exports, their imports, their channels of transport and communication, all reflect linkages of a bipolar character and I think that the time has come in which the developing countries need to modify this situation of dependence and diversify their linkages and exchanges with other parts of the global economy. I think the socialist countries offer an opportunity for new and diversified links but, above all, the greatest opportunity lies within the community of developing countries themselves where, through a process of greater economic co-operation among the developing countries, new linkages and new exchanges could be forged which would contribute towards a reduction of this historical dependence. Economic co-operation among developing countries of course is likely to proceed any way, but I think that a special effort is needed to give some momentum to this process, and at the Manila Conference I expect that the developing countries would have an opportunity of working out not merely a set of goals endorsing the principle of economic co-operation, but also of presenting a concrete programme to give flesh and blood and meaning to this concept. So I believe that the theme of economic co-operation among developing countries, the theme of collective self-reliance, would begin to gain momentum politically, and at Manila it may well occupy a place of importance in the context of the total agenda.

Trade and Development Board

20 March 1979

It was the early hours of this morning that saw the conclusion of the third session of the United Nations Negotiating Conference on a Common Fund under the Integrated Programme for Commodities. I am sure that you all would share with me a sense of satisfaction that it proved possible for the Member States of UNCTAD to reach agreement on the fundamental elements of the Common Fund. We have striven for this result for a long time now. In the course of our prolonged efforts we experienced setbacks, but we also experienced moments of hope and encouragement. But now at last we have reached the objective we set for ourselves—we now have a consensus on the basic elements of the Common Fund. There is still, to be sure, much work to be accomplished. The drafting and negotiation of the final Articles of Agreement of the Fund will be a complex and demanding task. But what we now have is the most important—I would say the essential—ingredient for the eventual establishment of the Fund, and that is an agreement on its broad character and its dimensions. We have, in other words, the foundation on which we could establish the Common Fund.

It is not my purpose to make any assessment of the results achieved. Indeed, many of us may hardly yet have recovered from the exertions of the last few days and hours. But no matter how one might react to the several issues that were specific to the agreement and were embodied in it, one cannot avoid the feeling of satisfaction that an agreement has indeed been reached, an agreement on an issue that has been of particular significance in the whole context of the dialogue between developed and developing countries.

The Common Fund, no matter how one looks at it, will represent an innovation in the institutional field. It will be an institution that will exercise its functions in the sensitive but vital area of the world trade in commodities and one which will have a multicommodity interest. It will be an institution towards the creation of which the developing countries played a pioneering role, an institution embodying a new pattern of representation in the decision-making process, and, above all, an institution to which the developing countries have themselves committed substantial resources. At the same time, these particular features will find expression within the framework of a co-operative endeavour, an international endeavour reflecting the interests of all the countries. The developed market-economy countries have responded positively to the need to improve the working of international commodity markets and to the setting up of mechanisms for this purpose. This has represented for many of them changes in previous policies which have involved much study, appraisal and analysis, and their response needs surely to be recognized.

The socialist countries of Eastern Europe have for long given their support to the concept of commodity agreements, but the Common Fund was for them, as much as it was for the other countries, an innovation to which they, too, have responded constructively. From China there has been consistent support for the objectives of the Common Fund and for the Integrated Programme, and this, too, was reflected in the work of the last few days.

I have mentioned countries, or groups of countries. But I think you will agree with me that no small part of the credit for what has been achieved must also belong to the many individual actors from the several groups, at various levels, who for a long time have addressed themselves to the task of reaching agreement with a singular sense of commitment and dedication.

This session of the Board is essentially concerned with UNCTAD V. I have said before, however, that a successful outcome to the Common Fund Conference would be particularly important in contributing towards a positive atmosphere at Manila. Well, we now know the outcome of that Conference, and we now have to ask ourselves how we can profit at Manila from the results of yesterday's meeting. We should take advantage of any improvement in the climate of international discussions so as to ensure that UNCTAD V will itself prove to be an event of major importance to the future of international economic co-operation.

Report to UNCTAD V

May 1979

The agenda for the fifth session of the United Nations Conference on Trade and Development is wide ranging. It includes within its compass virtually all the major concerns in the area of international co-operation for development, the major issues of relevance to the North/South dialogue, the essential themes of the New International Economic Order. No single issue dominates the agenda to the exclusion of others. No single issue has been the subject of intensive pre-Conference negotiations, as was the commodity issue prior to UNCTAD IV. For this reason, the fifth session needs to be seen as affording the international community an opportunity to progress along a broad front, to provide new orientations and directions for the 1980s and to give credibility and confidence to the very concept of international economic co-operation.

The issues incorporated in the agenda for the fifth session are relevant to many of the essential concerns of the international community in the current situation. They reflect the major problems presently facing the developing countries in the area of international economic relations. But they also reflect problems that must be of vital concern to the developed countries themselves. The problem of weak and fluctuating terms of trade continues to be one of the predominant concerns of the developing countries in the present context. The question of access to markets for the products of their emergent manufacturing sectors has acquired a new urgency against the background of a trend towards protectionism in the industrialized countries. The severe inadequacy of the prevailing network of financial facilities, and indeed the limitations of the international monetary system as a whole, have been underlined by the vast shifts in payments positions of developed and developing countries in recent times. The need for much wider economic co-operation amongst the developing countries themselves has come to be highlighted by the persistence of their dependence on a few metropolitan powers for trade, technology and finance. All these issues figure prominently on the agenda for the fifth session. Taken together with issues in the fields of technology, of trade between countries with different economic and social systems, of shipping, and with problems affecting specially disadvantaged categories of countries such as the least-developed countries, they make up a wide and well-rounded agenda for UNCTAD V.

The issues by themselves are not new. Indeed, it is important to recognize the continuity that exists between the fifth session and UNCTAD IV at Nairobi. The Nairobi Conference sought to give specific content to some of the themes of the New International Economic Order by launching a serious process of negotiations in a number of areas. The progress achieved and the further actions needed in these very areas must be central to the consensus of the fifth session itself. The session must approach these issues in the light of developments and perceptions that have emerged in the intervening period. The distinguishing feature of UNCTAD V would be not so much the difference in subject matter but rather the fact that the agenda for the fifth session provides—perhaps for the first time in an international conference—an opportunity for actions on a number of issues which, when taken together, could contribute to bringing about important structural changes in international economic relations and indeed in many aspects of the global economy itself. The theme of structural change pervades the agenda for the Conference. It is reflected in the issues that are crucial to each of the specific items of the agenda. More significantly, it is the subject of a separate agenda item itself.

The theme of structural change is one of the crucial concepts of the New International Economic Order. It signifies the conviction of the developing countries that the development process cannot progress adequately as a mere by-product of growth and prosperity in the developed countries. It also signifies their conviction that the development process requires more than the transfer of resources through aid or development assistance alone; that it requires rather changes in some of the prevailing mechanisms and systems that govern international economic relations. But what is also relevant in terms of the actions called for at UNCTAD V is that the theme of structural change needs to be seen as being of particular significance to the developed countries themselves. The developed countries are becoming increasingly aware that the problems of recession, unemployment, inflation and slow growth which they have faced for some years now are not merely of a cyclical nature and that certain basic changes of a structural character are needed for their solution. There are also the beginnings of a realization in the developed countries—and this is of vital importance to the future of the dialogue between developed and developing countries—that the growth and prosperity of the developing countries can contribute to their own recovery and that actions to accelerate the development process, far from being burdensome to the industrialized countries, could impart strength and vitality to their own economies. The dependence of the developing countries on the developed has for long been emphasized. What has received less attention is the growing dependence of the developed countries on the developing, not only as sources of essential supplies, but also as markets for their exports.

There are two specific aspects of the theme of structural change to which reference has been made in the agenda item dealing with that subject. One of these concerns the manner in which provision might be made for taking account of the recognized interdependence of issues in the field of money, trade and development in the formulation of policies both national and global. The other relates to the need for further evolution in the rules and principles that have hitherto governed international economic relations. In respect of the former, the Conference can take action relating to the establishment of an appropriate mechanism. In respect of the latter, the Conference could, by its responses and approaches, initiate a longer-term process that might eventually lead to a recasting of these rules and principles so as to make them more relevant to the needs of the time.

The fifth session of the Conference convenes against a background of disappointment and impatience regarding the slow tempo of progress in the dialogue on international co-operation for development and the paucity of results attained so far. This was strongly voiced in the recent Arusha Programme of the Group of 77.

Restructuring Commodity Markets and Trade

The restructuring of international trade in commodities was indeed the major issue at UNCTAD IV in Nairobi. The main result of that session of the Conference was the adoption of a comprehensive and far-reaching decision which endorsed the concept of an Integrated Programme for Commodities. The central theme of the Integrated Programme was the need to treat the problems of individual commodities within a common framework of principles, modalities and mechanisms and to establish a common institution for the financing, *inter alia*, of stocking operations that would result from commodity agreements to regulate international markets.

The Integrated Programme is made up of a number of interrelated elements which together shape the basic plan for the restructuring of international trade in commodities. It includes the regulation of commodity markets through the mechanism of the Common Fund and international commodity agreements as well as compensatory financing for fluctuations in export earnings. But it also embraces those elements of a development character which are aimed at a fundamental restructuring of international trade in commodities such as the export-oriented processing of commodities and the reorganization of marketing and distribution systems which would need to be developed within a longer-term perspective. In adopting the Integrated Programme the Nairobi Conference also authorized the launching of international negotiations both on individual commodities and on the Common Fund.

In the period since Nairobi, UNCTAD as an organization has been deeply concerned with the negotiating process. It has had a vast number of meetings—both preparatory meetings and negotiating conferences—on individual products and on the Common Fund. In the light of this experience the tasks facing the fifth session of the Conference fall into two categories. It must take stock of the results achieved so far in the process of negotiations and draw the lessons to be learned from it. But no less important, it must address itself to those aspects of the Integrated Programme which have not received particular attention since Nairobi. The Conference must in other words pursue the implementation of the Integrated Programme in all its aspects.

The basic elements of the Integrated Programme for Commodities are not confined to price stabilization measures. The Programme has other dimensions of crucial importance, dimensions to which relatively little attention has been paid since Nairobi. With the progress achieved on the Common Fund and the prospect of more rapid advance in the discussions and negotiations on individual products, it is important that UNCTAD V turn specially to these other aspects of the Integrated Programme.

One of these aspects is the need for developing countries to increase their share of, and improve their position in, the marketing, distribution and transportation of products. The many facets of this problem are elaborated in separate documents before the Conference. To a considerable extent the actions needed in this field have to be taken by the developing countries themselves but these could be facilitated by a framework of support and accommodation by the international community. Many important issues are involved in this area. For example, there are the questions that surround the very technique of marketing itself. Several commodities continue to be sold today through auctions and similar systems whose origin lie in much earlier times—when buyers were less concentrated and more open to the influence of competition than today. The manner in which these systems should evolve and be adapted is clearly a pertinent issue. Closely related to this is the fact that in the present context an increase of the participation of developing countries in marketing and distribution will effect their relationships with transnational companies which play a major role in commodity trade, relationships which need to be made more equitable so as to allow developing countries a more adequate share of the benefits of this trade.

Similarly, a complex of issues surround the goal of increasing the participation of developing countries in the processing of their products. These are part of the wider question of industrialization and include such aspects as access to markets in industrialized countries, relationships with transnational corporations and trade amongst the developing countries themselves. The problem of market access has acquired a new urgency against the background of the rising trend towards protectionism in the industrialized countries and therefore requires particular attention in the context both of the wider treatment of this issue and of specific solutions to commodity problems. The questions that surround the objective of enhancing the participation and share of developing countries in the transportation of commodities are similarly wide ranging. But they are particularly linked to the objective of increasing the participation of these countries in world shipping.

Compensatory financing is also a basic element of the Integrated Programme. The subject has received emphasis in proposals recently before the Joint Development Committee of the World Bank and International Monetary Fund calling for a study of possibilities relating to a globalized scheme for the stabilization of export earnings—a scheme that would reflect some of the principal elements of the Stabex scheme extended by the European Economic Community (EEC) to the African, Caribbean and Pacific (ACP) countries. In terms of the Integrated Programme, however, compensatory financing needs to be viewed as a supplement to, rather than a substitute for, instruments such as commodity agreements which aim directly at the regulation of prices themselves. When there is a malfunctioning of particular commodity markets, it is important to correct such malfunctioning so that patterns of production, consumption and investment are not wrongly influenced by extreme and erratic price movements. Compensatory finance can, however, usefully play a supportive role to market regulation—both because it may not prove possible to bring all commodities under international agreements that support prices and also because earnings of producers, which are affected by variations in the volume of exports as much as of prices, need also to be stabilized.

The existing compensatory financing facility of the International Monetary Fund is limited in many ways—in respect of its size, the conditions governing its use and the terms of repayment. A major revision of the existing facility is a possible option in the search for an adequate scheme. An alternative is the establishment of a new facility that, unlike the Fund facility, is specifically commodity-oriented. In such an event, consideration needs to be given to establishing such a new facility as an additional activity—a third window possibly—of the Common Fund. This would be a plausible course since the Common Fund would itself be a commodity-oriented financial institution concerned with more than one aspect of the commodity problem. Together with the second window, which would deal with measures of a developmental nature, an additional activity in the form of a compensatory financing facility would round up the character of the Common Fund and turn it into a truly comprehensive institution in the commodity arena. It would thus be relevant to view the issue of compensatory financing in that light.

Restructuring International Trade in Manufactures

Whilst the basic elements of relevance to the restructuring of international trade in commodities were incorporated in the Integrated Programme adopted at UNCTAD IV, the Conference at Manila will need to pay particular attention to the subject of trade in manufactures. The fundamental issues pertinent to this were already discussed at UNCTAD IV, where the need was stressed for a comprehensive approach that would extend beyond the requirement of market access alone and encompass requirements on the supply side relating to investment, production and technology. Such an approach setting out the basic aspects of the problem remains valid today.

However, in the period since Nairobi there has been mounting anxiety regarding one aspect of the problem—the increasing barriers to market access that have been emerging in the industrialized countries themselves. Such a trend, if it continues and accelerates, could menace the realization of one of the basic objectives of the development process itself—the industrialization of the developing countries. It is indeed one of the most negative developments of recent times, one that runs counter to a basic tenet of the whole post-war trading system firmly held to by the developed countries themselves—the need for an open system that would foster the flow and growth of trade between countries. Ironically, the trend towards the "new protectionism" coincided with what purported to be a major global exercise in trade liberalization—the multilateral trade negotiations. Although these negotiations have still to be concluded, and it is not yet possible to fully assess results, there can be little doubt that these have been robbed of their earlier promise by the contrary and pernicious phenomenon of restrictionism in trade.

The impact on the developing countries of protectionism in the developed countries is not confined to their trade in a handful of manufactured products—textiles, clothing, leather goods, footwear, etc.—of which they have been traditionally low-cost producers. It reaches out, or threatens to reach out, to whatever industrial goods are being produced in substantial amounts for export by the developing countries—steel, shipbuilding, electronics, in fact any such line as does emerge. Nor is the impact of protectionism of relevance only to a relatively few developing countries. It can, on the contrary, affect all countries as they progress on the path of economic transformation. Already a number of the smaller and less-industrialized developing countries with newly acquired manufacturing capacity are beginning to feel the impact of the current trends—often in the very products on which the more industrialized developing countries had earlier concentrated. The risk of protectionism poses major dilemmas for planning and industrial strategy in the developing countries. Up to now these countries had been admonished—by the international bodies and other advisers—for pursuing inward-looking, import-substituting, patterns of industrial development. They had been faulted for being insufficiently receptive to the benefits of private foreign investment. Yet, in pursuing the alternative course of an outward-looking pattern of growth they face the prospect of barriers to their exports, barriers that are sometimes defended on the very grounds of their punitive impact on foreign investors and transnational corporations.

It has to be recognized, of course, that the acceleration of the protectionist trend in developed countries is a result of the crisis of recession and unemployment recently experienced by them. Official policy in these countries has continued to express support for the principle of an open and liberal trading system where restrictionism is viewed as the exception rather than the norm. Departures from the open system have been a response to acute political and social problems particularly in the field of employment. Not seldom have the industries affected by competition from developing country imports been labour-intensive industries, established in economically backward areas, with wage structures inferior to those prevailing in other parts of the economy. The alternative opportunities available to labour—as well as to capital and management—in these industries have been reduced by the loss of dynamism in other parts of the economy in the background of the recession and the slow tempo for recovery. In such a situation protectionism was seen to offer a temporary shelter until the passing of the storm.

If protectionism in the industrialized countries is only a temporary phenomenon brought about by recession it could indeed be expected to fade away with a process of recovery in these countries. However, it is quite unlikely that this is the case. Apart from the possibility that the recession itself is not of a purely cyclical character, that it is rather a symptom of a deeper malaise requiring more fundamental changes of a structural kind in the industrialized countries—a process that can itself be hindered by protectionism—there is a more basic long-term issue that is related to the rising tempo of industrialization in the developing countries themselves. In the process of industrialization and economic transformation the developing countries will progressively acquire new capacities for production over an ever-widening range of products. This would find its counterpart in new capacities for export requiring market outlets. Whilst to some extent these outlets would need to be found in trade with other developing countries—a process which could itself gather momentum over time—they must in large part lie for some time to come in the markets of the industrialized countries. The problem, however, is that the industrialized countries are already possessed of production capacities for virtually the full range of manufactured goods. The accommodation of developing country imports is likely, therefore, to give rise to competition with prevailing activities, with all its concomitant problems. Moreover, the tendency is likely to increase rather than recede over time—as developing countries speed up their industrialization.

The fundamental answer to this problem cannot, however, be the perpetuation and intensification of protectionism in the industrialized countries. Such a course is not in the long-term economic interest of these countries themselves. It could also be strewn with the seeds of future global political convulsions. The industrialized countries will not gain by the perpetuation of their prevailing industrial structures. The resilience and growth of their economies require a dynamic process of change and adaptation, a continuing shift of factors of production from less-productive to more-productive activities, a continuing process of technological change and innovation. The essential problem facing the industrialized countries is not how to shelter domestic industries from competing imports from developing countries but how the frictions—political, social and economic—that would arise from a changing pattern of trade and industrialization could be minimized and dealt with. Fundamentally both the industrialized and the developing countries have a convergence of interest in a dynamic process of change and adaptation. They have a common stake, therefore, in policies and measures that facilitate this process.

Protectionism is inimical to the long-term interests of the industrialized countries for another reason as well. Whilst competing imports from developing countries may result in a loss of jobs in the sectors affected, new jobs are created as a result of exports to the developing countries. In fact, recent studies have indicated that imports from developing countries have had only a marginal impact on jobs in import-competing sectors. On the other hand, exports of manufactures from industrialized to developing countries have played a supportive role in dampening the effects of the recent recession. Illustrative of this is the fact that developing countries accounted for 30 per cent of the *increase* in the value of developed market-economy countries' total exports of manufactures between 1973 and 1977, in contrast to 15 per cent of the *increase* in such exports from 1962 to 1973, a period of unprecedented growth in international trade. In 1977 imports of manufactured goods by the developed market-economy countries from developing countries amounted to around $32 billion. At the same time, exports of these goods from developed market-economy countries to developing countries stood at around $125 billion. Quite clearly, restrictions on the earning capacity of the developing countries through protectionism or other means will have their impact on the purchasing power of these countries. They can contribute to a downward spiral of contraction in the developed countries themselves. Labour unions in the export industries of the industrialized countries should be as much interested in the issue of protectionism as are unions in the industries competing with imports.

For all these reasons, it is a matter of urgency that the international community—both developed and developing countries—address itself to the manner in which the protectionist trend could be arrested and reversed. The problem needs to be attacked from both the short-term and the long-term point of view. In the short term the pressing need is to ensure that barriers to trade with developing countries are not resorted to, save in the most exceptional of situations and as a last resort, and that when such barriers are imposed they conform to principles and disciplines that are broadly recognized by the international community. Such principles must underline the purely temporary character of the restrictions and a commitment to dismantle them early, the need to identify the instruments used, the need to avoid discrimination, the need for consultation with the parties affected, and the need for surveillance. Devices such as "voluntary export restraints" and "orderly marketing arrangements" do not come within the purview of GATT rules on tariff and non-tariff barriers. The same considerations which persuaded the international community to bring actions in the field of tariff and non-tariff measures under a framework of internationally accepted rules must apply to these other restrictive measures also. In the multilateral trade negotiations a serious effort was made to reduce substantially the ease with which developed countries could resort to such measures. But this effort appears to have largely failed. In any event the developing countries, and indeed the international community, should not find satisfaction in partial responses. There is a need to pursue the goal of an internationally accepted, effective and comprehensive framework to deal with the short-term aspects of the protectionist issue. This is a major task before the Manila Conference. Without such a framework there is the danger that protectionist measures introduced as temporary expedients will grow in intensity and assume a permanent character. The restrictions in textile imports provide a striking example— eighteen years have now elapsed since they were first introduced on a temporary basis!

The long-term aspect of the problem is even more fundamental. Whilst there may be strong compulsions to have recourse to protectionist measures as temporary expedients in a situation of crisis, given the convergence of interest in the avoidance of protectionism as a long-term phenomenon there is a vital need for policies and measures that ensure this result. As mentioned before, the rising export capacity of the developing countries can to a large extent and with mutual benefit be accommodated by the industrialized countries if there is a process of dynamic adaptation in the economies of these latter countries. The heart of the problem is how this process could be encouraged and accelerated by policy measures in the industrialized countries and how the social, political and economic frictions generated could be minimized. To a large extent these frictions would themselves be reduced by a process of change and adaptation which increases employment opportunities in the dynamic sectors of the economy. But policy measures aimed at such a goal could clearly be at cross-purposes with measures of protectionism that perpetuate the less-efficient industries and delay the process of change.

Despite the interest of the industrialized countries in appropriate policies of adjustment, the issue cannot be seen as a matter of largely national concern. The issues at stake concern the entire international community since they have a direct bearing not only on the future growth prospects of the developing countries, but also on the character of the entire international trading system in the future. For this reason, there is a need for the formulation and adoption of an internationally accepted framework of principles or guidelines, which will help bring harmony between national and international needs and objectives and thus provide a frame of reference for policy making. What is basically at stake is the future pattern of distribution of world industry and of trade in industrial products. In the absence of an adequate international framework to guide industrial policy, conflicts are likely to increase, leading to a waste of resources in both the developing and the developed countries. On the other hand, a framework of agreed principles, which includes an endorsement of

policies of adjustment and of adjustment assistance and which provides for consultation on issues of relevance to particular sectors of trade, will contribute significantly
towards dealing with the longer-term aspects of the problem of protectionism. In this
connection it is important to recognize that the provision of market access to developing countries should not be seen as being exclusively a matter involving the closure or
restriction of existing activities in the industrialized countries. Just as in the case of the
trade amongst the industrialized countries themselves there is also considerable scope
for intra-branch specialization in trade with the developing countries. Such specialization would help foster complementary rather than competitive relationships in respect of such trade.

The discussion above has centred round the rising trend towards protectionism in
the industrialized countries—what has been called the "new protectionism". The question may be asked whether the same considerations do not also apply to protectionism on the part of the developing countries. The answer has to be that there is no
exact parallel between the two phenomena. The rationale for protectionism in developing countries has been well recognized in terms of the "infant industry" argument—
extended also to take into account the wider limitations in terms of infrastructure of a
growing but weak economy. In the long term, such protectionism, which would still be
temporary but of much longer duration, can be seen as contributing to growth and
efficiency. The same cannot be said for the merits of protecting ageing industries—
except temporarily as a means of smoothing out the frictions that stand in the way of
adaptation to change. Protectionism in the developing countries could of course be
carried too far—to the detriment of growth and efficiency in these countries, and it is
right to draw attention to this danger. But here the criticism is of the incorrect use of
the instrument rather than of the instrument itself. From the international point of
view there is another, even more important consideration. Protectionism imposed by
the industrial countries can be directly restrictive to world trade by reducing the earning
capacity of developing countries and hence their capacity to import. Protectionism
imposed by the developing countries does not have quite the same effect since these
countries tend in any case to spend all their export earnings, and more, on imports—
mostly from the developed countries. The foreign exchange saved by restrictions on
some types of goods are utilized for imports of other types. Hence protectionism has
more of an impact on the pattern of imports than on their total.

The entire question of market access and how to improve it is of course the central
issue of the multilateral trade negotiations. It remains to be seen how far these negotiations will succeed in improving the access of developing countries to the markets of
the industrialized countries. But even on the most optimistic of assumptions there is
little likelihood that they will deal adequately and decisively with the problem of the
new protectionism. It is a problem therefore to which the Manila Conference must
turn. The evaluation of the multilateral trade negotiations is itself a subject on the
agenda for UNCTAD V. Although the final outcome of the negotiations is still to be
known there are already indications that their result will fall short of the expectations
of the developing countries in the light of the original statement of objectives in the
Tokyo Declaration. This underlines all the more the importance of follow-up action in
the aftermath of the multilateral trade negotiations.

Another item on the agenda in the field of trade in manufactured goods concerns the generalized system of preferences (GSP). It has for long been an objective of the developing countries to establish, more securely, the GSP as a recognized instrument of international policy. It is important not only to remove limits to the duration of the system, but also to extend its applicability and to alter its present purely unilateral character by subjecting it to a negotiating process. In this context, there have been suggestions, from the industrialized countries, for the introduction of a system of graduation in terms of which preferences will be reduced or withdrawn for the more advanced of the developing countries. It is easy to understand the logic of this suggestion. To the extent that preferences are extended to developing countries as a means of facilitating their exports, the rationale underlying them will cease to apply once individual countries emerge out of that category and join the ranks of the industrialized nations.

The essential question, however, concerns the point at which the transition will be seen to have taken place. The countries in the category of developing countries, despite the acquisition of manufacturing capacity, continue to remain far behind most of the industrialized countries in respect of levels of *per capita* income. If reaching the *per capita* income levels of the advanced countries is the criterion, it will take a considerable time before even a few of the developing countries pass the test of graduation. If, on the other hand, the signal is to be the very effectiveness of the GSP in stimulating exports from particular developing countries, this would run counter to the very purpose of the system, which is precisely to facilitate such exports until the economies of these countries are sufficiently transformed. Until such a point is reached, it is difficult to justify measures that would impair their progress. From this point of view, it would seem somewhat premature in the present context to depart from non-discrimination, one of the basic principles of the GSP and introduce the concept of graduation and differentiation among developing countries. It is relevant to note that whilst four developing countries—Argentina, Brazil, India and Mexico—with a total population of 829 million, account for more than half of the production of manufactures in the Third World, their share in the total of world manufacturing production is much the same as that of Italy with a population of 56 million.

The subject of restrictive business practices is also of relevance to the reform of the structure of international trade in manufactures. The use of such devices as "voluntary export restraints" and "orderly marketing arrangements" referred to earlier has led also to a greater use of private cartels and thus of restrictive business practices. The need for international action to regulate such practices, including those of transnational corporations, has been under intensive consideration in an *ad hoc* group of experts in UNCTAD which has been preparing a set of equitable principles and rules for this purpose. The fifth session of the Conference is called upon to consider, and take appropriate action, on the outstanding issues, and to determine the dates of the negotiating conference on this subject. Also before the Manila Conference is the wider question of review and follow-up action in respect of the Nairobi decision on comprehensive measures for the expansion and diversification of the trade in manufactures of developing countries.

Restructuring the International Monetary and Financial Framework

The restructuring of the international monetary and financial framework is another of the major themes of the Manila Conference. Indeed, world economic developments since Nairobi have only underlined the importance and urgency for action in this area. The prevailing weaknesses in this field are deeply relevant to the difficulties and crises of recent times. They have affected adversely the developed and developing countries alike and both groups have a common stake in adaptation and reform. The need for action covers a number of fronts.

In the first place, there is the need to revive or revitalize the discussions and negotiations pertaining to a reform of the international monetary system. It is already some years since some of the basic elements of the Bretton Woods system came to be seriously undermined, if not destroyed. It is already some years since a blueprint for reform was outlined and discussed in the forum of the International Monetary Fund. There has been even a wide acceptance of some of the principal features of a new system—including the nature and role of the special drawing right (SDR) as the principal reserve asset. Yet progress towards the actual reform of the system appears to have stalled. Instead, in the face of dislocations and disturbances, there has been recourse to *ad hoc* improvisations and makeshift arrangements, some of which run counter to the needs of more durable and fundamental reforms or serve, at least, to postpone them.

The basic requirements of a reformed system have been outlined on many occasions. They include the need for international control over the process of creating international liquidity and the corresponding need for the SDR to replace currencies as the principal reserve asset; the need—widely accepted but yet to be implemented—for the establishment of a link between the creation of SDRs and development assistance; the need for mechanisms that foster more balanced and speedy processes of adjustment with more symmetrical obligations as between countries with surpluses and deficits on current account; the need for more predictable and stable systems of exchange rates and for conditions that foster more orderly capital flows; and, not least, the need for developing countries to exercise a greater voice in the decision-making process.

The reform of the international monetary system will not be negotiated at the Manila Conference. But the Conference could make a significant contribution by spelling out the requirements of a reformed and global system and by giving a strong political thrust to the need for action in this realm. The absence of a coherent system can imply a heavy cost to the international community. The problems of inflation, unemployment and slow recovery from recession that continue to affect the developed countries are not unconnected with the failure to reform the international monetary system. Nor are the problems experienced by many developing countries through losses in their terms of trade and the real value of their assets owing to fluctuations in the exchange rates of major currencies. Many features of the current scene could have, in fact, consequences of a seriously disruptive or disturbing nature in the future. These include the increasing tendency for the creation of international liquidity to be assumed by the private sector instead of the International Monetary Fund, the emergence of conditions for disruptive movements of short-term funds, and the channelling of liquid balances by the private capital market to developing countries at excessively short maturities and high interest rates. If uncorrected, these features could severely undermine the prospects for sustained recovery and growth in both developed and developing countries and lay the foundation for deeper crises in the period ahead.

A second area in which action is urgently needed is related to the requirements of a better monetary system but is not wholly contingent on, and need not therefore await, the implementation of comprehensive reforms. This concerns the need to enhance the adequacy of the facilities at present available to the developing countries to help them cope with their balance-of-payments problems, and also to improve or modify the conditions which govern their use.

The underlying philosophy of the monetary system set up at Bretton Woods was that countries should subscribe to the maintenance of an open system of convertible currencies, stable exchange rates and the absence of restrictions on trade and payments. In this way, it was hoped to avoid a return to the mutually harmful policies of the pre-war period. To help countries desist from restrictions in periods of payments crises, they were provided with access to financial accommodations from the International Monetary Fund. These were to help finance short-term deficits and maladjustments until corrective measures of a non-restrictionist kind had their effect.

The relevance of this philosophy to the needs of developing countries was perhaps always in question. An essential need of developing countries is to be able to finance a level of imports commensurate with their development objectives. The ease with which they could subscribe in practice to the tenets of an open system depends on the extent to which this need is satisfied. When it is not, the short-term and limited amounts of accommodation that the Fund can provide offer little compensation. Indeed, it is hardly surprising that developing countries have often valued support from the Fund not because of its scale but because of the confidence which adherence to Fund precepts, in the field of discipline and conditionality, generates in other donors and providers of long-term finance.

The limitations of the facilities at present available to developing countries have in the recent period become particularly and forcefully apparent. During the last few years the payments gaps of the non-oil-producing countries taken together increased substantially, reflecting the multiple crises afflicting the international economy. Yet, despite valuable efforts by the International Monetary Fund to increase the resources at its disposal, the wider network of official facilities available to developing countries to cope with the new situation proved starkly inadequate. A limited number of developing countries was able to have recourse to private capital markets for accommodation—a process that was facilitated by the increased liquidity of the banking system, itself a reflection, in no small part, of payments imbalances and the continuing recession. This process has resulted in a significant acceleration of the volume of commercial indebtedness of developing countries, reflecting borrowings at short maturities and market rates of interest. For most developing countries, however, even this source was not available. Although to some extent additional accommodations were provided by the International Monetary Fund and other lending agencies, as well as donor countries, the amounts made available fell desperately short of requirements. In consequence, these countries have had little option but to curtail severely their import levels and so place in jeopardy their investment levels and development programmes. As a result, the targets and objectives of the Second Development Decade— internationally agreed upon—were put beyond reach.

The experience of recent times has brought into focus not only the question of the adequacy of the facilities available to developing countries to cope with their payments problems, but also the related issue of the adjustment policies which have hitherto conditioned the use of the Fund's resources. This issue has been the subject of a recent study by UNCTAD, undertaken with UNDP support.* The study questions the extent to which policies of internal contraction and adjustment in developing countries are a valid corrective or response to disturbances of external origin. It also sharply highlights the issue of the efficacy and relevance of short-term financial support in meeting problems of a more enduring structural character. A major conclusion of the study is that a gap exists in the prevailing network of facilities, a gap which needs to be filled by the establishment of a medium-term multilateral facility. Such a step could constitute an important part of the international effort to improve the existing system and to make it more responsive to the needs of developing countries.

In the context of the present discussion it is also relevant to point to another proposal before the Manila Conference—the establishment of an export credit guarantee facility. This would help meet a long-felt need and thus enhance the capacity of developing countries to promote their exports of manufactured goods. The limitations that developing countries have hitherto encountered in this field have placed them at a disadvantage in securing external markets for their products.

A third area which is relevant to the restructuring of the international monetary and financial framework concerns the treatment of debt problems. There are two aspects to this issue—the question of the actions to be taken to provide immediate or early relief for debt problems which have become burdensome and are impeding development efforts, particularly of the poorer countries, and the introduction of an internationally agreed framework of principles, procedures and mechanisms which will help in the future treatment of debt problems.

Both aspects of the problem have been the subject of attention in UNCTAD and will require action at Manila. The question of the official external debt of the developing countries was the subject of decision by the ministerial session of the Trade and Development Board in March 1978. On this occasion there was agreement to provide relief to the poorer developing countries by means of retrospective adjustments in the terms of their past official development assistance (ODA) debt so as to conform to the current softer terms being applied by donors. For the least-developed countries where grants are the current norm, this implies a writing-off of such debts; for the others, a scaling down and spreading of annual debt service charges. A few donor countries had taken action in this direction even prior to the ministerial session of the Board, but most of them have acted subsequently or announced their intention of doing so. By

---

* *The Balance-of-payments Adjustment Process in Developing Countries: Report to the Group of Twenty-Four.*

the end of 1978, eleven major creditor countries had committed themselves to convert into grants $6.2 billion of loans owed by the poorest countries representing an annual saving in debt service costs of $300 million over the next twenty years. The implementation of the actions envisaged at the ministerial session has, however, still to be completed. Not all major donors have detailed the steps they intend to take in this regard. In a number of instances, too, the determination of the beneficiary countries has fallen short of what was envisaged in the Board decision. The Manila Conference is called upon to review the implementation of this decision. It needs to be added that the question of the commercial debts of developing countries was not the subject of active discussion at the Board session in March 1978.

The second aspect of the debt issue concerns the adoption of an internationally accepted framework of practices and principles to guide debt operations relating to interested developing countries. At present, there is no uniform and internationally agreed set of principles to guide the treatment of the debt problems of the developing countries. There is no system that would ensure that countries in similar situations will receive similar treatment, no assurance that the remedial actions taken will pay sufficient attention to the wider developmental needs of these countries.

The question of principles and features was the subject of alternative proposals presented by the developing and the developed countries at the Conference on International Economic Co-operation at Paris. But though these proposals had several common elements, no agreement was reached. Since that time the question has been discussed in UNCTAD by an inter-governmental group of experts and significant progress has been made. The prospects are favourable therefore for reaching agreement on this issue and for the adoption of a multilateral framework of guiding features and principles. This is a subject before the Manila Conference. A suggestion has been made in this context for the establishment of an International Debt Commission made up of eminent persons who could objectively examine the overall position of debtor countries and be responsible for the effective and equitable implementation of the guiding features in the context of international economic co-operation at the request of these countries as a contribution to the process of organizing debt relief. Such an operation would pay heed to the relationship between debt problems and development needs and contribute to timely action well before the stage of default.

A fourth issue of relevance to a better structure in the monetary and financial field relates to the long-term transfer of resources to developing countries. This must be the focus of serious attention at Manila. The failure of the major donor countries to conform to the 0.7 per cent target for official development assistance has been cited as evidence of a serious lack of political will towards achieving the goals of international co-operation for development. Development aid has been one of the preferred instruments of the industrialized countries themselves and the failure to conform to international targets in this area must naturally be taken as a reflection of the degree of commitment of these countries to the needs of the development process. Some industrialized countries, particularly the smaller ones, have already reached this target and even surpassed it. But the focus will be sharpened on some of the largest donor countries whose performance has in fact shown a retrogression. Until the developed countries show a convincing improvement in their performance, the seriousness of their commitment to international co-operation for development will inevitably remain in question. The issues in the field of long-term resource transfers are not confined to the volume of official development assistance. They also touch on such questions as the untying of aid, the need for programme aid, the regularity and predictability of aid flows and the resource availability of long-term lending institutions. These are not new subjects. But the fact that they remain on the agenda for Manila is evidence of the shortcomings that persist in respect of this particular dimension of international co-operation for development.

The lack of coherence of international policy in the entire field of resource transfers has prompted the suggestion that there is now a need for a consistent and comprehensive framework for international financial co-operation. Such a framework would bring within its compass each of the major elements of relevance to financial co-operation for development—bilateral and multilateral aid and lending, debt policy, access to capital markets, balance-of-payments accommodation and so on. The essential objectives would be to ensure that the several instruments of financial co-operation are mutually supportive and, most important of all, that in sum they provide for a total of resource flows which is commensurate with the scale of resource needs for development. The basic elements of such a framework could, of course, evolve over time in the direction of a shift towards greater predictability, even automaticity, in resource flows and towards the forging of instruments appropriate to such a goal. The Manila Conference could give consideration to the form and characteristics of a suitable framework for international financial co-operation and initiate a process of consultation and negotiation that will lead towards its establishment.

The Thrust Towards Collective Self-reliance

The subject of economic co-operation amongst developing countries is another of the major issues before the Manila Conference. It will occupy a place of a particular importance on the agenda, both because it is central to the restructuring of international economic relationships—the theme of the Manila Conference—and because it has gained momentum in the political sense since UNCTAD IV in Nairobi. Collective self-reliance is one of the cornerstones of the concept of the New International Economic Order. It is a goal that is likely to increase in prominence in the 1980s.

There are two dimensions to the concept of economic co-operation amongst developing countries. The first relates to the need for extending and expanding trade and other linkages amongst these countries; the second to the need for them to co-operate with one another in bringing about changes and improvements in their relationships with the rest of the world. Each of these aspects is gaining in importance against the backdrop of the evolving international economic situation.

The strengthening of trade and other linkages amongst developing countries is crucial to any restructuring of international economic relationships because it is the means of reducing the economic dependence of these countries on the industrialized countries—for the most part the metropolitan powers of earlier times. It is also important because it offers, in large part at least, a solution to some of the problems they are likely to encounter in the process of economic growth and transformation. Quite clearly, the growing export surpluses of the developing countries cannot all be absorbed by the present industrialized countries even if there were no barriers to market access in these countries. Increasingly the developing countries must look to one another for markets and for sources of supply of raw materials and manufactured goods. Collective self-reliance, from this point of view, can become an engine of growth and development.

Trade amongst developing countries is likely to continue increasing spontaneously through the operation of market forces. But such trade, whether regional or inter-regional, is still of minor dimensions and the process of normal growth will be slow. Habit and the lack of adequate communications, are powerful obstacles that need to be overcome. The goal has therefore to be consciously pursued. It has to be fostered through policies and mechanisms specially fashioned for the purpose. This need for conscious actions is the essence of the concept of economic co-operation amongst developing countries.

There are several aspects of relevance to the forging of policies of co-operation aimed at intensifying trade and other exchanges amongst developing countries. First, there is the question of the breadth and coverage of co-operative activities. The developing countries span three continents. Many policies and instruments of co-operation will relate to small groups of countries, usually contiguous ones. Indeed, such examples of co-operation that now exist are largely of this kind and it is this category that lends itself to integration arrangements—the closest type of co-operation. But co-operation amongst developing countries should also be on the regional and interregional, or global, scale. Certain types of co-operative arrangements are in fact applicable over a wider canvas—common institutions, frameworks of rules and principles, trade concessions and so on. Indeed, the developing countries are so numerous and their territories so extensive that virtually any actions or institutions relevant to the international level generally can conceivably be applied also to the developing countries as a group. The concept of collective self-reliance can be taken to apply to co-operation at all levels. But the strengthening of the position of the developing countries as a group, and actions that involve co-operation amongst all such countries, must be an essential dimension, political no less than economic, of the concept. For this reason, special attention needs to be given to instruments of co-operation amongst developing countries applicable "across the board"—instruments such as schemes of trade preference and Third World institutions and actions in economic, financial and other fields. The major question that arises in this context is the way in which such instruments can be made consistent with and supportive of similar instruments designed to promote co-operation at regional and subregional levels.

A second aspect relates to the kind of instruments to be used to promote co-operation. There are, of course, a number of possible instruments some of which—such as a trade preference scheme—facilitate trade, and others—such as contracts—which promote it in a more direct manner. But whatever the instrument, if the objective is to overcome the weakness of developing countries in market competition with the developed countries, its efficacy would be enhanced if it incorporates the principle that developing countries would provide preferential or special treatment in favour of one another, within an accepted framework of rules and guidelines.

The third aspect is a related one. Systems or instruments of co-operation amongst developing countries must, whenever relevant, take account of differences amongst these countries. The successful treatment of this issue is crucial to the success of the whole endeavour. This is as true of the subregional and regional level as it is of the interregional level. The developing countries are not a homogenous group. They comprise countries at different levels of development and of different economic strengths. Co-operative arrangements which afford no protection to the weaker countries from the stronger will serve only to widen the gap between them and to increase tensions amongst the partners. The differentiation that exists amongst the developing countries can, however, be a strength rather than a weakness. The varying capacities and endowments of these countries offer a greater potential for mutually supportive development than would be possible if all countries were similarly placed and endowed. The movement of skills in recent times between developing countries is an illustration of this. So too is the prospect for beneficial exchanges in the field of appropriate technologies. But, nevertheless, a conscious and careful effort is needed to ensure that differences amongst developing countries lead to positive rather than negative results. This is an approach that must govern every effort to forge instruments of co-operation amongst developing countries. Existing systems of co-operation at regional or subregional levels already provide a fund of useful experience in the handling of this problem, and future initiatives should make use of the lessons they offer.

The other major dimension of economic co-operation concerns the co-operation of developing countries with one another in order to improve their relations *vis-à-vis* the outside world. Here again there are at least two aspects to the concept. One relates to co-operative arrangements among themselves that strengthen their position, in one way or another, in trading and related activities. The other refers to co-operation for the purposes of obtaining better results in the area of international negotiations.

There are a number of possibilities of relevance to the first category of co-operative arrangements. The essential principle here is combination on the part of developing countries to enhance their market strength. This principle can apply to a range of activities in the field of export and import ranging from joint ventures to common arrangements for import procurement. One of the most important prospects lies, however, in the field of commodity trade where producers, by co-operation in supply management, can improve—even transform—their present market strength.

Producer associations can also strengthen the negotiating positions of producers in international commodity agreements. But where feasible, they can go further and directly organize the provision of supplies to markets and thereby improve prices. In this connection, the adoption of articles of agreement for a federation of producer associations of developing countries is potentially a significant step.

Co-operation amongst developing countries in the area of international negotiation assumes a special importance in the context of the relations between developed and developing countries. The establishment of the Group of 77 in 1964 in the context of UNCTAD I was the first manifestation of co-operative activity of this kind. That the

Group of 77 has persisted, increased in number and appeared in many other international forums is a mark of its success. But in the current phase there are new challenges to be overcome. Issues in the field of international co-operation for development are moving away from the stage of the formulation of broad objectives to that of complex negotiations on specific issues. This requires that the developing countries succeed in forging common positions on such issues by reconciling conflicts of interest amongst themselves. This in turn calls for expertise and skill and a capacity, if needed, to increase their leverage by mobilizing their own power of action, sometimes by committing their own resources. Measures to improve the expertise and preparedness of developing countries in the negotiating process are therefore an important aspect of co-operation amongst these countries.

The issue of co-operation amongst developing countries has now passed beyond the stage of commitment to the general principle. At successive meetings of developing countries the several possibilities for co-operation have been identified and enunciated in specific terms. The feasibility of the many of these proposals has been examined in studies by UNCTAD itself. The essential need is to proceed with their implementation. The number of possibilities in this realm are vast and it is important therefore to establish priorities and concentrate attention on their realization. The launching of even a few important endeavours will give credence to the concept of collective self-reliance.

The content of co-operation amongst developing countries has essentially to be determined by these countries themselves. Yet the process must not be seen as an attempt at self-contained growth. Rather it must form part of any global strategy for development. In terms of specific aspects, it should attract support from the developed countries themselves. It is for this reason that economic co-operation amongst developing countries must remain a critical concern of the UN system and of UNCTAD in particular—in fulfilment of the aims which have been set out in successive General Assembly and UNCTAD resolutions. Ways need to be found that would enable developing countries to discuss amongst themselves and pursue co-operative arrangements within the framework and with the assistance of UNCTAD and other parts of the UN system. This process has at the same time to be made consistent with the concerns of other groups and fitted into a global strategy for development. The mounting tempo of interest and activity in the field of economic co-operation for development is in a sense a new phenomenon, to which UNCTAD needs to respond with new modalities—in close collaboration with the regional economic commissions and other interested agencies.

The Arusha Programme of Collective Self-reliance presented by the Group of 77 to UNCTAD V encompasses a number of specific proposals and activities which need follow-up work and action in terms of the short- to medium-term plan of global priorities which it contains. These include a global system of trade preferences for developing countries, the creation of joint ventures among them, co-operative arrangements amongst State trading organizations, co-operation in import procurement, the establishment of multinational enterprises, measures to strengthen the integration process, the establishment of Third World monetary arrangements such as payments and clearing arrangements, and the creation of Third World banking institutions. The

Manila Conference has to respond to this need by endorsing international support measures where relevant, including activities to be undertaken by UNCTAD in the period ahead. A number of specific programmes in UNCTAD await such endorsement.

Other Issues Before the Conference

There are a number of other important issues on the Manila agenda. These include the subject of technology, trade between countries having different economic and social systems, shipping, the special problem of the least-developed countries and the problems of other specially disadvantaged categories of countries—the land-locked and island developing countries. In one way or another, these issues form an integral part of the major issues discussed earlier. However, because of their special character they figure as independent items on the agenda, calling for particular decisions.

1. *Technology*

The issues in the area of technology are intimately linked to the problem of the economic and social transformation of developing countries, particularly in the direction of industrialization. The industrialization and development objectives of developing countries have major implications for national and international policies in the field of technology. There is an urgent need for reducing the technological dependence of developing countries—dependence which carries with it a number of serious constraints on their development efforts—and for building up an adequate technological capability in these countries themselves. This theme has been the concern of UNCTAD for some time. The Conference at Nairobi took certain decisions of major importance in the area of technology, particularly the decision to initiate a process of negotiation of a code of conduct on the transfer of technology. The decision at Nairobi also called on UNCTAD to make a vital contribution to the economic development and commercial aspects of the revision of the industrial property system—the legal arrangements and practices relating to patents and trade-marks—in the context of the revision of the Paris Convention being undertaken under the auspices of the World Intellectual Property Organization. The Conference at Manila will need to take stock of progress on both these fronts. Two sessions of the United Nations Conference on an International Code of Conduct on the Transfer of Technology have already concluded. The Conference at Manila will need to determine the further action called for in this area, taking into account the progress made at these sessions and the problems which still remain to be resolved. The decisions of the Conference will have a critical bearing on the completion of this important initiative.

There are other major issues in the area of technology before the Conference. Foremost amongst these is the subject of the transformation of the indigenous technological capability of the developing countries. The transfer of technology from the industrialized countries to the developing countries is a vital and important process whose efficiency and terms need to be improved to as great an extent as possible. But it needs to be recognized that improved terms and conditions of access to the technology of the developed countries will not by themselves suffice to strengthen the technological capability of the developing countries or to accelerate their technological transformation. For the attainment of these latter objectives complementary measures are required at national, regional and interregional levels in the developing countries themselves. These countries need consciously to pursue the goal of attaining their technological transformation through developing their own technological capacity. They need to adopt policies and establish institutions which aim at achieving such a goal. Such policies and institutions must serve to create a framework or infrastructure for the transformation of indigenous technological capability. The policies in this area must necessarily bear a close relationship to policies relating to the acquisition of technology from abroad. This requires moving from *ad hoc* policies to a comprehensive approach, including adoption of technology planning as an integral part of development planning. The Conference at Manila would be called upon to decide on the steps that can be taken in this regard and the support which the international community could extend to developing countries in their pursuit of this goal. Effective decisions in this area and a significant programme of work could be a major result of the Conference in the field of technology.

A related question pertaining to the problem of technology relates to what has been called the reverse transfer of technology from developing to developed countries—sometimes referred to as the "brain drain"—although such a flow is not confined to the movement of professional skills but also embraces middle-level talents and related skills. The reverse transfer of technology does undoubtedly pose problems for the developing countries affected by it. The overall questions in this area are complex and embrace a number of elements which are political and social as much as economic. But as long as the problem is of major dimensions and promises to remain so, or even increase in intensity, there is a need for the international community to address itself to it and to formulate acceptable approaches. The flow of skills and other manpower resources is not of course always of a negative character. In recent times there has been a particularly marked increase in the flow of human skills between the developing countries themselves. This has enabled some of them to benefit from the availability of expertise and skills in other developing countries. This is an aspect which holds promise for the whole theme of co-operation among the developing countries themselves. Flows of this nature have both their positive and negative aspects, and here again it would be timely for the international community to take stock of the problem and to formulate guiding approaches and policies to deal with it.

2. *Trade Between Countries having Different Economic and Social Systems*

An earlier section underlined the need of the developing countries to reduce their dependence on a few of the industrialized countries, mostly the former metropolitan powers. As mentioned, this dependence is a legacy of history but it persists to this day despite the evolution that has taken place in the political realm. One means of reducing this dependence is through trade and other linkages with the socialist countries of

Eastern Europe. The potential in this area is great. The socialist countries of Eastern Europe constitute an important element of the global economy taken as a whole. They themselves are in the process of growth and expansion, a process which cannot but offer increasing opportunities for specialization and trade. Since the growth of such trade cannot be left to the operation of market forces, it has to be consciously sought after and fostered. Already in recent years the rate of growth of trade between the developing countries and the socialist countries of Eastern Europe has been rapid, in fact, more rapid than the rate of growth of other elements of the total trade of developing countries. Nevertheless, in many cases, the base remains small and the potential remains great for the future.

The subject of trade between countries having different economic and social systems has been on the agenda of previous UNCTAD conferences and remains an important item on the agenda for the Manila Conference. The agenda for Manila refers to all trade flows arising from trade relations between such countries. There is a need to impart further impulse to this issue and to provide new orientations. The socialist countries of Eastern Europe can play a major part in the process of structural change and in a better ordering of international economic relations. They can make an important contribution to the restructuring of international trade as a whole, including trade between them and the developed as well as the developing countries. They can also play a significant part in the process of the industrialization of the developing countries through further intensification of their trade and economic co-operation with developing countries and the planned restructuring of industrial development. In recent times progress has been made in UNCTAD on selected aspects of trade and other economic relations between the socialist countries of Eastern Europe and the developing countries—aspects relating to the diversification of the form of co-operation (industrial co-operation, including joint ventures and tripartite co-operation, co-operation in planning, co-operation with respect to third markets, etc.), the multilateralization of payments arrangements and the utilization of the potential for trade with developing countries of the integration programmes of the socialist countries of Eastern Europe themselves. But the greatest gains in this area are still to be reaped, and a conscious attempt needs to be made by both the socialist countries of Eastern Europe and the developing countries to exploit to the full the potential in this area. This is a subject on which the Manila Conference could take important new decisions.

3. *Shipping*

The subject of shipping is another issue on which major initiatives could be forthcoming at Manila. This subject was not on the agenda for the fourth session of the Conference at Nairobi, largely because UNCTAD IV was convening shortly after the negotiation and adoption of the Convention on a Code of Conduct for Liner Conferences and the basic need was for the ratification by governments of the Convention in order to bring it into force. The time has now come, however, at UNCTAD V to focus attention once more on the question of shipping and to seek international action in support of the goals in this area.

The situation regarding the present status of the Convention on a Code of Conduct for Liner Conferences is one of the subjects on the agenda for UNCTAD V. Although the Convention has been ratified by a sufficient number of developing countries, to meet one of the requirements for bringing it into effect, the other condition of ratification by countries accounting for a specified total of tonnage, has yet to be achieved. This is an essential requirement and it is hoped that the developed countries which voted for the Code at the Conference of Plenipotentiaries would now proceed with the process of ratification. The Convention itself provides for a review after it comes into effect, but it would seem that the first step is to make the Code an effective legal instrument.

Besides the Code, the main issue in the field of shipping before the Manila Conference relates to the need of developing countries to build up their merchant marines and increase their participation in world shipping. Although since the first UNCTAD Conference in 1964, this has been a major goal of developing countries, actual performance has fallen far short of the objective, especially in the bulk sectors. The share of developing countries in the deadweight tonnage of the world merchant fleet is 8.6 per cent and although some countries have successfully expanded their merchant fleets, the overall share of the developing countries as a group remains unsatisfactory. There are a number of issues relating to the objective of enhancing the participation of developing countries in international shipping. One of these relates to possible measures to secure bulk cargoes for the fleets of developing countries. Another issue is the role played by the system of open registry and its implications for the development of the national fleets of developing countries. Yet another issue relates to the availability of finance for the development of merchant marines in developing countries, together with problems related to training of personnel. All these and other elements could form part of a new and concerted international policy in the field of shipping aimed at building up the merchant marines of the developing countries.

4. *Least-developed Among Developing Countries*

The special needs of the least-developed countries have received recognition and attention for some time now. UNCTAD, from its inception, has been the focal point for dealing with these problems, formulating special measures to solve them. There is already in UNCTAD an Intergovernmental Group on the Least Developed Countries, and UNCTAD recently broke new ground with a special meeting of officials from donor agencies with representatives of the least-developed countries. The meeting, which proved to be very useful, will be repeated in the coming year.

However, concrete measures to assist these countries still remain hopelessly inadequate. Indeed, paradoxically, despite the international endorsement of the need for special attention to these countries as part of the global attack on the problem of development, the performance of these countries in recent years has been poor, reflecting among other things the inadequacy of international support. In some cases, *per capita* growth rates in the least-developed countries have remained negative. On average, their growth performance has lagged far behind other countries—a result that does not square with the clearly stated desire of the international community to afford special attention to the problems of these countries.

UNCTAD V provides an opportunity to formulate and adopt a major new programme that is coherent and effective and aimed at problems of structural transformation of the least-developed countries. Such a programme would give credibility to the commitment of the international community to the development issue. It could represent a particularly important result of the Manila Conference. There is a proposal before the Conference for launching such a radically expanded programme, in two phases: viz. in the short term an immediate action programme aimed at providing an upward thrust to the economies of the least-developed countries, and in the longer term a substantial new action programme for the 1980s for the least-developed countries, with the objective of transforming their economies towards self-sustained development. This proposal would no doubt command the attention of the Conference.

5. *Land-locked and Island Developing Countries*

The problems of geographically disadvantaged countries have also received special attention in UNCTAD for a considerable period of time now, and UNCTAD has been the focal point for efforts to mitigate the geographic handicaps of land-locked and island developing countries.

The fifth session of the Conference provides an opportunity for the international community to reaffirm its support for specific action related to the particular needs and problems of the land-locked developing countries, as well as an occasion for land-locked developing countries and their transit neighbours to reiterate their commitments to co-operate fully with each other in identifying transit transport problems and in seeking effective co-operative solutions to them, with strong financial and technical assistance support for the actions identified.

With respect to island developing countries, further specific action is particularly needed in the case of smaller, more remote, island countries in order to offset their major handicaps in terms of transport and communications, great distances from market centres, highly limited internal markets, low resource endowment, heavy dependence on a few commodities for their foreign exchange earnings, shortage of administrative personnel, and heavy financial burdens caused by the location of small numbers of people in islands remote from one another and from main centres.

Extract from *Restructuring the International Economic Framework*

JUNE 1979 TO THE PRESENT DAY: TOWARDS A NEW INTERNATIONAL DEVELOPMENT STRATEGY

The two speeches which make up this section report on the proceedings at Manila, with frank discussion of the ways in which the Conference might be said to have fallen short of expectations, as well as of areas in which previous work was consolidated and further progress made. The agenda for the Manila Conference was deliberately wide ranging—partly to make plain the importance of the specific negotiable issues in their proper context and partly to affirm the true and complex interdepedence of all these issues. The need for general structural change thus emerges as the main theme of UNCTAD's concerns in the post-Manila period, and as the premise on which the Secretary-General bases his call that the time has come for the "rules of the game" to be comprehensively rewritten, for which the projected special session of the United Nations and the opening of global negotiations towards the end of 1980 might provide a beginning.

United Nations Economic and Social Council

6 July 1979

It is always a difficult task to make an assessment of an UNCTAD Conference, let alone provide a definitive verdict on it—one's assessment of the results is dependent on one's own expectations, on the yardsticks one uses, and naturally this can vary from individual to individual, from country to country. I recollect being in a similar position when I addressed the Economic and Social Council in the wake of UNCTAD IV at Nairobi. I said then that we would need to withhold judgement on the results of UNCTAD IV because in a sense that session of the Conference served as a launching pad for an extensive series of negotiations. The ultimate verdict or judgement on the Nairobi Conference would depend to a large extent on how those negotiations unfolded in the period after Nairobi. I said that, if the negotiations concluded with fruitful results, then, in retrospect, Nairobi would be seen to be a positive event. On the other hand, if the negotiations themselves proved to be inconclusive, the importance of Nairobi would be correspondingly reduced.

I think it is important to recognize and to underline the continuity that existed between the Nairobi Conference and UNCTAD V in Manila. It was prior to Nairobi, on the occasion of the sixth special session of the General Assembly, that the broad goals of the international community in the sphere of international economic relations were formulated and embodied in the concept of a New International Economic Order. UNCTAD IV, which was convened after that sixth special session, sought to give content or concrete form to some of these broad goals by endeavouring to translate them into specific arrangements or agreements brought about through a process of negotiations, even though this process might prove to be time-consuming and arduous.

At Nairobi, the focus in respect of the launching of negotiations fell very sharply on one or two issues. The problem of commodities was particularly underscored, because at that point in time it was felt that the question of the developing countries' trade in primary products was a crucial aspect of their international economic concerns, and an aspect where the attention of the international community was needed to deal with many long-standing and important problems. As a result of this concentration on the commodity issue, the Nairobi Conference gave endorsement to the concept of an Integrated Programme for Commodities and authorized the launching of negotiations, both on individual commodities and on a Common Fund. There were other negotiating processes that were also launched at Nairobi, although they were not highlighted so much at that point in time. We cannot forget that it was the Nairobi Conference that initiated the negotiations that are expected to lead up to an International Code of Conduct on the Transfer of Technology. Similarly, it was the Nairobi Conference that launched the negotiations on restrictive business practices that are at present under way. Again, it was Nairobi that gave a particularly strong impetus to the concept of economic co-operation amongst developing countries reflecting the theme of collective self-reliance.

Convening as it did three years after Nairobi, the Manila Conference took place at a time when many of the initiatives launched at Nairobi—and many of the negotiating processes—were still under way, they had not all been brought to a final conclusion. At the same time, when the Manila Conference was being prepared, the multilateral trade negotiations were also in process, and for all these reasons it proved difficult to apply the focus to any single issue which would form the dominant theme of Manila. For that reason, it seemed necessary to present and structure the Manila Conference, not in terms of a specific focus on a single issue, but in terms rather of a wider range of issues where the international community would be invited to pay attention to the needs of the international economy in these several areas. It was not the intention, given the state to which issues had evolved, to seek out of the Manila Conference specific actions or decisions of a substantive character, specific solutions in respect of these several issues. But at least it was expected that at the Manila Conference there would be some endorsement of an extension of the negotiating process into the new areas covered by the items placed on the agenda. In that way, Manila was seen as providing an opportunity with which to complement and complete the negotiating process launched at Nairobi.

At the Manila Conference, particular emphasis was given to those issues that were not the subject of concentrated attention at Nairobi. The need to progress on some aspects of the commodity problem not covered in the post-Nairobi phase was underlined. Similarly, attention was given to such problems as the rise of protectionism in the recent period—an issue which was causing concern to the international community and to the developing countries. The need for a reform in the framework of money and finance was also highlighted as one of the issues on which an ongoing process of negotiations needed to be launched. Similarly, problems in the area of economic co-operation among developing countries, problems in the field not only of the transfer of technology but also of technological transformation, problems in the area of shipping, in the field of the least-developed countries, in the field of relations between countries having different economic and social systems—all these were seen to be issues on which new processes could usefully be initiated at Manila.

But apart from the listing of these issues as subjects for international dialogue, discussion and negotiation, it was one of the distinctive features of the Manila Conference that these issues were set against the canvas of a wider awareness of the need for more basic fundamental changes in international economic relationships. That is why what has come to be called the theme of structural change came to be the underlying theme of the Manila Conference. That is why it figured not only as a thread running through the individual agenda items, but as a separate and specific agenda item by itself. In this way, it was sought to make of Manila a particularly distinctive event in which the essential needs of the international community, in the field of co-operation for development in particular, could be highlighted as part of an ongoing process of change and evolution in prevailing systems, mechanisms and of relationships.

Now we have seen the conclusion of the Manila Conference. As I said earlier, it is not my purpose to make an assessment this afternoon, nor is it my intention to attempt an exhaustive enumeration of all the results of the Manila Conference. Suffice it to say that, in respect of a number of issues, the Manila Conference did take decisions on the basis of consensus. In respect of other issues, the Manila Conference took decisions on the basis of voted agreements. In still other areas, the Conference was unable to take decisions and referred the pending issues to the permanent machinery of UNCTAD, particularly to the Trade and Development Board. As I see it, in the aftermath of Manila, the important task for the international community—and for UNCTAD itself—is to build on the positive decisions that were taken, to pursue the work that has been launched and to create new structures on the foundations that have been laid. It is in this way that I should like to approach the period following the conclusion of the Manila Conference and the tasks that remain to be undertaken in the light of that event.

In my view, in three critical and crucial areas, the Conference at Manila did succeed in providing openings at least for the international community to involve itself in the period ahead in important consultations, even negotiations. If these ongoing consultations and negotiations unfold in a positive and constructive manner, they could provide a crucial and important complement to the process started at Nairobi and open up the way for an assessment of the Manila Conference which in retrospect might seem to be useful. First of all, in the area of international trade in commodities, the Conference at Manila did succeed in adopting, by consensus, a somewhat comprehensive resolution which not only endorsed and affirmed the objectives and the activities pertaining to the Common Fund under the Integrated Programme for Commodities, and to the ongoing efforts to arrive at individual commodity agreements in respect of a number of products, but also provided new dimensions in respect of facets of the commodity problem which, though figuring in the Integrated Programme, had not received particularly sharp attention after Nairobi. In particular, the Manila Conference did endorse the objective of building or working towards what has been called an international framework of co-operation in two very vital areas—in the area of the marketing and distribution of commodities, and in the area of the processing of these commodities. The resolution called not only for studies on these issues on the part of the UNCTAD secretariat; it also called for the establishment of an international framework of co-operation which presumably can only be brought into being through a process of deliberation, consultation and negotiation between Member Governments. I think that this is a very significant development, because up to now the machinery of UNCTAD has given its attention to the need to regulate commodity markets and prices through individual commodity agreements and through the Common Fund. With the new resolution we turn our attention to other, perhaps even more dynamic, aspects of the commodity economy—the aspects of marketing, distribution and processing which are inherent to the very structure of world commodity trade. If, in the period after Manila, this resolution enables the international community to arrive at definitive and useful results in this realm, then I believe that the Conference itself would prove to have been significant. The problem of marketing and distribution of commodities touches on a variety of aspects, including the role of transnational corporations in international commodity trade. Similarly, the question of the processing of commodities touches on such vital issues as access to markets and the question of the emergent trend of protectionism. So you can see that these aspects do bring within their compass a number of key problems which are of central importance to the whole question of restructuring international economic relations.

Secondly, the Manila Conference also produced, through consensus, a resolution dealing with the vital subject of protectionism and structural adjustment. The question of protectionism was, of course, one of the issues which was given great prominence at Manila. This was inevitable in the context of recent developments. I believe that the very fact that the protectionist issue came to be the subject of particularly sharp focus, the very fact that it was the occasion for an expression of views on the part of the different constituents of the international community, this in itself was of value from the point of view of the contribution made by the Conference. But, more specifically, the resolution itself did provide for action on two fronts. It called upon UNCTAD, within its intergovernmental machinery, not only to review and identify problems, but to formulate recommendations on what has been called the general problem of protectionism. Likewise, the resolution called upon the intergovernmental bodies of UNCTAD to formulate general recommendations on the question of structural adjustment. You will perhaps agree with me that these resolutions carry within them the seeds of somewhat extensive negotiating processes. After all, the general problem of protection-ism on which we have been invited to make recommendations is very much linked to the entire question of the way in which the future world trading system evolves in the light of the industrialization of the developing countries as well as other parts of the international economy. The task of formulating recommendations on this very funda-mental issue does open up prospects for the involvement of governments in a new area of activity which can hopefully bring out positive and meaningful results, and I would say the same of the mandate given to pursue the question of structural adjustment. What is interesting about the resolution adopted at Manila is that it recognizes, by combining these two issues in a single decision, the very intimate link between protectionism and the problem of structural adjustment. So, here again, I think it would be true to say that at Manila at least potentially a process has been launched, a process that could lead the international community to positive results.

Thirdly, the Manila Conference also pronounced itself on certain issues in the field of money and finance. The Conference adopted by consensus a resolution on the transfer of real resources which reflects the current thinking of the international com-munity in respect of this very important issue. The resolution embraced the question of bilateral assistance, multilateral assistance, the role of private capital flows and also the question of what has been described as the massive transfer of resources. But at the same time, the Conference adopted a resolution, not by consensus but by vote, pertaining to aspects of the more fundamental question of the reform of the inter-national monetary system itself. This resolution identified a number of requirements for the future evolution of the monetary system and for the first time called upon UNCTAD to establish an intergovernmental group of experts to deal with fundamen-tal aspects of this problem, particularly those aspects which bring out the relationships between the evolution of the monetary system and issues in the field of trade and development. UNCTAD, as you know, has always contributed to the ongoing debate on the reform of the monetary system; it has not been the forum, and it is not envisaged that it would be the forum, where negotiations on the specifics of monetary reform take place. Nevertheless, the invitation by the Conference for governments to engage themselves in UNCTAD on this issue, I think, opens the way for UNCTAD to make a very useful contribution in the future to the whole debate on the reform of the global monetary system. I hope that this opportunity will be grasped by Member States and that we would be able to fulfil the expectations that are embodied in the resolution.

Well, these are three critical areas—commodities, world trade in manufactures and protectionism, and the area of money and finance—in which the Manila Conference initiated, or served as a launching pad for, negotiating processes of one kind or another. There are, at the same time, a number of other areas in which the Conference took decisions by consensus relating not perhaps to new negotiations but to some-what extensive and multifaceted programmes of action. In the field of technology, the Conference adopted two resolutions unanimously, which pertain to the reverse flow of technology and, perhaps even more important, to the very fundamental issue of the technological transformation of developing countries. We have always seen this subject of building up the technological capability of developing countries as constituting the reverse side of the coin to the transfer of technology. UNCTAD is already involved in the negotiation of an International Code of Conduct on the Transfer of Technology, and that it should now turn its attention to the technological transformation of developing countries is, I think, an important and appropriate result of the Conference. In regard to the Code itself, the Conference was unable to resolve the wider issue of the character of the Code, whether it should take the form of a legally binding instrument, or of guidelines, but it did endorse the convening of the negotiating Conference in its second round and referred these issues to that Conference. It is our hope and expectation that progress would be made at the resumed session on the negotiation of an International Code of Conduct on the Transfer of Technology.

Then, again, in the area of economic co-operation among developing countries, the Conference at Manila did produce an important decision by consensus setting out the parameters of an extremely extensive programme of activities in this field. I am happy to be able to say that the Conference was able to break the impasse or deadlock which had prevailed earlier regarding the ability of UNCTAD to call meetings of experts from developing countries—these meetings have now been authorized, as also has the need for UNCTAD to give support to many aspects of co-operation among developing countries which were called for by the developing countries at their Arusha meeting.

In the area of the least-developed countries, the Conference was again able to arrive at a far-reaching resolution giving new support to the least-developed countries, a resolution which in a sense could constitute a new attack on this problem, which I have described on many occasions as constituting the core of the world's poverty problem. The Conference resolution envisages the convening of a global meeting on the problems of the least-developed countries at a later date. Parallel to this were consensus decisions on the problems of land-locked countries and island developing countries, all forming part of the category of specially disadvantaged countries.

In the area of shipping, there were some decisions taken by consensus and others taken by vote, but it is important to note that at Manila it seemed possible at long last to bring the Convention on a Code of Conduct for Liner Conferences into legal effect, because at Manila, announcements were forthcoming of a number of countries taking decisions to ratify the Convention. I believe that we have now some fifty-six countries, representing about 75 per cent of world tonnage, that have signified their decision to ratify the Convention, and this makes it possible to bring the Code of Conduct into legal effect and for UNCTAD to undertake the follow-up work pertinent to the coming into effect of the Code itself.

I would like also to mention in this connection another important decision taken at Manila on the basis of consensus, and that is the decision on the role of UNCTAD, a decision which recognizes the contribution which UNCTAD could make to the ongoing negotiations in the field of international economic relations, which recognizes the need to give to UNCTAD a degree of flexibility and of adequacy in the availability of resources, and also the need to strengthen and rationalize the governmental and internal structure of UNCTAD itself in order to make it a more effective instrument of the General Assembly in the treatment of international economic issues.

There were areas in which UNCTAD V failed to arrive at decisions and referred resolutions to the Board. On the subject of trade between countries having different economic and social systems, a resolution was adopted affirming the decisions taken at UNCTAD IV, but referring to the Board the draft resolutions submitted to UNCTAD V. So it is one of the tasks before the Trade and Development Board to pick up this issue from where it was left at Manila in the hope that some decisions will prove possible in the future.

Similarly, a draft resolution relating to the question of the adoption of common features to deal with the problems of the reorganization of debts of interested countries was similarly referred to the Board although, in my opinion, there was quite a degree of consensus on the content of these features themselves. Though there was disagreement on the institutional mechanism to be set up to provide surveillance of the application of these features. I hope, and I must say I am somewhat optimistic on this score, that the Trade and Development Board or the relevant machinery of UNCTAD will be able to resolve this issue in the course of the period ahead.

There were a number of other draft resolutions also referred to the Board for action. The Board has also been requested to make an evaluation of the multilateral trade negotiations because the Conference was unable to do so—and the Board is to make such an evaluation on the basis of a report by the Secretary-General of UNCTAD together with other relevant documents.

But having said this, one of the prominent failures of UNCTAD V was its failure to reach agreement on what I referred to earlier as the over-all agenda item dealing with the wider issue of structural change itself. I was myself, and I have said this on other occasions, somewhat disappointed at this result because it is my feeling that had we succeeded in arriving at a consensus on this agenda item the image of the UNCTAD Conference would have proved to be vastly different. Because of the importance of this issue, because of its many dimensions, there was naturally a particular public interest in the discussion of this item, and the fact that the Conference was unable to produce a result did naturally contribute to the feeling of disappointment and dissatisfaction with the over-all result of UNCTAD V. This situation is an unfortunate one in a sense because in my view we came somewhat close to a consensus on the operational parts of a draft resolution relating to this agenda item. What proved difficult to secure at Manila was agreement on the preamble; in the concluding stages of the Conference time proved to be too short, given the complexity of the issue and the timing of the proposals, to make it possible for the Conference to arrive at a decision. However, this issue is not a dead one, it is, I hope, still very much alive, and has been referred to the Trade and Development Board for action. I hope that the Trade and Development Board at its next session will turn its attention to this important issue with a view to arriving at a constructive and positive conclusion.

These in brief are some of the highlights of the Conference. I have tried to list some of its successes and some of its shortcomings. Of course, it is not a comprehensive enumeration of the results, or a fully fledged assessment of the outcome. I do feel, however, that in looking at UNCTAD V one must give some importance to the very fact that the Conference did devote itself to the very wide range of issues that formed its agenda. The very fact that basic issues pertaining to structural change, pertaining to fundamental changes in prevailing relationships, formed the subject of international discussion by governments at an international conference—I think this itself will impart its influence on the climate of world thinking in the future. It will have its impact on the way in which the international dialogue evolves in the period ahead. From this point of view, I think it is important to see UNCTAD V not just as a specific isolated particular event, but rather as part of an ongoing process, part of a process where a contribution was made to the ongoing discussion and dialogue and debate on crucial issues. It is hoped that from this point of view the influence of UNCTAD V will continue to be felt in the period to come. The results of UNCTAD V undoubtedly reflected the mood of the moment. No one can say that as a result of UNCTAD V we have now a vastly changed climate in regard to relations between developed and developing countries. Such a change in climate might still be forthcoming as a result of the way in which the ongoing negotiations and discussions unfold. From that point of view, UNCTAD V may still be seen to have contributed to it; but as at this moment of time we cannot say that the event itself brought about this result. It is true that, had the perceptions of the various problems been stronger, the results themselves might have been more markedly different. But I do think it is important to set UNCTAD V in the perspective of the wider canvas against which it took place.

It has been said that one of the reasons for failure to reach agreement on the wider issue of structural change at the Manila Conference was the inability to arrive at a consensus on how to deal with the energy issue. This has been the subject of much comment in the aftermath of the Manila Conference. But you will appreciate that there had been no in-depth preparation with a view to taking up this issue at Manila as one of the particular items on the agenda. The energy question is certainly a complex one. There are many facets to the issue and it is not surprising that the Manila Conference, concerned as it was with a wide range of issues, was unable to deal with this issue in the way that has sometimes been expected. The energy issue has many dimensions. To the oil-producing countries, its facets include the need to safeguard the real value of their earnings, the need to safeguard the real value of their reserves, the need to safeguard the rate of depletion of their natural resources, the need to give an impetus to the process of development and transformation. To the industralized countries, the energy issue has also many facets—the need to bring about viable patterns of consumption, the need to ensure regularity of supplies, the need to ensure stability in financial markets. To the non-oil-importing developing countries, the energy issue implies and involves the need for cushioning the balance of payments problems that face them, the need for them to have access to financial resources to promote their development process, the need for support in their efforts themselves to explore and conserve energy. For all groups of countries, the energy issue is deeply concerned with progress on the technological front. Given the complexity of these subjects, it is not surprising that the energy issue could not have been dealt with in Manila under the over-all theme of structural change, or interdependence. I feel that there are possibilities for co-operative relationships in respect of this problem within the developing countries themselves and between the developing countries and the developed countries. But I believe that the basic theme of Manila, the basic themes of structural change, of interdependence, of the need for an evolution in the rules and principles governing international economic relations—these will remain of relevance in the period ahead. They cannot but continue to dominate the dialogue on international co-operation in the period to come. They must inevitably influence both the flavour and the content of the international development strategy for the future.

In conclusion, one last observation. In the current context, I often hear it said that the crisis, and the difficulties facing many parts of the world economy, serve as a constraint to adequate responses to problems concerning development, to problems of relevance to the North/South dialogue. The growth and prosperity of the developing countries needs to be seen as a potential instrument for promoting the economic recovery of the global economy itself. The development needs of the developing countries should not be seen as an additional constraint in a difficult economic situation. On the contrary, they should be seen as an opportunity—as an instrument—for bringing about a revitalization of the global economy itself. The strengthening of the economies of the developing countries cannot but contribute to the expansion of world trade and to the markets of all other Member States of the global economy. The strengthening of the developing countries, therefore, not only by the transfer of resources, but by the more fundamental changes needed in prevailing relationships, should therefore be seen as forming an integral and inherent constituent part of the interests of all groups of countries of the international community.

Trade and Development Board

8 October 1979

This session of the Board is convening for the first time since the fifth session of the Conference and inevitably its work will be influenced by the many processes that took place at Manila. The Board is also convening at a time when many vital and crucial issues are under active consideration, in the context of both the preparations for the International Development Strategy and the proposal for a new and comprehensive round of global negotiations put forward by the non-aligned States in Havana and subsequently the Group of 77 in New York. These are issues to which UNCTAD could contribute in many important ways.

For all these reasons I think it important that the Board at this session should look to the future and prepare itself for the tasks that lie ahead and I would like to focus here on the tasks facing UNCTAD in the aftermath of the Manila Conference.

These tasks fall into three broad categories. First, we need to finish what was started earlier, not at Manila but at Nairobi. We have been engaged in a number of negotiations launched at Nairobi. Many of these have still to be brought to a successful conclusion and the accomplishment of that task should be seen as one of the important responsibilities facing UNCTAD in the period ahead.

Secondly, whilst seeking to accomplish the post-Nairobi negotiating responsibilities, we should also address ourselves to the new mandates given to UNCTAD at the Manila Conference, pursuing these mandates and building upon them. That is the second task facing UNCTAD in the period ahead.

Thirdly, I feel that the Organization—and the Trade and Development Board in particular—has to turn to the unfinished business arising out of Manila, to the many issues not settled at Manila but referred to the Board for decision and action.

In discharging these three tasks UNCTAD's future work will prove of relevance to the contribution that UNCTAD will make to the events forthcoming next year, namely, the preparation and adoption of the strategy for the Development Decade, and the thrust towards a new round of global negotiations.

In respect of the post-Nairobi negotiations, there has as you know been criticism about the slow tempo of progress experienced in achieving adequate results. I am convinced that the speed of progress in these negotiations will be profoundly influenced by the determination and resolution of governments to make rapid progress and arrive at early conclusions. Yet, to the extent that the negotiating process that has been launched has proved to be complex, embracing a number of difficult and intricate issues, a period of gestation was inevitably necessary before these negotiations could bear their final fruit. It is my hope that, in the light of the activities that we have undertaken in the years since these negotiations were first launched, this period of gestation is now largely behind us and that we can reap the benefits of the work done and progress made so far and bring these negotiations to a successful conclusion before too long.

The second of the major tasks facing UNCTAD is the pursuit of the new mandates that have arisen out of the fifth session of the Conference. Manila was an event where we sought to extend the negotiating processes launched at Nairobi. The agenda for the fifth session was structured to make such a process possible. It touched on most of the key issues of relevance to trade and development, and indeed to international economic co-operation, and attempted to treat them in the context of the need for structural change, for basic changes in the mechanisms, structures and relationships that have hitherto governed international economic relations.

The results of Manila are of many kinds, some positive, some not so positive. The positive results of UNCTAD V are of two types, and UNCTAD needs to pursue the mandates given in respect of both of them. On the one side, the mandates arising out of the Manila Conference relate to action to be taken by governments that would involve negotiations or consultations within the intergovernmental mechanisms of UNCTAD. The other mandates given at Manila extend not so much to intergovernmental negotiations at this stage as to intensive action programmes that have to be implemented. Each of these tasks has arisen out of the Manila Conference and needs to be taken in hand with vigour and resolution.

The mandates which relate to intergovernmental action, sometimes even to negotiations, extend to three categories of issues. It is important that we distinguish these and prepare for the work that has been entrusted to us in each of these areas.

In the first place, the fifth session of the Conference adopted by consensus a wide-ranging resolution on the commodity problem. It not only endorsed and reinforced the thrust of the negotiating process launched under the Integrated Programme for Commodities, but also underlined dimensions of that Programme that had hitherto not received adequate attention. In particular, the Conference called upon UNCTAD to work towards a framework of international co-operation pertaining to the marketing and distribution of commodities, and also to their processing. Up to now, the emphasis of UNCTAD's work in the field of commodities has been very largely on the regulation of markets. The new mandate invites us to turn to the structural aspects of the commodity economy and to deal with very fundamental and dynamic issues. This decision would lend body to, and in a sense complete, the character of the Integrated Programme. The marketing and distribution of commodities involve many fundamental issues, including the role of the transnational corporations as actors in this process. The processing of commodities also involves fundamental issues touching on problems of access to markets and of protectionism. On both counts the questions arising in respect of this resolution are of very great importance. By launching on a process in this area UNCTAD would be breaking new ground and taking new initiatives. We in the secretariat would pursue the studies needed to make the intergovernmental process of negotiation and consultation as fruitful as possible.

I would also refer in this connection to the resolution in the commodity area whereby UNCTAD was requested to study compensatory financing in the context of the Integrated Programme for Commodities. This was a resolution that was adopted by vote, but a few days ago at the meeting of the Development Committee I attended in Belgrade a decision was taken by consensus which is of relevance to UNCTAD's work in this area. That Committee decided, in the light of steps already taken by the International Monetary Fund to improve the existing compensatory facility, to return at the end of one year to the problem of further extensions in the area of compensatory financing, in the light of the evolution of negotiations in UNCTAD on the Common Fund and of the study which UNCTAD is to undertake on compensatory financing. The International Monetary Fund has been asked to extend full technical co-operation in respect of this study. I was very pleased at this decision of the Development Committee. It gives a new emphasis to the importance of the UNCTAD study. Thus in the area of commodities Manila has indeed launched new processes, some of which involve negotiations.

There is a second issue concerning which the Manila Conference launched a potential negotiating process, namely, the subject of protectionism, which was one of the key issues at Manila. It was seen not just as a short-term problem likely to disappear with a return to an upswing in cyclical activity but rather as a more basic problem related to the way in which the international economy would evolve, particularly in the light of the industrialization of the developing countries. As UNCTAD V followed very closely on the multilateral trade negotiations, there was some reluctance to deal with specific proposals that had already been covered by those negotiations or were still in progress. Nevertheless, the Conference was able to pronounce itself on some of the more fundamental aspects of the problem of protectionism and structural adjustment and adopted, by consensus, a decision which asked UNCTAD to make a regular review of problems in the field, to formulate recommendations on the general problem of protectionism, and to formulate general recommendations on the problem of structural adjustment. This resolution can be a very challenging mandate to UNCTAD and to its intergovernmental bodies. After all, the general problem of protectionism is intimately linked up to the manner in which the world trading system will evolve in the future, given the numerous trends at work, particularly the industrialization of the developing countries, the continued development of the socialist countries, and the dynamics of change and adaptation in the market economy countries.

Is the post-war framework that had existed up to now adequate to deal with these evolving changes? If so, is there a need for a reaffirmation in the present context of this framework in the light of the changes that are taking place? If, on the other hand, the answer is no, what changes are needed and what changes could be introduced into the framework established at the end of the Second World War? These are very important, critical questions. It is particularly significant and valuable that the problems of protectionism and structural adjustment were brought together at UNCTAD V within the ambit of a single resolution, because these issues are intimately linked together in the search for any viable solutions. I believe that the Board will need to address itself to the question of how it would respond to this very important mandate given to it at Manila.

Then there is a third issue which involves intergovernmental activities which also arises out of the decisions at Manila, namely that of money and finance. Here there were two important decisions. One of these, adopted by consensus, related to the transfer of real resources. The second concerns the reform of the monetary system. Although the decision in question was subject to a vote, it was also subject to negotiations although these were not brought to a final conclusion. The relevant resolution calls for the establishment of an intergovernmental group to deal with certain fundamental aspects of the reform of the monetary system, particularly in the context of the evolving needs of trade and development. This resolution is an opportunity for governments to look at some of the more basic long-term issues relevant to the evolution of the international monetary system, rather than to the specific issues that are the subject of activities, negotiation and consideration in the forum of the International Monetary Fund at the present time. By looking at the longer-term issues UNCTAD would be able to make a constructive contribution of value to all forums in the context of the discussion and negotiations on various aspects of international monetary reform. UNCTAD has a long history of involvement in international monetary issues and is particularly equipped to deal with this problem in the setting of its relationship to money, trade and development. After all a sound trading system would hardly prove possible in the absence of a sound monetary system. If governments were to approach the work of the intergovernmental group within this constructive framework then this group could indeed make a very useful and vital contribution.

These three areas on which there were decisions at Manila—the areas of commodity structure, protectionism, and money and finance—are all areas where some of the most critical problems of our time have emerged. They are crucial to the future evolution of the world economy and central to the concept of a new international economic order. If UNCTAD is able to fulfil the mandates given to it at Manila in these areas it will be able to contribute enormously to the search for co-operative solutions and the further evolution of the framework which has governed international economic relations up to the present time.

The mandate of Manila extends to action programmes in other crucial areas. Manila saw the launching of an imaginative programme to deal with the problems of the least-developed countries. This has to be implemented in two phases and involves the convening of a world conference on the least-developed countries. UNCTAD has to give a maximum of attention to the implementation of this very important decision. We have been able in UNCTAD to play a useful, and I hope leading, role in dealing with the problems of the least-developed countries. We have to maintain the momentum in this area and to translate the many proposals and themes into concrete actions. Manila also saw the adoption of programmes of relevance to the land-locked and island developing countries and in this area, too, we have to address ourselves to the task of implementation.

Then, again, there was an important decision at Manila pertaining to the problem of technology, including a wide-ranging resolution on the subject of technological transformation. This, too, is a work programme which UNCTAD has to implement with the utmost effort and seriousness in the period ahead.

Decisions were also taken at Manila on the subject of shipping. We have to convene an expert group on the subject of flags of convenience and this we propose to do in the near future. There have been decisions on other dimensions of the shipping problem, on the problem of bulk cargoes, and here again we look forward to fulfilling the tasks that have been given to us.

One of the major decisions taken at UNCTAD V relates to economic co-operation among developing countries. What emerged from Manila was a very important action programme for UNCTAD to implement in the period ahead. It endorses the need for UNCTAD to convene a number of meetings of developing countries at the regional and interregional level to give real content to the many concepts pertinent to the theme of economic co-operation among developing countries. I have been impressed by the degree to which this theme of ECDC has received increasing emphasis in all the gatherings of developing countries convened in recent times. This is a subject that is gaining importance as time goes by. From now on the thrust would need to be directed towards the implementation of many of the proposals that have already been made. We in UNCTAD look forward to playing the very crucial and indeed pivotal role that has been assigned to us in the decisions taken at Manila in the field of ECDC.

Then, too, we need to turn to what I have described as the unfinished business of Manila—to the issues on which no decisions were taken but which were referred to the Board or the permanent machinery for follow-up action. These include resolutions on trade between countries with different economic and social systems, on debt, on a framework of financial co-operation, on many issues in the field of trade in manufactures, on the evaluation of the multilateral trade negotiations and so forth. In some cases—the question of common features in respect of debt is one—substantial progress has already been made and probably a consensus is not far away. But it has still to be reached and this is a challenge before the permanent machinery of UNCTAD. In other cases major efforts are still needed before the issues dealt with at Manila can be translated into concrete decisions. I have mentioned some of these issues. In particular we need to give particular emphasis to the issue of trade between countries with different economic and social systems. Although the decisions taken at Nairobi, which were far-reaching, were reinforced and endorsed at Manila, there is scope for much greater progress in this area. If this progress is to be realized there is need for understanding and a fresh imaginative approach on all sides. I hope that at this session of the Board we shall be able to register progress in this area.

Perhaps the most significant and most publicized issue left for the Board to deal with in the aftermath of Manila, is that covered by what was item 8 of the Manila Conference, and which is now item 3 on the agenda for the Board.[1] I believe that the failure of UNCTAD V to deal successfully with this item, dealing with the big issues of interdependence and structural change, was very largely responsible for the image of UNCTAD V as a conference which failed to live up to expectations. Despite this failure to reach final agreement, I felt that agreement was not far away at Manila and that a consensus was emerging on the operational part of that item, in which UNCTAD was asked to set up a mechanism of global consultations assisted by a high level group of experts to deal with issues relating to the interdependence of issues and to structural change. Unfortunately at Manila it was not possible to reach agreement on the preamble to this operational part. I hope that at this session of the Board it will be possible to complete action in respect of this issue. It would be significant if the Board were to take a positive decision regarding the operational side of that resolution—the setting up of a continuing mechanism to deal with the global issues—and to authorize UNCTAD to prepare for this as a regular event in the calendar of UNCTAD meetings unfolding year after year. It is important that this proposal for a system of global consultations within UNCTAD on an annual basis should not be seen as conflicting with, and should not be confused with, the proposal that has been made for a new round of global negotiations to deal with issues pertaining to development. As we see it, the global consultations envisaged in UNCTAD would involve the setting up of a regular procedure, not a negotiating activity intended to arrive at final conclusions settling matters that have been the subject of discussion within the international community. The consultations would rather be an opportunity to review developments unfolding on the international economic scene from the point of view of the various groups of countries that are members of UNCTAD and of the international community, the developing countries, the socialist countries, and the market economy countries. Such a review, preceded by a thorough documentation of trends and by advice from high-level technical experts, will fill a need in the present context. The issue of interdependence is on the agenda of each of the regular sessions of the Board, but the latter's time-table does not permit of this issue being dealt with in any great

---

[1] Evaluation of the world trade and economic situation and consideration of issues, policies and appropriate measures to facilitate structural changes in the international economy, taking into account the interrelationships of problems in the areas of trade, development, money and finance with a view to attaining the establishment of a new international economic order and bearing in mind the further evolution that may be needed in the rules and principles governing international economic relations and UNCTAD's necessary contribution to a New International Development Strategy for the Third United Nations Development Decade.

depth. The establishment of a process of global consultations will help rectify this deficiency. The results of these consultations would serve as a valuable input to discussions in all forums, including the global negotiations that have been proposed. I hope that governments will see the proposal for establishing a system of global consultations in this light. A positive decision in this regard will go far towards completing the action needed in respect of the unfinished business of UNCTAD V.

It remains for me now to refer to two forthcoming events with which UNCTAD and the Board would need to be very intimately involved. It is important that UNCTAD organizes itself to make a very important contribution to the preparatory work now being undertaken towards the formulation of an international strategy for development. You will recollect that in respect of the Strategy for the Second United Nations Development Decade, UNCTAD was able to make a very vital contribution. I have been given to understand in New York that this contribution was really crucial to the final success of the General Assembly in evolving a strategy for that Second Decade. All parts of the UN system have been invited to contribute to the work on the Strategy for the Third Development Decade. But at the conclusion of the recent meeting of the Preparatory Committee on the Strategy a decision was specifically taken requesting the Trade and Development Board to make UNCTAD's contribution available to the Committee before its next session. This very specific invitation to UNCTAD needs a response on our part. It provides us with an opportunity to contribute towards the formulation of the Strategy in a very important way. This is as it should be in that so many issues that form part of the Strategy are vitally linked up with matters with which UNCTAD is so directly concerned. I do not know what form the Strategy will take, but I believe that it will attempt to outline the goals which the international community will need to adopt and pursue over the Decade. I also believe that it will need to extract from these goals what I would call a negotiating content, which would involve the setting up of machinery for future negotiations. If under the Strategy such a framework for future negotiations was established and a schedule set up for the unfolding of these negotiations, these decisions would be of extreme relevance to UNCTAD itself. I also understand that the proposals that have been made for global negotiations would involve their launching after the adoption of the Strategy and would be seen as an approach towards implementing the elements of the Strategy. It is too early to anticipate the structure of these global negotiations, but it has been emphasized by the Group of 77 and the nonaligned countries that these negotiations would not only not delay any of the ongoing work that is in hand—any of the ongoing negotiations—but would, on the contrary, reinforce these negotiations and draw upon them. Thus in regard to these proposals for a new round of global negotiations UNCTAD must prepare itself to make the contribution expected from it from all sides. It is important that UNCTAD prove of maximum assistance in each of these processes—the Strategy and the proposed negotiations for the future. We have to make our contribution, not only as a secretariat, but as an intergovernmental body. Both arms of UNCTAD will need to be mobilized in order to achieve success in this realm.

The issues embrace many dimensions, as I have indicated. The global negotiations are to be linked up with a number of issues including the problem of energy. Yet, as I said in my address to the Economic and Social Council and to the meeting of the non-aligned countries, the energy issue itself has many facets, many dimensions. Some of these, such as those which relate to issues of relevance to the international monetary and financial system, are areas in which the involvement of UNCTAD even in pursuit of its existing responsibilities could prove to be of help. Accordingly, no matter from what standpoint they are approached, the processes that are being contemplated for 1980 are likely to prove to be of the utmost importance. It is crucially necessary that we made every effort to ensure the success of each of these processes. A great deal is at stake for the international community and we cannot afford to see these processes fail.

All this relating to the substantive tasks before UNCTAD brings me to the role of UNCTAD as an organization. The challenge facing us in the period to come makes it all the more important that we look to the efficacy of UNCTAD as an organization. We had an important resolution on this subject at Nairobi, but I believe that progress in the improvement of UNCTAD as an organization, in restructuring its institutions, in rationalizing its work, did not prove to be as rapid as we would have liked in the post-Nairobi period.

We have now had another major resolution on this subject at Manila, going beyond what has been adopted before. This resolution calls for the establishment of an *ad hoc* committee addressing itself particularly to this aspect of the institutional improvement and reform of UNCTAD. We in the secretariat, and I myself personally, attach a great deal of importance to the work of this *ad hoc* committee. We look forward to giving it all our support and assistance. If this process is based on a premise that is shared by all—that UNCTAD has to be adapted to contribute in the period ahead to the resolution of the critical issues facing the international community in all the areas that fall within its competence—then I believe that we could really move forward in a very important and a very decisive way.

I believe it important in my concluding remarks to underline the fact that this session of the Trade and Development Board is convening in the context of a particularly critical situation affecting several parts of the international economy. The developing countries are particularly affected by the current crisis. This was the recurring theme of all the speeches that I heard recently at the Belgrade Conference. There will be no easy solution to the problems facing the international economy. We cannot be so optimistic as to expect that there would be a spontaneous upturn in the cycle of economic activity. The problems that have been brought to the forefront in the context of the current crisis are proving to be of a more fundamental and deep-seated character and call, in turn, for more basic solutions. I think that there is a growing understanding of this fact on all sides. To the extent that there is indeed this understanding, I believe that the work of UNCTAD in the period ahead will become, not just more relevant, but in fact more crucial to the needs of the international community. The universal appreciation of this role for UNCTAD will help ensure that it will be successful in discharging the mandates and responsibilities entrusted to it at Manila. It is for these reasons that I have said that this session of the Trade and Development Board is a particularly important one, and on that score I want doubly to wish it all success.

PART IV

Sectoral Issues

SECTION 1

COMMODITIES

The Integrated Programme for Commodities, for which UNCTAD received a negotiating mandate in May 1976, is a five-point programme of which two points were
subsequently taken up as the subject of detailed preparatory and actual negotiating
meetings. These two elements were the proposals for a Common Financing Fund and
for agreements, based on stocking, for individual commodities. The two sub-sections
below deal respectively with an examination and description of the Integrated Programme proposal as a whole and the progress of the negotiations for a Common
Fund, and with the meetings, either preparatory or full negotiating conference meetings, on a number of the eighteen commodities originally put forward as suitable
subjects for international commodity agreements of the conventional kind. The Common Fund is not yet in its final operational form, for the articles of agreement need
still to be translated into a legal constitutional document; of the many individual
commodities on which meetings aimed towards securing an international agreement
have been held, rubber is the only one for which an agreement has as yet been
finalized, though others may be close to this stage. The material in this section covers
the case for comprehensive, interrelated reform of trading relations, details of the
proposed new mechanisms tabled by the secretariat from time to time and discussion
of the characteristics of various individual commodities and their particular importance in the trade of the developing countries, as well as giving an overview of the
nature and progress of negotiations in these fields since 1976.

Conference of Developing Countries on Raw Materials, Dakar

4 February 1975

I believe that historians will come to regard this as a very significant occasion. This is the first time that the developing countries—the countries of the Third World—are meeting to address themselves primarily to the problem of raw materials. It is fitting that they should do so because the production of raw materials, or primary products, or commodities, as they are sometimes called, remains basic to the economies of most developing countries. This is indeed a legacy of the colonial past reflecting the way in which the countries of the Third World were fitted, albeit in a peripheral fashion, into the old economic order. It is proper that the striving for a new economic order should begin with the problem of raw materials since it is here that there is a need to break away from old patterns and to establish new relationships which will greatly strengthen, and indeed transform, the economies of the developing countries. I would venture to say that since trade in primary products is still the major source of external resources for the Third World, their very success in industrialization, and in development in general, is contingent on a sound and satisfactory situation on this front. The need is for changes of a wide-ranging character—extending beyond the issue of prices alone and embracing major structural reforms in such fields as marketing and distribution, the processing of products and even patterns of ownership. Over the last decade there has been a tendency to deal with the problem of the external resource requirement of developing countries through aid, because this would have required a minimum of interference with existing mechanisms, but this approach has been barely successful and it is now necessary to turn towards solutions in the area of trade.

Action in the field of primary products is a basic need, but it has acquired a new relevance and a new urgency in the current economic situation. I am deeply concerned about the present indications. Already the prices of commodities other than petroleum have declined on average about 40 per cent below the peak levels they enjoyed in early 1974. The OECD in its assessment of the economic outlook for 1975 has indicated that its members could expect to gain as much as $7\frac{1}{2}$ billion from a prospective deterioration this year in the terms of trade of the developing countries other than oil producers. As you are well aware, the short-term answer to the problems of the

153

developing countries most seriously affected by adverse price relationships has been the provision of emergency aid and other forms of financial accommodation. But I would venture to say that the new aid mechanisms—the emergency fund, the oil facility, the proposed third window of the World Bank, helpful as they are, would themselves prove inadequate if the external resource base of the developing countries is seriously undermined by a collapse in commodity prices. Indeed, the very list of most seriously affected countries will need to be further expanded. In today's situation I would consider action to deal with the commodity question as part of an attempt to arrest the growth of recessionary forces—to prevent these forces from harming the developing countries and from further aggravating the global situation itself.

You will agree that despite the verbal endorsement of the objective of commodity stabilization throughout innumerable international conferences over the last two decades, actual results have been negligible—a mere half-dozen commodity agreements, not all of them working satisfactorily. The piecemeal approach to commodity problems pursued in the past proved too narrow, too commercialized in concept, and too far removed from the wider dimensions of the commodity question to provide the momentum needed for success. A new approach must remedy this difficulty and be more comprehensive and more multidimensional in scope. It should reflect the new situation of a greater capacity for action on the part of producers of primary products and new developments in financial resource availabilities within the Third World—as has been pointed out in the document submitted by your Intergovernmental Group.

In response to the need for a new approach and for effective action in the field of raw materials or commodities, and in pursuance of the resolution of the sixth special session of the General Assembly on the Establishment of a New International Economic Order, UNCTAD had proposed what is described as an integrated approach to commodities. At the fourteenth session of the Trade and Development Board, last August, I received a unanimous mandate to further elaborate upon the several facets of such an approach. The proposal that UNCTAD has made in recent weeks in documents circulated to its members is based on five elements which, taken together in appropriate combinations, would amount to a more comprehensive, and in our view, a more effective attack on the commodity problem than has been envisaged before. The elements are:

First, the establishment of international stocking arrangements covering a wide range of commodities. It is our belief that such stocking arrangements could make an effective contribution towards the stabilization and strengthening of commodity prices.

Second, a common financial fund for commodity stocks which would be open to investments from various sources and which would offer investment outlets for developing countries with financial surpluses.

Third, a system of multilateral commitments between buyers and sellers to purchase and supply within acceptable price ranges.

Fourth, as a residual measure, an expanded and effective system of compensatory financing for countries suffering from a shortfall in real earnings.

Fifth, a new thrust in the field of the processing of primary products which would result in a new dynamism in the commodity sector.

UNCTAD has also carried out much work on the problem of indexation and will produce further studies on that subject.

I do not wish on this occasion to elaborate further upon the modalities of the integrated approach. At this stage there is a need for flexibility and adaptation; but in spirit the new approach is a reaction to the failure of earlier prescriptions. The new approach does not preclude the treatment of commodities on an individual basis if their particular problems might be resolved in this way. But the basic thrust of the integrated approach is a recognition of the fact that the problem of raw materials or commodities is not just a problem of one or even a few products taken in isolation, but a general one covering a major sector of the global economy that is of intimate concern to the developing countries. This is indeed recognized by the very fact of this meeting and by the recent proposal to include commodities in general in the tripartite talks that are now envisaged. Besides the fact that the problems of many commodities could be dealt with in terms of common principles and even common instruments, there is a possibility that a comprehensive approach could strengthen negotiating positions. We need also to remember that many developing countries are also importers of commodities and cannot find satisfaction in such partial approaches which will strengthen the commodities they import but leave unattended the commodities they export. By looking at commodities together, as far as possible, we have a safeguard against this.

The integrated approach is, of course, part of the package of policy measures provided for in the Action Programme and as such it goes hand in hand with measures to expand the trade in manufactures and to deal with the transfer of technology.

The Integrated Programme on Commodities will be taken up next Monday in the Committee on Commodities of UNCTAD, which is the forum for dealing with this problem within the UN system. I believe that the meeting of the Committee on Commodities is a critical one that can influence the tone of many of the crucial international assemblies that are to take place this year. I consider it significant that this meeting of the developing countries on raw materials should convene before next week's session of the Commodities Committee. One of the characteristic features of the commodity situation has been that the sellers have been more numerous, more dispersed, and less well organized than the buyers. I have said on other occasions that one should not equate the efforts of producers of primary products so to organize themselves and to co-ordinate their policies as amounting to the establishment of cartels. There is already much concentration on the buying side of commodity markets and the joint efforts of producers could provide an offset or a countervailing power to this—a development which would result in a better rather than a monopoly price.

No one can fail to take cognizance of at least two major developments which are potentially of the greatest relevance to attempts to deal with the commodity problem. The first of these is the growing awareness of the developing countries of the inherent strength they can command through the development of their capacity for joint consultation, co-ordination and action. There is no better evidence of this than the convening of this very meeting here in Dakar. The second development is the changed financial resource pattern within the developing countries with the accrual of financial surpluses to many oil producers which are in need of secure and remunerative investment outlets. The Integrated Programme for Commodities has been conceived as a global programme involving the co-operation of producers and of consumers, of developing and of developed countries alike. Although some of the facets of the Programme are capable of being implemented by producers alone, no one would exclude global solutions if they lead to more co-operative and enduring solutions: but these solutions cannot but be enhanced if out of this meeting the countries present here, demonstrate clearly the will and the ability to assert themselves in a constructive way and demonstrate also that they would be supported in their endeavours by the influence and the resource potential of a part of their membership.

Committee on Commodities

8 December 1975

I do not wish on this occasion to dwell at any great length on the substance of the issues of relevance to the commodity question, but to make some brief observations on what seems to me some aspects of the issues that have crystallized or were in the process of becoming crystallized over the period of debate or discussion we have had in recent months. On the occasion of the July meeting of the Committee I already referred to the fact that there seems to be an emerging consensus on the need for some type of action to deal with the commodity problem. The several announcements that have been made in various forums and in various capitals bear witness to this emerging consensus. However, there is still a need to bridge the gap and to arrive at a consensus on the type of action that is needed in order to bring about an effective solution to the commodity problem. I am aware that on this question of the type of action needed, the governments of member countries have still to take up final positions, but already there seem to be at least two broad approaches, which are still some distance apart and which need in one way or another to be brought closer together. On the one hand, there would seem to be the approach which favours solutions to the commodity problem through the adoption of measures that would require perhaps a minimum of intervention in existing structures, in existing market mechanisms, seeking to correct whatever malfunctioning there is through financial and other devices which would themselves involve as little intervention as possible in the structures and mechanisms themselves. It is true that even this type of approach contemplates the initiation of new arrangements to govern trade in certain selected commodities, but it seems to me that it does not go so far as to recognize the need for a regime of regulation covering as large a number of commodities as possible. This approach is, indeed, still somewhat of a selective kind. At the other end of the spectrum, there is the approach which views solutions to the commodity problem as requiring some substantial intervention in commodity markets and some basic changes in structures, not necessarily to displace the markets themselves but in order to reinforce their working and to provide for ceilings and floors in prices. As to the operations of these markets, this type of approach would anticipate some kind of regulatory regime to govern world trade in commodities.

The UNCTAD proposal for an Integrated Programme for Commodities does indicate the regulation of commodity markets, covering as many commodities as possible, as being of particular interest to developing countries. From that point of view the Integrated Programme does put the accent on the comprehensive character of the approach that it has adopted. It regards the commodity problem not as the problem of an individual commodity here or there, which needs to be attacked in isolation, but as a problem which is common to a wide range of products and which is reflected in the working of an entire sector of the economies of the developing countries. It is for this reason that the Integrated Programme seeks to include in its ambit as many commodities as possible, because it is based on the conviction that solutions for individual commodities, if they are not similar to the solutions for other commodities, would not succeed in creating a totally equitable situation in which the producing countries are all, in one way or another, able to enjoy the benefits of an attack on the commodity problem.

There are some points which I feel I ought to make in regard to the Integrated Programme in the light of previous discussions and debate. The first point is that, whilst the Programme itself is made up of five basic elements, each of which we believe are of similar importance, there are two of these elements which in our view constitute the core of the Programme. These two elements are the proposal to establish a range of internationally owned stocks covering a large number of commodities, and the proposal to establish a Common Financial Fund. The first is based on our belief that the instrument of stocking could be an important device for dealing with the problems of a number of commodities, a device which has not by and large been exploited to its full potential in the past. This proposal does not of course exclude the initiation of other measures to deal with the commodity problem, both for those commodities for which stocking is not appropriate for various technical and other reasons, and even for commodities where stocking is appropriate, but where other measures could be introduced to reinforce and buttress the solutions to their problems. We believe that the arrangements for individual commodities would need in fact to be multidimensional; they cannot hinge exclusively on the proposal for stocks alone. At the same time, however, we believe that the stocking concept is of primordial importance for a large number of these commodities and should therefore be utilized to as large an extent as possible. The proposal for the Integrated Programme and for the establishment of stocks does not of course deny the need for a case-by-case approach, as has sometimes been stated in criticisms of the Integrated Programme. We feel that it is necessary to look at the problems of individual commodities on a case-by-case, product-by-product basis, when stocks are established, when price ranges have to be determined and decisions have to taken about the location and quantity of stocks, or about other dimensions of the commodity problem. But whilst we do envisage a case-by-case approach for commodities, we seek to place this approach within the broader framework of a total programme, under the umbrella of a system of principles and common instruments which are applicable to a range of commodities. We do not wish to see the approach to the commodity problem decimated in terms of a number of isolated actions which do not add up to a meaningful attack on the global problem of commodities and of raw materials.

The second of the basic elements of the Programme is the proposal for the establishment of a Common Financing Fund, which for a variety of reasons, we believe to be of vital importance. On the one hand, we are convinced that there would be considerable financial economies in the adoption of a device in which financial resources are pooled and made available for the purposes of financing individual stocking operations. We feel that these economies would be much greater than those that would be effected if attempts were made to secure finance for individual commodities on a case-by-case basis. However, we believe that the significance of the Common Financing Fund goes far beyond that of financial economies alone. Such a Fund could have a dynamic impact on the whole approach to the solution of the commodity problem. It would be the one institution that would be able to take an overview of the commodity problem, no matter how limited its immediate operations are—an institution that is sorely lacking today. I believe that it would make a great difference to the prospects for reaching agreements, for initiating measures on individual commodities, if it were known in advance that a pool of financial resources was available. The existence of such an institution would serve to bring together producers of commodities, consumers of commodities and other investors such as the oil-producing countries—should they decide to support the fund—in one single body in which international responsibility for dealing with the commodity problem could be highlighted. Without such an institution, I fear that we run the risk of falling back on past approaches and repeating the frustrating experience of the past, an experience of failure to reach agreements on a large number of commodities. So from that point of view, we feel that the proposal for the Common Financing Fund is perhaps the key integrating element of the Integrated Programme.

In our proposal we have, of course, also included as one of the prime elements of the package a suggestion for the establishment of a strengthened system of compensatory financing. On the occasion of the July meeting of the Committee, I expressed some of our views on this element of our package, on why we considered it to be of importance and on its place within the full set of measures that we have suggested. We believe that the proposal for compensatory financing is an important one, largely because the other measures that we have proposed, such as the measures for stocking, for multilateral commitments and so on, may not successfully reach out to all the commodities of concern to developing countries or to all the countries which are dependent in one way or another on the production of commodities. So we felt that there was a need to buttress the integrated programme through the provision of a facility for compensatory financing.

In another forum, the Committee on Invisibles and Financing Related to Trade, we drew attention to the need to bring about substantial reforms in the existing facility of the International Monetary Fund for the compensation of receipts of developing countries in the light of their total balance-of-payments experience. In the current crisis, when a large number of developing countries are experiencing deficits of unprecedented magnitude in their balance of payments, there is an urgent need for some kind of relief and for the initiation of mechanisms by which this relief might be provided. We saw in the compensatory financing facility the opportunity to provide such a mechanism, and we have suggested a reform of the facility which goes beyond the compensation of shortfalls in commodity earnings alone and extends to compensation for shortfalls in other sectors of the trade of developing countries, including trade in manufactures, and to compensation for balance-of-payments difficulties that arise out of an increase in their import prices. So we have in fact made proposals for a rather comprehensive reform of the IMF facility taking into account not only the problems arising in the commodity sector, but all the other facets of the balance-of-payments problems of developing countries.

Having said that, I should like also to assert that, in the context of the commodity issue as we have presented it to you in the Integrated Programme, we see compensatory financing as essentially a supporting device, as a residual device, which is in no way a substitute for the action needed for the direct regulation and strengthening of prices. So from the point of view of our approach to the commodity problem, we do not see compensatory financing as providing a total answer or even as occupying the centre of the stage.

The Integrated Programme has, of course, other elements to it, though I do not propose to elaborate upon them on this occasion. There is a proposal for the establishment of a system of multilateral commitments, where necessary, and for initiating a new thrust in the area of the processing of primary products. The General Assembly in its resolution at the seventh special session also highlighted two other issues which are of central concern to the commodity problem and on which it has given a specific mandate to UNCTAD to further advance its work. The first of these relates to the question of the marketing and distribution of commodities, which is part of the whole drive to bring about structural changes in the commodity economy of the developing countries. We in the secretariat of UNCTAD are addressing ourselves to this question; we have already initiated much work in this regard and we hope to present the results in due course to the member governments.

The other element in the package of measures pertaining to the commodity problem which was highlighted by the General Assembly relates to the issue of indexation. I should like to say that in our integrated programme we see the question of direct indexation as very much a part of the price-fixing exercise that we contemplate for individual commodities. We feel that any attempt to introduce direct indexation presupposes the establishment of mechanisms to bring about the effective regulation or control of prices. We believe that the objective of establishing commodity prices which are deemed to be fair and equitable cannot be sustained in a world of continued and incessant inflation, and that provision must therefore be made to change these prices themselves in the light of the changes in relative prices. If you have a situation in which inflation is proceeding apace, at a rate which reflects percentages expressed in double digits, then no price which is accepted as being fair and equitable today will remain fair and equitable in a period of 10 or 12 or 24 months hence. So I believe that, as long as this inflation is an element of the international economic situation, there will be a need for measures to bring about continuing adjustments to the prices of commodities if they are to remain fair and equitable and thereby fulfil the objectives that were envisaged when these prices were established.

These are some of the substantive issues relating to the Integrated Programme which may be of relevance to the deliberations of your Committee in the course of the next two weeks. In the paper that I have presented to you,[1] I have drawn attention to the negotiating requirements for the commodity package. As we see it, the process of arriving at a decision in the field of commodities would need to proceed in two phases. In the first of these phases, we envisage that some basic decisions would be taken on

---

[1] Document TD/B/C.1/193.

the fundamental aspects of the Integrated Programme itself, on the proposal to establish a range of stocks for a number of commodities and regarding the establishment of a Common Financing Fund. In the next phase, after these decisions have been taken, it would be necessary to launch, *pari passu*, a series of negotiations on two fronts: negotiations connected with the establishment of the Common Financing Fund itself, and with its modalities, and negotiations on a number of individual commodities which, hopefully, would have been identified during the first phase. These negotiations would seek to arrive at decisions on minimum and maximum prices and the amounts of stocks to be held and so on, in the light of the availability of finance as provided for by the Common Financing Fund.

It has sometimes been suggested that a decision on the Common Financing Fund cannot really be taken until the individual commodity negotiations have matured and until the need for stocking and the financial requirements for stocking have been firmly established. In our view, such a sequence is not necessary or called for. We believe that, in all the studies that we have made, we have established the need and the rationale for stocks for a large number of commodities, which we have identified in fairly concrete terms. We have also tried to indicate in broad terms what would be the financial requirements for these stocks, and whilst in the course of individual negotiations it may be necessary to adapt and modify these estimates in the light of specific problems that might emerge, I think that the evidence is sufficiently clear, on an overall view, to justify a decision to establish stocks and to establish the mechanisms to finance these stocks. You will recollect that the International Monetary Fund itself has already adopted an overall facility for the financing of buffer stocks, a decision which did not have to await protracted negotiations on the justification of stocks for individual commodities. It was based on a conviction that there was a need for stocks, in general, for the treatment of commodity problems, and we believe that in the light of those considerations, it would be feasible to take a decision on the establishment of stocks and to enter into negotiations for the establishment of a Common Financing Fund for these stocks at the same time that negotiations proceed apace in relation to individual commodities.

Preparatory Meeting for the
Negotiation of a Common Fund

29 November 1976

I do not need on this occasion to underline the crucial importance of the work that you are now initiating. It is well recognized that the Common Financing Fund for Commodities is in many senses the centrepiece of the Integrated Programme. It is true that the negotiations on individual products that we have commenced have themselves many new features compared to past experience. They are taking place within a framework of common principles and objectives; they are organized as part of a single exercise; they are to be conducted within a well-defined time frame; they are also to be subject to surveillance or monitoring by the *ad hoc* Committee that has just been established. We envisage also that the content of the commodity arrangements that may be set up as a result of this ongoing process may also have innovative elements as compared to the past, in the sense that they may be somewhat more multidimensional in character than has been the case before. But despite these innovations in regard to the approach to individual commodities, it is, I think, true to say that the major innovation of the Integrated Programme was the proposal to establish a Common Financing Fund. It was a major innovation because it is basic to the concept of the Common Financing Fund, as determined and outlined initially by the secretariat, that this fund would itself play a major role in helping to bring about arrangements that would stabilize and improve the markets for individual products.

The essential rationale that underlies the proposal for a Common Financing Fund is basically simple. It is well recognized that commodity markets are subject to violent fluctuations which impose grave difficulties and cause serious disruptions in the producer countries, many of which are developing countries.

I could hardly think of any planner in a developing country whose plans have not gone awry because of the frequent, and sometimes unexpected aberrations that occur in commodity markets. The essential rationale behind the proposal for a Common Fund is simply that these violent fluctuations and disturbances could indeed be moderated or modified, if not eliminated altogether, if there could be some concerted international action specifically devoted to that end. The action itself is not inherently of a complex kind. It is essentially that measures be taken to support markets in periods when prices are in the process of falling or collapsing—measures taken through international action—and also, as a corollary that measures be taken to moderate a runaway upward spiral of prices in periods during which sudden short-term curtailments occur in regard to supplies. The objective of the Integrated Programme, and of the Common Fund which is an instrument of the Programme, is basically to provide a floor to the downward movement of commodity prices, as well as a ceiling, so that in the end result you will have a regime of commodity markets which operate and function with greater smoothness, greater regularity and greater stability.

The idea which lies behind the concept of international action to support markets, the idea behind the concept of buffer stocks for this purpose is not, of course, a new idea. It has for long been advocated by experts and analysts and writers on commodity problems, experts and analysts who are by no means confined to developing countries alone, and who have seen in the concept of buffer stocks a mechanism that could work in the interest of the international community as a whole, embracing both producers and consumers. But despite the long history of advocacy of buffer stocks, the concept itself has failed to be implemented on any significant scale. I do not wish on this occasion to dwell at length on the complex reasons for this failure, but I believe myself that the unsuitability of products for stocking in a technical or physical sense is not, and has never been, a major factor behind the failure to establish and implement proposals and ideas for buffer stocks. It is true that there are some commodities, and these are by and large exceptional, which are totally unsuited for stocking. But most commodities are, in one way or another, capable of being stocked, particularly if one admits the principle of the rotation of stocks. It is a fact that despite the failure to set up buffer stocks as a mechanism to stabilize markets through international action, governments of consumer countries—in particular affluent and powerful countries—have themselves succeeded in establishing stocks for a wide range of commodities for reasons of national security or for strategic objectives. It is also a fact that, despite the failure to set up stocks as a stabilizing mechanism for international action, the private trade has succeeded and continues to hold substantial stocks of a wide range of commodities. So I do not believe that the physical or technical factor is the essential reason for the lack of success in the past with respect to the implementation of schemes for buffer stocks and commodity stabilization.

I think the reasons lie elsewhere. In part, they are bound up with the absence in the past of an adequate will—a political will, if you like—to initiate commodity arrangements, a failure to see the importance of the commodity issue as a major problem in the economic arena. A large part of the reason for the failure of past efforts to establish stocks under the aegis of commodity agreements was probably the difficulty of overcoming the very vital, central and crucial factor of the financing of these commodity stocks. I do not think that I would be wrong in saying that until the proposals for an Integrated Programme for Commodities were presented, even the principle of a common sharing of responsibility between producers and consumers for the financing of commodity stocks was not a universally accepted one. Up to now none of the commodity agreements in existence recognize the concept of producer-consumer sharing of financing burdens on an obligatory basis. In the international agreement on tin, there is provision for voluntary financing by consumers, but the principle of compulsory contributions has still to be written into any international agreement. In a sense there has been an interaction between the failure to establish buffer stocks and the failure to reach commodity agreements. If stocking is ruled out as a mechanism, whether for financial or for other reasons, then the whole burden of adjustment of commodity markets falls on such other instruments as export regulation and production control, with all the difficulties and the disruption these imply for countries, particularly in the short run. So I think that there is a link between the lack of success in establishing arrangements for stocking and the relatively small number of international commodity agreements that have been concluded over the last two or three decades.

The proposal for a Common Financing Fund for commodities is basically an attempt to face up to, and to overcome, one of the major difficulties that has stood in the way of stocking arrangements, and indeed commodity arrangements, in the past. It is basically a proposal to make financial resources available for stocking in so far as problems on that score had up to now inhibited the successful conclusion of commodity arrangements. We had proposed that finance be made available for the purpose of stocking through the medium of a single institution, called a Common Financing Fund, for several reasons. On the one hand, we are convinced that in many important ways it would be more economical in the utilization of finance if resources could be mobilized and provided through a single institution rather than through a variety of individual commodity bodies. The needs of different commodities for stocking are not likely all to occur simultaneously, and a Common Fund, which constitutes as it does a pool of financial resources, would be able to take account of this factor and manage with a quantum of financing which would be less than if the needs for each individual commodity were to be mobilized for contingencies on an individual basis.

We feel also that the proposal for a Common Financing Fund will help to relieve the burden on governments, both of consumer and of producer countries, in making subscriptions available to the financing of buffer stocks. This is because in establishing a Common Financing Fund we would be establishing an institution which is capable of having access to markets for the borrowing of financial resources. The total financing needs for the stocking of commodities would not therefore need to be provided by way of governmental subscriptions, with all the difficulties this would impose upon member governments. A large part of these needs could be harnessed and could be mobilized by having recourse to financial markets, by providing an outlet for investment funds which is capable of offering to the investor both a security for his investment and an adequate rate of return. We have elsewhere estimated as a broad approximation that the total financial cost of stocking the commodities mentioned in the list adopted at Nairobi was of the order of about $6 billion. In the past, where it was implicitly assumed that the burden of financing commodity stocks should rest with producers, this figure would imply that producer countries would have to find, out of their own resources, $6 billion. Even if the principle of sharing resources between producers and consumers is now recognized, and this $6 billion were to be distributed, say, on an equal basis, half of the total cost would need to be found by the producers. But under the proposal for the Common Financing Fund we have envisaged that something like one-third of the total financing need be made available through subscriptions, and again roughly half, let us say, be made available by producers. This means that the claims on Member Governments by way of subscriptions, in so far as producer countries are concerned, or the developing countries are concerned, would really be one-sixth of the total instead of 100 per cent—or even 50 per cent in the case of an equal sharing of costs by producer and consumer governments. Of course, it is possible to envisage arrangements to mobilize funds on a commodity by commodity basis, arrangements which would also be predicated on some concept of borrowing. But we feel that a single institution with a representative membership, a viable method of operation and the prospect of self-financing activities, would be better able to mobilize resources in the markets through borrowing than a variety of individual commodity bodies. That is why we feel that on the financial side a Common Fund for the financing of commodity stocks has a great deal of merit and much to underscore its utility.

But we have on several occasions made it clear that we do not see the Common Financing Fund as being exclusively a financing device in the narrower sense of that term. We see the Common Financing Fund as providing a stimulus, serving as an impetus, to the successful establishment of individual commodity arrangements. We see the Common Fund playing this role because by its very existence it would ensure that individual arrangements for commodities and the quest for solutions to the problems of individual commodities will not be thwarted, will not be frustrated, by the lack of finance. By ensuring the availability of finance we feel that the prospect for concluding arrangements on the other complex aspects of individual commodity problems, would be enhanced. That is why we have called the Common Financing Fund a "catalyst". That is why we have described it as the integrating element of the Integrated Programme. And that is why, also, we feel that the establishment of the Common Financing Fund should, in terms of time, be parallel to, if not actually precede, the negotiations on individual commodities rather than take place at the conclusion of a series of individual commodity negotiations. We attach importance to this because we want to avoid the vicious circle of possible failure: no Common Fund because there are no commodity agreements and no commodity agreements because there is no Common Fund. By the early establishment of the Common Financing Fund we feel that the prospects for the successful conclusion of individual commodity agreements would be immensely enhanced. But at the same time, whilst we do attach importance to the early establishment of the Fund, we do not wish to imply that the monies mobilized for this Common Fund would, in one way or another, remain idle and unused pending the successful negotiation of commodity arrangements. We have provided, in our own suggestions for the mobilization of financial resources, that whilst prior commitments would be made of financial resources for the Fund, the actual call on these commitments could be harmonized with the need for disbursement, as this need emerges in the sequence of successfully negotiated and established commodity arrangements. So we are not asking governments to pay in funds which would remain unused and immobilized pending commodity negotiations that have yet to mature. We feel that the actual call on resources could be synchronized with the actual need to disburse these resources as and when commodity arrangements are finalized.

The concept of the Common Financing Fund has, of course, been under active discussion for a long period. What this preparatory meeting is called upon to examine is not a new proposal; it is one that has been on the table, so to speak, for over two years now. But despite the discussion and debate and analysis and examination of the

Common Financing Fund that has taken place over these last two years, I still think that there remain a number of misunderstandings, a number of misconceptions, which in a sense stand in the way of a sharp focus of attention on the real issues pertaining to the establishment of a Common Fund. It may be of some use to refer to, and hopefully to dispel, some of these misconceptions, so that they need not take up the time of this preparatory meeting. One of the most general misconceptions, which in my view extends not only to the Common Financing Fund but also to the Integrated Programme as a whole, relates to its potential benefits to different groups of countries, to what I call the distributional impact of the Programme and of the Fund which is its instrument. I have heard it said that the Integrated Programme and the Common Financing Fund would not essentially benefit developing countries because developed countries are the major exporters of commodities. It is true that if commodities such as grains and a whole array of minerals are included in the reckoning, the greater share of world commodity exports is enjoyed by the developed countries. But the Conference has deliberately sought to be selective in the choice of products to be brought under the aegis of the Integrated Programme. It has deliberately singled out those products which are of major interest to the developing countries. For example, if one were to take the ten core commodities which we originally presented as being particularly suited for stocking, we feel that the statistics of incidence are quite revealing. Thirty four per cent of the world's exports of this group of products is supplied by some sixty developing countries with a per capita income of less than $300 per annum. Another 28 per cent of this group of products is exported by a group of developing countries with per capita incomes of $300 to $500, and still another 22 per cent is supplied by developing countries with a per capita income of between $500 and $900. So 84 per cent of world exports of this group of products is supplied by developing countries with a per capita income of $900 or below. On the other side of the coin, 51 per cent of the imports of these products are bought by developed countries, countries with a per capita income in excess of $2500 per annum and a further 28 per cent by countries with a per capita income of between $1500 and $2500. So there can be little doubt as to who are the sellers and who are the buyers of the group of commodities that are included in the Integrated Programme. Now it is true that the list extends beyond those ten commodities to which I have referred and embraces products where, in some cases, there is a significant degree of production and of export by the developed producer countries. But it should not be forgotten in this context that one of the purposes of the Common Financing Fund is to support the holding not only of internationally owned stocks, but also of nationally owned stocks within the aegis of commodity agreements, support which could be extended to the developing countries producers of these commodities, countries which by themselves would not have the financial strength to establish and sustain national stocks of their own.

Another common misconception about the Common Financing Fund and the Integrated Programme is that in some broad way it is seeking to establish a regime of bureaucratically administered prices which would, in one fell swoop, dispense with the existence and operation of markets. This, of course, is a gross misunderstanding of the underlying concept of the Programme and of the Common Fund, because the basic objective of the Programme is not to dispense with markets but to improve their functioning by providing them with greater stability, by establishing limits to the excessive declines in prices that take place under the unregulated market system and to the excessive price increases that also occur under that same system. A smoother, more stable, functioning of markets would in my view enable them to satisfy more efficiently, more effectively and more constructively the needs of both producers and consumers.

Then, again, it is sometimes said that the objective of the Integrated Programme is in one way or another to raise prices indiscriminately and thereby bring about income transfers from consuming to producing countries. But we have made it patently clear that the question of prices in regard to individual products would not be determined *a priori* in terms of the Integrated Programme in general. They would, on the contrary, be determined in the process of negotiation between producers and consumers in the context of negotiations for individual commodity negotiations, representing as they do both producers and consumers, to give effect to these broad objectives, to translate them into specific and agreed prices.

Fears have been expressed that the Integrated Programme, and the process of stocking in particular, would in one way or another lead to burdensome surpluses of commodities, to over-production of products and, eventually, to a potentially disrupting situation in commodity markets. But these fears again are based on assumptions that are not in my view valid. They are based on the assumption that the prices themselves would have in one way or another been wrongly established. They are based on the assumption that the establishment of stocks is the only mechanism for dealing with commodity problems and that recourse would not be had to other, supplementary, mechanisms which aim at regulating supplies and bringing them into better balance with demand. We have consistently recognized that the establishment of buffer stocks would not do away with the need for supplementary measures. On the contrary, such supplementary measures may, in certain circumstances, be needed in order to make the stocking operations effective. But we feel that the stocking operation would facilitate the adoption of these measures by providing a breathing space, by creating a market situation of relative regularity against which these other, more basic and long-term measures, could be designed and implemented. Although voices are raised about the fear of over-production, it is also the case that in other contexts fears are expressed about the possible shortage of raw materials and proposals made to facilitate the flow of investment to ensure that these supplies would be forthcoming on a continuing basis.

It is, perhaps, worthwhile to ponder over the question of what really is the problem in the field of commodities that we need to worry about. Are we fighting against the problem of over-production or are we concerned with the problem of prospective shortages? I would like to draw your attention to the fact that, despite the existence of commodity agreements, in the case of cocoa, in the case of tin and in the case of coffee, the immediate picture is not one of burdensome surpluses. It is, on the contrary, one of an inadequacy of supplies even to render some of the operative aspects of the pricing arrangements insufficiently effective.

It has also been suggested that in one way or another the concept of the Common Financing Fund is intended to create a multipurpose supranational authority which would dabble indiscriminately and directly in commodity markets. This, again, is patently not the case, and in the concept of the Common Financing Fund as we have expressed it, we see the fund operating through individual commodity councils, which in turn have been established through the conclusion of successful commodity agreements. It is these individual commodity bodies that will intervene in markets, utilizing resources, should they so wish, obtained from the Common Financing Fund. It is true that we have suggested that, as an exceptional but temporary measure, some provision be made to deal with an emergency situation. Pending the establishment of commodity arrangements, should the world witness some catastrophic decline in commodity prices which calls for urgent and immediate action, then for that contingency alone we have suggested that some provision be made for the Fund to intervene in commodity markets on a temporary and strictly limited basis, and on terms which would have the approval of its membership. But our basic concept is that the Fund would not be a body dealing with commodities directly, but one which would act through established commodity councils that have been created through individual agreements. However, the individual commodity bodies would not be under any compulsion to seek finance from the Common Fund. If individual commodity bodies are able to mobilize resources in any other way, they would of course be free to do so. But we feel that it would be in the interests of individual commodity bodies, in the interests of individual commodity arrangements, that they make provision for recourse to the Common Financing Fund, should they feel the need for such finance. This is the essence of our proposal and the way in which we see the relationship between the Common Financing Fund and the individual commodity bodies.

If a Common Financing Fund is to be established, as indeed I hope it will, such a fund would need to possess a constitution, embodied in specific, precise articles of agreement. In the paper which the secretariat has presented to you, we have attempted to set out what, in our view, are the main issues which the constitution or articles of agreement of a fund should reflect, and to convey our own thinking of what might be the character of some of these articles of agreement. We have not, of course, attempted to present to you anything like the darft of a constitution for the Fund. At this preliminary stage we have tried to identify the headings, the issues, on which decisions would be needed. In some cases we have ourselves pointed to possible alternative decisions in regard to specific issues. But more generally we have tried to present to you our view of what might be provisions which would contribute to an efficient and effective institution. We have pointed out, first, the important need to determine what would be the functions, what would be the objectives, of the Common Financing Fund. We have indicated that, although the financing of buffer stocks would be the primary, or major function of the Common Fund, it could be envisaged that the Fund would undertake such other activities as member governments might wish to entrust to it. But we have stressed, at the same time, the importance of ensuring the self-financing nature of the stocking operations of the Fund by providing, on a differentiated basis, for the treatment of its financing accounts for stocking, on the one hand, and for other activities, on the other.

Another decision which would need to be reflected in the constitution of the Fund would be its financial capacity, an estimate of what would be its financing needs. Here again, we have provided to you our best estimate possible, which we feel would be in the neighbourhood of $6 billion, but which could be divided into an initial amount of $3 billion in the first phase. We have to address ourselves to the question of what should be the ratio of capital to borrowing in respect of the fund. I said earlier that the capacity to borrow would be one of the significant features of this new institution, and in the paper that we have presented to you we have suggested a ratio of capital to borrowing, of subscription to borrowing, of 1:2, and we have also suggested mechanisms and instruments which would make the fund an attractive investment outlet to potential lenders, including Member Governments.

A fund, when established, would also need to incorporate provisions on decision making and management structure. On this issue we have, as on previous occasions, pointed to the importance, in our view, of the Fund having a decision-making and management pattern different from the traditional pattern that has hitherto been reflected in international financial institutions. We have earlier given a number of variants, a number of alternative possibilities. There might be others, but this again is an issue on which governments would need to focus before they could pronounce on the constitution of a fund. We have also to take some view, and ultimately decisions, on the method of operation of the Fund. As I said a moment ago, in our view this Fund would operate through individual commodity councils. We have to take a view and adopt decisions on the relationship between the Fund and those commodity bodies that already exist or will come into existence. We have suggested that, in its lending activities, the Fund would need to operate in terms of a certain set of ground rules which would set out the terms on which it would lend to commodity bodies. But this is not to suggest that the Fund would itself pronounce on the substance of individual commodity arrangements. It would only set out the terms and conditions with which those who wish to borrow from the Fund would need to comply. Under each of these headings, and under other headings as well, we have made certain suggestions, but these are variations, alternatives, that are possible, and what we would wish most of all is that we have a reaction on the part of governments indicating what they feel is the best and most acceptable solution or provision under each of the respective heads.

Distinguished delegates, you are aware that these preparatory meetings which we are now holding have to lead up to a negotiating conference, which must take place not later than March next year. I believe that the time-table that was adopted at Nairobi is of particular importance. It is, in a sense, a significant aspect of the total agreement, the total compromise, if you wish, arrived at in Nairobi. This time-table and the procedures envisaged imply that at this meeting, and at the subsequent preparatory meetings to be held, there is a need to proceed in an expeditious, purposeful and business-like fashion. As I said earlier, we have already had a long period of general debate and discussion on the concept of the Common Fund, and it is not the purpose of these meetings to repeat that discussion. We need from now on a debate and a discussion that is focused on the specifics of what might be an acceptable Common Financing Fund. It is true that, at Nairobi, some important consuming countries expressed some hesitations and uncertainties that they had regarding a Common Financing Fund. But the agreement to embark upon a negotiation for a

Common Financing Fund signifies, I think, the good faith of these countries to take part in this process with the will to search for acceptable solutions. As I have said also on other occasions, it is hardly conceivable that governments would have agreed to take part in a negotiation for a specific objective such as a Common Financing Fund if that very objective was in itself objectionable or anathema to them. So I feel that the negotiating procedure that has been set up does provide governments with an opportunity to clarify the problems they have in mind, to overcome whatever hesitations, to dispel whatever uncertainties, they might have in the course of the elaboration and elucidation of the specifics of the Fund itself. In other words, I do believe that when one comes to negotiate a Common Financing Fund one has to do so on the basis of what would be the chief features of an acceptable institution. One cannot, obviously, envisage the negotiation of something other than a Common Financing Fund; one cannot negotiate a non-fund. For this reason, if one has the task of negotiation in mind, it is important to focus, as early as possible, on the principal issues under the several heads that we have indicated, or possibly others, issues that in one way or another help determine the character and constitution of the new institution that is being negotiated. I feel, therefore, that the preparatory meetings should endeavour to lay a solid basis for the negotiation that is to come, to try and resolve, to clarify, as many issues as possible, and to leave a minimum of unresolved issues for the final negotiation itself. I hope that the delegations present here will approach their task in that light and that at each successive step we would have facilitated the task of the negotiating conference.

I have spoken in somewhat broad terms and referred to what in my view are some of the salient issues pertaining to the question of the Common Financing Fund. But we need at all times to bear in mind that this process that has been launched in respect of the Common Financing Fund, as well as of the Integrated Programme for Commodities, is a process which has been awaited and watched with a great deal of expectation in the world outside. There is a growing awareness of the fact that the issue of commodities, of primary products, or of raw materials, is a central issue in the context of the wider problem of development, a central issue of concern to relationships between the developed and the developing countries. The negotiating framework that has been authorized by the Nairobi Conference provides, in my view, a unique opportunity for the international community to contribute towards the resolution of the vexed problem of commodities and the developing countries' involvement in trade in commodities.

By launching a successful attack on the commodity problem, the international community would do a great deal to improve the position of developing countries, not just in financial terms but in the wider context of their economic and political stability. If this opportunity is not grasped, if this opportunity is lost, then I cannot but see that the consequences would be most profound indeed. I have said on a previous occasion that the whole concept of an Integrated Programme for Commodities, the concept of the Common Financing Fund, is based on, is predicated upon, the concept of co-operation between producers and consumers. It is this concept which is now being put to the test in the series of negotiations that are under way. If the negotiations succeed and result in constructive conclusions, then the concept will be strengthened and reinforced for the future, it will gain a new vitality. But if these negotiations fail, if they lead to frustration, then inevitably the concept itself will come into question and all groups of countries would have to ask themselves whether they do not have to seek other ways and other avenues of meeting their problems—however difficult and however uncertain these other avenues might turn out to be. I am myself confident that, despite all the problems that lie before us, despite all the complexities, despite all the difficulties, the international community and the governments represented here will see the opportunity that lies before them and grasp it in a constructive way. For that reason I remain hopeful that the enterprise that has now been launched will lead to successful conclusions and that by the time of the conclusion of the negotiating phase of the Integrated Programme for Commodities we shall have succeeded in bringing about a better situation in regard to the whole area of commodity problems, particularly as they affect the developing countries.

With that last thought before you, I should like once again to convey to you my satisfaction at the commencement of your work and my very best wishes for the future of your work and for the successful accomplishment of the very important task that lies before you.

United Nations Negotiating Conference on a Common Fund under the Integrated Programme for Commodities

7 March 1977

The Common Fund is a central element in the Integrated Programme and, as such, is a key element in the quest for structural change in the realm of commodities. I have on several occasions in the past expounded upon the rationale of the Common Fund and on its relevance to the Integrated Programme as a whole. I do not wish on this occasion to repeat these arguments and to cover ground that has been gone over before, but I should like to say once more that we see the Common Fund as a crucial element for helping to bring about arrangements to stabilize and strengthen commodity markets through market intervention and through such other measures as may be agreed upon. We see it as an instrument that can make the difference between success and failure.

The concept of a Common Fund is predicated on the belief that the periodic and catastrophic declines in commodity prices that are so disruptive of the global economy, and for the producer countries in particular, should be averted in the future through international agreements to intervene in commodity markets when prices collapse. At the same time, the corollary to this is international action through market intervention in periods of excessively high prices as well. In principle, such international action—in the framework of commodity arrangements—could be conceived of for a wide range of commodities, rather than for just a few taken in isolation. Such action would involve the acquisition of supplies in periods of surplus and the disposal of these supplies in periods of shortage. It involves, in other words, the acquisition of stocks as an inherent part of the process of the stabilization and improvement of markets.

I am making this point because questions have often been asked about the importance and feasibility of stocking as an instrument of international commodity policy. In particular, measures such as export quotas and production restraints have sometimes been proposed as alternatives to stocks. But it is important to appreciate that, in periods of surplus, virtually all corrective measures involve, in one way or another, the withholding of supplies. If this is done through export quotas, the burden of stock accumulation has to be borne by producers nationally, with all that this implies for them. If the curtailment of production is the main instrument, this is disruptive of employment and is also ineffective for correcting short-term imbalances because of time lags—at least in so far as agricultural commodities are concerned. So the problem is not always one of a simple juxtaposition of the holding of stocks and other alternatives. It is rather a question of the overall effectiveness, and of the incidence of the burden, of a policy of stabilization.

It is, of course, true that the intensity and duration of a decline in prices might be such that these sources available for international intervention in markets might not by themselves suffice to meet the objectives of market regulation. In such a situation, stocking would need to be supplemented by other supportive measures. But even in this case a policy of market intervention through stocking would afford a much-needed breathing space for the introduction of these supplementary measures. In this connection there is another point to be made which, I believe, is of particular relevance to the consuming countries. The conventional instruments of export quotas and production restraints, even if effective in supporting floor prices, do not provide a means for the defence of price ceilings in periods of physical shortage. It is essentially a policy of stocking—involving international stocks or internationally co-ordinated national stocks—that could meet this latter objective as well.

Even if there is a wider acceptance of the need for stocking as an instrument of international commodity policy, there is still the question of the financing of these stocks. It is, of course, possible that individual commodity stocks could be financed separately and this has led to the suggestion that the need for a Common Fund should be examined at the end of the process of commodity negotiations—only after other possibilities have been fully explored and examined. The merits of a Common Fund as against individual commodity funds have already been argued on several occasions. It is our belief that a Common Fund can be significantly more economical of financial resources than the sum of individual commodity funds, because of the varying incidence of individual commodity cycles. It has also been pointed out—and this is of particular importance to the poorer developing countries—that a Common Fund would impose a far lighter burden on contributing governments than individual funds because of the better prospects that a Common Fund would have of mobilizing a large part of its resources through borrowings rather than through subscriptions. In particular, governments which are potential lenders, but which have no major interest either as producers or as consumers of a particular commodity, are more likely to invest in an international institution dealing with a range of products than in individual commodity funds.

But, besides all this, there is a major practical problem in the context of individual commodity negotiations, caused by uncertainty about the availability of finance. These individual negotiations cannot, in practice, leave open the question of financing. They must either proceed on the assumption that funds for stocking will be available from some central source and take this into consideration in the arrangements that are agreed upon, or assume otherwise and seek other arrangements for the mobilization of finance. This is why it is vitally important that the issue of the Common Fund be settled in good time and in advance of the conclusion of individual agreements. As I have said before, individual commodity arrangements would not be pre-empted from introducing their own financial provisions. There could be no compulsion to borrow from a Common Fund, but it would make a world of difference to the negotiators of individual arrangements if they knew in advance that they had a choice—a choice between seeking finance from a Common Fund or of adopting other means of financing. The decision could then be left to individual commodity negotiations on the merits of the alternatives before them. Without prior knowledge of the availability of finance from a central source, it is difficult to see how, in practice, such a deliberate choice could be made. This is why I have been somewhat puzzled by suggestions that have been made which treat the Common Fund as a kind of residual element whose justification can only be determined after the process of negotiations on individual commodities is completed. The existence or otherwise of a Common Fund must surely make a crucial difference to the character of the individual negotiations themselves.

It is these considerations that underline the supreme importance of making rapid progress on the negotiation of the Common Fund and that is why I believe that the Nairobi resolution provided for the negotiation of a Common Fund at a date that is well in advance of that foreseen for the completion of negotiations on individual products.

The final shape and character of the Common Fund can, of course, only emerge through the process of negotiation of the Fund itself. Since the Nairobi Conference, much work has been done to spell out the specific aspects of a Common Fund. The secretariat of UNCTAD has itself produced several papers of a technical character on the various aspects of the Fund. For the purposes of the present conference, the secretariat has presented a broad document outlining what might be the approach to the constitution of a Common Fund. The proposals are largely of an illustrative character, intended to assist governments in the task of reaching agreement on the characteristics of a fund. In the course of the last few months we have had three preparatory meetings on the Common Fund, which have provided an occasion for member governments to express their views. The Group of 77 have presented their preliminary position on a number of specific issues concerned with the Common Fund. Other groups and countries have also expressed their broad approaches. It now remains to undertake the task of bringing about a reconciliation of views in the context of the negotiation of the Common Fund itself. There has to be a meeting of minds on each of the basic elements of a fund—on its objectives and purposes, its mode of operations, its financing structure and its pattern of management and decision making. This Conference is the occasion for bringing about such a meeting of minds. It is the opportunity for governments to negotiate the specific characteristics of a Common Fund, taking due account of their various interests. It is only in the context of such an approach that this Conference can make the progress that is so crucially needed.

I believe we are close to a creative and constructive step forward. I trust that all Member governments will grasp the historic opportunity that has come their way. A successful outcome of this Conference will be a milestone in international economic relations and will represent a major contribution towards dealing not only with development problems, but also with the problems of the world economy as a whole. It is an opportunity that must not be lost. This Conference is the first major event in the field of international economic relations to take place in 1977. Its results could well change the whole climate of relations in the period ahead. Its success would engender a new spirit of international co-operation. I have no doubt, distinguished delegates, that your awareness of the issues at stake will be amply reflected in the outcome of your work. I wish you all success in this very vital and important endeavour upon which you have now embarked.

Ad hoc Intergovernmental Committee for the Integrated Programme for Commodities*

11 July 1977

This Committee was set up as a unique instrument, one which was not to be found before, to exercise some kind of overall surveillance on the progress of the negotiations under the Integrated Programme, and to monitor this process on a continuing basis. From that point of view, it is this Committee alone which would be able to view the ramifications of the several individual negotiations in the wider context of their implications for and their significance to the Integrated Programme as a whole.

Well, whilst this Committee itself is of outstanding importance, I think that this particular session of the Committee is also of some significance. This session is meeting, so to speak, at some point, perhaps a mid-point, in the evolution of the Integrated Programme, in the schedule of the Programme, as envisaged at Nairobi. This is, therefore, a useful point of time in which to reflect on the experience so far and to try and draw whatever lessons there might be which could be of use for the second subsequent phase of the meetings under the Integrated Programme.

---

* (Extract.)

I have been struck by two basic factors which have emerged in one way or another since the Nairobi Conference. These two factors or developments are not necessarily consistent with each other, and that is one question to which we might address our minds. The first of these factors is that there does seem to be, or seem to have been, after Nairobi a continued reaffirmation in the international community of the central importance of the commodity issue in the entire setting of relationships between developed and developing countries. This factor or development has, I think, emerged strongly in the months that have elapsed since the Nairobi Conference. At each of the successive meetings that took place since Nairobi—in Colombo, in Mexico, in Delhi, in Guatemala on a regional basis, and more recently in Libreville, the developing countries meeting either as a whole or in their regional groups have missed, no opportunity to endorse and emphasize their commitment to the Integrated Programme. Since Nairobi, too, we have seen the Member States of OPEC pronounce their support for the Integrated Programme and to give indication of their willingness to underline and endorse it in every feasible way.

On the side of the developed countries too, I discern some strong progress in relation to responses to the commodity question since Nairobi. In recent months we have witnessed affirmations of this new position on the part of the developed countries—such occasions as the summit meeting of the countries of the European Community in Rome, the industrial summit of the OECD countries in London, and, in the last few weeks, the ministerial meetings of the OECD countries in Paris. On each of these occasions the developed countries have underlined their sensitivity to the importance of the commodity issue, their willingness to participate in the quest for solutions and their endorsement of the concept of a Common Financing Fund. So on the broad political front it does seem that the whole concept of the Integrated Programme for Commodities has not moved backwards; if anything it has moved forward since the Nairobi meeting.

But given this development on the political side, one has to turn to the second of the factors to which I referred earlier, the second of the developments, which is not in full conformity with the trend on the political front. We have not been able to witness commensurate progress in translating the political commitment into specific arrangements, into specific action. We have, since the launching of the Integrated Programme, held already a number of preparatory meetings and meetings of other kinds in regard to both individual commodities and to the Common Fund at which there has so far been very little evidence of any major progress towards translating the political willingness of governments into concrete workable specific actions. We have already had some twenty-four meetings of one kind or another under the auspices of the Integrated Programme; these meetings have occupied something like twenty-six weeks up to now and already we have disseminated in the context of these meetings something like ninety-five documents touching on one aspect or another of the Integrated Programme.

But despite this immense concentration of attention on the Integrated Programme as a negotiating process I think it is true to say that we have still no reason to be satisfied, still no reason to be complacent at any rate about the progress achieved so far. In the case of the Common Fund the negotiating conference held in March, which succeeded at least two preparatory meetings, turned out to be almost wholly inconclusive. In the case of the individual commodities, we have had preparatory meetings on a number of them, we have established expert groups on several of them, but with the exception of perhaps rubber, it would appear that we are still far from a clear vision of what action is to be taken to help strengthen and stabilize the markets for those products.

So there is this inconsistency, this dichotomy so to speak, between the political thrust at the general level and the actual experience at the technical level when the hard issues of commodities are being discussed. And I think that the major challenge in the period ahead in the next phase of the Integrated Programme is to bring about this consistency between the political will to act and the technical effort of designing and bringing about effective results. I think that the situation as it exists for the moment does have within it some promise of success in this endeavour. In regard to the Common Financing Fund we have seen, as a result of the Conference on International Economic Co-operation which was concluded in Paris, a unanimous commitment on the part of the participants, both developed and developing countries, to the principle of the establishment of the Fund, and also a commitment to strive to the utmost to bring about constructive results when the Common Fund meeting reconvenes in November. I think that this decision in principle is immensely helpful because it takes us away from the earlier sterile debate of whether or not there should be a Common Fund and enables us now to concentrate on the character and the details and the manifold aspects of the Common Fund itself.

Ad hoc Intergovernmental Committee for the Integrated Programme for Commodities

10 July 1978

This meeting provides an opportunity to review progress in terms of the Integrated Programme for Commodities and, particularly, in respect of its two main components: the negotiations and preparatory meetings on individual products, on the one hand, and the discussions pertaining to the Common Fund, on the other.

You will recollect that, after the suspension of the second session of the United Nations Negotiating Conference on a Common Fund under the Integrated Programme for Commodities in December last year, I was requested, both by the General Assembly and by this Committee, to enter into consultations with governments with a view to bringing about an early resumption of the Conference. At the same time, it was indicated quite naturally that such a resumption should be on a basis which afforded a fair prospect of success. I would like to say that, since the adoption of those resolutions I have engaged in a series of intensive consultations, in the capitals of both developed and developing countries and here in Geneva. I would like to avail myself of this opportunity to give to this Committee my assessment of the situation that has resulted from these consultations.

The second session of the Conference was suspended because of a failure to reach agreement on two basic issues: the question of the Common Fund being empowered to finance measures other than buffer stocks through the mechanism of a second window, and the question of the financial structure of the Fund. In regard to the financial structure of the Fund, the discussion was centred around the question whether resources should be contributed directly to the Fund by governments, or whether its resources should be derived exclusively from individual commodity agreements. There is also a third which is central to a successful agreement on the Fund but which was not the subject of an intensive exchange of views in the course of the last session, namely the question of the voting structure of the Fund and decision making. This is a crucial element on which some agreement or consensus would be necessary before a successful agreement on the Common Fund could materialize.

In the course of my consultations in the capitals and here in Geneva I expressed to all the parties concerned my own view that an eventual agreement on the Common Fund was not conceivable if the financing of other measures was not provided for and if the financial structure of the Fund was predicated essentially on the pooling of deposits from individual commodity agreements.

On this question of the financial structure of the Fund, the secretariat of UNCTAD has had the benefit of informal discussions with representatives of the banking community. As a result of these discussions, we were encouraged to believe in the soundness and, indeed, the desirability of three important aspects of a possible financial structure for for Fund.

The first was that the Fund would need to have significant resources contributed through direct contributions from member governments. There is, of course, no mechanistic method of determining an appropriate level for these direct contributions. In this regard, a balance needs to be struck between the need to ensure that the claims on governments are not excessive and at the same time the need to make the Common Fund both a successful borrower in the capital markets and an effective lender to individual commodity agreements. In the context of the aggregate requirements for the financing of buffer stocks for the wide range of commodities listed in resolution 93(IV), which the Common Fund might eventually be called upon to finance, it was felt that a foundation capital for the Fund of around $500 million would be appropriate.

A second factor, and a very important one, was that the Common Fund can indeed be successfully structured so that it could serve the purpose of being a major sources of finance for commodity stocks. You will recollect that one of the main objectives underlying the initial proposal of the secretariat for a Common Fund was to help relieve governments, in particular the governments of developing countries, from having to bear what might be a fairly significant financial burden in the financing of buffer stocks. A fund that does not serve the objective of providing such relief will not, in fact, fulfil this basic consideration underlying the initial proposal of a Common Fund. The discussions that we have had with the banking community indicated that it was possible for a Common Fund to offer to finance as much as three-quarters, i.e. 75 per cent, of the costs of buffer stocks which form part of individual commodity agreements, provided that such a Common Fund was properly structured and endowed with the appropriate borrowing instruments; namely, the collateral of stock warrants, and the guarantees or callable capital contributed by the member governments of individual commodity agreements as backing for any loans extended by the Common Fund to these agreements.

A third point which emerged in the course of our discussions with the banking community was that it would significantly strengthen the financial viability of the Fund and its attractiveness to the capital markets if the guarantees or callable capital contributed by countries members of individual commodity agreements were pledged directly to the Common Fund rather than to the commodity agreements to which they relate.

The consultations I have had with representatives of governments and with others on these and other related aspects of the Common Fund have left two broad impressions in my mind.

My first impression is that there does seem to be a universal desire on the part of governments to bring this issue of the establishment of a Common Fund to a successful conclusion. I think that there is a desire to see the Fund eventually established, and I consider that this is a situation which augurs well for the prospects of future work on the Fund.

The second impression that I have brought with me is that, whilst there has been a considerable degree of movement in regard to the basic elements of the Fund, relative to the situation that prevailed in December, we have still not reached a point of being able to say that there is now complete agreement or consensus in regard to all the key aspects of these elements. The principle of a second window, for example, seems to have gained much wider acceptance since the suspension of the Conference in December, but it cannot be said today that every country is now without hesitations in respect of this issue. Moreover, some countries are of the view that the scope and modalities of the second window for the financing of other measures need still to be defined on an agreed basis, with greater precision. Similarly, on the question of the financial structure of the Fund, whilst there seems to be greater acceptance today of the concept of direct contributions of at least relatively limited amounts to cover, for example, administrative costs, differences remain concerning the need for larger contributions to meet other specific needs. Apart from the need for agreement on the appropriate magnitude of direct contributions, a consensus would also be required on a formula for the contributions by member governments of any agreed amount.

There is now a much greater appreciation of the importance of having a ratio of cash resources to borrowing on the part of individual commodity agreements which would not place too excessive a burden on governments. There is perhaps also, in that context, a better understanding of the potential value to the Common Fund of having guarantees or callable capital pledged directly to it. However, it cannot be said that on these issues there is as yet a complete meeting of minds on matters of specific detail.

The question that we should now ask ourselves in the light of these developments is what indeed should be the steps that we should next take. In this respect, I should like to say that, although there has been evidence of progress—I certainly do not have the impression that the issue of the Common Fund is in a state of hopeless deadlock—I do feel, nevertheless, that it is unlikely that such progress could be vastly accelerated in the period to come in the absence of a specific decision to reconvene the Conference and of a specific date for such resumption. Not unnaturally, we cannot expect governments or groups to be inclined to make firm commitments regarding the several aspects of the Common Fund or the various possibilities, in a situation of continuing uncertainty in regard to the reconvening of the Conference and in regard to the date for such reconvening. Moreover, the kind of consultations which I have had have been more useful from the point of view of eliciting broad reactions rather than of securing statements of firm and definitive positions. For these reasons, I feel that it would help further progress on the issue of the Common Fund if a decision is now taken regarding the reconvening of the Conference and if a date is set for such reconvening. It is quite important that work towards a consensus and towards a meeting of minds on the basic elements of the Fund should continue between now and the reconvening of the Conference itself. Such work might perhaps proceed through the medium of small groups or a representative, though still hopefully informal, character.

If a decision is taken to reconvene the Conference, it is important that the question of the most appropriate date for such a resumption be viewed in the light of two basic factors:

The first factor is the view which I have previously expressed to this Committee and which I feel is shared by all of you, namely that the Conference should not be delayed for an excessively long period. This is important not only because of the urgency of the issue of the Common Fund and the need to sustain momentum but also because, as I have said on previous occassions, of the need to avoid having the Common Fund negotiations meshed in too closely with the preparations for the fifth session of the Conference at Manila. Such a situation would cause difficulties in the preparations for the Conference. There is also the consideration that, if a breakthrough on the basic elements of the Common Fund could be secured before the Conference, this would, by itself, help improve immensely the atmosphere for the fifth session of the Conference itself. I feel, therefore that, for these reasons, we should set a date that is in advance of the time when the preparations for UNCTAD V, both on the part of the various groups and on the part of the secretariat, begin to get in their stride. On the other hand—and this is the second factor—I recognize that in choosing a date it is important to allow for a sufficient period of time for governments to reflect on the issues before them; to continue the work in the various capitals; and to determine the positions that they would take in order to ensure the success of the Conference. A decision on the date has to be based on a recognition of both these factors, namely the need to convene as early as possible and at the same time the need to allow sufficient time for adequate preparatory work for the resumed Negotiating Conference.

I have looked at the possible dates that might suggest themselves for the reconvening of the Negotiating Conference, particularly from the point of view of the availability of conference facilities. In this respect we do have serious problems arising out of a particularly heavy calendar of UNCTAD meetings in the months to come. But I have ascertained that it would be possible to make available both conference space and conference services for a session of the Negotiating Conference in the months that follow the latter part of September, provided that such a reconvened session is of a relatively short duration of about two weeks. Whilst this possibility exists from the point of view of the availability of conference services, it needs clearly to be recognized that the resumed Conference, no matter what date is chosen, cannot altogether avoid a degree of overlap with other important meetings or negotiations that are to be convened by UNCTAD in the period ahead. I have found, for example, that if the session is convened in the last two weeks of October, such a session would be possible from the point of view of conference services but would overlap with the initial part of the United Nations Conference on an International Code of Conduct on Transfer of Technology. There would be a similar overlap if the Conference were to be convened later, in the month of November, for example, either with the latter phase of the Conference on a Code of Conduct or with the scheduled United Nations Conference on Natural Rubber. Besides this, whatever the choice of date, there would be need for some rearrangement of the dates of some of the other scheduled meetings of other UNCTAD bodies.

Before I conclude these remarks, I would like to return to the question of discussions on individual commodities. The document before you has set out the picture in this respect; but I would like to underscore some points which I think are of relevance to the assessment that you intend to make of the progress of preparatory meetings under the Integrated Programme.

The first observation I wish to make is that it is still very much my view that the relatively slow tempo of progress in respect of invidual products has been due in no small part to the failure up to now to move decisively towards the establishment of the Common Fund. It has always been my view that meeting on individual commodities taking place in isolation are not likely to lead to concrete results, as past experience has demonstrated so amply. The very purpose of proposing a Common Fund was precisely to introduce a new element into the situation that could provide a strong enough stimulus towards the attainment of agreements on invididual commodities. I do believe for this reason that success with regard to the Common Fund would contribute immensurably towards bringing about a better situation with regard to progress on individual commodities.

A second observation is that there is need now for a more definitive approach to the actual mechanisms that are needed in the case of individual commodities in order to stabilize commodity markets. The preparatory meetings that we have had concerned themselves with a whole complex of issues; but it is my feeling that there has not been enough focus on the actual steps needed to stabilize markets; on what minimum and maximum prices might be; and on how these could best be defended. Progress in this respect would be enhanced considerably if producer governments, no less than consumer governments, addressed themselves to the issue of the arrangements that they would wish to propose as a basis for the preparatory discussions and negotiations on individual products. In the absence of specific initiatives of this kind, it is hardly surprising that the discussions in preparatory meetings tend to be inconclusive and lacking in sharp focus.

I am particularly glad that the *ad hoc* Committee is reviewing the progress on individual products in what I may call a single session. Not only was this one of the basic purposes of the Committee but it was also inherent in the whole concept of the Integrated Programme that individual commodities and their problems should not be seen in isolation but that they should fall within a common umbrella, a common framework of principles, objectives and even modalities. The present session makes it possible to review progress on individual commodity negotiations as a single process and to see whether any lessons could be drawn which are of general applicability outside of the specific and sometimes technical problems of individual products. Such conclusions would undoubtedly be of value for our future work.

One of the proposals before this Committee is the need to extend the time-table set for the conclusion of negotiations under the Integrated Programme. The Nairobi resolution set the end of 1978 as a terminal point for the negotiations on individual commodities. I believe that the establishment of such a deadline was important in order to sustain the momentum of activity in the field of individual commodity discussions. From that point of view, I think you will agree that this deadline has served a valuable purpose. But I think you will also agree that Member Governments would hardly have expected that by the end of 1978—a little more than two years after the conclusion of the fourth session of the Conference at Nairobi—it would in fact have been possible to bring to a successful conclusion negotiations on a range of commodities numbering as many as possible up to eighteen, and to embody these in successful international commodity agreements. It is hardly to be expected that within two and a half years or so, we would succeed in achieving results for eighteen products, results that took virtually two decades or more to bring about in the case of three or four products. I feel, therefore, that whilst every effort needs to be made to change the general picture prevailing so far in the field of discussions on individual commodities and to direct them towards successful negotiations for specific agreements, we should not draw excessively negative conclusions from the experience gained so far. I believe that, given success in regard to the establishment of the Common Fund, negotiations on individual products would move into a new and more decisive phase. It is from this point of view that we have suggested to you that the deadline for the conclusion of negotiations under the Integrated Programme be extended for another year; allowing at the same time an opportunity for the Conference at its fifth session in Mainla to review progress in respect of the Programme as a whole.

United Nations Negotiating Conference on a Common Fund under the Integrated Programme for Commodities

14 November 1978

I am pleased indeed to welcome you all to the resumed second session of the United Nations Negotiating Conference on a Common Fund. The resumption of this Conference is an event that has been long awaited; it is an event whose outcome is being watched with more than ordinary interest by the entire international community. I trust you will all agree with me when I say that the time has now come to move decisively towards the establishment of an institution whose creation has been supported in principle by all Member Governments. Two previous sessions of this Conference failed us in this regard. The present session is an opportunity to make amends, an opportunity to demonstrate that the Member States of UNCTAD do have both the will and the negotiating capacity to take a major step forward in the field of international economic relations.

It is my belief that there are now sufficient grounds for reaching an agreement. When the first session of the Conference took place in March last year there was no universal acceptance of even the principle of the Common Fund. By the time of the second session in November there was agreement on this principle but still no common view on even the broadest questions pertaining to the character of the Fund. There were, it is true, some specific proposals that were presented at that time, but the distance between them appeared too great to permit of any consensus. Today, the situation is considerably different. Since the suspension of the Conference last November, there has been much reflection on the part of governments and of country groups on the several questions pertaining to the character of the Fund. There has been an exchange of views through the medium of informal consultations, through discussions in capitals, and through contacts and exchanges of various kinds. These processes have helped to bring about two results, each of a positive character. They have served to elaborate upon and enlarge the area of understanding on some of the key aspects of the Common Fund itself. Even more important, they have served also to increase the awareness of the political importance of achieving results in a wider context of the dialogue between developed and developing countries.

In a background note presented to this resumed session of the Conference the secretariat of UNCTAD has endeavoured to point to the basic issues which need to be settled in order to provide a foundation for drafting the final articles of agreement of the Fund itself. These basic issues fall broadly under three heads: the objectives and purposes of the Fund, and in particular the issue of the second window to finance measures other than stocking of commodities; the question of the financing and of the capital structure of the Fund; and the question of management and decision making. In each case the note has attempted to set out the major points on which agreement is needed and where relevant to indicate in the light of the consultations the approaches that might result in possible solutions.

When the second session of the Conference was suspended last November there was no agreement even of principle on the question of a second window for the financing of "other measures". As I have stated on other occasions, I did in the course of my discussions convey my view that an agreement on the establishment of a second window was a necessary condition for a successful agreement on the Common Fund itself. The informal consultations and other discussions were not, of course, occasions for governments to make commitments or definitive statements of position. But it is my impression that there is now a wide understanding that such a second window must indeed be part of the Common Fund itself and that the Fund should play a significant role in the financing of measures other than stocking in the field of commodities. I believe that this is a constructive development which augurs well for a successful agreement. What is more, I believe also that there is already much common ground between governments on many of the purposes and modes of operations of the second window. It is true that some issues remain to be settled, issues relating to a more precise definition of purposes as well as to contributions to the second window. But I think there is already a sufficient understanding to provide a good foundation on which to build.

Whilst on the subject of the several purposes of the Fund, I would like to clarify a reference made in the secretariat's note to the possibility to enabling the Common Fund to finance the holding of national stocks in situations in which commodity agreements have yet to be established. This is not a proposal that is intended to circumvent the need for the producer–consumer consensus that is normally embodied in international commodity agreements. Rather, it is intended to deal with situations of crisis where commodities and the countries dependent on them may be in serious difficulty but where, although both producers and consumers are agreed upon the need for action, time is insufficient for the negotiation and conclusion of full-fledged commodity agreements. In such a situation we have felt that the Common Fund should not be preempted from action if there was indeed a consensus that such action was urgently needed.

The issue of the capital structure of the Common Fund and of finance is, of course, of crucial importance. Here again, the meeting in November last year failed to reflect any agreement, even of principle, on the question of direct contributions to the Fund. Since then, it is my view that there has been significant progress. Although once again there have been no firm commitment, I feel that there is now a wider appreciation of the importance of confirming the principle of direct contributions as an essential element of any agreement on the Fund itself. A number of issues, I would say crucial issues, remain, however, to be settled relating in particular to the size of the contributions, as well as to the manner in which they would be distributed among member governments.

I have sometimes been asked about the extent to which the design of the Fund as now contemplated represents a departure from the original concept presented by the secretariat. The original concept, you will remember, envisaged a fund that would eventually mobilize about $6 billion to meet the expected needs of all commodity stocks under the Integrated Programme. It was felt that by making such finance available, the Fund would play a catalytic role in helping to bring about commodity agreements. Under the design now contemplated, the Fund would remain in a position of being able to mobilize resources of roughly this order of magnitude and would therefore be able to offer to finance the bulk of the requirements for stocking under each commodity agreement. In this way the Fund could still be a catalyst in helping to bring about these agreements. Under the present design, however, although the Fund would offer to finance the individual commodity agreements (ICAs) in advance of the finalization of the agreements, the actual raising of the funds needed for lending to ICAs would occur as and when the need is established through the creation of the ICAs themselves. This is because the borrowing instruments needed by the Fund to raise resources in the markets—the collateral—would become available with the establishment of individual commodity agreements. In the original proposals, the possibility was left open for the mobilization of the requirements for stocking in advance of commodity agreements through direct government subscriptions and possibly, although this was not made explicit, through borrowing as well. But as I have indicated, the practicability of and indeed the need for direct contributions of the amounts originally contemplated came into question, as also did the issue of the security which the Fund could offer to back up its borrowing operations outside of that provided by commodity agreements.

There is a further point that should perhaps be mentioned. The present design envisages that the Fund could provide, as I said before, 75 per cent rather than the full requirement of commodity stock financing—the residual 25 per cent being provided by member governments of the individual commodity agreements (ICAs). The original proposals, however, themselves anticipated that as much as one-third of the total requirements for stocking be contributed directly by governments to the Common Fund itself. The essential difference here is that under the present design the portion of the financial requirements for stocks that will be met by direct contributions will be provided by the members of the commodity agreements as the latter emerge, rather than by the membership of the Fund in general.

I have dealt at some length on financial issues because these are of crucial importance to the current negotiations. But there is also the third set of issues which would need to be resolved on this occasion. These relate to questions of management and of decision making. These are subjects on which relatively little was said at the earlier sessions of this Conference. During the informal consultations, however, there was some discussion of these matters and I have the impression that, although we are still some distance from a specific solution, there is now a wide understanding of the principles on which such a solution might possibly be based.

There is no doubt that Member States will respond to the challenge before them. The Common Fund, and the Integrated Programme for Commodities of which it is a part, is not an exercise in aid or assistance from the rich to the poor. It is, on the contrary, predicated on the concept of a co-operative endeavour on the part of the entire international community, which has a common interest in imparting strength and stability to world commodity markets. The special character of the Common Fund was strikingly demonstrated at the Nairobi meeting of UNCTAD IV itself, when a large number of developing countries themselves came forward with pledges of financial contributions, some in specific terms and others more generally. There have been similar pledges of support from some developed countries as well. The member countries of OPEC have themselves taken, at virtually all their meetings, the opportunity to endorse their commitment to and support for the Fund. All this lends credence to the prospect of a soundly conceived and financially strong fund to which the developing countries have themselves committed their own resources. It is a facet of the Fund which I am sure will not be lost in the arrangements that finally come to be established.

I have previously stressed the importance of achieving a positive result on this occasion as a prelude to the fifth session of UNCTAD to be held in Manila next May. I am sure you will agree that a successful outcome at the end of the next two weeks would contribute immeasurably towards improving the atmosphere of the entire dialogue between developed and developing countries. It we succeed on this occasion in laying a solid foundation, we could set in motion the follow-up work that would be needed, and thus present the Manila Conference with a record of solid achievement and accomplishment. If this were to happen, the Conference in Manila could look forwards rather than backwards, and concentrate on the task of building a new order and of giving strength and substance to the concept of international economic co-operation in the years to come.

B. Individual Commodities

United Nations Cocoa Conference
22 September 1975

It gives me much pleasure to declare open the United Nations Cocoa Conference of 1975. This event is one which gives me very great satisfaction. The International Cocoa Agreement of 1972 was the first full-fledged commodity agreement negotiated in the forum of UNCTAD. Other agreements have been re-negotiated in UNCTAD, but the Cocoa Agreement remains the only *new* agreement which was concluded successfully under UNCTAD auspices. There is, of course another—more personal— reason which reinforces my satisfaction: I was myself closely associated with the Cocoa Agreement as the Chairman of the 1972 Conference and I am very happy to be once more in the presence of so many friends and so many familiar faces. The discussions and activities of the previous Conference are still very vivid in my memory, and I count it as one of the most constructive endeavours in which I have had the privilege of participating.

The present Conference convenes in a setting very different from that which prevailed in 1972. In recent months there has been an unprecedented degree of interest throughout the international community in the commodity problem as a whole. It has been a subject of intensive discussion and debate, not only in UNCTAD but in several other bodies, and this has demonstrated a growing awareness of the crucial importance of the commodity issue in world trade and development. I think it is true to say that there is now emerging a broad consensus on the need for some kind of action to help strengthen commodity markets and world trade in commodities, and I believe this consensus sets the stage for progress towards agreement on the type of action that would be needed for dealing with these problems.

The seventh special session of the General Assembly, which ended barely a week ago, paid a great deal of attention to commodity trade; this issue loomed large throughout the negotiations that took place in New York. The Assembly arrived at a consensus on several of the issues pertaining to trade and the problems of developing countries, and there was a constructive mood in evidence throughout the session. I believe that these are good auguries for this Conference.

UNCTAD has been particularly concerned and active in the commodity field as the initiator of a whole set of proposals for dealing with the complex issues involved. UNCTAD has presented, several months ago, an Integrated Programme for Commodities comprising a number of elements which, taken together, aim at bringing about a significant improvement in commodity trade. It is not my intention now to elaborate upon these proposals; I believe that most of you are well aware of their content. By and large, they seek, among other things, to establish a range of internationally managed commodity stocks, and to provide for a Common Financing Fund to which contributions will be made by producers and consumers as well as other investors. The Programme also envisages a network of multilateral commitments, a system of supporting compensatory financing and new initiatives in the area of processing of commodities. I believe that the Integrated Programme proposed by UNCTAD has aroused a good deal of interest and that it remains the only comprehensive and detailed set of proposals in existence for tackling the commodity issue in general.

The meeting which has opened today will, in many ways, be a test of the new mood which prevails for dealing with the commodity problem, of the willingness to act and to reflect the many concerns that have been expressed about commodity issues; it will be a test of the capacity to fulfil objectives which have now been increasingly endorsed. The co-operation between producers and consumers which was embodied in the first agreement needs, I believe, to be extended to reflect, as far as is relevant and practicable, the new thinking and the new realities that have emerged since the first agreement was concluded.

The UNCTAD secretariat has presented to you in its background document[1] some of the themes which, in our view might form the subject of your deliberations. I do not wish to take up your time by repeating at length the substance of our observations and comments. Briefly, we have tried to point out that the first agreement has already

---

[1] TD/COCOA/4/2.

provided a valuable basis for, and experience of, close and constructive co-operation between producers and consumers. It remains a very good foundation for the work of this Conference. It is, of course, true that the operative mechanisms of the first agreement have not been put to the test because of market developments. Despite having been revised once, both the minimum and the maximum prices that were established in the first agreement remain below the prices that have prevailed in the market throughout the period of the agreement. Thus, while the agreement made provision for the accumulation of a cocoa buffer stock, no physical stock has in fact been built up, although substantial financial resources have accrued to the management of the stock. I believe that today the stock could claim credit for a sum of something like $52 million, an amount which has been increasing as the months go by.

This 1975 Conference could concentrate, amongst other things, on some key issues pertaining to the revision of the existing agreement. One of these issues concerns the level of prices—not only the adequacy of the price range that has been set, but also the question of how to maintain an adequate and relevant price range against a background of continuing and unabated inflation. As you well know, a price range set in nominal terms would no longer remain a stable range in real terms when relative prices are changing rapidly. I think therefore that the question of the maintenance of the stability of a price range, not just in nominal but in real terms, is one of the basic questions to which you would need to give attention in the course of your deliberations.

There is also the question of the buffer stock mechanism and how to increase the efficiency of the system as envisaged in the first agreement. The mechanism provided for the first Cocoa Agreement was not of the conventional kind. It was not designed to intervene actively in the market to protect the agreed price range; it was, in fact, intended as an outlet for some of the excess supplies over and above the quotas that might be set. This type of mechanism reflected some of the constraints that were in existence at the time the first agreement was negotiated—in particular, the absence of any provisions for the pre-financing of stocks and also the desire, which was strong at that time, to avoid providing what might have been incentives to over-production. Consequently, the mechanism provided for phased payments for stocks, based on a low level of initial payment. I believe that, in the course of your deliberations, these provisions should be reviewed, and perhaps reconsidered, with the aim either of providing for a type of buffer mechanism which is more effective in practice than the existing one or, at least, of adapting the present mechanism with a view to eliminating some of the provisions which do not appear to be relevant in the present context. The concept of low initial payments is one of the particular issues you might wish to review in that context. I think the basic objective, which you all share, is to establish a stocking mechanism that would be effective in defending a price range that has been agreed upon as being in the interest both of the producers and of the consumers.

I believe also that this Conference should be concerned with the need to make participation in the Cocoa Agreement as universal as possible. As you know, the United States of America, which is the largest consumer and importer of cocoa, was not a participant in the first agreement. I, for one, have been encouraged by the statement of the US Secretary of State at the seventh special session of the General

Assembly, regarding the approach which his Government intends to adopt towards commodity agreements and its desire to participate in this Conference with a view, presumably, to becoming a full member of the agreement. A commodity agreement is stronger if the range of its membership is greater, and I hope that significant progress will be made in this regard as a result of this Conference.

I should like to end by referring to the co-operation which the UNCTAD secretariat has enjoyed with the secretariat of the International Cocoa Organization. We are particularly glad that they are collaborating with us in the servicing of this Conference. We have enjoyed very close and cordial relations with that Organization over the past two years and I am quite confident that this co-operation will not only continue but be strengthened in the period ahead.

Not only as the Secretary-General of UNCTAD, but also as the Chairman of the 1972 Cocoa Conference, you have my warmest wishes for the success of your deliberations. I feel confident that the foundations laid in the past will be strengthened as a result of your work and that you will respond to the new spirit pervading approaches to commodity problems by concluding an effective, strong and successful international agreement for cocoa. I would like to pledge to you the fullest co-operation and assistance of the UNCTAD secretariat in your efforts to this end.

International Tin Council

1 July 1976

I am very pleased indeed on behalf of the Secretary-General of the United Nations to convene this first session of the International Tin Council under the Fifth International Tin Agreement and to welcome all of you here this morning.

The Tin Agreement has a particularly long history, and I know that in many phases of the evolution of this Agreement UNCTAD itself has been very closely associated with your work. But I believe that this is the first occasion on which the United Nations has served as the depositary of the legal instruments remitted by governments who wish to participate in the Agreement. Hence this is the first occasion on which the United Nations has had the privilege of convening the first session of the Council. My pleasure at this event is, of course, immensely great, but I do wish to express on behalf of all of you our thanks to the Government of the United Kingdom, which has in previous years acted as the depositary of the legal instruments and which earlier undertook the task of opening these sessions of the Council.

You will, of course, shortly receive a report regarding such matters as signatures to the Agreement, the deposit of the appropriate instruments, and notifications of intention to deposit such instruments. But I think I could anticipate this report by expressing satisfaction at the response which has been forthcoming from member governments. I do, of course, hope that where governments have hitherto limited themselves to notifications of intent, they will follow this up by the deposit of the necessary instruments themselves.

I would like to express my pleasure and deep satisfaction at the notification of intention to ratify the Agreement which has been made by the Government of the United States. The United States is the largest consumer and importer of tin and this will be the first occasion on which it would be participating in the Agreement. I think you will all agree with me that this step taken by the United States does augur very well indeed for the future of the Agreement itself.

This first session of the Tin Council is convening in the immediate aftermath, so to speak, of the fourth session of UNCTAD which concluded in Nairobi almost a month ago. I believe that this is the first of the commodity meetings taking place after the Nairobi session. As you are well aware, the subject of commodities loomed large in Nairobi. I think it was the focus of attention of participating governments, and the results of the Nairobi Conference will inevitably be assessed in terms of what has been decided upon in the arena of commodities. At Nairobi we did secure endorsement, on the basis of a consensus resolution, for what we have called the Integrated Programme for Commodities. The Nairobi resolution endorsed the objectives and mechanisms of the Integrated Programme, and authorized a series of operational steps which are intended to bring about the implementation of the Integrated Programme. This would involve UNCTAD, the UN system, and many Member States of the United Nations in very intensive activities in the realm of commodities in the months to come. It is an immense challenge but one which we, for our part, look forward to with great enthusiasm and anticipation.

There are many links between the decision taken at Nairobi on the Integrated Programme and what you yourselves have been doing within the framework of the Tin Agreement.

As you perhaps know, tin is one of the commodities that are included in the Integrated Programme. But the Integrated Programme and the resolution on commodities has made amply clear that where there are already international agreements in force—as is the case with tin—all future activities would be in accordance with the procedures that have been established by these agreements. In the case of commodities for which there are no agreements, the resolution calls upon myself, as Secretary-General of UNCTAD, to convene new meetings for these commodities with a view to arriving at agreements should such agreements prove to be feasible.

A second link between the Integrated Programme and the International Tin Agreement relates to the role of buffer stocks. A primary element of the Integrated Programme is the proposal to establish a series of internationally owned stocks covering a wide range of commodities. In proposing the programme, we felt that the instrument of commodity stocks has up to now been inadequately used by the international community as a mechanism for imparting strength and stability to commodity markets. The Tin Agreement has, of course, been the one exception where a buffer stock has, from a very early stage, played a central role. I think I could say that we in UNCTAD, in evolving the integrated programme, drew on the experience of the Tin Agreement and on the concepts embodied in it. So I believe that the Integrated Programme owes a debt to the Tin Agreement in respect of some of its basic features.

Another element common both to the Integrated Programme and to your own experience pertains to the financing of commodity stocks. I have been very encouraged to learn that offers of contributions to the financing of commodity stocks have been forthcoming from five consuming countries as at present. As you know, we have attached a great deal of importance to the question of financing commodity stocks. We feel that one reason why the instrument of stocking has not been widely utilized in the past relates to the difficulties experienced in regard to raising finance. Hence we have been encouraged by the innovations and the progress that you have made in the International Tin Agreement. One of the elements of the Integrated Programme to which we have attached primary importance has been the proposal for the establishment of a Common Financing Fund for commodities. This proposal for a Common Fund did indeed attract a great deal of attention at Nairobi. In one way or another, it became the centre-piece of the whole discussion on commodities in Nairobi. In the course of the fourth session of UNCTAD, we received a number of pledges of support for the Common Financing Fund and a number of countries indicated their support in quantitative terms. These countries were not confined exclusively to the developing countries or to the producing countries. In some cases they included consuming countries as well. The concept of the Common Financing Fund also received pledges of support from the Member States of OPEC. The result of all this is that in the resolution on the Integrated Programme for Commodities, accepted at Nairobi, I have been authorized to convene—not later than March 1977—a Negotiating Conference on the Common Financing Fund. It is our hope that this Conference will prove to be successful and that it will lead to the establishment of a Common Financing Fund.

It was our intention in proposing this Fund that the resources available to it would be extended to individual commodity bodies. Should the Common Financing Fund be established, as I hope and expect that it would, it would follow that the International Tin Council would be one of the bodies which would be eligible to draw upon it—should it consent to do so. I believe that in the Fifth Agreement you have made provision in one of your articles for having recourse to financing from sources such as the Common Financing Fund. I am glad that such provision already exists.

There is still another connection between the International Tin Agreement and what was decided in Nairobi on the Integrated Programme. Your Agreement provides, and I think this has been an innovation, for a regular but flexible mechanism to review prices from time to time in the light of changing circumstances. In the Nairobi resolution there was similar recognition of the need to review prices from time to time in respect of all the commodities for which arrangements are brought about in the future. In the Nairobi resolution it was specifically recognized that the price levels set for commodities should take account of world inflation and of changes in the world economic and monetary situations. It was also recognized that the periodical review of these price ranges should take into account, amongst other things, the movements in the prices of imported manfuactured goods, exchange rates, production costs, world inflation as well as in levels of production and consumption. I think that this language incorporated in the Integrated Programme for Commodities is new. But in a broad way it has already been anticipated in your own provisions embodied in the International Tin Agreement.

We expect the next eighteen months to two years to be a period of very intense and heightened activity in the arena of commodities. We have received a mandate to convene a large number of meetings on individual products. These will be part of a single exercise, be conducted within a given time frame and be subject to overall monitoring or surveillance by machinery to be specially created in UNCTAD. I hope very much that these initiatives would bear fruit and that as a result we would help bring about a better situation in commodity markets which serve the interests of all the participants—both the producing and the consuming countries.

I feel myself that your own Agreement will grow from strength to strength. What you have already achieved is a milestone in the field of international commodity policy. For this we need to extend credit to all the participating governments as well as to all those who have been involved in the management of the Tin Agreement on a day-to-day basis. I wish your deliberations all success.

I have very great pleasure now to declare open this the first session of the Council under the Fifth International Tin Agreement.

Preparatory Meeting on Copper*

27 September 1976

This Preparatory Meeting is the first of the meetings on individual commodities to be convened after the Nairobi Conference. Copper is one of the most important of the commodities which enter world trade. It is a commodity that is of vital interest to a number of developing countries, although it is also a product that is produced by a number of developed countries. Copper is an indispensable raw material to the importing consuming countries, and for this reason I think that there is a strong common interest in the establishment of a satisfactory situation pertaining to the market for copper.

Copper is a commodity which has been particularly susceptible to wide fluctuations in prices; indeed, as the evidence before you shows, the range of price fluctuations in copper has been greater than the range displayed by most other commodities. This instability causes persistent problems not only for the producing countries, whose economic and social well-being is dependent on copper. It is also a cause of difficulties for the consuming countries, where the volatility of prices affects not only the costs of production but the prospects of the availability of supplies over a long period. I think there is now a growing recognition of the fact that the smooth flow of investment in the realm of commodities is in one way or another assisted by a situation of strengthened stability in commodity markets.

---

* (Extract.)

It is I believe a recognition of the importance of finding remedial measures for copper that prompted the Integovernmental Council of Copper Exporting Countries (CIPEC) at its Ministerial Conference in November 1975, to decide to work towards an international stabilization arrangement for copper. Similarly, it is an awareness of the importance of greater stability that prompted the International Wrought Copper Council, which represents the copper transforming interests in the principal importing countries, to display an interest in the idea of a stabilization system which includes amongst its elements the concept of a buffer stock. These developments do, I believe, pave a way for the future search for arrangements in the field of copper.

It is our view, and I hope it is a view that is shared by all of you present that, despite the inevitable problems that might arise, copper is a commodity which is technically amenable to stabilization arrangements. We are convinced that arrangements could be instituted to render stability to the copper market by means of certain mechanisms which include a buffer stock system as an important element. We believe that the establishment of a buffer stock for copper is a feasible proposition and that a system of interventions in markets to prevent prices from reaching levels that are considered too low or levels that are considered too high is desirable. We believe that such a system, if supported by other supplementary measures, could offer a solution to the problems of copper. The Integrated Programme for Commodities does itself lay stress on the establishment of stocks as an important component of the Programme, and I think that copper is a case where this concept of stocking could be of particular relevance.

The Integrated Programme for Commodities pays particular attention, as you know, to the question of the financing of stocks. In the past the problem of finance has been one of the elements, I would even say one of the difficulties, which has stood in the way of the negotiation of commodity agreements. We ourselves, in formulating the Integrated Programme, sought to meet this problem of finance by providing for a common financing fund for commodities. In doing so we sought to relieve members of individual commodity agreements (they have been producers in the past, they may be producers and consumers in the future) from the burden of securing the finance for the stocking operations themselves, at least in part. The concept of the Common Financing Fund is based on mobilizing financial resources over a wide range. It is based on having recourse to borrowed funds from the money markets of the world. In this way we felt that the problem of mobilizing resources for the financing of buffer stocks could be dealt with more effectively and with less cost to individual countries. But the Common Financing Fund is not intended itself to act or intervene or dabble in commodity markets. In terms of the Integrated Programme, this would be the task of individual commodity bodies set up as a result of agreements between producers and consumers. The Common Financing Fund would only lend resources to such bodies. The bodies so established should be authorized to have recourse to the Fund should they desire such recourse. So the Fund itself is intended to assist individual bodies. We do not see that there is a compulsion for such bodies to seek recourse to the Fund if they felt that in one way or another they were not in need of such recourse, but it is our belief that the availability of resources made possible by the establishment of the

Fund would be of help to individual commodity bodies in the pursuit of their stabilization arrangements.

As you know, parallel to this series of meetings on individual products, we have been asked by the Nairobi resolution to convene a number of meetings pertaining to the Common Financing Fund itself. We intend to convene the first preparatory meeting on the Common Financing Fund this year, perhaps in November, and in terms of the resolution we aim at convening the Negotiating Conference on the Common Financing Fund not later than March 1977. In your deliberations, in your approach to finding solutions to the problems of copper, I would like you to bear in mind the parallel meetings that are taking place and the time-tables of meetings that are being drawn up for these meetings. It is important that these two sets of meetings should be of relevance to each other, that they should support and in one way or another reinforce each other. It is only in this way that one can take advantage of the common conception that has been incorporated into the Integrated Programme for Commodities.

Preparatory Meeting on Jute, Kenaf and Allied Fibres

25 October 1976

I am pleased to declare open the Preparatory Meeting on Jute, Kenaf and Allied Fibres and to extend to all of you a very warm welcome. As you are aware, the Preparatory Meeting on Jute, Kenaf and Allied Fibres is the second of the meetings on individual commodities convened within the framework of, and pursuant to, the resolution of the Nairobi Conference, resolution 93(IV), on the Integrated Programme for Commodities.

The resolution on the Integrated Programme has, so to speak, two prongs to it; one of these relates to a series of preparatory meetings, which are expected, in as many cases as possible, to lead to negotiating conferences on a number of individual products, including those that have been listed in the Nairobi resolution itself. The second prong of the Programme is the negotiations that would pertain to the establishment of a Common Financing Fund. We are expected to hold the Negotiating Conference on the Common Financing Fund not later than March next year, and that Conference will itself be preceded by preparatory meetings, the first of which we intend to hold possibly in November of this year.

The purpose of the present preparatory meeting is to work towards arrangements pertaining to jute, kenaf and allied fibres which would contribute to both the stabilization and the strengthening of the prices of these products, and also to setting the industry producing these on a firm and viable basis. It is my hope that the preparatory meetings to be undertaken will eventually lead to a negotiating conference, which will formulate specific measures and specific arrangements to impart strength, stability and viability to the markets for jute and allied products.

I do not need to underline the importance of this meeting, and the importance of jute as a commodity in the Integrated Programme. Jute is a depressed commodity, which is subject to rapid contraction of consumption in traditional markets, and indeed, contraction of world trade, largely, but not entirely, because of displacement by synthetic substitutes. It is a product exported by few countries, but these are amongst the poorest in the world in terms of per capita income. It is a striking fact that jute constitutes the life-blood of one of these countries and accounts for over 80 per cent of its export earnings. It is thus the source of livelihood for tens of millions of people engaged in the production of raw jute and jute goods and also in the ancillary services associated with the industry.

The problems of jute have, of course, been under close scrutiny for the past fifteen years, or so. Despite these past attempts at arriving at remedial measures, the effective action that has proved possible has so far remained somewhat limited. Up to now assistance for jute has been rather of an *ad hoc* nature, made available either by individual donor countries, or by international financial institutions. You will recall the previous discussions in the FAO Study Group on Jute, which go as far back as 1962. In the period 1968–70, there were discussions on the possibility of establishing international stabilization reserves for jute. But although stocking arrangements were, even at that time, accepted as being an appropriate mechanism—perhaps the most appropriate mechanism—for stabilizing the price of jute, it did not prove possible to institute such mechanisms largely because of a lack of funds, and particularly of funds from consuming countries.

The prospects today for reaching effective agreements are, in many ways, better than in the past. There are new circumstances which suggest that such action might prove to be feasible. The prospect for establishing jute on a more viable basis has been strengthened of late by the rise in the prices of synthetic substitutes, and the prospect that they might increase still further over the next decade or so. At the same time, there are significant possibilities of reducing the cost of production of jute fibre and jute goods, of improving their technical qualities and of finding new uses for them through research and development and promotional efforts. The prospects for success at this point in time are also enhanced by the fact that these meetings on jute are taking place within the framework of a wider attack on the commodity problem, a framework that is embodied in the Integrated Programme for Commodities. There is, I believe, a greater awareness now on the part of the world community of the importance of the commodity problem in general and of the need to adopt remedial measures in this realm. This focus of attention should extend to the problems of the jute industry, and I believe that the fact that these problems are now being considered, not in isolation, or in a fragmented way, but as part of a wider effort to improve the working of world commodity markets, will help impart not only greater awareness of the importance of the problems, but also greater political will to take action in this field.

An element which might contribute to success in the quest for solutions for jute is, of course, the attempt to mobilize financing for the establishment of stocks by means of the negotiations on the Common Financing Fund. The lack of finance has, in the past, been an obstacle to the institution of stocks for jute. The fact that we are now trying to find an overall remedy for the problem of financing of international stocks could be an additional element which would contribute to the success of the attempts to reach agreements on jute. It is also important to emphasize that the remedial measures taken for jute would need to be appropriate to the particular conditions facing the jute-producing industry. I have time and again emphasized that the fact that we are having an Integrated Programme for Commodities does not imply that there could be single common solutions for all commodities. Rather, there is a need to find solutions which are specific to the individual commodities, which are tailored to their needs, and which take account of their particular problems. We believe that in the area of jute and allied products, the need is for a somewhat comprehensive action programme which would be aimed at, and which would succeed in, revitalizing the jute industry.

The secretariats of UNCTAD and FAO have placed before you a document which they have jointly prepared containing ideas regarding remedial action that might help governments to determine the basis of an effective action programme for jute. That document reflects our view that an action programme on jute can best be undertaken within the framework of an international commodity agreement on jute and jute products, which would perhaps have wider dimensions than those that have hitherto been contemplated. We feel that a stocking arrangement for jute and jute products is both technically feasible and economically desirable. Such an arrangement could play a crucial role in improving the competitive position of jute. It would naturally help provide greater assurance in respect of the stability of prices. No less important. It could help impart confidence regarding the future of jute to the final users, who could be given a greater assurance of the reliability of supplies of jute and jute products at competitive prices. Such an assurance has been lacking in the past. We believe also that a stocking arrangement for jute would provide a valuable breathing space until the longer-term measures aimed at cost reduction, product improvement and demand expansion could bear results. An international agreement on jute and jute products would provide a framework for co-operation among producer and consumer countries, in respect of not only the establishment of stocks, but also other essential elements such as measures to reduce costs and to initiate more intensive research and development and promotional activities.

If we are to make progress as regards action on jute, there must, first of all, be a new willingness to act on the part of the international community. The circumstances in which this meeting is taking place, the background that has led to its convening, are a manifestation of such a willingness—which has nevertheless to be expressed in terms of firm commitments and specific arrangements. If the Preparatory Meeting is able to agree in principle on an action programme for jute and jute products, and on the follow-up procedures that are to be taken from now on within a short time span, then it may well indeed be possible to proceed to a negotiating conference which would given some kind of contractual endorsement to the measures agreed upon within a relatively early period, hopefully even within a period of one year. This could be a goal in this and the succeeding preparatory meetings that would be initiated in regard to jute.

As indicated earlier, the arrangements that are contemplated would need to be multidimensional, taking into account not only the need for the establishment of buffer stocks, but also other elements aimed at improving and reducing costs and improving access to markets—which is an important element—and also improvements in other fields such as marketing, distribution and so on. You have a great deal before you for study, and I wish your meeting every success. I would like to express my particular thanks to the FAO secretariat for their wholehearted co-operation in the preparation of this meeting. There has been very close and constant collaboration between the officers dealing with jute in the two secretariats. This collaboration has extended not only to the preparation of the basic document, but also to all aspects of the preparatory work. This is a matter of very great satisfaction to me, and I look forward to the continuation of this collaboration in the future work to which this meeting will surely give rise.

United Nations Sugar Conference

18 April 1977

There is no need to emphasize the great importance of the task upon which you are now embarking. For the developing countries, sugar is a commodity of vital importance as an export, and at the same time it claims a very considerable part of their foreign exchange for imports. As an export earner, sugar from the developing countries reached $9 billion in 1975, and in that year it had overtaken coffee as the leading commodity other than petroleum. Nearly $3 billion was spent on imports by developing countries, a cost surpassed only by wheat. These facts alone indicate the key role of sugar-market conditions for developing economies, and the pervasive effect that market instability can have for balances-of-payments equilibrium, management of the domestic economy and employment. Sugar has also, of course, its special connotation in the context of world food problems, so that the ends that can be achieved through an agreement on international trade will have their wider impact on this fundamental issue. There can be no doubt on all of these grounds of the urgency and importance of the task before this Conference.

International co-operation in the sugar industry has a long history dating back to the beginning of this century. Since 1945 alone, eight UN sugar conferences have been held, but I think it is right to say that this Conference, the ninth UN Sugar Conference, convenes under very different circumstances to those of the previous conferences.

I believe it would not be an exaggeration to say that the past three years which have elapsed since the failure of the 1973 Sugar Conference to negotiate an international agreement with effective provisions, have represented an unusually eventful period for the world sugar economy. Drastic changes took place during this relatively short period, not only in the course of prices, but also in supply and demand relationships, in the usage of substitutes, in sugar consumption and in sugar policies pursued by individual countries.

I do not think I am wrong in saying that developments over the last three years have not been in the real interest of any section of the world sugar economy, whether importers or exporters, developed or developing, cane or beet growers. I need hardly elaborate on major features of the situation—the unprecedented price explosion in 1974, the drastic fall in prices in 1975–6, the inroads into sugar end-uses made by sugar substitutes (some of which are now under scrutiny), the erosion of the purchasing power of sugar-exporting countries, and the increased pressure for the protection and subsidy of sugar production in some developed countries. Above all, the instability suffered by sugar exporters and importers in the 1970s, together with the still uncertain future in this respect, has been especially damaging to the prospects of sound and rational development planning of investment and human resource use in the many developing countries with a substantial dependence on this crop.

In the field of policy, the most striking development since the 1973 Conference has been the modification or disappearance of arrangements that had come to be regarded as almost permanent features of international trade. These changes have meant that the international system of trade in sugar has become more integrated, or less fragmented, if I may so express it. There have, of course, been new arrangements between groups of countries, and in the manner of regulating imports into particular countries. It is also a fair judgement that there has been a growing interest among both exporters and importers in making their outlets and source of supplies more certain and more predictable as to price through bilateral contractual arrangements. These policy developments also point to the need for co-ordinated international action for effective stabilization of the world market.

In this connection, the issue of universality of the International Sugar Agreement deserves special attention. It would be truistic to say that a commodity agreement is stronger the greater the range of its membership, or that the new International Sugar Agreement should be as universal as possible. I recognize that the Sugar Agreement has had a very representative membership in the past. Nevertheless, it is to be hoped that these negotiations will succeed in attracting wider participation taking account of the encouraging fact that all major sugar producers and consumers are participating at this Conference.

May I add that I myself have also been encouraged by recent statements by representatives of major countries regarding a new, positive approach towards international commodity agreements in general. It seems to me that the International Sugar Agreement with wide representation of both producers and consumers might prove to be one of the best to start with practical implementation of this new approach.

It is clearly the prerogative of governments to decide here what kind of agreement is wanted, and how best to put the type of intervention selected into effect.

As you all know, the secretariat of the International Sugar Organization, with the help of an intergovernmental preparatory committee, has accomplished a very difficult task in preparing a comprehensive draft of a new International Sugar Agreement. This draft undoubtedly will serve as a valuable working document for your deliberations and should allow the Conference to make an expeditious start on the business of negotiation.

I have noted that the draft prepared by the ISO secretariat as a working document for this Conference envisages the establishment of a stabilization mechanism linked to minimum and maximum prices. Within the price range action will be based on a system of export quotas and minimum national stocks. I feel detailed attention needs to be given to the role of stocking to facilitate the working of a quota-type agreement to stabilize the market, especially since quota systems mean withholding of supplies, with all the consequential costs for producers. It must also be recognized that it is essentially a policy of stocking that provides the means for the defence of price ceilings in situations of shortage, as in 1973–4.

There is, of course, the question of financing of these stocks. This question has been made a key aspect of the Integrated Programme for Commodities, both in the context of negotiations on invididual commodities and those on the Common Fund.

In this regard, it will be appropriate for me to comment briefly on the negotiations on a Common Fund, since the Negotiating Conference ended here only two weeks ago. There have been various appraisals of its results. The Conference has not taken concrete decisions on the scope and institutional features of the fund. The Conference has not completed its work, and this Sugar Conference will thus not be able to see precisely what relevance the Fund would have for arrangements on sugar. But I would like to emphasize that there were strong indications from all sides of a commitment to negotiate towards the establishment of a Common Fund. The Negotiating Conference is to be resumed not later than November this year with the aim of reaching a conclusive result. Therefore, I, for one, think that the Common Fund will in due course become a financing instrument that could facilitate and strengthen the operation of international commodity agreements, existing and to be concluded. You will not wish to exclude this possibility in framing the arrangements on sugar for the next few years.

I should like to acknowledge the co-operation which the UNCTAD secretariat has had with the Executive Director and secretariat of the International Sugar Organization in the preparations for this Conference.

In concluding, may I wish you every success with the very important task of negotiating and concluding an effective, strong and durable International Agreement for Sugar.

United Nations' Natural Rubber Conference

13 November 1978

The task upon which you are now embarking is one of great importance. Natural rubber is one of the most important commodities exported by developing countries. In 1976 developing countries exported $2.2 million worth of natural rubber and in value terms natural rubber ranks as second amongst all agricultural raw materials and sixth amongst all commodities exported by developing countries. Natural rubber production is concentrated in a few countries of Asia and Africa which depend on exports of it for a major part of their foreign exchange earnings income and employment. Natural rubber production is very labour intensive and the industry provides a livelihood for about 15 million people, most of whom are small farmers. Natural rubber also plays a very important role in the economies of the rubber-consuming countries particularly in the transportation sector which accounts for about two-thirds of all the natural rubber consumed by these countries.

From its very inception the natural rubber industry has been plagued by the problem of price instability which has adverse effects on both producers and consumers. The instability of natural rubber prices causes export earnings and incomes to fluctuate widely, thereby distorting investment priorities and making economic planning and plan implementation extremely difficult. At the same time natural rubber price instability introduces a large element of uncertainity into the costing and pricing decisions of rubber manufacturers. This has encouraged them to substitute natural rubber with stable-priced synthetic rubbers whenever this has been technically feasible. As a result, over time, there has been a sharp secular decline in natural rubber's share of the world elastomer market.

The problem of natural rubber's price instability has been studied in various international forums for a very long time. The Stevenson Scheme and the International Rubber Regulation Agreement of the inter-war years represent two early attempts to arrive at an international solution to this problem. The International Rubber Study Group (IRSG) discussed the draft of an international natural rubber agreement based on buffer stocks at its tenth meeting in Copenhagen in 1953, but the group could not arrive at a consensus on the matter. Since then the stabilization of natural rubber prices has been discussed at many subsequent meetings of the IRSG but these discussions have not produced any concrete results. For a number of years the FAO has been advocating that natural rubber prices should be stabilized so as to improve natural rubber's competitive position. In addition, during periods of exceptionally low prices major producing countries have intervened unilaterally in the rubber market.

Recent events and new circumstances indicate that the prospects for concluding an effective agreement on natural rubber are much better today than they have ever been in the past. The competitive position of natural rubber has improved significantly as a result of the sharp increase in crude-oil prices and the associated increases in the costs of production of synthetic rubbers. Recent studies show that even on the basis of relatively favourable assumptions there is likely to be a natural rubber shortage of 0.5 to 1.0 million metric tons by the year 1990. As a result of the massive long-term research and development effort into natural rubber production and processing the technology to alleviate such shortage is readily available. But the great diversity of the industry, the small size and limited resources of individual small holders and the large element of uncertainty with respect to the future course of prices and profits have all combined to hinder the adoption of the latest technologies.

Producing countries have been fully cognisant of the fact that if the benefits of these productivity improvements are to be fully realized it will be necessary to introduce a measure of price stability into the market for natural rubber. To this end, after more than two years of intensive consultations and numerous economic and technical studies, within the auspices of the Association of Natural Rubber Producing Countries, Malaysia, Indonesia, Thailand, Sri Lanka and Singapore signed the ANRPC an international agreement on natural rubber price stabilization in Jakarta in November 1976.

Recognizing the positive role and benefits that could accrue from consumer participation, the producing countries solicited the participation of consumers in a wider producer–consumer agreement within the context of the UNCTAD Integrated Programme for Commodities (IPC). Since then seven meetings on rubber have been held within the framework of the IPC. The consensus reached in these meetings has made it possible to schedule this United Nations Negotiating Conference on Natural Rubber.

The task upon which you are now embarking is one of special significance not only because of the needs of natural rubber, but also because of the fact of the eighteen commodities covered by resolution 93(IV) on the IPC, rubber is the first, and so far the only, commodity to reach the stage of a negotiating conference within the framework of the IPC as such. In this respect the meetings on rubber have been quite different from those on other commodities under the IPC. At the very first preparatory meeting producers and consumers agreed that measures designed to reduce excessive price volatility in the international market for rubber would be in the interests of both producers and consumers. Having identified the problem, they moved expeditiously towards considering the actual mechanisms required to stabilize the natural rubber market. Unlike the preparatory meetings on other commodities which have concerned themselves with a whole complex of issues and related technical and economic studies, from the outset the direction of the rubber meetings was action-oriented, and focused towards an international agreement to stabilize natural rubber prices. This enabled governments to dispense with the wide-ranging studies that have characterized the preparatory meetings on other commodities and to concentrate on an exhaustive dialogue about the specific elements of an international agreement to stabilize natural rubber prices.

At the Third Preparatory Meeting on Rubber governments unanimously agreed to request the convening of a Negotiating Conference on Natural Rubber. To this end they set out the main elements that should be considered as a basis for these negotiations. Governments agreed that an international buffer stock, large enough to ensure its effectiveness, should be the central element of a price stabilization agreement. They also agreed that the pricing provisions of such an agreement should be cast so as to promote long-term equilibrium between the demand and the supply of natural rubber. Finally, they agreed that there should be a balance between producers and consumers in the rights, obligations and benefits deriving from an international agreement on rubber.

The rubber-producing countries can justly claim a substantial part of the credit for the rapid progress made in the preparatory meetings on rubber. Having concluded a price stabilization agreement amongst themselves, they put forward a concrete and detailed set of proposals for a wider producer–consumer agreement. Having clearly set out their basic position they provided in depth clarifications of the principal elements of their proposals. To keep the preparatory meetings in sharp focus the producing countries met frequently amongst themselves both in Asia and here, in Geneva, to air their views, weigh the merits of different alternatives, to iron out their differences and to forge a strong united position. Hence in the working document for this Conference the producing countries as a group have put forward a single coherent set of draft articles of an International Natural Rubber Agreement.

Representatives of the consuming countries have also been engaged in intensive preparatory work, including field visits to some of the producing countries to acquaint themselves first hand with the situation of natural rubber. Although the consuming countries do not yet have a common position, reflected in the different options contained in the conference document, none the less there is a substantial measure of convergence on some of the main issues. The principal outstanding issues appear to be the pricing provisions and the size of the buffer stock. Producing countries are seeking an agreement with fixed floor and ceiling prices. Consuming countries, on the other hand, appear to be in favour of an automatic or semi-automatic mechanism for adjusting the price range in keeping with underlying market forces.

With respect to the buffer stock, the producing countries and a number of consuming countries are in favour of a buffer stock of 400,000 tons which could be supplemented by borrowing. One major consuming country, on the other hand, is in favour of 700,000 ton buffer stock fully supported by government contributions. Buffer stocks of these magnitudes could pose a considerable financial burden for individual producing and consuming countries. The question of the size of the buffer stock is inseparable from the mode of its financing. In this regard I would like to remind you that the United Nations Negotiating Conference on the Common Fund is scheduled to resume tomorrow. The intensive consultations that I have with governments and others indicates that there does seem to be a universal desire on the part of governments to bring the issue of the establishment of a Common Fund to a successful conclusion. One of the principal questions to be resolved is the cash borrowing ratio that will be required of individual commodity agreements that associate with the Common Fund. Our own work in the secretariat, supported by advice from leading bankers, indicates that a properly structured Common Fund could finance up to 75 per cent of the financial requirements for stocking, leaving governments in those ICAs to find the remaining 25 per cent. It is my hope that the results of the Common Fund Conference would contribute meaningfully to reaching agreement on the questions of the size of the rubber stock and on its financing.

I wish you every success in the very important task of negotiating and concluding an effective, strong and durable International Agreement for Natural Rubber. I pledge you the fullest support and co-operation of the UNCTAD secretariat in your efforts towards this end.

SECTION 2

MANUFACTURES AND TECHNOLOGY

Industrialization and the transfer of technology, on which the building up of an industrial base must to some extent depend, are given crucial importance within the UNCTAD programme, for it is recognized that industrialization is essentially the ultimate objective of the development process. The extract which follows, an extended discussion of the question and of its international aspects, which fall within UNCTAD's sphere of competence, is taken from the Secretary-General's Report to the fourth session of the Conference at Nairobi. It was at that Conference that a mandate was achieved for the secretariat to conduct negotiations on two separate topics within this area, towards a Code of Conduct on the Transfer of Technology and the preparation of a set of equitable principles and rules on restrictive business practices, including those of transnational corporations. There has been steady progress in both series of meetings, as mentioned in several speeches in Part III, and agreements seem likely to be reached on both issues in the very near future.

Report to UNCTAD IV

May 1976

Although trade in commodities is of major importance to the developing countries and needs for that reason to be restructured, it cannot be the aim of a New Economic Order to perpetuate the commodity economy of these countries, even in a vastly strengthened form. A sound commodity sector must be regarded as the base, the springboard, for the further transformation of their economies, generating a large part of the resources needed for this purpose; but the transformation itself must inevitably be in the direction of industrialization. Industrial growth must indeed be the more dynamic and the more rapidly expanding element in the development process. The efforts of the developing countries to industrialize, however, need to be supported by a structure of international economic relations that is more conducive to their industrialization and to the enhancement of their technological capability.

In recent years several criticism have been directed against the industrialization process in developing countries. Industrial development is alleged to have resulted in the neglect of agriculture, to have made too small a contribution to employment, to have imposed excessive strains on the balance of payments, to have distorted the structure of prices and costs, to have disrupted the environment, to have failed to meet the basic needs of the mass of the population, and to have contributed to the maldistribution of income and wealth. But these criticisms, whatever their validity, must not lead to the erroneous conclusion that the countries of the Third World should eschew, or at least relegate to a lower order of priority, their goal of industrialization, for that would mean the perpetuation of their economic backwardness. The need, on the contrary, is to draw the lessons from recent experience and to devise new approaches and new policies that would overcome or reduce this backwardness and result in more appropriate patterns of industrialization that would also serve to accelerate the process of economic and technological transformation.

The primacy of the industrialization objective was strongly reasserted at the Second General Conference of UNIDO held in Lima in March 1975. That Conference in fact adopted some bold and ambitious goals for the future industrial development of the Third World. Perhaps the most striking of them was the target for the share of developing countries in world industrial production by the end of the century— twenty-five years from now. While their present share is about 7 per cent, the target share for the year 2000 is as high as 25 per cent.[1]

The realization of a target of this magnitude has major implications for the pace and pattern of industrial development in the developing countries in the period ahead. It implies that industrial expansion will accelerate from the rate of some 6–7 per cent per annum attained during the 1960s to about 10 per cent per annum in the next twenty-five years. Such a rapid expansion must be accompanied by changes in strategies that pay attention not only to the volume of industrial output but also to its structure and content, with particular emphasis on meeting the essential needs of the mass of consumers. These changes must seek to overcome past deficiencies and ensure that industrial development contributes more directly to the relief of such major social problems as widespread poverty and unemployment. They must also seek to exploit to the full the potential linkages between agriculture and industry, so as to ensure that growth and development in the different sectors of the economy are mutually reinforcing. Above all, they must make a massive contribution towards enhancing the technological capacity of the developing countries and the technical and managerial skills of their peoples. The rapid and accelerated expansion of industrial capacity will have major implications for the transfer of technology to developing countries and the growth of their technological self-reliance. On the one hand, it will generate an increasing demand for technology, while, on the other, the resulting diversification of the structures of production could contribute to the process of creating a self-reliant technological base.

The attainment of the industrialization targets also has far-reaching implications for trade in industrial products. Although the satisfaction of domestic needs will be a major determinant of the future pattern of industrial growth, it is scarcely conceivable

---

[1] See *Lima Declaration and Plan of Action on Industrial Development and Co-operation,* UNIDO publication PI/38, paras, 12 and 28.

that such growth will be directed to the domestic market alone. That would imply a sacrifice of the potential benefits of specialization and trade. If past experience of both the industrialized and the developing countries is any guide, trade in industrial products will need to expand even faster than industrial output. Preliminary estimates of the magnitudes involved in achieving these targets indicate that the volume of exports of developing countries in manufactures will have to increase twentyfold in the next quarter of a century at an annual rate of some 12 per cent compared to the current rate of about 10 per cent. As a result, exports as a proportion of gross output would probably rise from 10 per cent in 1972 to 18 per cent by the turn of the century.

This raises major questions about the capacity of the global system to accommodate these increased trade flows and about the adequacy of the present framework of policies. These additional exports from the developing countries would need to find outlets in three categories of markets: inevitably, a substantial part of the total would continue to be directed to the developed market-economy countries, which enjoy high levels of purchasing power; at the same time, there would have to be an acceleration of exports to the socialist countries of Eastern Europe, whose trade with developing countries has already grown fast, albeit from a relatively small base; but in addition, there would surely need to be a vastly enhanced level of trade among the developing countries themselves, reflecting increases in both supply and demand in these countries. The realization of each of these prospects has implications for policy. It cannot be assumed that the necessary trade flows will occur spontaneously within the present framework of barriers and other constraints to trade. There is a need, in fact, for a whole complex of new policies that would go well beyond the approaches of the past and would be consistent with the changes in the world industrial structure that the new goals for industrialization imply.

It should be one of the major tasks of the United Nations Conference on Trade and Development at its fourth session to lay the foundations of an adequate response to the challenge posed by these new policy orientations. So far, the major thrust of policy affecting exports of manufactures from developing countries to developed countries has been in the area of trade liberalization and improved access to markets. The quest for free access must surely continue since it is without doubt of fundamental importance. But there is at the same time a need to add new strands to a global policy in this field, based on a recognition of the fact that there are other constraints to the flow of manufactured exports from developing countries. It cannot be presumed that, once liberalization is achieved and all doors are opened, the forces of the market will suffice by themselves to bring about the required increase in exports from developing countries.

In the case of market access, many of the relevant issues are under consideration in the multilateral trade negotiations. The basic needs of the developing countries in this area have for long been set out by UNCTAD, both in its secretariat documents and in the debates and resolutions of its intergovernmental bodies. The main goals have been the elimination of tariff and non-tariff barriers in developed countries and the establishment of an effective system of generalized preferences in favour of the developing countries. These goals continue to be relevant. Although earlier global efforts at trade liberalization, such as the Kennedy Round of tariff negotiations, resulted in a significant reduction of tariff barriers in general and provided a strong impetus to the expansion of trade among the developed countries, they made relatively little progress in dismantling the protective system that has impeded the access of products of particular interest to the developing countries. The correction of this anomaly must be one of the prime goals of the developing countries in the current multilateral trade negotiations.

The generalized system of preferences (GSP) was proposed at the first session of the Conference in 1964, and its acceptance in principle at the second session, in 1968, was regarded as one of the major positive achievements to the credit of UNCTAD. Since that date schemes of generalized preferences have been introduced by virtually all the developed market-economy countries—most recently by the United States of America, whose scheme entered into force on 1 January 1976. Most of the socialist countries of Eastern Europe also participate in the GSP and have taken other measures to promote imports from developing countries. The GSP—consisting of voluntary, non-binding offers made by developed countries outside of any contractual partnerships with the beneficiaries—has been of undoubted value, since it has, over the range of products covered, resulted in the lowering or removal of tariff barriers to exports from developing countries. However, its beneficial impact has been limited and its full potential has not been realized. There are two main reasons for this: the limited coverage of the schemes, which still do not as a rule embrace processed agricultural products, and the system of limitations and safeguards whose incidence tends to fall particularly heavily on just those products for which the developing countries have a sizeable productive capacity and a comparative advantage. It is true that the schemes have been progressively improved, and that preference-giving countries may be expected to make further improvements, but the basic limitations just mentioned have yet to be overcome.

In terms of its original conception the GSP aimed, as its name implies, to afford an advantage to developing countries in the markets of the developed countries in the form of preferential duty margins applicable to their exports in relation to the exports of other developed countries. The logic of the system is analogous to that of the protection of nascent domestic industries from outside competition during an "initial" period of learning and growth. Nevertheless, in practice both the impact of and the scope for protective treatment of this kind have been reduced by the emergence of common markets and free-trade areas among the developed countries themselves, developments which epitomize the liberalization of trade among developed countries. In such situations the GSP has continued to be of relevance not so much because of the competitive edge it gives the developing countries in the markets of the developed countries, as because of the leeway it offers for avoiding discrimination against them in these markets, through a partial and selective liberalization of trade in favour of the developing countries, i.e. for products where total liberalization under the MFN principle is considered undesirable or impracticable.

It is at the same time this very feature that constitutes the crux of the problem of establishing a fully effective GSP. The main constraint on total liberalization under the MFN principle is the impact on domestic industry, and it is therefore not surprising that the partial liberalization under the GSP has been in precisely those areas where the impact on domestic industry was minimal—in other words, where the developing countries' capacity to export was not so great as to create problems for domestic industry. It is when such problems are created that the need for qualifying limitations is felt. It follows that unless steps are taken to meet the problem of competition from imports facing domestic producers in the developed countries, major progress in improving market access for the industrial products of developing countries will hardly be possible. This is all the more true in the context of the developing countries' inability to offer sizeable reciprocal benefits by way of compensation.

The above conclusion is of particular significance in the light of the new targets for industrialization in developing countries, which imply not only an expansion in the volume of their exports but also a progressive enlargement of the range of these exports. Unless the industrial structures of the developed countries themselves evolve in a complementary fashion, so as to accommodate a greater volume and variety of manufactured imports from developing countries, there will in all probability be a continuation, and even an intensification, of the prevailing barriers to market access. This raises the central question of industrial adjustment and structural change within the developed countries themselves. So far, this aspect of the industrialization targets of developing countries has not loomed large in the consideration of long-term industrial policy in the developed countries. Yet if problems are handled only as they arise there can only be disruption in trade, damaging to the developed and the developing countries alike. The problems must be anticipated and taken account of in the long-term industrial policies of the developed countries.

The need for adjustment assistance has for long been recognized in international discussions on the problems of the developing countries in manufactures. The Lima Plan of Action adopted by the Second General Conference of UNIDO[1] includes far-reaching proposals for a system of consultations between developed and developing countries in the area of industrial restructuring and location. These requirements have, however, still to be woven together into a complementary set of measures aimed at improving access to the markets of developed countries. These measures need to be given an operational context by, for example, specifying industrial sectors or subsectors that could be the subject of consultations and establishing a time-table for them. The process would need to be supported by research, study and analysis. It cannot, of course, be accomplished in a short time, for difficult and fundamental problems are involved, many of which are of a long-term nature. The social, political and technical issues that would arise in this connection are not to be underestimated. International action in this area should be so organized that it would gather momentum over time and result eventually in the harmonization of industrial development policies of the developed and the developing countries. The deliberations of the Conference at its fourth session could make an important contribution towards the evolution and implementation of a programme of action for the achievement of these objectives in the field of industrial development policies and international trade in manufactures.

---

[1] See footnote on page 204.

Another dimension to the problem of market access that needs also to be taken into account is the question of restrictive business practices as they affect both the imports and the exports of developing countries. For some time this aspect has been under active consideration in UNCTAD, and as a result of the work done by expert groups and by the secretariat, a basis now exists for the Conference to launch initiatives aimed at bringing about intergovernmental negotiations in this field. The negotiations will need to cover such aspects as equitable principles and rules governing the use of restrictive business practices and will call for a three-pronged approach involving governments in both developed and developing countries and enterprises themselves. The negotiations should also focus on improvements in the collection and exchange of information in this area and the establishment of procedures to facilitate consultations between governments in developed and developing countries where particular problems concerning their interest arise.

As mentioned before, the new goals for industrialization will require a rapid acceleration of trade among the developing countries themselves and with the socialist countries. The former is an aspect of an overall policy for co-operation among developing countries to achieve self-reliance, which is discussed in Section 3 below. As pointed out in Section 3, the intensification of trade relationships among the developing countries will require new policies and institutions in order to remove or reduce existing obstacles and actively promote these relationships. In this context a system of trade preferences extended by the developing countries to one another could play a prominent part. With respect to trade with the socialist countries of Eastern Europe there is a vast potential yet to be exploited. Here, too, there is need for a complementary evolution of industrial structures, which is rendered easier by the economic systems in these countries, in which the practice of medium-term to long-term planning makes it possible to allow in broad quantitative terms for imports of manufactured goods from developing countries. The development co-operation policies of these countries could also serve to promote the over-all objective. The supply of industrial equipment and technology to developing countries could be linked to the purchase of the products of the enterprises so established on a far greater scale than hitherto. In addition, there are increasing opportunities for tripartite industrial co-operation arrangements involving also enterprises in developed market-economy countries for the provision of technology or financing. In all respects there is scope for a system of consultations and policy co-ordination.

The question of securing wider access to markets is, however, only one side of the coin. Unless the developing countries are, in fact, able to supply the products desired by those markets, they will scarcely be able to take advantage of any improved access that is offered. A host of well-known constraints operate on the supply of manufactured goods by developing countries, and their elimination is central to the achievement of the new targets for global industrial output. They lie at the heart of the problems of industrial development. The developing countries already have a wealth of experience of the difficulties encountered in exporting industrial products: tariff and non-tariff barriers; inadequacy of credit and of access to credit insurance; limited access to technology on appropriate terms; restrictions imposed by transnational corporations on exports to various markets; and the paucity of communication and

contact with importers in developed countries. There are also the limitations sometimes posed by faulty policies pursued by the developing countries themselves that
result, for example, in inappropriate exchange rates and non-competitive cost structures. A comprehensive international strategy for trade in manufactures needs to take
account of these problems and to comprise policies—particularly those which could
be the subject of international co-operation—that tackle these important limitations,
otherwise emphasis on market access alone will prove one-sided and inadequate. This
is a field that calls for the closest collaboration between such intergovernmental
bodies as UNCTAD and UNIDO.

An area of central concern to industrialization and to the supply of manufactured
exports—and indeed to the development process in virtually all sectors of the economy—is that of technology. Technological transformation is the core of development,
and its absence implies the perpetuation of economic backwardness. Yet the developing countries encounter numerous obstacles in their efforts to acquire, develop and
apply technology, and there is as yet an inadequate international awareness of these
problems. The conditions governing the transfer of technology from the developed to
the developing countries could, in particular, be vastly improved. This is a field which
is studded with restrictive business practices and in which the costs incurred by
developing countries are exorbitant. Payments by developing countries for imported
technology may now come to as much as $3–$5 billion per year. If developing countries were to continue their present degree of dependence on imported technology for
the attainment of their industrialization goals by the end of the twentieth century, and
if the terms governing its acquisition were to remain unchanged, these outlays could
rise by 20–35 times. The conclusion is clear. There is a vital need for a vastly intensified effort to reduce the technological dependence of the developing countries, and
towards this end action is required on two fronts. On the one hand, it is necessary to
establish a greatly improved framework to govern the transfer of technology from the
developed to the developing countries; on the other hand, the indigenous technological capacity of the developing countries needs to be strengthened. The two are closely
interwoven strands of a global policy in the realm of technology.

The United Nations Conference on Trade and Development can take decisive
action on both these fronts and thus establish the basis for comprehensive action in
regard to the technology problem as a major element of a global development strategy. The first necessity is for the establishment of a sound legal, juridical and policy
framework to govern the transfer of technology and the use of industrial property. The
main elements in such a framework are a code of conduct for the transfer of technology and the revision of the international patent system. There has already been
notable progress in each of these fields. The drafting of an outline for an international
code of conduct governing the transfer of technology has already been undertaken in
intergovernmental bodies of UNCTAD. The Conference could take major decisions
on the status of such a code—whether it should be legally binding, a set of guidelines,
or a combination of the two—and at the same time establish modalities for its adoption. Significant progress has been made in UNCTAD in exploring and broad issues
involved in the revision of the industrial property system. UNCTAD initiatives have
already clarified the main issues relating to the revision of international standards and

national legislation on industrial property and set out the guidelines for reforming patent administration. These initiatives have formed the background to the inter-governmental negotiations now taking place within WIPO to review the Paris Conven-tion for the Protection of Industrial Property so as to reflect the interests of develop-ing countries. The establishment of an effective code of conduct for the transfer of technology and a reformed patent system that is more responsive to the needs of development would go far towards creating an over-all framework—legal, juridical and economic—for the transfer of technology to developing countries.

The restructuring of the legal environment would help to remove some of the major constraints on the development of the technological capabilities of developing coun-tries, thereby reducing their technological dependence. To be fully effective, however, it would have to be supplemented by a comprehensive programme of action at the national, regional and international levels. With the new framework, the way would be clear for establishing a new focus of attention on promoting the technological capacity of the developing countries themselves and on the adoption of measures needed to strengthen their technological independence. There would need to be several elements in such a package. The requirements on this point have been outlined in the documen-tation submitted to the Conference. They include the establishment of national, sub-regional, regional and interregional centres for the transfer and development of tech-nology, which could play a catalytic role in increasing the technological capacity of developing countries and in establishing necessary linkages with national centres for the transfer and development of technology.

Policies of simple import substitution have now run their course for many develop-ing countries. Often, the share of imports in total domestic sales has not lessened, and balance-of-payments pressures have intensified. What has occurred is a change in the structure of the external accounts—shift from imports of consumer goods to imports of technology, either directly, in the form of know-how, or indirectly, in the form of intermediate products and capital goods. Clearly, without the adoption of coherent policies for building up national technological capabilities, and without supporting measures that selectively link up with the positive influences of the international economy and break away from its negative influences, it would be impossible to sustain the vast expansion that is required in the industrial output of the developing countries.

Some progress has been made towards formulating a comprehensive programme of action for enhancing the national technological capabilities of developing countries. Some of the more important elements of such a programme are summarized in the policy paper before the Conference.[1] The main elements of the programme include various measures to be adopted by developing countries at the national level, such as the elaboration of technology plans, coherent policies on the transfer and development of technology, and the establishment of national institutional machinery. Equally important is the co-operative action that has to be taken by developing countries in the field of transfer and development of technology.

---

[1] TD/190 and Corr. 1 (reproduced in *Proceedings of the United Nations Conference on Trade and Develop-ment, Fourth Session*, vol. III (*op. cit.*).

There has been a significant measure of intergovernmental agreement on a number of points. These include formulation of national plans and development of policies for the integrated transfer and development of technology and the interlinking of such plans and policies with other parts of the national administrative machinery. Concrete ideas have evolved in regard to the types of institutional structures needed, their role and functions, and the linkages called for at the subregional, regional and inter-regional levels. The importance of new initiatives for particular sectors, including pharmaceuticals, and in the matter of the reverse transfer of technology ("brain drain") has been accepted. Quite clearly, the ideas about what needs to be done have now been identified in terms of concrete areas of action. However, no agreement has been reached on how to go about these urgent tasks. The developed countries, for their part, need to translate the major decisions agreed upon by the world community into positive action. This is the gap to be bridged in the process of intergovernmental consideration which lies ahead.

In the whole field of industrialization and technological transformation, the objectives of developing countries impinge closely on the activities of the transnational corporations, which in turn touch upon many facets of the development process: the production and export of primary and manufactured products; the marketing and distribution of such products; the provision of technology; banking and investment; and shipping and other modes of transport. Any global strategy for development, any new international economic order, must take into account the present and future roles of such corporations. There are both positive and negative aspects to their present role. On the negative side lies in particular the intensification of the dependency of developing countries on the developed countries and the constraints that these corporations have placed on the development process through their use of restrictive business practices and their control over the volume and pattern of production and trade, the cost and price structures, the choice of technology, and even through their adverse impact on the political and social life of the developing countries. On the positive side lies the contribution of their capital, technology and managerial skill to the acceleration of the development process. In consequence, a framework for their operations must be devised to remove the constraints on development and thereby enhance their contribution. While certain aspects of the activities of transnational corporations are dealt with in other parts of the UN system, an important contribution to the total UN effort in this area must be made by UNCTAD, given its major role in implementing the new international economic order. In establishing new directives the Conference will thus need to keep in mind the issues arising from the activities of transnational corporations so as to ensure an effective contribution by UNCTAD to the total UN effort.

In order to achieve a more broadly based economic development in developing countries, including the goals set by the Second General Conference of UNIDO, a comprehensive programme for promoting the exports of developing countries in manufactures needs to be adopted, together with complementary measures designed to reduce their technological dependence and lay the foundations for an independent and viable indigenous technological capability in those countries. The United Nations Conference on Trade and Development should consider adopting a broader policy approach than hitherto to promoting the manufactured exports of developing countries. This approach should cover not only improvements in market access, supported by appropriate long-term industrial adjustment measures in developed countries and more effective regulation of restrictive business practices and of the activities of transnational corporations, but also action by the developing countries themselves to improve their ability to supply an increased volume and variety of industrial products to the world market.

Decisive action by the Conference is also needed to establish the basis of a comprehensive attack on the problem of the technological dependence of developing countries. The Conference should consider adopting a programme of action in this area which translates agreements on policies into concrete institutional machinery such as the establishment of regional and subregional centres for the transfer and development of technology. In this regard, the Conference should consider measures for strengthening the advisory and technical assistance functions of UNCTAD in the field of transfer of technology. The Conference should also decide on the legal status, as well as the modalities for the establishment, of an international code of conduct governing the transfer of technology and make appropriate recommendations regarding the revision of the international industrial property system.

Extract from *New Directions and New Structures*
for Trade and Development

SECTION 3

MONEY AND FINANCE

This section deals with the analysis of the interdependence of money and finance and trade, and thus with the crucial importance to the developing countries of an effective transformation of the international monetary and financial system. Four aspects of the situation are treated: the problem of the external indebtedness of the developing countries; the question of resource transfers to developing countries; the question of support for developing countries with balance-of-payments difficulties; and the issue of general reform of the monetary system as a whole. It is in the first of these areas that important steps were taken to improve the terms of aid transfers and thereby lessen the debt burden for a certain number of developing countries at a ministerial meeting of the Trade and Development Board in March 1978. UNCTAD has also made significant contributions to the formulation of proposals for action in other areas, all drawn from the comprehensive analysis of the working of the international monetary system and its effects on developing countries, as presented here.

Committee on Invisibles and Financing Related to Trade

27 October 1975

I should like to concentrate here on the relationship between the work of this Committee and the preparations for the Fourth Conference to be held next May. At the beginning of this month, the Trade and Development Board finally adopted, on the basis of a consensus, the provisional agenda for the Conference, and as a result the stage is now set for putting all the preparatory work for the Conference in hand. I should very much like to see this Committee take advantage of the present opportunity precisely to elaborate upon and prepare in advance the issues that would come up for decision at Nairobi. The provisional agenda for the Fourth Conference includes one broad item entitled "Money and finance and transfer of real resources for development" which is very much at the heart of the concerns of this Committee. It also includes a general item on trends in international trade and development under which a review of developments in the international monetary field would be made.

The item on money and finance and transfer of real resources itself identifies four basic issues on which the Conference is expected to focus its attention. The first is the question of the debt problem of many developing countries. The second is the question of the long-term external financing needs of the developing countries. A third issue is that of the growing short-term balance-of-payments deficits which the developing countries are facing. There is, finally, the fourth issue, that of the further evolution of the international monetary system and the way in which a new and reformed system might be established. In respect of each of these issues, I think it would be appropriate for the Committee to reflect on what useful results might be possible and desirable at Nairobi and how the Committee could advance the issues with the objective of significant, useful and effective action at the Conference. This is, I think, one of the major tasks which the Committee should set itself at the present session.

In asking oneself what results are desirable and possible at Nairobi it is very important to keep well in the foreground the vastly changed economic situation facing the international community. This situation is in many ways fundamentally different from that prevailing five or ten years ago. For that reason, the questions to be asked, the answers to be provided and the solutions that have to be drawn up, need to differ from what might have been appropriate at some earlier period. Today we are witnessing major stresses in virtually every sector of the international economic system. The Bretton Woods system has undergone what is, in all probability, a basic breakdown. The members of the international community are faced with the phenomenon of balance-of-payments difficulties whose quantitative dimensions are quite unprecedented. The spasmodic character of international capital flows has become more pronounced, and we see from time to time alternative phases of gloom and euphoria in these markets. We are witnessing a deceleration in the growth of international trade as well as very dramatic, and perhaps basic, changes in the relative prices of commodities and of other goods which enter into international trade. We are also witnessing fluctuations in levels of production and employment in developed market-economy countries, with a fairly active and vigorous boom being followed by a recession which has proved to be deeper than anything experienced in the whole post-war period. We continue to see inflation carrying on in a virtually unabated fashion, accompanied by changes in the relationship between price levels and levels of employment, changes different to those we have been accustomed to experience in the past. These basic changes in the international situation are not, I am sure, accidental, nor are they the result of a temporary combination of unusual events that may be expected to disappear in the period ahead. The changes, I believe, reflect more deep-rooted developments which are pervading the international economy and the international community at large. They reflect, among other things, changes in the distribution of economic and social power, both within societies and between the societies and nations that form the international community.

The moral that I would draw from all this is that in seeking solutions we must endeavour to reflect these changes. We need to go forward from approaches which might have been valid five or ten years ago and seek out new orientations which are more responsive and more relevant to the present stituation. I believe that if no such new solutions are found, then the crisis that faces us will intensify and the external economic environment will not foster development but will become a major constraint to the process of development, not only for the world economy, but also, and more particularly, for the developing countries. From this point of view, I think that we have to approach the problems facing us as ones calling for action which goes beyond the current problems of the countries that are, or have been, most vulnerable to these changes. We have to look for solutions which have a wider relevance and which aim at protecting the developing world as a whole against major dislocations in the world system.

Let me now take the first of the issues which form part of the agenda item on money, finance and transfer of real resources—the problem of external indebtness of developing countries. I dare say that in a normal world, or a world which we have been accustomed to regard as normal, the occurrence of debt crises and debt problems may be viewed as sporadic events affecting a mere handful of countries from time to time. If that were so, there would be some logic in approaches which attempt to deal with these problems as exceptional ones, calling for improvised remedies relevant to the particular cases at hand. These remedies, as we have known them in the past, were by and large intended to discourage any lassitude on the part of borrowers and any laxness in the ways in which they managed their financial problems and systems. In the present context the debt problem is seen to assume a more general character. Today, the problem of external indebtedness facing many developing countries is not due exclusively, or even mainly I would say, to internal mismanagement, wrong decisions and lax attitudes. It is a reflection of more deep-seated and far-reaching developments in the international economy. Many of the debt problems of developing countries are a reflection of the fact that they have had inadequate access to official aid to support their development efforts, which had induced them to seek credits on terms and conditions that have not always been appropriate and which have resulted today in the emergence of problems in servicing these credits. To some extent, too, the debt problems of developing countries are a reflection of the malfunctioning of capital markets, where the resources needed by developing countries have not always been available to them in terms of the interest rates and the maturities they require for coping with their own situations. Most important and significant of all, the debt problem of the developing countries today is to an increasing extent a reflection of the serious payments disequilibrium that has emerged in the last year or two, in turn reflecting the imbalances in the world economy. I think that any approaches and solutions to this problem would have to take account of the changed nature of the problem. I am not saying that the debt problems of the developing countries could be reviewed in some broad over-all fashion leading to a single and unique solution. Without doubt, there is a need to look at the specifics of individual cases, but there is also a need to combine the approach to specific problems with more general approaches which take account of the broader dimensions and of the many-faceted character of the debt problem as it has emerged in the context of the situation of developing countries. There is, of course, a need for a differentiated approach. There is, for example, a difference in the type of remedy which might suggest itself for those countries whose external indebtedness today is a reflection both of their dependence on past official borrowing and of the inadequacy of flows of official assistance. For these countries there are difficulties in the way of marked acceleration of official development assistance.

It would be logical to consider measures to alleviate debt as one means of sustaining the flow of official development assistance in the current context. Mention has been made of the various ways of dealing with the problem of debt service burdens arising from past official development assistance. Suggestions have been made, for example, for a selective moratorium on debt service payments for those countries whose debt problems need very much to be looked at in the context of their over-all assistance needs. Then, again, there are countries for whom the problem reflects not so much their need for concessional assistance as the fact that they have been obliged to have recourse to forms of borrowing in private capital markets that have not always been appropriate. This has led to a bunching of their indebtedness, to a heavy concentration of debt obligations with short maturities, for which particular and relevant solutions would need to be found, solutions which may lie, for example, in the direction of refinancing debts with a view to bringing about a better distribution of their maturity pattern. These solutions would have to be sought in ways which, of course, would not in any way impair the credit standing of the borrowing countries.

These are just some of the issues which come up in the context of the debt problem. As you know, some months ago we had in UNCTAD a successful meeting of an expert group on this subject, where some initial steps of a positive character were taken. On the basis of a consensus, this expert group was able to identify some broad principles which might fashion approaches to dealing with the debt problem and also to make suggestions regarding the institutional approaches for treating this problem. I think that the results of that group could be built upon and the whole question of debt, and how it could be treated, advanced a stage further so that at the Nairobi Conference a fairly decisive step could be taken to solving this very urgent and critical problem.

To turn to the second of the issues under this broad agenda item of money and finance and transfer of real resources for development, namely, the question of the long-term flow of resources to developing countries; the most striking need in this context is to accelerate the flow of official development assistance, the growth of which has not fared sufficiently well in the recent period. In fact, it has been estimated that if official development assistance continued around its present levels for the remainder of the Second Development Decade, then the growth prospects for the non-oil-exporting developing countries would not be particularly bright. In fact, it has been estimated that if there is no significant acceleration of the flow of official development assistance to the non-oil-exporting developing countries, those countries as a whole will not be able to look for anything more than perhaps a 2 per cent annual improvement in their per capita income for the rest of the Decade. What is worse, for that group of countries, which have been categorized as most seriously affected, the growth prospect in percapita terms is in fact for very little growth and in some cases even for a negative growth. This is certainly a case for concern in regard to the prospects for development over the remainder of the Decade. It underlines the need for new approaches, for new modalities, and above all for a political will to increase the flow of resource transfers to the developing countries as a whole. At various times, and throughout the documents that are before you, suggestions have been made for new mechanisms and new instruments which might help to achieve this objective. One of these instruments, which has been discussed for quite some time now, is the greater use of interest subsidies in order to increase the net flow of capital to the developing countries. Another possibility is to find ways and means of further strengthening the capital base of the development banks which make long-term resources available to the developing countries. There are other ideas of a more far-reaching character, and perhaps of a more long-term character, ranging from suggestions for the introduction of some kind of taxation, perhaps on international trade, trade in consumer durables and non-renewable resources, to taxes even on incomes, which could increase the total of resources available for development. Mention has been made of the need to bring about a greater automaticity in the flow of these resources. An old UNCTAD proposal for establishing a link between special drawing rights and resources for development has some of the elements of automaticity. But in this whole area of long-term resource transfers to developing countries, there is now a very urgent and compelling need for some new thinking, for new approaches, because without doubt we are now in an impasse in this field, and if we do not emerge from it the implications for the development process in general and for the prospects for developing countries will be very serious indeed.

In the context of the long-term flow of resources, there is also the new phenomenon that has emerged in recent times, and that is the resources made available by the oil-exporting countries to the developing countries. I understand that, right now, consideration is being given to ways and means by which this flow could be further augmented so that the developing countries would enjoy a measure of protection against the problems they encounter in the field of resource availability as a result of external help.

A third issue under this agenda item of the Conference is the problem of short-term resources to meet the payments deficits of the developing countries. In this field, there seems to be a basic change in patterns and in dimensions, relative to what we have experienced before. Barely two or three years ago, the developing countries as a whole (that is, the non-oil-exporting developing countries) were accustomed to deficits of relatively moderate dimensions which they succeeded in grappling with in one way or another, either by the use of reserves or by recourse to external borrowing of various kinds. But today, the size of the deficits has grown enormously. From one of about $6 billion two or three years ago, present estimates set the existing and potential deficit over the next few years at $35–37 billion. This is a basic change in the situation, and there is a very compelling and urgent need for finding ways and means of financing these deficits. They are not being estimated as far as I know on the assumption of a very ambitious growth rate for the developing countries; in many cases they are based on objectives which remain, if anything, very modest indeed. The one thing that does appear quite clearly is that the existing facilities and the existing institutional arrangements for coping with deficits of these dimensions are hopelessly inadequate. The facilities that were set up under the Bretton Woods system have proved to be of great value to the developing countries from time to time, but by and large they were based on a diagnosis of the problem very different to what we are experiencing now. The problem facing the developing countries in the realm of their balance of payments is not so much a reflection of sporadic difficulties in the field of individual commodities of importance to them. It is not so much the outcome of changes in the weather, leading to poor crops; nor is it the outcome of inappropriate, inadequate or badly conceived domestic policies. It is, on the contrary, a reflection of the deep-seated changes taking place in the international economy and the price movements that are unfolding on various fronts, to which I have already referred. In this context, there is surely a need to ask ourselves not only whether the existing facilities continue to be appropriate and adequate, but also whether new facilities could not be established which are more responsive to the problems as they are emerging at the present time. There is a need, perhaps, to see the case for financing the balance-of-payments deficits of the developing countries as not just some kind of temporary support to enable internal adjustment policies to take effect and to unfold themselves, but as part of a global counter-cyclical policy which aims at meeting the problems caused by the world recession that we are now facing. It will be recalled that when the developing countries encountered exceptionally large payments deficits on current account as a result of the increase in oil prices, it was correctly and quickly recognized that this particular problem could not be dealt with by internal measures of contraction in terms of adjustment which would, in fact, have had negative and cumulative effects. Rather, it had to be dealt with through measures aimed at the recycling of resources so as to enable the importing countries to sustain their level of imports and their levels of economic activity.

I think that this experience is relevant to the present recession-induced deficits of the developing countries, since the solution is not so much internal contraction or internal adjustment on the part of these countries as provision of the wherewithal for them to sustain their levels of activities in the face of world recession. This approach would be consistent, as I have said, with the very objective of stimulating the process of recovery, because any resources made available to the developing countries to meet their current payments situations would help sustain and augment the level of world trade, and in that way contribute to the recovery process in the developed countries themselves. And if this is true, then there are implications for the type of mechanism that would need to be established in the present context. The type of mechanism should provide for a resource availability much larger in quantity than what we have been accustomed to in the past. It would need to recognize that these resources would have to be made available on a long-term, rather than on a short-term, basis and that the kind of conditions attached to the use of these resources in the past would no longer be relevant to the problems confronting the developing countries today. In a situation of global recession, in which there is idle capacity in the developed countries, unemployment and a slowdown in economic activity, the real cost of such a counter-cyclical policy—of a strengthened mechanism of the kind that I have referred to—would be very low indeed, even for the developed countries. It is an issue which thus needs to be looked at in the present context of how one is going to face up to these enormous deficits of the developing countries as a result of the disequilibria in their balances of payments.

Lastly, among the issues under this agenda item for the Fourth Conference is that of monetary reform. The agenda speaks of the need to review the requirements for evolving an international monetary system that would foster development and world trade, having particular regard to the interests of the developing countries. UNCTAD, in the past, has made a contribution to the debate and discussion on international monetary reform, particularly at the Third Conference, in Santiago. Some very important decisions were taken, decisions pertaining to support for the SDR link and also for the need to enhance the participation of the developing countries in the decision-making process. But, unfortunately, I think it is also true to say that the whole momentum for reform of the international monetary system has been lost and that there is now need to give it a fresh impetus and to outline even more clearly and strongly than before the basic needs of a new and reformed system, adequate to the needs of the world economy, and in particular to those of the developing countries. In the present system there are several asymmetries, if I may use that word, in the way in which different groups of countries have been dealt with. For example, there is an asymmetry between the way in which the reserve centres and their problems are dealt with and the way in which the problems of other countries are dealt with, and there is an asymmetry in the way in which the deficit countries and the surplus countries are dealt with in regard to mechanisms of adjustment. In a wider context, there is an asymmetry between the industrialized countries and the primary producing countries in respect of the transmission of the forces at work in the world economy and their impact on balances of payments in the two groups of countries. The developing countries are particularly vulnerable to payments problems which have their origins in inflation and recession in the developed countries. In any reformed monetary system, attention would need to be paid to removing or reducing as far as possible all these asymmetries and that the developing countries would need to receive the greater part of newly created international reserves and newly created liquidity. It is one of the paradoxes of our time that in the last few years the developing countries have benefited minimally from the creation of international reserves and liquidity. The bulk of this creation has taken the form of an increase in the use of reserve currencies and perhaps, more recently, of the revaluation of gold, an action in which the developing countries were, unfortunately, not in a position to participate. A reformed monetary system would also need to take account of the need for greater resources for the developing countries to meet their payments disequilibria, the dimensions of which have grown, as I have indicated a moment ago. A new system would perhaps also need to take a new view of the adjustment mechanism, with a better understanding of the processes at work and their impact on the balance of payments of the developed countries, on the one hand, and the developing countries, on the other. Finally, the new system would have to give greater recognition to the role of the developing countries in the decision-making process. It would have to be a system which is universal in membership and one more responsive to the actual problems facing the international financial community at the present time.

Not all these issues which will come up at the Conference would be relevant or ripe for immediate action, but some of them would be. I think that the debt issue is one on which the Conference could generate action of a fairly urgent and operational character. The question of establishing new mechanisms to meet the financing needs of developing countries is another one on which some early action might be possible. In the case of new approaches to resource transfers of a long-term character, the Conference might be able to generate some new thought and launch programmes of work which would unfold and have their impact in the period ahead. In the case of monetary reform, and also of resource transfers, the actual negotiations would continue to take place within the forum of the International Monetary Fund. But, as in the past, the Conference could give some kind of stimulus to the negotiations that take place in these forums and help by identifying the elements of the new system that would be conducive to the needs of development, in particular of the developing countries.

Trade and Development Board

23 January 1978

The forthcoming ministerial meeting of the Trade and Development Board, which will take place from 6 to 10 March, is an event to which we in UNCTAD attach the greatest importance. It will be the first meeting of the Trade and Development Board at that level and it will deal with the problems of the external indebtedness of developing countries, including the debt and related development and financial problems of the least-developed, the developing island and developing landlocked countries. This shows clearly that all Member States of UNCTAD recognize these problems as meriting international attention at a high political level.

The issues arising in connection with the external indebtedness of developing countries are, of course, not new. They have been dealt with extensively in UNCTAD and in other forums over the past five years or even longer. Much analysis has been carried out during that period, and the report of the Intergovernmental Group of Experts on the External Indebtedness of Developing Countries on its second session, summarizes the various views on this matter. If the issues seem familiar, however, there is not as yet a clear consensus on what their solutions might be. I myself think that the possible solutions in this area will require political initiative at a high level in developed countries. For this reason I am hopeful that the forthcoming ministerial session of the Trade and Development Board will succeed in moving forward in an area which has up to now been one of the outstanding stumbling blocks in the North/South dialogue.

The current session of the Trade and Development Board will greatly contribute to the success of the ministerial meeting if it succeeds in identifying the outstanding issues and the possible solutions in the clearest and most succinct manner so that between now and March governments could reflect anew on their positions and come forward with new approaches that might provide a basis for a consensus.

Looking at the issue in a historical perspective, I feel that some progress has been made over the years and I sincerely believe that we do have today the elements on which we could build a future agreement. I think that there is already a broad measure of agreement on several aspects of the issue, namely, that:

(a) The exceptional current account deficits that most developing countries experienced in the recent past are not due to domestic mismanagement or overspending. Rather, they are externally induced as a result of the twin processes of inflation and recession at the global level.

(b) Increases in, or even maintenance of, levels of world economic activity and trade require that these deficits should not be suppressed through containment of domestic development but that they should be financed through long-term flows on appropriate terms and conditions.

(c) The medium-term development prospects of the least-developed, landlocked and island developing countries and other MSA countries appear to be particularly unfavourable. Net transfer of official development assistance to these countries must therefore be substantially increased if they are to meet minimum development objectives over the medium run.

(d) The phenomenal growth of private capital markets in recent years has contributed to increased availability of external financing for those middle-income developing countries which currently meet market criteria of credit worthiness. Measures designed to improve access to capital markets by developing countries and to avoid bunching of short-term debts will not only serve the interests of these countries, but will also secure the stability of the financial markets.

(e) When a debtor country is faced with need for debt reorganization, arrangements to be agreed upon in a multilateral framework should safeguard both the legitimate interests of the creditors as well as the development objectives and the welfare of the people of the debtor country.

The Intergovernmental Group of Experts on the External Indebtedness of Developing Countries, which met in July and December last year, has dealt most usefully with the task of examining the various proposals which have been submitted for the consideration of the Board. Seen in the context of the consensus elements that I have just sketched out, the issues before us may be usefully considered under three broad headings:

(a) international measures relating to the outstanding official debt of certain categories of poorer developing countries;

(b) the scope of official intermediation in increasing the availability of private funds to developing countries on appropriate terms and conditions;

(c) agreement on the establishment of international guidelines for future debt reorganization.

The issues before us appear to be in different states of readiness in respect of decision making. The subject of the external indebtedness of the poorer developing countries has been examined exhaustively in the past two years and I think it is now ripe for a political decision. What is needed here is the adoption of a scheme that will meet the needs of all parties involved, irrespective of their economic and social systems. In the light of the memorandum submitted by Sweden at the last session of the Intergovernmental Group of Experts and the informal reactions of governments to that memorandum, I am inclined to believe that a satisfactory agreement can be reached by adopting a course of international action which would safeguard the flexibility of the donor countries to determine the volume of overall assistance and the distribution of such assistance among recipients and, at the same time, result in an increased net transfer of resources to the poorer developing countries in the form of quickly disbursed funds, on improved terms and conditions.

One way of meeting these broad objectives could be, for example, for the donor countries to agree to extend their current standards regarding terms of assistance to outstanding bilateral official debt. As you know, developed countries have agreed to provide assistance to least-developed countries primarily in the form of grants. Currently, credits to MSA countries are very often on terms equivalent to, or even better than, IDA terms. On the other hand, current debt service payments of developing countries reflect terms of assistance prevailing some ten or fifteen years ago. On the whole, these terms are significantly harder than those now considered appropriate for the poorer developing countries. A case can be made, I believe, for the terms of outstanding official loans incurred in the past to be brought into line with current norms.

We in the secretariat have examined the implications of such an *ex post* correction of terms of the official outstanding debt of the least-developed, landlocked and island developing and other MSA countries. We have come to the conclusion that, while the over-all volume of assistance, its terms and its distribution among recipient countries will continue to be determined by individual donors, this approach would go a long way towards reducing the debt service burden of the recipient countries. For example, if the official bilateral debt of least-developed, landlocked and island developing countries were to be converted into grants, and if the outstanding official bilateral debt of other MSA countries were to be recalculated so as to increase its implicit grant element from 53 per cent to 76 per cent,[1] then the total average annual saving in debt service outflow from these countries in each of the next five years would be more than $600 million.

It should be noted that this approach would raise the grant element of total past official assistance, including grants, from about 75 per cent to about 87 per cent, which is consistent with the target recommended for terms of assistance in resolution 150(XVI) of the Trade and Development Board. In making these calculations, the terms I referred to earlier were applied uniformly to all donor countries. However, in

---

[1] Payments on the outstanding debt are computed on the following terms: 1 per cent interest rate, forty years maturity with annual amortization schedule of 10 per cent over the first ten years, 20 per cent over the second ten years, 30 per cent over the third ten years and 40 per cent over the remaining ten years, and no grace period.

implementing such a proposal some flexibility should be introduced to take into account differences in performance by donor countries with regard to the share of grants in their aid flows. Thus, for donors for whom their share of grants in their total aid flows is larger, the required adjustment in their terms of past lending would be correspondingly smaller.

The question of possible international measures regarding private capital flows to developing countries is a complex one. I think it is fair to say that we have not as yet reached a common understanding as to what exactly could be, or should be, done. On the other hand, our thinking has evolved considerably since Nairobi and there is a broad consensus; I think that the subject matter must be seen now in a broad and global framework. In the past, there was a tendency to examine the issue in the somewhat narrow context of the size of the external debt and debt service payments of debtor countries. But it is becoming increasingly clear that absolute magnitudes of the debt or debt service payments are relatively meaningless unless they are seen in the context of prospects for the world economy, for international trade, for prices and for liquidity. For example, it is now realized that the accumulation of commercial borrowings by many developing countries has largely been made possible by sizeable and persistent savings on external account in other parts of the world. The fact that many developing countries have been able and willing to absorb such savings is in itself a positive factor. For one thing, transfer of these savings from the rest of the world to many middle-income developing countries contributes to the avoidance of further deflation in the world economy. For another thing, increased borrowing by developing countries, under appropriate terms and conditions, can make a significant contribution to their development.

The question then arises as to why the increased commercial debt of developing countries has become a matter of international concern. The reason is not related so much to the size of the external debt as to the form in which external financing is made available to developing countries. On the one hand, it is recognized that the gestation period of investment processes in developing countries is relatively long, and consequently the adjustment cannot be seen as a short- or medium-term objective. On the other hand, private capital markets largely comprise commercial banks providing loans to developing countries at short or medium maturities. The inconsistency between the gestation period of the investment process in developing countries and the maturities at which funds are being made available is a matter of concern to all parties involved, not only to the debtor nations. It is relevant to the stability of the international financial system as a whole. There seem to be two major ways in which the problem can be tackled. In the first instance, various measures can be taken to improve access by developing countries to bond markets. However, such measures, if successful, will have their impact only in the longer run. This has led many observers to suggest that some official intervention to improve the functioning of the private capital markets may be required. This intervention may involve, for example, the establishment of a multilateral facility which would operate on commercial terms in both its borrowing and its lending. It would make available medium-/long-term balance of payments loans and thus would contribute to avoidance of difficulties arising from the bunching of short-term loan repayments, would enhance security for

the creditors and would reduce uncertainties for the borrowers. It should be emphasized that mechanisms of this nature would also serve to strengthen and supplement
private capital markets. It needs to be recognized that the recent expansion of the
balance of payments support facilities in the IMF does make a positive contribution
in this realm. But the scale of the problem and the nature of the adjustment process
point to the need for measures that are substantially additional to the existing
facilities.

I believe that action in the fields of development assistance and capital markets
would significantly facilitate the debt management of developing countries and, at the
same time, enhance the financial system. On the other hand, I should perhaps emphasize that such measures, if they are to be successful, should go hand-in-hand with
concerted international policies regarding a more satisfactory adjustment process at
the world level, and avoidance of deflation and increased protectionism. Above all,
they should complement international measures designed to stabilize and strengthen
the markets for primary commodities and to strengthen the purchasing power of
exports of developing countries.

Apart from the need to deal with the immediate problems of the developing countries in the realm of external indebtedness, there is need also for a more long-term
framework of policy within which the international community could approach the
debt issues in the period ahead. There is, in other words, a need to reach an international understanding as to the norms that may apply so as to resolve debt crises in
a consistent and equitable manner, with due regard to the legitimate interests of
creditors and the development objectives of the debtor countries. This is the third
major issue to which the ministers will have to pay priority attention. Work at the
technical level has amply shown that there is a good deal of common ground in the
various proposals made. At the same time, negotiations in this area at the last session
of the Intergovernmental Group of Experts were brought to a halt apparently because
many experts had no authority to negotiate. This is an additional reason why the
Trade and Development Board at its current session should pay particular attention
to this issue with a view to identifying the broader objectives that could form the basis
of common norms or international guidelines for future debt-rescheduling operations.
This would provide a useful basis for the ministerial session to reach agreement on the
broad principles, whose details may then have to be worked out later on by an
appropriate intergovernmental body. Let me emphasize, once again, that in my view
the establishment of an international policy framework for debt renegotiations is an
indispensable component of a more stable and productive financial relationship
between developed and developing countries.

I began my remarks by stressing the importance of the first meeting of the Trade
and Development Board to be held at ministerial level. It is an important innovation
in the institutional framework of UNCTAD and a major initiative in the dialogue
between the developed and developing countries. That ministerial session of the
Board, concentrating on the debt issue, would be expected to be a major turning point
in respect of the debt problems of developing countries. There would be, and I think
rightly, a very deep and keen sense of frustration if significant progress was not
achieved at that meeting. As we approach the fifth session of the Conference and

prepare for a policy framework for the 1980s, for the Third Development Decade, it is extremely important to start with a common understanding of the importance of the development of developing countries for the stable and balanced growth of the world economy and of the need for a clear demonstration on the part of the international community as a whole of a common commitment to ensure that acceptable levels of development are achieved. Your work this week and the ministerial meeting in March are not therefore of transient importance but will constitute a crucial step towards this objective and towards the building of a more just and equitable international economic order.

I began my remarks by stressing the importance of the first meeting of the Trade and Development Board to be held at ministerial level. It is an important innovation in the institutional framework of UNCTAD and a major initiative in the dialogue between the developed and developing countries. That ministerial session of the Board, concentrating on the debt issue, would be expected to be a major turning point in respect of the debt problems of developing countries. There would be, and I think rightly, a very deep and keen sense of frustration if significant progress was not achieved at that meeting. As we approach the fifth session of the Conference and prepare for a policy framework for the 1980s, for the Third Development Decade, it is extremely important to start with a common understanding of the importance of the development of developing countries for the stable and balanced growth of the world economy and of the need for a clear demonstration on the part of the international community as a whole of a common commitment to ensure that acceptable levels of development are achieved. Your work this week and the ministerial meeting in March are not therefore of transient importance but will constitute a crucial step towards this objective and towards the building of a more just and equitable international economic order.

Trade and Development Board

6 March 1978

I have much pleasure in addressing this first meeting of the Trade and Development Board at the ministerial level. I am keenly aware of the unique, indeed historic, nature of this occasion, and on my own behalf and that of the UNCTAD secretariat I would like to extend a very warm welcome to you all.

This meeting is a major event in the context both of the ongoing dialogue on the establishment of a New International Economic Order and of UNCTAD itself as an organization. It is the follow-up to Conference resolution 90(IV), adopted at Nairobi, which decided, *inter alia*, that the Trade and Development Board should meet at ministerial level every two years between sessions of the Conference. I believe that this new institutional arrangement will provide Member States with an effective forum to discuss and resolve important policy issues and will thus enhance the possibilities of stable economic growth for the world economy as a whole and, in particular, for the developing countries.

In pursuance of Conference resolution 94(IV), also adopted at Nairobi, and in the light of subsequent preparatory meetings, the provisional agenda for this session deals with the question of the external indebtedness of developing countries, including the debt and related development and financial problems of least-developed, developing island and developing landlocked countries.

The issue before us is a complex one and has remained a stumbling block in the international dialogue on development problems. It was discussed at the fourth session of the Conference in Nairobi, without success; it was dealt with extensively—though yet again unsuccessfully—at the Conference on International Economic Co-operation in Paris. Yet, since then, there does seem to have been a discernible evolution in thinking and a better appreciation of the various viewpoints. The preparatory meetings for this session of the Trade and Development Board have succeeded in identifying the outstanding issues and have thus established the groundwork for a decision at a high level. I believe that there are now sufficient common elements on the bais of which this meeting can produce a constructive consensus. Such a positive outcome will transcend the area of international financial co-operation and will certainly improve the climate in all ongoing negotiations in the field of economic relations between developed and developing countries.

The total outstanding debt of developing countries has been increasing at a rate of about 20 per cent per annum. At the end of 1977 it may have reached the mark of $250 billion—or of $340 billion if undisbursed loan commitments are included. Debt service payments during that year appeared to have claimed as much as 21 per cent of the merchandise exports of non-oil-exporting developing countries.

Impressive as these magnitudes may be, they do not by themselves provide a sufficient basis for a full assessment of the problems at hand. There is now a general recognition that the question of external indebtedness must be seen in the broader framework of the interdependence of forces that affect the productive capacity of a country as well as the components of its balance of payments. A problem may be said to exist when a country's foreign exchange resources, in real terms, originating in exports of goods and services and in long-term capital inflows, continue to be insufficient to accommodate both the financing of imports needed to sustain development as well as reverse flows on account of interest and amortization payments and profit remittances. In the past, there was controversy around the possible trade-off between a downward adjustment of the development process and early debt reorganization. Some considered that, in the first instance, the brunt of adjustment should take the form of a scaling down of development programmes; others considered that early debt reorganization would be the appropriate solution if medium-term development prospects were to be safeguarded and if longer-term debt-servicing capacity were to be improved. In the absence of international norms regarding minimum development objectives, on the one hand, and the conditions justifying "debt reorganization", on the other, problems of this kind have to be—and have been—resolved on an *ad hoc* basis which could result in an unequal treatment of countries facing similar situations. In the light of useful discussions and contributions at meetings of the Intergovernmental Group of Experts on the External Indebtedness of Developing Countries, I am inclined to think that substantial progress has been achieved towards a common understanding of the issues involved and that it might now be possible to establish internationally agreed guidelines that would safeguard both the development process of the debtor countries seeking relief and the interests of the creditors.

Yet the question of appropriate remedial measures is but one aspect of the problem at hand. An effective international strategy to deal with the question of external indebtedness should also encompass international measures designed to avert debt service difficulties. Seen in this broader context, the question of external indebtedness is interlinked with the functioning of the world economic system itself. It is to the financial aspect of this problem that I would now like to turn.

The dramatic increase in the external indebtedness of developing countries has its origins in the exceptional balance of payments deficits on current account that many developing countries have experienced in recent years as a result of the processes of recession and inflation at the global level. The financing of those deficits made it possible for a number of developing countries to cushion—to some extent—the impact of external events upon their development programmes; it also serves as a counter-cyclical service for the world economy in a period of recession.

On the other hand, the financing of the exceptional balance of payments deficits was predicated—implicitly at any rate—on the view that deficits would be of a transient or cyclical nature. The relatively short maturities at which funds were made available reflected to a large extent that presumption. But against a background of several successive years of recession and unabated inflation and with no assurance of a reversal of these trends, it is possible, indeed probable, that those deficits might continue and even increase in the years to come. The question therefore arises whether the financial devices that were intended as intruments in the course of a normal business cycle may now prove sufficiently resilient to withstand the pressures over the longer run.

The time has perhaps come to look into the issue in its proper perspective. I am inclined to think that the traditional dichotomy between short-term balance of payments financing and long-term development finance, if it ever had any validity in the case of developing countries, is now at least rather blurred. The need of developing countries for balance of payments adjustment assistance on a continuing basis for a long time to come and their need for development finance to underpin fundamental restructuring of their economies seem to me to be convergent and to require functional integration. On several occasions I myself expressed the view that perhaps the establishment of a multilateral mechanism to provide adequate longer-term balance of payments financing to developing countries on terms and conditions consistent with their structural problems might usefully supplement the role of private capital markets and enhance a development-oriented adjustment process.

The fact that a number of developing countries have been successful so far in financing a good part of their externally induced deficits should not obscure the significant adjustment that did take place in several developing countries through the containment of domestic expenditure. Indeed, adjustment at the expense of the development process has been significant and widespread and has contributed to the shortfall in the annual growth rates of GDP of developing countries as a group, in comparison to the target set forth in the International Development Strategy. The cost of such adjustment to the development process has been particularly pronounced in the case of low income per capita developing countries which depend upon official assistance to finance their external capital needs.

It is indeed most unfortunate that Official Development Assistance has failed to rise towards the 0.7 per cent target. In fact, as a ratio of the GNP of DAC member countries, it declined from 0.42 per cent in the period 1965–7 to 0.33 per cent in 1976. Against this discouraging background, many countries in the category of the least-developed countries or the most seriously affected countries had little choice but to cut back their development programmes. The average annual rate of growth of GNP of the least-developed and MSA countries as a whole was only 3.1 per cent during the period 1973–6 and the medium-term prospects continue to appear discouraging. In these circumstances, it will be apparent that governments would find it increasingly difficult to meet even their minimum needs of development—indeed, the needs of millions of their people and, at the same time, to service their past official debts which, on the average, claim about 14 per cent of their annual export earnings.

Current debt repayments, of course, reflect terms of past loans committed and disbursed many years ago when the current world economic situation and its adverse impact on developing countries could not be foreseen. In most instances, the terms of past assistance tend to be significantly harder than those currently adopted as appropriate by the donor countries themselves. Thus, in the case of the least-developed countries, DAC member countries are now agreed to provide assistance essentially in the form of grants. Other developing countries with relatively low income per capita receive bilateral assistance on terms equal to or even more favourable than IDA credits. For developing countries as a group, the grant element of total ODA commitments by DAC member countries increased from 85 per cent in 1972 to 89 per cent in 1976. The question therefore arises whether the terms of past official bilateral assistance should not be brought into line with currently prevailing norms that are generally considered more consistent with the debt-servicing capacity of the low income per capita developing countries.

In my remarks, I have placed emphasis on the financial aspects of the question of external indebtedness because I wish to explore the possibility of certain practical solutions that may be considered at this session of the Board. But before I do so, let me say that the problem of external indebtedness in its wider ramifications cannot be successfully resolved in the longer run without significant progress on a much broader front. I am convinced that avoidance of debt crises and the smooth functioning of the international financial system would require that the world economy moves back to its full employment growth potential; that international trade becomes again open and dynamic with full access to markets for the exports of developing countries; that markets for primary commodities be strengthened and stabilized; and that barriers to access to capital markets, especially bond markets, are removed, at least in the case of developing countries.

I am, of course, aware that in the short period of time available to us it would not be possible to discuss and resolve the problem in all its aspects. Moreover, the issues that can be raised under our agenda appear to be in different states of readiness in respect of decision making. In the light of the dicussions that took place in the preparatory meetings, as well as in informal consultations, I am inclined to think that perhaps the Board might wish to concentrate its deliberations on three key issues.

The first issue, and certainly the most urgent one, relates to the possibility of taking international measures in favour of the least-developed, developing landlocked, developing island countries and other most seriously affected countries.

Recently, Sweden, as well as Canada, the Netherlands and Switzerland, have taken measures to alleviate the debt burden of developing countries with relatively low income per capita. These developments, as well as a memorandum submitted by Sweden at the second session of the Intergovernmental Group of Experts on the External Indebtedness of Developing Countries, have encouraged me to think that perhaps a solution may be obtained that would meet the basic objectives of the proposals made by developing countries and, at the same time, take fully into account the views expressed by developed countries with regard to debt relief—in other words, a solution that meets the needs of all parties concerned, irrespective of whether they are creditors or debtors or of their economic and social systems. In this connection, the Board may wish to consider the possibility of reaching an agreement on the basis of which each developed donor country will take all necessary measures to increase the grant element of the outstanding official debt owed to it by the group of developing countries mentioned above to a level that is consistent with current norms of terms on ODA.[1] Within this broader objective, the conversion of the outstanding loans of the least-developed countries into grants would seem appropriate.

In operational terms action along these lines could be analogous to the implementation by the DAC member countries of the terms target they have set for themselves in connection with new disbursements of ODA. The effect of such action would be to reduce significantly the debt service payments of low income per capita developing countries. Tentative estimates by the secretariat indicate that the reduction in annual debt service payments may exceed $600 million.

The second issue relates to the possibility of establishing a set of common norms that can provide a basis for future debt reorganization at the request of individual debtor countries. The subject matter was discussed by the Intergovernmental Group of Experts on the External Indebtedness of Developing Countries, and I believe that views are converging to the point that an eventual agreement can be envisaged. There are, of course, some outstanding differences in points of view mainly revolving around the balance to be struck between obligations and responsibilities of creditor and

---

[1] Trade and Development Board resolution 150(XVI) recommends a grant element of 90 per cent for ODA disbursements to developing countries. In 1976 the grant element of ODA commitments by DAC members to developing countries and multilateral agencies was 89.3 per cent; in the case of least developed countries, the grant element of official bilateral development assistance was 92.1 per cent. Since the grant element of ODA includes grants, the retroactive adjustment of the terms of outstanding loans may take into account cumulative disbursements of grants in the past.

debtor countries, but I feel that the outstanding differences could be resolved if provision is made for work to continue, possibly through an Expert Group.

The third issue relates to the broader question of the external indebtedness of developing countries, the functioning of the private capital markets and the possible role of official financial intermediation. While no concrete proposal appears to be ripe for consideration at this stage, the Board may wish to decide to keep this matter on its agenda for future consideration, taking into account suggestions that the Member States may wish to make during this session.

If we succeed in reaching an agreement in the main areas that I have just outlined, I am sure that this session of the Trade and Development Board at the ministerial level will have a profound and lasting effect in the entire field of international financial co-operation.

Meeting of Ministers of the Group of 24

4 March 1979

We would probably have to go back to the 1930s to find a period in which the world economy was in as serious a disarray as it is at the present time. We are confronted by a bewildering array of inconsistencies in international economic policy. The international community, in the first place, continues to search in vain for a reconciliation between the needs of financial stability and those of world development. At the last meeting of the Interim Committee, great hopes were placed on prospects for what was described as a better balance within the industrial world, a balance which was to be secured by an acceleration of growth rates in Western Europe and Japan and a slowing down of the economy in the United States. Whether or not this kind of readjustment will lead to a stabilization of currency relationships—and there is little enough sign even of that—it leaves a serious question as to the implications for developing countries, which have already experienced over a prolonged period the adverse repercussions of the stagnation combined with inflation that have gripped the industrial world. The UNDP/UNCTAD study[1] documents the disruptive impact of the developments of the past several years upon the economic growth of developing countries. Particularly worrying is the impact on capital formation, which has dropped sharply in a number of these countries, and upon levels of real earnings and real wages which have in several cases been declining at rates without precedent in the past thirty years.

A second major inconsistency, clearly related to the first, arises out of attempts by countries to achieve and maintain financial stability in a world of currency instability.

---

[1] *The Balance-of-payments Adjustment Process in Developing Countries: Report to the Group of Twenty-Four.*

One cannot help wondering at times whether we are running the system or whether the system is running us. Certainly the flexibility of exchange rates which, it had been hoped, would remedy the growing international disequilibrium of the 1960s has itself created a whole new set of problems, and has raised the question whether financial stability is even possible under conditions where speculative short-term capital movements can rule the roost in the exchange markets over prolonged periods.

A third inconsistency relates to the asymmetrical behaviour of prices of manufactured goods and primary commodities. Prices of manufactures have been increasing mainly as a result of cost factors in the industrial countries, while commodity prices have exhibited wide fluctuations mostly around a downward trend. I believe that the international economic system cannot function smoothly without effective mechanisms to stabilize prices of commodities and strengthen and regulate commodity markets. In this connection, I believe that the international community still needs to give a great deal of priority to the implementation of the Integrated Programme for Commodities which was intended to improve the working of commodity markets and in that context to proceed rapidly with the establishment of the Common Financing Fund.

A fourth inconsistency, on which the report also dwells, is that between the surplus and deficit countries. On the one hand, the surplus countries maintain, not unreasonably, that their surpluses are structural in character, and that structural adjustment takes time and organizational imagination. On the other hand, while the surplus countries are permitted an indefinite period of time in which to adjust their surpluses downwards, the international community insists on the adjustment of the counterpart deficits within the standard periods provided for under arrangements conceived from an entirely different point of view. Since the international community obviously accepts the fact that the structural surpluses will continue, the only effect of its insistence on asymmetrical adjustment in the deficit countries is to shift these deficits backwards and forwards from one country to another, with a deflationary impact upon the system as a whole.

A fifth inconsistency lies in the distribution of the burden of adjustment as between rich and poor countries. For reasons that are pointed out in the report, the burden of adjustment falls most heavily on those countries that are least able to bear it. Thus the over-all impact on the international environment has been perverse, and a disproportionate share of the burden of adjustment has been shouldered by the developing countries in general, and the poorest among them in particular. In the absence of adequate concessional finance, stabilization programmes have often arrested the development process in those countries and have impinged with particular severity on the poorest groups, notwithstanding international efforts to ensure that the position of these groups should receive special protection. There is an urgent need to reverse the trends of concessional flows and ensure that low income per capita developing countries are provided with adequate concessional finance from both multilateral and bilateral sources.

Finally, while the international community, as mentioned earlier, often requires prompt adjustment in countries faced with balance-of-payments deficits, it tolerates increasingly restrictive trade measures in the industrial countries that frustrate the efforts of the deficit countries to adjust. These restrictive measures are sometimes defended as a means of giving the industrial countries adequate time in which to adjust to imports from low-wage countries. In the case of textiles, the period of adjustment since the first international textile arrangement has already lasted over sixteen years, with no end in sight. No such stretching out of the rate of adjustment is possible in cases of balance-of-payments difficulty calling for structural changes. Moreover, as the report points out, while great emphasis is placed on exchange rate realignment as a means of correcting external imbalance, by improving the export competitiveness of the countries concerned, the efficacy of the exchange rate weapon is continually eroded by the growing wave of protectionism that removes products of export interest to developing countries from the influence of the price mechanism and the forces of competition.

I have listed six major inconsistencies in the present configuration of international monetary policy and one could no doubt add others. Inevitably such inconsistencies generate great conflicts and tensions in the system, and it is the weakest and poorest countries that are least able to fend for themselves in the policy vacuum that results.

The report suggests ways of dealing with some of these problems. It suggests that improvement of the adjustment process in developing countries requires the creation of an international environment conducive to this end—including the maintenance of high levels of economic activity, the stabilization of commodity markets and assurance of access to markets. And it recommends that the conditionality provisions of the Fund should be substantially eased, and that the resources available for official balance of payments support should be considerably increased. This would make it possible to undertake the structural changes required for a truly meaningful adjustment process, and would reduce the pressures upon developing countries that result from external forces for which they are not responsible or, at least, are not wholly responsible.

These are very far-reaching recommendations requiring careful study and consideration. There has been a remarkable evolution of the entire philosophy and method of operations of the IMF since Bretton Woods. In the course of that period the Fund has traversed the entire spectrum from a situation in which drawings upon its resources were subject to a relatively lenient regime that did not include any requirements for agreement with the Fund on the economic policies to be pursued by member countries, all the way to the opposite extreme at the present time whereby the conditions imposed on drawings have caused many, if not most, countries to regard recourse to the Fund as a last resort to be contemplated only under conditions of extreme pressure. It has been argued that the present rules of conditionality are actually reducing the effectiveness of the Fund's co-operation with its member countries. Whether or not this is true, it does appear that the pendulum has swung too far, and that a strengthening of the relationship between the Fund and member countries would require re-examination of the conditions now applied to drawings on the Fund.

I understand that the Executive Board of the IMF has just agreed on new guidelines of conditionality and this, of course, is relevant to what I have been saying.

While the new decision is encouraging as far as it goes, it obviously does not deal—nor was it intended to deal—with the full range of problems set out in the report. One would even have to say that had the new decision been in effect throughout the period covered by the report, the essential difficulties described in the report would not have run a materially different course. We are still very far from a situation in which it could be said, as the report suggests in its fifth recommendation, that the adjustment process is firmly established in the broad context of long-run development. Negotiations between member countries and the Fund as to the adjustment measures and policies required in connection with stand-by arrangements, whether for one year or longer, do not yet explicitly address the question of ensuring consistency between short-run and long-run objectives, and above all of minimizing the disruption of development programmes. There is still much to be done before one could feel satisfied along these lines.

I need hardly say that the work of the Fund in this field is of the highest importance to us in UNCTAD in bringing about better arrangements for world trade and development. The need for co-operation between international institutions in the solution of problems that cut across their responsibilities is illustrated in the point that I made previously about the inconsistency between the prolonged measures of trade restriction applied by industrial countries and the prompt adjustment of the balance of payments required of the deficit countries affected by such restrictions. Payments problems are inextricably linked to problems in other fields, notably those of trade, long-term capital flows, employment and development. Surveillance over and management of the world economy require much more than the kinds of consideration that are presently taken into account in the context of the adjustment process. What is needed here is not merely a reconsideration of the Fund's assessment of its own role in these matters, but a concerted movement towards greater consistency of purpose in the international community as a whole.

NEW LINKAGES AND NEW DIRECTIONS
IN TRADE AND ECONOMIC RELATIONS

This section deals with the topic commonly known as economic co-operation among developing countries (ECDC) and with trade flows and trade relations between the developing and the socialist countries. The fostering of increased trade exchange among developing countries, and between them and the socialist countries is seen as vital in the attempt to break down the current predominantly bipolar nature of economic relationships in the world economy, by which the developing countries deal with the industrialized countries almost as two blocs, and relatively very little takes place in the way of economic exchange in other directions. The attempt to encourage trade between developing countries also has strategic value with respect to the weight that the developing countries are able to bring to bear in international discussions with the industrialized countries. This section includes a part of the Report of the Secretary-General to the fourth session of the Conference at Nairobi and a recent speech, of March 1980, in the course of which a number of the specific schemes which have been proposed by the secretariat for discussion and action in this area are discussed.

Report to UNCTAD IV

May 1976

The urge towards collective self-reliance of developing countries is the expression of a deeply felt desire by the countries of the Third World to reduce their dependence on the developed countries to strengthen their capacity for joint action and to play a part in the building up of the external framework within which development takes place. Self-reliance, let alone collective self-reliance, does not imply autarchy. It does not seek to build a wall of containment that seals off the developing countries from the outside world, but aims rather at mobilizing the resources of these countries to accelerate the development process and to transform the mechanisms and institutions that have hitherto governed international economic relations.

The logic of the concept of collective self-reliance is indeed compelling. Over a long period of history the countries of the Third World have had their economies linked to metropolitan countries in a bipolar, two-way relationship, which virtually excluded their trading among themselves. While many of their demands in the realm of international economic relations are directed at removing the constraints, within the bipolar relationship itself, that impede their efforts at development, there is a growing awareness that the mere intensification of this two-way flow as a means of solving their problems is both undesirable and impracticable. It is undesirable because it might serve to reinforce the dependency relationship; and it is impracticable because it is scarcely conceivable that the existing industrialized countries will provide an unlimited outlet for the vastly increased volume of tradable goods that the developing countries will be able to provide in the future. There will inevitably need to be "horizontal" links as the developing countries acquire a greater capacity to meet each other's needs. Moreover, the slowing down of the rate of economic growth in the developed countries makes it even more necessary for the developing countries to strengthen their mutual economic links in order to accelerate their own progress.

That is why the concept of collective self-reliance or co-operation among developing countries must assume a major significance in a new international economic order. The increasing presence of the developing countries on the international scene and the evolution of modalities for mutual collaboration at the international level—reflected, for example, in the existence of the Group of 77 and of the group of non-aligned countries—have underlined the importance of the concept and given it a new vitality. The concept itself embraces two basic elements: co-operation among developing countries to establish common positions and to apply a maximum of leverage so as to increase their bargaining power in negotiations and joint action *vis-à-vis* the industrialized countries, on the one hand, and efforts to strengthen and intensify trade, investment and technological co-operation among themselves, on the other. Each of these elements needs to be woven into a coherent policy or strategy for collective self-reliance.

The work programme of UNCTAD provides several vantage points for a strategy aimed at enhancing the bargaining strength of the Third World and developing new countervailing power in the international economic system. The proposed integrated programme for commodities, considered in the previous chapter, provides a framework for modes of collaboration that would not only improve the bargaining position of the Third World in commodity markets, but also develop new markets within the Third World for both primary and processed products. The Integrated Programme takes the idea of economic co-operation beyond the concept of territorial contiguity and approaches it in terms of resources. It provides effective mechanisms for co-operation on an intercontinental, Third World scale. The export of manufactures is another vantage point. In this area, developing countries would need to work out new instrumentalities for providing access to one another's markets and, even more important, for establishing a viable framework for the creation of multinational enterprises. Technology is another major field with high potential for diverse forms of Third World collaboration. The proposals under consideration in UNCTAD have as their objective the creation of a network of regional centres which could trigger a programme of technological exchange that could play a key role in promoting the collective self-reliance of developing countries.

Indeed, each of the major items on the agenda of the fourth session of UNCTAD involves the concept of the self-reliance of Third World countries in the effort to restructure international economic relations and changes the present pattern of bipolar dependence. The economic dependence of the developing countries derives from relationships that are enmeshed in the structures of production and marketing which straddle the Third World as a whole. The emergence of the transnational corporations as a major economic power calls for strategies that make joint action and bargaining possible on an interregional front encompassing the entire Third World.

As regards the second major element in the collective self-reliance of developing countries—the strengthening of trade and other exchanges among themselves—such exchanges are at present at minimal levels. In 1974, trade among developed market-economy countries accounted for 73 per cent of their total trade, while for the socialist countries of Eastern Europe the proportion of intra-trade was 51 per cent. In contrast, the corresponding figure for trade among developing countries was only 20 per cent. Nevertheless, the long-term potential for expanding trade among the develoving countries themselves is enormous. With their extensive territories, spanning three continents, and their vast populations they have the basis, in terms of both demand and resources, for radically transforming and vastly expanding their mutual trading relationships. The Third World, if China is included, contains over two-thirds of the earth's population. A growth of national income of 7 per cent per annum can create markets by the turn of the century exceeding the present output of the developed market economies or equal to more than two-thirds of current world output. If China is excluded, the proven reserves of non-renewable resources in the Third World amount to two-thirds of the world total (or one-third if petroleum is left out of the account). One part of the Third World, comprising the oil-producing countries, has become a major lender to the developed market economies. The Third World countries are also providers of skilled manpower to the developed countries—over 30,000 migrants annually in the early 1970s.

The so-called differentiation among the countries of the Third World—the lack of homogeneity in respect of levels of development, resource endowments and so fourth—has often been cited as a divisive factor that could undermine the unity of developing countries in international negotiations. Yet it would appear that it is precisely this very differentiation that holds forth the greatest promise of effective co-operation among the developing countries in trade and in other fields. The very fact that countries are at different levels of development, are favoured with different resource endowments, and are possessed of different levels of skills and other aptitudes, provides a major opportunity for mutual help and the adoption of complementary policies of development. The task would be more difficult if all countries were in a similar situation in respect of each of these factors. At the same time, their need for patterns of development that are responsive to problems they share in common in one way or another also enhances the prospect for co-operation. The developing countries need, for instance, to establish the types of industry that cater to the consumption requirements of the mass of their populations. The scope for exchanging their surpluses with each other appears to be far greater than the possibility of sale in the markets of the industrialized countries, where demand patterns are more sophisticated. For similar reasons, there may be scope for wider exchanges of the more relevant types of technology.

While trade among developing countries is likely to increase spontaneously even within the existing framework, it is unlikely that a major reversal of the present directions of trade will take place without a conscious and deliberate effort. The historical links tying the developing countries to the industrialized countries are too strong to be supplemented by the working of market forces alone. There must be a cohesive policy and a programme of action that will sweep away some of the obstacles standing in the way of the development of mutual trade and co-operation and will establish new facilities and institutions for promoting it. The concept of collective self-reliance must not remain a mere philosophy. It must be given operational content in the shape of a systematic and interrelated programme and of a well-articulated and mutually reinforcing set of measures.

Until quite recently, the idea of co-operation among developing countries was understood to mean schemes for regional co-operation and integration. In the present context there is a need, while strengthening the regional approach, to add a further dimension in terms of co-operative action and arrangements that could operate over a wider area—particularly among the countries to the Third World as a whole. These wider arrangements, besides facilitating co-operation among the countries of the Third World as a whole, should also provide additional support for co-operation on a regional and interregional basis.

The essence of such global, Third World arrangements would be the provision of special advantages by the developing countries to one another, advantages that would be absent in their dealings with the outside world. The identification and elaboration of the instruments suited for this purpose is one of the most important tasks at present, one that calls for research, analysis and study. Already, some broad possibilities have been suggested which are worthy of consideration and elaboration, although much work remains to be done before they could be translated into action.

The establishment of a payments scheme for countries of the Third World would enable them, to a great extent, to dispense with the use of scarce currencies in their dealings with one another. This would involve both clearing arrangements and arrangements for the settling of balances in a unit of account acceptable for the purchase of goods and services throughout the Third World. Beyond certain limits, the balances may need to be settled in convertible currency, for which in turn margins of credit in such currency may be provided. The corollary would be the removal or reduction of barriers which at present impede trade among Third World countries, to the extent that these barriers have been occasioned by payments difficulties.

An international framework to facilitate the flow of financial resources among the countries of the Third World could significantly strengthen their resource base. At present, many oil-producing countries have a surplus of financial resources that require investment outlets; in the future, there may be other developing countries in a similar position. Nevertheless, the organized investment outlets today are almost exclusively in the industrialized countries, a situation that results in a net transfer of capital from the Third World to these countries. The oil-producing countries have responded to the needs of other developing countries through an encouraging expansion of official aid flows, but they have still too few opportunities for productive investments that afford them both security and an adequate rate of return. To some extent, multilateral financial institutions like IMF and the World Bank have served as a channel for the recycling of the surpluses, and the petro-dollar has played a similar role. Although there is scope for the continuance and even strengthening of these links, there is also a need for some direct mechanisms for providing the investing countries with access to investment outlets in the developing countries. Such a development will hardly occur spontaneously. It will need to be facilitated by new mechanisms and institutions within the Third World that would guarantee adequate rates of return and security of investment. The establishment of appropriate instruments could constitute an important element in a system of co-operation among developing countries.

Another possibility would be a system of trade preferences granted by the developing countries to one another, based on the principle of preferential treatment of developing country imports in the markets of each developing country *vis-à-vis* imports from the rest of the world. It is possible to conceive of several variants of a preferential system, some of them more far-reaching than others. At one extreme would be a system which affords duty-free access to all developing-country imports. This could be modified, as in the GSP schemes of the developed countries, by limiting free access to a selected list of items, subject to safeguards. At the other extreme would be a system that allows a fixed preferential margin of duty below MFN rates, as was embodied in the Commonwealth preferences system. In between there are a host of possibilities, including a multilateral round of trade negotiations among developing countries with the idea of establishing a "most-favoured-developing-nation" concept. The practical details in respect of these and other options need to be worked out, but any preferential scheme covering Third World countries as a whole would need to make allowance for, and be consistent with, two requirements: the need for special preferences among members of regional groupings and the need for protection for the economically weaker countries.

Some of the instruments for further co-operation among developing countries— such as a preference system or a payments arrangement—are in the nature of facilitating mechanisms. As such, they have a direct value and are also of political significance, since they serve as an institutional expression of the concept of co-operation among developing countries "across the board". However, for co-operation to be fully effective the instruments would need to be supplemented by direct measures that involve collaboration in specific activities. The documentation before the Conference identifies a host of activities which afford such opportunities, at least for groups of developing countries. The activities cover a wide range, including finance, transportation, the pooling of imports and, above all, co-operation in production through such instruments as multinational enterprises. The potential in these and other areas is promising and needs to be exploited to the full, which would call for a variety of new institutional arrangements and systems. These activities should not be viewed as isolated and self-contained but should be brought into an over-all framework for co-operation among developing countries, a coherent and mutually reinforcing system of co-operative policies and actions.

Expanded economic exchanges between the socialist developing countries and the rest of the Third World should also form part of a comprehensive strategy of collective self-reliance. Including China, the socialist developing countries contain one-third of the total population of the Third World, while their share of the total gross product of the Third World is in the region of 30 per cent. The growth of the economies of the socialist developing countries, the expansion of their markets, and the process of structural and technological transformation of their societies offer immense possibilities for exchanges with other developing countries in the fields of trade, industrialization and technology. Forging the appropriate instruments and devising effective modalities for economic co-operation between these two groups of developing countries are challenges to which these countries need to respond through their own collective efforts.

Co-operation among the countries of the Third World must also include measures designed to expand food production on a vast scale and thereby eliminate the food deficits of many developing countries, as well as their present dependence on the developed countries for food aid. Indeed, national and co-operative action to this end is central to the concept of self-reliance. The over-all food deficit of the Third World has grown dangerously in recent years, and a major concerted effort by the developing countries themselves is urgently needed to avoid a further deterioration in the food situation. In this effort, the full support of the international community will be required.

A comprehensive system of economic co-operation among all countries of the Third World needs to be formulated and implemented by the developing countries themselves. The organizations within the United Nations, and UNCTAD in particular, can contribute to such an effort. While the UN regional commissions in the Third World are equipped to promote regional collaboration, it is in UNCTAD that the modalities of interregional collaboration can best be evolved within the United Nations. UNCTAD has already, through the medium of an expert group and in secretariat studies, spelled out many of the elements of such a system. The system itself must constitute an essential element of a global policy for development and should be recognized as such by the international community as a whole. The concept of collective self-reliance is not inimical to global co-operation. On the contrary, it can reinforce such co-operation by enhancing the strength of the Third World countries in the global system.

The requirement of the socialist countries of Eastern Europe in world trade extend well beyond their relationships with the developing countries. At successive sessions of UNCTAD these countries have pointed to the obstacles which stood in the way of an expansion of their trade with the rest of the world and which included discriminatory treatment in the markets of several developed market-economy countries. The socialist countries of Eastern Europe have consistently laid stress on their endorsement of the principles governing world trade adopted at the first session of the Conference[1] and on the need to give practical expression to these principles.

---

[1] Recommendation A.I.1.

The fourth session of the Conference will give consideration once more to the issue of trade relations among countries having different economic and social systems. As in the past, it is likely that the main emphasis will be on relations between the socialist countries of Eastern Europe and the developing countries. The evolution of these relations must constitute an important aspect of a new international economic order. It must be seen as an essential part of the need for developing countries to modify the historical patterns of trade and other relationships which have resulted in an excessive dependence on the developed market-economy countries and to take advantage of the growing productive potential of the socialist countries for mutually beneficial exchanges. Trade with the socialist countries of Eastern Europe, like trade among the developing countries themselves, will add new dimensions to the role of the developing countries in the world economy.

The trade of the developing countries with the socialist countries of Eastern Europe has grown at a faster rate than their trade with the rest of the world and has thus constituted a relatively dynamic element in developing country trade flows. However, this rate of increase has stemmed from a narrow base. In 1974, trade between these two groups of countries accounted for only about 4 per cent of the total trade of the developing countries and about 15 per cent of the total trade of the socialist countries of Eastern Europe. The rapid growth of trade between these two groups largely reflects the results of conscious efforts to establish trading relations, mostly by means of bilateral agreements. But it is doubtful whether the present dimensions of this trade will increase appreciably unless there is a vigorous and purposeful effort to give fresh impetus to its expansion. Such an effort would require the adoption of various innovative approaches and modalities, as a part of a new policy for development co-operation between the developing countries and the socialist countries of Eastern Europe, a policy that would embody the latter's response to the development problem.

In each of the areas of trade and development co-operation the socialist countries of Eastern Europe can make a significant contribution—in arrangements to strengthen and stabilize commodity markets, in measures to increase imports from developing countries and in the field of the transfer of capital resources and technology. In some cases, such as commodity arrangements, the socialist countries could participate with other countries, both developed and developing, in common instruments and institutions. In others, special mechanisms and modalities would need to be established to take account of the systems and practices of the socialist countries.

In the case of trade, for example, its volume would obviously not be determined by the operation of market forces, but would reflect conscious decisions by governments or foreign trade organizations to make deliveries and purchases abroad. For this reason, the over-all economic plans of the socialist countries would be one of the major determinants of levels of trade. This implies in turn that a major expansion of trade with the developing countries—to be achieved mainly through long-term trade and economic agreements—should form part of the basic planning objectives of the socialist countries and be reflected in the several targets of their plans, both over-all and sectoral. The CMEA countries have in recent years made considerable progress in the harmonization of their medium-term to long-term economic plans in order to give content to the growing integration of their economies. These efforts could in turn take account of, and make allowance for, bold new objectives in the field of trade expansion with the developing countries. One of the difficulties that the socialist countries of Eastern Europe are likely to face in incorporating any major new target for trade with developing countries is the lack of knowledge and certainty about the volumes of production of exportable goods in the developing countries. This calls for a mutual exchange of information and consultation on the plans of the developing countries themselves, a process that has yet to develop in a systematic way.

The main instrument for implementing the trade policies and objectives of the socialist countries of Eastern Europe *vis-à-vis* the developing countries has in the past been bilateral agreements which set out the mechanisms for trade and payments. Such bilateralism has been of undoubted value, since it opened up new channels of trade that would not otherwise have been possible. It has enabled participating developing countries to diversify and enlarge the markets for their traditional exports, to establish markets for non-traditional exports, as well as to diversify the sources of their imports. Nevertheless, there were also constraints implicit in the bilateral system, one of which was the accumulation of credit balances. While this accumulation could in principle have been of advantage to both parties, it would have been of particular value to the developing countries if there had been at least the possibility of utilizing accumulated credit balances in their trade with other socialist countries.

Some of the constraints have since been removed, and multilateral payments facilities are available for trade with socialist countries; these facilities should be taken advantage of to a greater degree. The developing countries themselves need to play an active role in expanding trade with the socialist countries. Although the trade relations of the socialist countries of Eastern Europe with developing countries are growing, the limited number of such relationships in the past was one of the factors that stood in the way of a more rapid expansion of trade between the two groups. While the socialist countries need to make a vastly extended effort to purchase imports from the developing countries, the latter need to make special efforts in turn to purchase imports from the socialist countries. The whole network of traditional trading links still exerts so strong an influence that special efforts are needed to modify it. While the developed market-economy countries as a whole can expect that virtually any increase in foreign-exchange earnings of the developing countries will eventually result in greater purchases from the developed countries, the socialist countries of Eastern Europe can have no such assurance. This might cause no special problem if they were participants in a fully multilateral system of trade and payments that would enable them to offset deficits with the developing countries by surpluses with the developed market-economy countries. As long as this is not possible, they will have a continued interest in a two-way flow of trade with the developing countries.

The socialist countries of Eastern Europe have been a source of capital transfers to the developing countries, which have taken place under the aegis of bilateral programmes. Many features of the aid programmes of the socialist countries have proved to be of value to the developing countries. Two such features are the provision of assistance to help build up the manufacturing sector of developing countries—a sector for which it has not always been easy to find external capital, particularly when the enterprises in question are state-owned—and the introduction of arrangements under which the output of the plants established is exported to the socialist countries concerned, often in part settlement of the credit obtained.

In the present context there is scope for a further broadening of the co-operation policy of the socialist countries of Eastern Europe. This improvement should take account of the present and future needs of the developing countries. The policy could reach out on many fronts. In respect of the short-term needs of developing countries there are, in particular, two areas in which the socialist countries could make a positive contribution. One is the relief of the debt problems of the developing countries. The global dimensions of this problem have now reached serious proportions and the need for some kind of remedial action is being increasingly recognized. To the extent that service payments on account of credits granted by the socialist countries of Eastern Europe are an important element in the total external outlays of a developing country in payments difficulties, debt relief measures could be of particular value—even if the credits themselves were on relatively easy terms. These relief arrangements could be made either in conjunction with other creditors or independently.

Another short-term need concerns the exceptionally large payments deficits which the developing countries—other than the oil producers—are now experiencing. This is today a major problem which calls for measures by the international community to enable the developing countries to finance their imports. The socialist countries of Eastern Europe could make a contribution towards these measures by, for example, granting credits on highly concessional terms to developing countries for the purchase of a wide range of their import requirements from the socialist countries—a range that will extend well beyond capital goods and machinery alone. Such a step would be a positive contribution towards assisting the developing countries in the current crisis.

There is a parallel need to increase the flow of long-term capital. Capital flows on concessional terms from the socialist countries of Eastern Europe represents like flows from the developed market-economy countries, a minute part of their GDP, and an acceleration of these flows must be an important element of the co-operation policy of the socialist countries. At the same time, there is a need to improve the mechanisms and modalities that govern these flows, so as to reduce the gap that now exists between commitments and disbursements. Moreover, greater use should be made of the promising system of linking the supply of capital and technology to developing countries with the purchase by the socialist countries of the output of the assisted enterprises. New opportunities are also opened up by the prospect of tripartite arrangements between socialist, developed market-economy and developing countries. The scope for such arrangements has been widened by the relaxation in international tensions and the corresponding improvements in relations between the socialist countries of Eastern Europe and the developed market-economy countries. The question of tripartite industrial collaboration was studied by experts at an UNCTAD seminar, held in Geneva in December 1975, which was able to point to a host of opportunities in this area.[1]

---

[1] See "Report of the seminar on industrial specialization through various forms of multilateral co-operation" (TD/B/599) (mimeographed).

Another related issue is the possible multilateralization of capital flows from the socialist countries of Eastern Europe. Although the socialist countries are contributors to UNDP, they are not, with one exception, members of the World Bank or of regional development banks. Even apart from the question of future relations with these bodies, there is the issue of the scope for multilateralization among the socialist countries themselves. This should be possible within the institutional framework established for purposes of integration among the socialist countries. Indeed, a start has already been made in terms of the International Bank for Economic Co-operation and the International Investment Bank. But in the period ahead there is room for making considerably wider use of this type of mechanism.

Extract from New Directions and New Structures
of Trade and Development

Preparatory Meeting on Economic Co-operation Among Developing Countries, Geneva

17 March 1980[1]

This meeting is a particularly significant one for two reasons. For us in UNCTAD it is breaking new ground because this is the first occasion on which UNCTAD has been able to convene a meeting of the experts of developing countries to discuss issues pertaining to economic co-operation amongst the developing countries. But even more important, in my view, is the fact that this meeting will begin to turn its attention to the problem of, and the need for, implementing programmes and policies and measures in the field of economic co-operation amongst developing countries.

In recent years the theme of economic co-operation among developing countries has been gaining momentum on the political front. As far back as early 1976, when the developing countries were meeting in Manila in preparation for the fourth session of the Conference, a good deal of attention was given to the problem of economic co-operation among developing countries as part of the endeavours of the developing countries to achieve a new international economic order. Subsequent to the Nairobi session, where authority was given to establish within UNCTAD a committee on

---

[1] Annexed by decision of the preparatory meeting taken at its first meeting, on 17 March 1980, after noting the financial implications thereof.

economic co-operation among developing countries as part of the permanent machinery of our Organization, there was a meeting in Mexico City of ministers of developing countries which was devoted solely to the subject of economic co-operation amongst developing countries. On that occasion a number of possibilities for co-operation were identified and a strong request was addressed, not only to UNCTAD but to the UN system as a whole, to help in the elaboration of the issues involved.

Since then, there has also been the meeting of the ministers of developing countries at Arusha, when the several possibilities in the field of co-operation among developing countries were put together in the form of a short- to medium-term programme of action. And then, again, after the Arusha meeting and the fifth session of UNCTAD at Manila, the heads of state of the non-aligned countries met in Havana and while they endorsed the Arusha programme they themselves added new dimensions to the concept of economic co-operation amongst developing countries by adopting a decision on policy guidelines for the reinforcement of collective self-reliance.

All these developments have completed the initial phase of economic co-operation among developing countries when the importance of it was recognized and endorsed, and the possibilities were identified. We have now to proceed to the next and crucial phase of giving content to these proposals, of embarking upon a process of implementation and of concrete measures of co-operation amongst developing countries. This interregional meeting was preceded, as you know, by very useful and important meetings at the regional level on all three continents—in Montevideo, Addis Ababa, and Manila—and is, in a sense, a convergence of the regional meetings aimed at combining the regional perspectives into a single interregional format which would be relevant and useful to the developing countries as a whole.

Basically, three important issues have been identified and placed before you for your attention. First of all, there is the question of how to launch a new system of trade relations amongst the developing countries within a format of preferential arrangements. The GSTP—the Global System of Trade Preferences among Developing Countries—is intended to create, in a sense, a new system, a new framework, which will facilitate, sponsor and encourage trade and other exchanges amongst the developing countries. I believe that the concept of the GSTP is important for two reasons. On the one hand, it aims at facilitating and intensifying trade exchanges amongst developing countries through the introduction of a system of preferences. This in itself has economic relevance and economic significance to the way in which the world trading system of the future will evolve. But the concept of a GSTP has another important dimension, and that is a political dimension, because the GSTP is intended to be, and will be, a system that will reach out to the developing countries as a whole. It will be, in a sense, a measure of ECDC which is across the board. Much of the real work on ECDC will, or course, have to take place within groupings of countries at the subregional level, the regional level and so on. But if these are supplemented by measures which have a global significance, which are, as I said, across the board, this will help to give cohesion to the concept of co-operation amongst developing countries; it will serve to give content to the idea of collective self-reliance on the part of the Third World as a whole.

There are many issues concerning the GSTP to which you will need to give attention—its character, its form, the modalities for its negotiation and so on. It is my own view that the GSTP concept should be approached in somewhat broad terms, because I do not think that the concept of preferences need be confined to tariff preferences, important as these are. There are other facets, other dimensions to the concept of preferences which could also be taken into the reckoning in fashioning and moulding a system of Third World preferences in the field of trade and related areas.

You also have on your agenda the issue of co-operation amongst State trading organizations in developing countries. The basic fact which gives importance and relevance to this concept is that the developing countries do experience the phenomenon of having substantial sectors of their economies engaged in trade through governmental and semi-governmental enterprises. If one looks at the facts country by country, region by region, one cannot help being impressed by the very important and, in a sense, growing role played by State trading enterprises in the economies of the developing countries. Given that fact, it is not only important to find ways and means by which these State trading enterprises can co-operate, but we should also see how the opportunity provided by the fact of State trading enterprises can be exploited to pursue and promote the wider concept of co-operation amongst developing countries.

Also on the agenda is a third issue—the establishment of multinational marketing enterprises amongst the developing countries. Although in recent years there has been a political evolution in the Third World leading up to decolonization and independence, the economic structures of many if not most of the developing countries are still oriented towards the former colonial or metropolitan powers. The mechanisms of trade, the institutions through which this trade is conducted, are still profoundly characterized by the relationships established in an earlier period. By the establishment of new joint ventures amongst developing countries, in-roads would begin to be made into this historical system and new instruments and modalities would begin to be created which would reinforce and enhance the growing economic strength and presence of developing countries on the global economic scene. So here again there is a vast and significant potential extending to a number of items which are the subject of trade amongst developing countries. The potential in respect of commodity trade is particularly important because up to now the developing countries have retained methods and instruments of commodity trade which are still a legacy of the past. Whatever is done to establish multinational enterprises amongst developing countries in the field of marketing will supplement the whole thrust of UNCTAD and the international community in bringing about the restructuring of world trade in commodities and primary products. Again it seems to me that there is an important potential here which needs to be grasped and exploited to the full.

The theme of economic co-operation among developing countries has been gaining momentum in a political sense in recent times. In so far as the eighties are concerned, the essential changes that are likely to take place will embrace three areas. I feel myself that the eighties will witness some basic changes in the international framework of trade as we have known it up to now. The trading system set up at the end of the Second World War has been deeply disturbed and undermined by a number of events, and there is a need for a new framework in my view, that, in one way or another will begin to come into operation in the eighties.

It is also my feeling that the eighties will witness basic changes in a second area concerning the system of monetary and financial relations that has prevailed up to now. Here, again, the framework that was brought into being at the conclusion of the Second World War has been disrupted and disturbed by the march of events. At this moment there is perhaps nothing which can be described as a coherent and cohesive framework or system. But I feel that in the eighties the quest for a new system will proceed apace and before the decade has run its course we shall see many changes and many reforms in the framework of monetary relations and financial systems as we know it today.

But no less important than the changes that are likely to come about in these two areas are the prospective changes in the area of trade and exchange amongst the developing countries themselves. The whole concept of economic co-operation among developing countries will and must be one of the key issues for the coming decade. It has to find a place in every strategy of development, and it must be reflected in any changes that take place in the workings and evolution of the world economic system.

At the sixth special session of the General Assembly, the importance of collective self-reliance was endorsed. In fact, structural change and the theme of collective self-reliance were perhaps the two basic strands of the whole concept of a New International Economic Order. The developing countries saw in collective self-reliance a means by which they themselves would acquire an important place in the workings of the international economic system. Collective self-reliance was seen as a method of giving weight and presence to the developing countries as participants in the global system.

The theme of collective self-reliance has to be seen as a necessary ingredient in any solution to the crisis facing the developing countries and the world economy of today. In the past, it was possible to envisage the development process benefiting, so to speak, from the rapid growth and expansion of the industrialized countries. This, in fact, was the experience of the post-war period up to the seventies, and the industrialized countries themselves were able to achieve rapid rates of expansion. Today, it is clear that we cannot predicate the development process of the future on the continuation of high rates of growth in the industrialized countries. There are many factors and developments which will act as constraints on the capacity of the industrialized countries to grow and expand at the tempo of the past. The eighties will be a period in which the industrialized countries will be experiencing a slower tempo of expansion, and we therefore have to find ways and means of maintaining the development process and the rates of growth and expansion in the countries of the Third World despite this scenario of constraint and slow growth in the main industrialized centres. It seems to me that an important part of the answer, apart from the restructuring of the framework of international economic relations, is the pursuit of ECDC. If you take each of the issues of central importance to development, I do not think that a total solution can be found to them outside measures to strengthen and invigorate economic co-operation among developing countries. I do not think that all the surpluses of the developing countries in the field of manufactures, as they proceed along the path of industrialization, could be absorbed in the markets of the industrialized countries of today. To an increasing extent, as time goes on, a growing proportion of these surpluses will have to find outlets and markets within the countries of the Third World themselves. I do not think that the instrumentalities, modalities and mechanisms for financial and monetary co-operation can be confined to relationships between the developing and the developed countries only. Increasingly they must reflect the concept of co-operation amongst the countries of the Third World. Inevitably, no matter how one approaches the challenge of the eighties, one must ensure that ECDC, or collective self-reliance, and TCDC all form an important and increasingly dynamic part of the answers and solutions to the problems of our time.

The very fact of differentiation amongst the developing countries, which is sometimes used as an instrument for division, could serve, on the contrary, as an instrument to foster and encourage co-operation and trade and other exchanges amongst the developing countries. The fact that the countries are at different stages of development, that they have different resource endowments, different endowments of skills and different capacities to produce manufactured goods, capital goods, raw materials and so on, would all serve to make it possible to establish a process of co-operation and exchange amongst them. If all the developing countries had similar economies the prospect for complementary and mutually beneficial exchanges might be less than would be the case with the existing differentiation. So I think that we ought to look on the heterogeneity within the countries of the Third World as a possible instrument and as a prospect of enhancing the process of co-operation amongst the developing countries themselves.

Of course, ECDC to some extent would take place spontaneously. Although, to a certain extent, trade amongst developing countries is likely to intensify on its own, I do not feel that the full potential can be seized if everything is left to the spontaneous operation of market forces. ECDC has to be consciously pursued, it has to become a policy instrument of governments, it needs new instruments, new mechanisms, new facilities, perhaps even new institutions, if its full possibilities are to be seized and utilized. So we have to promote the prospect of ECDC. It has to be pursued with vigour, relentlessly and resolutely.

ECDC, of course, needs to be brought within a framework of principles. We have already witnessed the emergence of ECDC activities at a number of levels, particularly at the subregional and regional levels. We have seen very welcome efforts at co-operation amongst groups of countries in Latin America, Africa, and Asia. But there is a need at this point to spell out a broader framework of principles which would give momentum to these efforts of co-operation amongst countries at the subregional and regional levels, and weave them into a coherent system of co-operation that will be meaningful at the interregional or global level and be applicable to developing countries as a whole. There are many problems that need to be faced in this context. We have to find ways and means to give support to the weaker countries to find principles that will strengthen the efforts of developing countries to co-operate at the subregional and interregional levels whilst participating in a wider framework at a global level. These are all parts of the task that faces you in elaborating a set of principles to be brought together into a coherent framework.

I have just returned from a meeting of the ministers of the developing countries which took place in New York on the subject of a round of global negotiations aimed at making a breakthrough in what is believed to be the current impasse in the field of North/South relations. It is very significant that the ministers who met to consider the agenda for the global negotiations thought it very important to include in their programme of work the subject of economic co-operation among the developing countries themselves. And it is significant that one of the decisions taken by the ministers was to set up a new open-ended intergovernmental group of the developing countries on the subject of ECDC, which would serve in a sense, as a focal point, for the organization of ECDC activities in all their dimensions.

So, with the advent of the global negotiations and the new emphasis on the theme of collective self-reliance at the political level, your work has assumed a new importance, relevance and significance. That is why I would like to say that I, and all of us in the secretariat of UNCTAD, look forward to your endeavours with a great deal of anticipation and expectation. You will be able to provide one of the major building blocks for the future evolution of ECDC. May I therefore wish you every success, and pledge to you the full co-operation and support of the UNCTAD secretariat. As you know, the whole UN system has been called upon to give its support to the programme of ECDC.

Subsequent to your meetings, the permanent committee of UNCTAD on EDCD will shortly be convening, and the subjects which are the themes of this particular meeting will also be those taken up by the ECDC Committee. The ECDC Committee encompasses the full membership of UNCTAD. It comprises the developed countries and the socialist countries, and whatever you are able to identify as necessary supportive action for ECDC will be of relevance and help to the work of the permanent committee. So, in addition to advancing the process of co-operation among developing countries, this meeting will also serve to prepare the position of the developing countries for the meeting of UNCTAD's permanent committee, and help to identify the support which you would want the rest of the international community and the UN system to extend to future work in this realm.

Statement to the Council of Ministers, First Organization for African Unity Economic Summit, Lagos

26 April 1980

I thank the Government of Nigeria for its warm hospitality and value this opportunity to visit this great country, which has played such a vital role in the emancipation of Africa. It is truly fitting that Nigeria should host this first economic summit of African nations.

I should like first of all to salute the birth of the new independent state of Zimbabwe. You well know the enormous significance of this event and what it means in the context of the goals and aspirations of the entire people of Africa. The freedom of Zimbabwe is the reward for relentless and unremitting struggle against powerful odds. It is the expression of the capacity of a people and of their leaders to assert an indomitable will and a capacity for action. It is as joyous an event for the peoples of the Third World as it is for the peoples of Africa and of Zimbabwe itself.

Mr. President, you are meeting here today to give concrete expression to the concept of the unity of Africa; to reinforce political co-operation with economic co-operation. In the context of developments in the international economic sphere there is hardly a need to argue the overriding validity of this goal. When reflecting upon the prospects for development in the 1980s and beyond, we need to be sharply aware of the vastly changed scenario which faces the developing countries in the period ahead. The entire framework of international economic relations and mechanisms as we have known them since the end of the Second World War has been undermined and disrupted. We cannot plan for the 1980s—as we tended to do for the 1970s—on the assumption of a smooth and spontaneous expansion of the world economy, of the economies of the industrialized countries or of world trade. We have instead a new context, at once a more difficult and a more challenging one. We have the prospect of a declining tempo of growth and expansion in the industrialized countries with the implication that the development of the Third World—despite the persistence of so many historical linkages—can no longer be a by-product of the dynamism of other growth centres. We have the prospect of physical constraints on the availability of many national resources—energy is only the most obvious of them—that are vital for development. We have the prospect of the malfunctioning of the earlier mechanism that served to ensure the flow of trade and capital. In short we have witnessed the end of an epoch and stand on the threshold of a new period, a new era whose basic character would be different from what we have known before.

The need for the developing countries in this context is not one of reconciling themselves to these limitations by lowering their ambitions and slowing down the tempo of development. The challenge on the contrary is how to accelerate development to levels unattained in the past despite this changed scenario. There are basically two approaches, two answers, to the problem which the developing countries must pursue relentlessly and singlemindedly. One of these is to restructure the international economic framework itself so that the mechanisms and systems that govern international economic relations are more directly beneficial to the developing countries, more reflective of their presence on the international economic scene, more conducive to the development process. The other is to widen the arena of economic co-operation amongst the developing countries themselves so that their growth, their expansion, is not so hopelessly dependent on the fortunes and experiences of other parts of the world economy. It is these considerations that lend particular significance to your efforts; it is these considerations that, in my view, will mark this economic summit of African nations as a historic point, a historic event, in the thrust towards a new international economic order.

There are in my view three dimensions to the concept of co-operation amongst developing countries, the concept of collective self-reliance, and it is in terms of these that I visualize the significance of your endeavours.

First of all, it is amply clear that economic co-operation amongst developing countries must be founded on co-operation at the subregional and regional or continental level. This must be the foundation, the basis, of the wider concept of collective self-reliance on the part of the developing countries taken as a whole. In this context you can already be proud of what you have begun to do in the African continent. It is indeed encouraging that there are already so many efforts at co-operation and integration amongst groups of countries at the subregional level: already 80 per cent of the Member States of Africa are participants in regional groupings and co-operation efforts. In this respect you are much in advance of Asia, where the process of regional co-operation and integration has been far less extensive. And now you have set your sights on co-operation in terms of the African region as a whole. It is a challenging and an exciting concept. It is of vast significance politically as much as economically; it is a tremendous manifestation of the awakening of consciousness, a development which is an encouragement to the countries and peoples of the Third World as a whole. A great tribute is due to the organizations and individuals which inspired and processed this concept—the OAU, our sister organization the ECA, the many intellectuals, officials and political leaders who spelled out the approaches and perspectives of this endeavour.

Nowhere more than in Africa do we find the paradox of development and underdevelopment more manifested. Nowhere is the juxtaposition more stark, between an enormous potential in terms of human and national resources and the actual level of use and of development. This is a legacy of history, of the colonial past, of the several linkages that have geared this continent to other centres of economic power. It is this legacy which you are not striving to change—I am convinced that the approaches and priorities you have fashioned are valid. The emphasis, in fact the insistence, on self-sufficiency, on food, on manpower development, on transport and communications, on technology and industrialization, on money and finance—all in terms of co-operative actions and interchanges within the context of the African region as a whole—reflect the imperatives for self-reliant development in Africa. The aims in those areas have to be pursued on many points and at many levels—nationally, subregionally and regionally across the continent—each consistent and supportive of the other. Their fulfilment will require policies, facilities, mechanisms and even institutions. They must profit from the differences as much as from the similarities within this vast and diverse continent. Sound policies and correct solutions are vital to success. But, the basic ingredient as you well know is the political commitment of the governments and peoples of Africa to co-operative and self-reliant development over the canvas of the continent as a whole. It is this commitment that stands out most vividly in the very convening of this economic summit of African States. It is upon this that you will need to build in the future. The concept of an African Economic Community is dramatic and inspiring. It is a goal that would fashion your approaches and your perspectives for the future. In the period ahead you may face problems and even experience frustrations. Regional co-operation and integration amongst developing countries are not, as is the case in Europe, for example, the culmination or the crowning of a historical process where trade and other linkages had already intensified. The rationale of co-operation amongst developing countries is on the contrary to reverse this past trend of history and to proceed from a situation in which the prevailing interactions are minimal. The challenge is therefore great but so is the potential and the prospect of reward.

The second dimension of the concept of collective self-reliance which I wish to underline relates to the need to link up and harmonize efforts at co-operation amongst developing countries at subregional and regional levels with the efforts of these countries to co-operate as a larger group. There is both the need and the scope for such co-operation "across the board" so to speak, embracing the developing countries as a whole. It is indeed one of the major strands running through the vision of a New International Economic Order. UNCTAD itself since its inception has been involved in assisting the co-operative efforts of the developing countries and the subregional and regional levels—first in Latin America and now increasingly in Africa. But UNCTAD is also now at the centre of the drive to give meaning and content to collective self-reliance over a wider canvas. The developing countries as a group, at successive meetings in recent times, have spelled out the possibilities and the priorities on this front. Only a few weeks ago in Geneva an interregional meeting of experts from the developing countries endorsed a number of major initiatives in this realm—initiatives that relate to the negotiation and establishment of a generalized system of trade preferences for the developing countries as a group, to the establishment of multinational marketing enterprises and to the promotion of co-operation amongst State trading organizations of developing countries. A preparatory regional meeting in Africa provided one of the major building blocks for this endeavour, and the contribution of African countries in the future will be crucial to success. The strengthening of trade and other linkages amongst developing countries as a whole, aid programmes and measures towards this end are important both on economic and political grounds. But I am convinced that fulfilment of this goal would be fostered, should even be predicated upon, the strengthening of co-operation at the regional and subregional levels. That is why I feel that your efforts at this meeting dealing with co-operation in Africa have a wider significance and a relevance to the thrust for collective self-reliance on the part of the Third World as a whole.

The third dimension to the concept of collective self-reliance relates to strengthening the collective bargaining power of the developing countries in recording and restructuring of the international economic framework. The present framework is now in need of change and these changes must embrace many crucial areas. The world trading system embracing trade in commodities, in manufactures and in services needs to be recast. So too does the present monetary and financial system. These objectives have been critical to UNCTAD's thrust in recent times. As you know, we have been engaged in crucial negotiations on many fronts. Developing countries have rightly shown their impatiences, their sense of frustration with the slow tempo of progress. But this should not result in defeatism or a sense of helplessness. With perseverance and singlemindedness success can be achieved. The negotiating processes on the Integrated Programme for Commodities on the Common Fund, on the code on the transfer of technology, on multimodal transport, and in other areas, reflect proposals and initiatives of the developing countries. They do not reflect objectives set out by the developed countries as in some other negotiations. This makes the task more difficult but it does not imply an inability to achieve results. Indeed, after a long and complex negotiating process the possibility of success is now closer at hand. Only the other day the UNCTAD negotiation on rules and principles to regulate restrictive business practices was brought to a successful conclusion with a consensus on the final result. This took nearly three years of work. The work on the Articles of Agreement on the Common Fund has made considerable headway and the negotiating conference will now reconvene in June this year. The concept of a second window for which the countries of Africa in particular fought hard is now accepted and there is every prospect that the target for contributions will be reached. The struggle to regulate individual commodity markets has been difficult. There have been some gains but also many frustrations but we have to stay with the issues till results are finally achieved. The key to success is the strength, the unity and the organizational and negotiating capacity of the developing countries, and this is a vital aspect of collective self-reliance. This has been true in UNCTAD's experience, it will also be true in respect of the future global negotiations on North/South issues.

I have spoken of the three dimensions of the concept of collective self-reliance. I would like before I conclude to refer to a facet of this question that is common to each of these dimensions. This concerns the need to pay particular attention to the problems of the least-developed countries. This issue has begun increasingly to absorb the attention of UNCTAD. It was the subject of a wide-ranging resolution at Manila. The General Assembly has now endorsed the convening of a global conference in 1981 on the least-developed countries, and the Secretary-General of UNCTAD has been designated the Secretary-General of the Conference. Most of the least-developed countries are in the African continent. It is in these countries that one sees the core of the poverty problem. It is for this reason that the needs of these countries have to be given special and adequate attention in the pursuit of collective self-reliance at all levels—at regional and subregional levels, at the level of co-operative arrangements amongst developing countries taken as a whole, and in restructuring the framework of international economic relations. I should like to assure this meeting of UNCTAD's full commitment to this very important goal.

I am encouraged and gratified by the close and co-operative links we have not only with UNCTAD's Member States in Africa but also with African institutions. We have benefited closely from the interest and support of the secretariats of the OAU headed by Secretary-General Kodjo. Needless to say, we have intimate working links with our sister organization, the ECA, and with its Executive Director, Mr. Adedeji. We have co-operative arrangements with subregional co-operative institutions and their secretariats. We have participated in technical assistance activities in many fields. All these must grow in the future. Your programme and plan of action will point to new possibilities. I want to assure you of our commitment to help in every possible way.

May the quest of co-operation and collective self-reliance in Africa meet with all success.

SECTION 5

THE LEAST-DEVELOPED COUNTRIES

The Manila Conference gave a new impetus to the work of UNCTAD concerning the special needs of the very poorest and most disadvantaged countries of the Third World. The following speech outlines the nature of those special needs and gives some details of the programme of action to be pursued by the secretariat in the period ahead.

Intergovernmental Group on the Least-developed Countries

4 February 1980

Since this Group last met, the economic situation of most of the least-developed countries has continued to stagnate, but there have been important developments which now give hope for real improvement. The idea, which was first put forward at the second session of this Group in July 1978, of a Substantial New Programme of Action for the 1980s for the least-developed countries has become a very serious undertaking by the international community since that time. Indeed, one of the most important achievements at UNCTAD V was its decision to launch a Comprehensive New Programme of Action for the Least-developed Countries in two phases: first, an Immediate Action Programme (1979–81) and, second, a Substantial New Programme of Action for the 1980s. The momentum of that decision was maintained with the convening by UNCTAD of a Group of High-level Experts in November 1979 whose far-reaching recommendations on the elaboration of this Programme are before you.[1] Of especial significance is the decision of the General Assembly last December to convene a United Nations Conference on the Least-developed Countries in 1981 with the broad objective of "finalizing, adopting and supporting the Substantial New Programme of Action for the 1980s".[2] In accordance with that General Assembly de-

---

[1] Cf. the report of the Group of High-level Experts on the Comprehensive New Programme of Action for the Least-developed Countries (TD/B/775—TD/B/AC.17/13).
[2] General Assembly resolution 34/203, paras. 1–2.

cision, the present Intergovernmental Group has been designated by the General Assembly to act as the Preparatory Committee for this Conference. Furthermore, the Secretary-General of the United Nations has designated me as the Secretary-General of the forthcoming Conference.

It is clear that the international community is very seriously concerned about the lack of progress in the least-developed countries and is determined to make an extraordinary effort on their behalf in the coming decade. This is an issue on which there is broad consensus and support from all sides. Clearly, the new International Development Strategy for the Third United Nations Development Decade must include special and vigorous efforts for the poorest and weakest developing countries in addition to the general measures for all developing countries.

The economic situation and prospects of the great majority of the thirty countries now classified as least-developed countries are bleak indeed. Using constant dollars at 1976 prices, the gross domestic product of the least-developed countries taken as a group has grown from a level of $123 per capita in 1960 to only $140 in 1978, and would reach only $152 by 1990 if the past long-term trend were to continue.

All of us have been aware of the great gap between the developed and the developing countries, which continues to be one of the central challenges of our time, but the international community is perhaps less aware that the least-developed countries are rapidly falling behind the group of developing countries as a whole. In 1960, at the beginning of the First United Nations Development Decade, the average per capita income of the least-developed countries was only one-third of the average for all developing countries; by 1978 it had fallen to one-fourth the general average; and if the trends of the past two decades continue, by 1990 the least-developed countries will average only one-fifth of the per capita income of the entire group.

This grim picture also extends to all of the major economic sectors. For example, agricultural production per head of population has actually declined on average in the least-developed countries from an estimated $69 per head in 1960 to $65 in 1977. This is all the more disquieting in that the least-developed countries are especially heavily dependent on agriculture, with more than 80 per cent of their population employed in this sector. It is noteworthy that output per worker in agriculture in the least-developed countries, taken as a group, is now less than half that in all developing countries. Clearly, far greater efforts must be made than in the past in order to reverse this unsatisfactory situation.

The contribution of the manufacturing sector is especially weak in the least-developed countries and, indeed, the small size of the manufacturing sector has been one of the criteria used to define the least-developed countries. Manufacturing output amounted to only $13 per capita in 1977 as compared with $96 for all developing countries and with enormously higher figures in the developed countries.

The purchasing power of the exports of the least-developed countries, expressed in per capita terms, has actually declined during the past decade, from a level of $22 in the late 1960s to only $18 in 1979. It is especially worth noting that the increase over the past decade in the flow of concessional assistance to the least-developed countries has been more than offset in real terms by the decline in the purchasing power of the exports of these countries. The volume of imports of the least-developed countries amounted to only $35 per head in 1979, i.e. only one-third the level of other developing countries.

The Group of High-level Experts which met last November to review the Comprehensive New Programme of Action for the Least-developed Countries stressed that the low level and the near stagnation in the per capita volume of imports of the least-developed countries is one of the most serious factors inhibiting development and growth in the least-developed countries by sharply constricting the in-flow of necessary resources. The international community can play a key role in assisting the least-developed countries to overcome their structural handicaps through measures to expand their exports and particularly by providing concessional assistance in much larger volume.

The Substantial New Programme of Action for the 1980s, launched at Manila for the least-developed countries, stresses the importance of structural change and at the same time urges support for much more adequate standards of health, nutrition, housing and education, as well as job opportunities, particularly for the poorest of their populations. The Programme further emphasizes the importance of supporting the bold and imaginative projects that might most effectively make for fundamental structural change. Finally, the Programme also stresses the need to cushion the impact of emergency situations, so that the effects of natural disasters and unforeseen shortfalls in resource mobilization can be quickly overcome and not allowed to impede the pace of economic progress, as has too often been the case in the past.

Action to overcome the stagnation facing most of the least-developed countries will unquestionably call for intensive efforts on their own part. However, strengthened domestic efforts will require special support from the international community. In most of the least-developed countries, the administrative skills necessary to mobilize and organize development efforts on a large scale are in particularly short supply. The usual rules of the game for international assistance must be adjusted to the actual situation in these countries so that they can better move to improve their planning, organization and training capabilities and thus to achieve the capacity for real self-reliance.

A key element in the Programme launched at Manila was the emphasis on a first phase of the Comprehensive New Programme of Action, namely the "Immediate Action Programme" for the period up to 1981 when the new development decade formally begins. This Immediate Action Programme lays particular stress on an immediate effort to greatly expand assistance for the least-developed countries in order to meet their critical situation, with two essential aims: first, to provide an immediate boost to their economies and immediate support for projects for the provision of the most pressing social needs; and, second, to pave the way for much larger, longer-term development efforts. The General Assembly has just requested this Intergovernmental Group to monitor progress under the Immediate Action Programme, and the first substantive item on the agenda of this particular session is to respond to the General Assembly's invitation to donors, as well as to least-developed countries to the extent of their possibilities, to inform this session on the steps they are taking to implement the Immediate Action Programme, including particularly the steps being taken to provide immediate financial support for preparations by the least-developed countries for the Substantial New Programme of Action for the 1980s.

A second major purpose of this session of the Intergovernmental Group is to review the findings and recommendations of the Group of High-level Experts. We were particularly fortunate in being able to arrange for an especially distinguished group of participants in that meeting, and we believe that their report has moved consideration of the entire Programme forward in a very positive manner. The experts had available to them the results of a number of studies on individual least-developed countries which represent a first inquiry into the development possibilities that the Substantial New Programme for the 1980s might act upon. These studies, because of the limited time available for their preparation and the difficulties in most of the least-developed countries in undertaking a careful analysis of their development possibilities over the next decade without special resources for this task, are in most cases no more than suggestive and reflect only a very preliminary look at this important subject. The Group of High-level experts themselves urged that the work begun in these case studies and in the other background studies be continued and intensified so as to provide a more concrete and detailed basis for the further elaboration of the Programme for the 1980s for the least-developed countries.

Like the Group of High-level Experts, this session of the Intergovernmental Group will also have available a number of serious and important contributions from various organizations in the UN system, and particularly those responsible for key economic sectors. The continuing support of these organizations for this common effort on behalf of the least-developed countries will be essential.

The high-level experts, in their recommendations, have made it clear, as they state at the beginning of their report, and "the continuing prospect of totally inadequate levels of living in the least developed countries is intolerable".[1] This Intergovernmental Group will wish to consider the various specific recommendations of these experts and particularly their call for expanded external resources flows. The experts stress the need "to mount a programme of sufficient size and intensity to make a decisive break from the past stagnation and the bleak prospects facing the least developed countries".[2] Moreover, they note that "the resources required for the massive achievement of significant and progressive change in the least developed countries are well within the world's capacities".[3]

The report of the Group of High-level Experts will play an important role in the further elaboration of the Comprehensive Programme for the least-developed countries. Indeed, the third major purpose of the present session of the Intergovernmental Group has to do particularly with the preparation of recommendations on the least-developed countries for consideration by the Trade and Development Board in its own contribution to the preparation of the new International Development Strategy, as requested by the General Assembly. The Trade and Development Board has estab-

---

[1] TD/B/775, para. 1.
[2] Ibid., para. 65.
[3] Ibid., para. 71.

lished a High-level Intergovernmental Group on this matter,[1] which is currently meeting and whose report will be considered by the Board at its eleventh special session. I feel that recommendations by your own Intergovernmental Group, which is devoted entirely to the problems of the least-developed countries, would be welcomed by the Intergovernmental Group on the Strategy and by the Board itself. A text, based on the recommendations of the Group of High-level Experts, is before you.

A fourth major purpose of the present session of this Group is to begin the specific work of preparation for the United Nations Conference on the Least-developed Countries. This Group, in its capacity as the Preparatory Committee, might wish to begin its work by considering five broad subject areas for the Conference, as suggested in the note on "Issues for consideration" which is before you:[2]

(a) First, the Conference will need to review and assess development potentials, bottlenecks and assistance requirements of the least-developed countries, based on a careful survey by the governments of each of these countries of the development possibilities which they might be able to realize under the Substantial New Programme of Action for the 1980s. It is essential that the governments of the least-developed countries begin this assessment process as soon as possible so that results can be reported to the Preparatory Committee. It is clear that this very process of preparing such an assessment will itself play an essential role in beginning the planning process in each country for a serious and substantial programme for the 1980s.

(b) A second task of the Conference should be to achieve further specific agreement on providing specially liberal and flexible modalities for assistance to the least-developed countries that take account of their special difficulties in preparing assistance projects and programmes and in implementing them rapidly and effectively. Furthermore, such modalities should take fully into account the special need for such countries for support of local-cost financing, recurring costs, and programme support, as well as specific projects.

(c) A third purpose of the Conference should be to review sectoral programmes prepared by the relevant bodies of the UN system in order to help meet the more ambitious targets now contemplated for the least-developed countries.

(d) A fourth subject should be consideration of a programme of economic co-operation among developing countries on behalf of the least-developed countries.

(e) Finally, the Conference will need to agree on detailed proposals regarding institutional arrangements for the implementation of the entire Programme of Action for the 1980s, including modalities for co-ordination at the global and country level, for review of progress and monitoring of performance of donors and of the least-developed countries themselves, and for ensuring the adequacy of flows of assistance and other support for the Programme.

---

[1] High-level Intergovernmental Group on the Contribution of UNCTAD to the preparation of the New International Development Strategy.

[2] TD/B/AC.17/12.

This is the first session of the Intergovernmental Group acting as the Preparatory Committee for the Conference, and it can only be expected to begin the preparatory process. Other sessions will be needed in order to discuss and agree on the whole array of substantive and administrative preparations for the Conference. It is clear from all that I have said, however, that the present session of this Intergovernmental Group has a very important task to perform. Most particularly, it should provide the opportunity for a serious dialogue among all of the parties who are now clearly committed to a common effort to overcome once and for all the structural handicaps of the least-developed countries.

The Structure of the
United Nations System and the
Role of UNCTAD

The speeches in Part V cover a wide range of issues. They are centred on the role of UNCTAD in the UN system, which entails discussion of the structure of the system as a whole and examination of the nature of international economic negotiations, in both their substantive and procedural aspects. The close relationship between the type of activities that UNCTAD is mandated to carry out and the institutional machinery and procedures which must be made available for the organization to carry out its role effectively is explored at some length. The discussion is based on the Secretary-General's observations of the many negotiating meetings held under UNCTAD's aegis during his period of office, and the reader will find several imaginative suggestions for ways in which the organization might more effectively conduct negotiations and thus continue to be the main forum in which the quest for a new international economic order for development is pursued.

Ad hoc Committee on the Restructuring
of the Economic and Social Sectors
of the United Nations System

1 March 1976

I believe that in recent times the considerations which, to a large extent, determined a limited role for UNCTAD in its early stages are now being progressively modified. I believe that the development issue has now entered—more than ever before—into the consciousness of the international community as a major factor in international economic relations, as a major issue where continued progress is needed, progress which should lead to new understandings, new arrangements and new agreements. I feel also that the image of the role of UNCTAD as serving primarily as a pressure house for the Group of 77 is also changing. The Group of 77 was born in the context of UNCTAD but it is no longer confined to the forum of UNCTAD. In recent years one has seen the Group of 77 emerging in many of the other forums both within the United Nations and perhaps even outside it. All this means that it is no longer only in UNCTAD that the organized "pressure" of the developing countries has to be faced. It is a phenomenon that is emerging in virtually every other forum as well. From this point of view I do not think that one can avoid this pressure of the 77 by going outside of UNCTAD. It is no longer the only body where the combined pressure of the 77 is manifested and for that reason it need no longer be viewed as a mere forum which serves the purpose of acting as a safety valve or a debating house rather than one in which specific business is done.

Applied to this, of course, is another very important development. The General Assembly itself is beginning now to take a particular interest in economic and social affairs. The sixth special session was a very strong manifestation of this trend. So, also, was the seventh special session. In a sense the General Assembly is now playing the role that UNCTAD itself and its Conference used to play in the past—the role of setting out general policies, of formulating priorities, of establishing guidelines, of determining the broad thrust which the international community should make. In this context there is now a new opportunity for UNCTAD, an opportunity to serve as the instrument of the General Assembly, to follow up the broader policies enunciated by it, to take them up for further elaboration, to concretize them and to translate them into specific agreements through a process of consultation and negotiation. This is a process that could indeed be best carried out with the help of the expertise that a body like UNCTAD can provide, expertise which is contained both in its intergovernmental machinery and in its secretariat. So in the new setting there is this opportunity for UNCTAD to respond to the new responsibilities which the General Assembly has itself undertaken and to serve as its instrument, its negotiating arm, in the area of trade and international economic co-operation.

I should like to take advantage of this opportunity to give my reactions to the proposals of the UN system that were made by the Committee of Experts, the Group of 25. The Group of Experts, if I understood their proposals correctly, envisaged the establishment of some kind of centralized structure within the UN system which could take an overview of the broad process of development and of the part which the United Nations is playing in that process. From the point of view of this latter objective, the report suggested a merging of various elements of the system which at present appeared to be somewhat fragmented, and proposed the creation of a centralized unit dealing with research and policy, covering virtually the whole canvas of development issues. At the same time, the expert group envisaged the continued functioning, and perhaps the strengthening, of bodies charged with different sectors of the international economy and even considered the possibility—although, if I remember aright they did not make a firm recommendation on it—of the eventual establishment of an international trade organization as a new sectoral body.

Now, as far as UNCTAD is concerned, the ambiguity lies in the fact that, if UNCTAD were to merge in one way or another into a new centralized structure within the UN secretariat, it would not be available for a merger, or for evolving, into an international trade organization. It seems to me that the one merger is somewhat incompatible with the other. The expert group also made a second observation about which, again, I encountered some difficulty. The expert group suggested that the new central structure that it was advocating should be given an opportunity of proving itself during an initial period of two years. This was described in the report as "an insurance policy". Pending that opportunity to prove itself, the Group suggested that UNCTAD should remain as it is without any part of it being merged into the central structure. Well, I had the difficulty of visualizing how the proposed central structure over this two-year period could, in fact, prove its efficacy if UNCTAD remained as it was and the central structure did not deal with some of the basic issues in the field of development with which UNCTAD is now concerned. If, on the other hand, some aspects of UNCTAD's work were taken over by the central structure, then, of course, UNCTAD would not remain as it is. On the contrary, it would be considerably weakened.

This led me to reflect on the possibility of envisaging for UNCTAD a role which does not altogether eschew some of the constructive suggestions made in the Report of the Group of Experts. Thus, I have no views on the desirability or otherwise of the suggestion to centralize the operational functions of the UN system. But, in regard to its work in the field of development, I feel that it would be useful to make a distinction between two kinds of contribution which the United Nations is making. If one reflects on this one finds that, on the one hand, the United Nations is involved in a massive effort of giving guidance, financial assistance and technical aid in respect of issues where the action and the decision making is primarily national. This is true of many of the subjects which lie at the core of the development process and for which the UN system has been giving support through technical assistance and through policy guidance by several departments of the system. If one looks at the range of issues covered by the UN system, ranging from population to water control, from food production to industrial structures, from planning to national resource management and so on, it is evident that a major effort of the United Nations is to help national efforts, to help decision making at the national level. On the other hand, there are those aspects of the development process where the action is primarily international, where the decision making is international, aspects which cover what I call the international framework for development, the external environment within which development takes place. Here you enter into the area of relations between the States, calling for continuous negotiations brought about through processes of consultation, discussion and even hard bargaining. In this area the role of the UN system has been to foster, to make possible, to service, the task of intergovernmental negotiations leading hopefully to new arrangements and new agreements.

I feel that in any restructuring of the UN system it would be useful to keep this distinction in mind although, of course, it is not a hard and fast one, for there are inevitably areas of overlap, there are obvious linkages, between the two. From this point of view I feel that perhaps the UN system needs a three-pronged division, one which is concerned with operational activities, technical assistance, capital aid and so on, another which is concerned with the substantive policy guidance which the UN system can give to countries *vis-à-vis* their national effort, and a third which is concerned with the negotiating function of the United Nations pertaining to the reform and revision of the international framework for development. I feel that a triple structure of the United Nations reflecting these distinctions might be of some value in considering the way in which the system as a whole might evolve. Now UNCTAD has, of course, to a large extent been that part of the UN system which has concerned itself with the international framework for development. I think that in the period ahead we ought to ask ourselves how this role of UNCTAD could be more clearly identified and further reinforced and strengthened so that UNCTAD could serve the UN system more effectively and efficiently than it has done in the past. If, for example, one looks to the aftermath of the Paris Conference there would undoubtedly remain a need for a continuation of the kind of discussion, of the type of consultations, that have been launched. After the conclusion of the Paris dialogue there would need to be some forum which could, so to speak, pick up the threads of that discussion, and I believe that it would be proper for this body to be within the UN system rather than outside it. So if one looks at the future role which a body like UNCTAD could play there are many possibilities, there exists a great potential and there is a need to reflect these opportunities in the specific suggestions that are being made for the restructuring of that body.

On two things I am fairly clear in my mind. One is that UNCTAD would need more than ever before in the period ahead to maintain and strengthen the relationship and link it has with the General Assembly. I think it is right and proper that the General Assembly should be the body which gives the political orientation to policy, which gives the push, which gives the thrust. It should be for UNCTAD to respond to this and to serve the General Assembly by elaborating and following up the general policy roles which it has proclaimed. Likewise, I feel also that *vis-à-vis* its relationship with the Economic and Social Council there is nothing in what I have visualized that should preclude the Council from playing the role it was intended to play as the co-ordinator of the whole system, looking after not only the international framework for development but also the work of the United Nations in regard to the national issues and in regard to its operational activities. I see that in any future restructuring of the United Nations it would be quite consistent to enhance the role of a body like UNCTAD as a negotiating instrument whilst the Economic and Social Council serves as the co-ordinating authority of the United Nations system in the economic and social field.

There is one last but important issue I should like to refer to. The agenda for UNCTAD since its very inception—from the first Conference itself—has included the proposal for the establishment of what was then called an international trade organization. This proposal has been under review for a considerable time and I believe that it will continue to figure on the agenda for UNCTAD and particularly at the fourth session of the Conference in Nairobi. Not so long ago I presented to the Trade and Development Board the thinking of the UNCTAD secretariat on the issue of what we call a comprehensive trade organization. I indicated there that since the first Conference there have been many changes in the international scene which make it pertinent to reconsider the need for moving towards the establishment of a comprehensive trade organization. The present institutional structure in the field of world trade and development is somewhat fragmented. We have UNCTAD dealing with many dimensions of the problem of trade and development and we have GATT dealing with some of the contractual aspects of international commercial policy. In the period ahead I think it will be important for the international community to ask itself the question whether the earlier proposal to have a single organization dealing with the whole field of trade and development should not be revived.

After all, there are many changes in the world's scene which make it necessary to reconsider some of the "rules of the game" which underlie the present arrangements governing international trade. When the GATT was originally formulated, the socialist countries were very much on the periphery of international economic relations, and their needs and problems were not taken account of in the rules of the game that were then established. The concerns of the developing countries did not also loom large at that time. Since then, of course, the requirements of these groups of countries have assumed a new importance. Some of them have been recognized to some extent in the legal instrument of GATT but more by way of modifications, adaptations, waivers and exemptions rather than by a reconsideration of the central structure of the rules of the game themselves. I think that at some point the international community will need to ask itself whether these rules that were formulated many decades ago continue to be relevant in their present form—even for the developed market economy countries— whether they are not in need of revision, reappraisal and restructuring and whether, eventually, a new set of rules of the game would not be needed, rules which would also need to be reflected in a new organization which is not just UNCTAD absorbing GATT or GATT absorbing UNCTAD but one which represents a merger of both UNCTAD and the GATT.

I believe that the need to consider this issue of a comprehensive trade organization, dealing not only with trade in its narrower commercial dimensions, but also with the wider aspect of trade and international economic co-operation, or trade and develop- ment, will assume significance in the period ahead. I know that it may be difficult to bring about structural changes as long as the multilateral trade negotiations are in progress. But there is, of course, a need to look to the period beyond that and to start the process of giving consideration to the evolution and eventual creation of a new comprehensive organization in the field of trade and development or trade and inter- national co-operation. The thinking that I have regarding the immediate strengthen- ing of UNCTAD as a negotiating instrument of the General Assembly does not, of course, assume a decision regarding the creation of a comprehensive trade organiz- ation but it must clearly be consistent with it, and permit an eventual movement towards such an organization.

Ad hoc Intergovernmental Committee on the Rationalization of UNCTAD's Machinery

7 February 1980

We are all aware of the changes that have taken place within UNCTAD arising out of the new emphasis in recent years on the resolution of issues through a process of negotiation. I think that this a welcome evolution. I have on every occasion under- lined that UNCTAD has two faces so to speak. It must play the role of being a source of new ideas, a generator of new thinking, a source which provides stimulus to govern- ments and to the international community in regard to the issues at stake and the solutions or approaches that might help in dealing with them.

As time has gone by we have also increasingly placed a sharp focus on the other face of UNCTAD, and that is that it should be not only a forum for debate but also one in which serious business is done, where concrete agreements are arrived at, decisions are taken, and arrangements adopted, some of them of a complex character. At all times UNCTAD needs to retain the importance of each of these aspects which are inherent in its nature.

I have been giving thought to some of the basic problems which we encounter in fulfilling each of these responsibilities and in responding to the demands made of us in terms of each of these aspects. I think that it would be helpful if I were to think aloud rather than make definitive proposals and to express to you as frankly as I can how I see the various issues as they concern the future work of UNCTAD.

In reflecting on the role of UNCTAD one of the first thoughts that comes to mind is that we are not an organization or a secretariat which is engaged in a task of day-to-day decision making. We are not administering programmes in a routine fash- ion, a process which would call for day-to-day decisions of one kind or another. We are not an organization which is administering or exercising control over any policy; we are not issuing permits; we are not issuing warrants or licences which are the basis for other actions. The way in which the organization and the secretariat are structured cannot parallel the manner in which an organization with a different kind of task would be structured. Our essential role is to service an intergovernmental body which in turn sets up other intergovernmental bodies, sometimes for debate, sometimes for negotiation. And it is inherent in that task that the way in which we respond to the demands placed upon us needs to have a certain degree of resilience or flexibility, reflecting the nature of those demands. One conclusion that we have come to is that we cannot structure UNCTAD in a bureaucratic fashion, to discharge routine responsibilities, particularly of an administrative kind. We have to structure UNCTAD in order to meet the needs of a multilateral forum whose primary task is providing facilities for the consideration of major international issues, and where relevant facilitating decisions.

One has also to take into account the fact that, even amongst Member Governments, there may be different conceptions of what is meant by the "effectiveness" of UNCTAD. Some governments would like to see UNCTAD playing a highly activist role, spearheading the changes in international economic relations which call for responses from Member States. This is a process in which some groups or countries may have to make concessions, agree to changes in the *status quo*, and in which other groups of countries are seeking new ground on which to move forward. It is inherent in this task that the governments' approach to the role of the organization would tend to be influenced by the extent to which they share in the perceptions which underlie the essential work of UNCTAD. You can structure UNCTAD to make it very effective as a spearhead for the implementation as rapidly as possible of the concepts of a new international economic order. You can equally structure UNCTAD in a way which makes it take a somewhat more cautious and conservative position, in which the tempo of change would reflect the difficulties and the varying attitudes of governments. Thus we have to recognize the fact that it is not going to be easy to obtain a common perception on the part of governments as to really how UNCTAD should be structured in order to enhance its delivery capacity; there are likely to be divergent views of what this delivery capacity should be.

I feel myself that, although the problem which has arisen lies in the enormous escalation in the workload of UNCTAD, in the proliferation of meetings, in the demands made on the time of delegations and the capacities of the secretariat, and so on, this phenomenon is not inherently a negative development or something to be deplored. I consider it a positive sign that an increasing number of issues are coming up for discussion, debate and negotiation within UNCTAD. Had there not been decisions by governments to try to establish a Common Fund to implement an Integrated Programme for Commodities calling for discussions and arrangements for eighteen products, to establish a code of conduct on the transfer of technology, to work towards the adoption of universally applicable rules and practices on restrictive business practices, to work towards a convention on multimodal transport and so on, then clearly the workload on UNCTAD would to that extent have been reduced. We would have seen a much smaller number of meetings and the pressure on delegations and the secretariat would have been immensely reduced. Nevertheless, we would not be playing the role which is really expected of us, and that is to make progress in the area of improving the international economic framework. So we ought not to be too self-critical because heavy demands are being made on the organization. This is a reflection of the way in which issues have evolved in the international context and of the fact that UNCTAD has tried to respond to new challenges. I do not think that the problem is that too many issues have been brought up for negotiation in UNCTAD. The problem is perhaps that once certain issues have been brought for negotiation this process itself has taken an inordinate length of time, has not been organized and structured in an efficient fashion, and that, as a result, the goal itself has been retarded, leading to a great deal of disillusionment and frustration. I believe that it is important to be clear as to what the problem is. In my view, it is not that we are being asked to take up a number of important issues for negotiation and that we have set up mechanisms to undertake this task. The problem is that these mechanisms themselves are not functioning as effectively and as rapidly as they might. This is the problem to which we should address ourselves in order to see whether we can make the negotiating process more decisive and more effective.

The reasons for the somewhat protracted, time-consuming processes of negotiation that we have experienced fall into two categories. On the one hand, we ought to recognize that, in many cases, what we are trying to arrive at is not a resolution but a complex agreement incorporated in a lengthy text of a legal character, calling for ratification by Member Governments. Inevitably there is going to be a requirement of time before the final result can be achieved. The second type of reason behind the delays and difficulties is logistical. I am not exaggerating when I say that the pace at which the international community is able to progress in arriving at new decisions *is* limited by the logistical capabilities of the UN system, and that is one reason why decision making is taking so long.

As to the substantive problems, I feel that much more could be done to make faster progress at actual negotiating conferences or preparatory meetings if there were a greater degree of pre-conference preparation, exchanges of views and consultations, not only between the secretariat and Member Governments but also among Member Governments. I am afraid that this process is at the moment minimal. The secretariat's own ability to play a role in a process of pre-conference preparation of issues, not in the sense of document preparation but in the sense of helping governments to narrow the gaps between them, is not what it could be. That is why I suggest that if the secretariat were equipped and geared to play a more effective role in helping to identify issues and to move government positions close to each other—partly by maintaining closer contact with capitals—the issues themselves would be more advanced when they are brought to the negotiating table. On the part of governments, too, the way in which issues are prepared for discussion prior to a negotiation leaves much room for improvement. It is no secret that, although the time given for negotiating exercises is relatively limited, sometimes two or three weeks, a great deal of this time is taken up by the groups themselves in preparing their positions. It has struck me very forcibly—and I am sorry to have to say this—that actual interchanges between groups of governments of a negotiating kind are getting less and less, and more and more time of negotiating conferences and other meetings is taken up within the groups in their efforts to arrive at common positions. Usually it is only in the latter stages of a conference that there are any effective exchanges of a negotiating character on the part of governments. We are following a pattern now in which there is a plenary in which some general statements are made and then a long period of conference time is taken when the groups are in caucus trying to arrive at common positions and when these common positions are eventually reached we are at the concluding stages of the conference. No wonder that the process of negotiation and the final resolution of issues takes time. To some extent this can be alleviated, if not solved altogether, if the groups themselves are organized and have more capacity and more assistance and facilities to enable them to undertake the preparations prior to a conference. But even given the best of pre-conference work, we have to face the fact that it is only when a conference convenes that we have the whole participation of Member Governments, including representatives from capitals. And one often finds that the work done by groups in caucus prior to the conference has to be reopened in order to respond to the concerns and needs of the delegations accredited to the conference itself. I do not know how this problem can be resolved but it is a problem—and one that lies at the heart of a good deal of the delay and difficulty that we have experienced in arriving at some kind of decision. A conference once adjourned can take six to nine months to reconvene with the prospects of similar delays if further rounds are needed. In this way, a year or two could easily pass by and in the meantime there is a chorus of complaints about the slow tempo of progress.

As to the logistical side, it is proper for this Committee and for all governments to ask themselves how this logistical capacity of the organization could be improved. I was very happy to see a number of very constructive suggestions coming out of the several working groups relating to documentation, the interpretation facilities, the schedule of meetings and so forth. I would like to consider these in a very positive manner because I feel that there is room for improvements, which can be made by redesigning the present way of doing things, and also by either acquiring more resources or organizing the use of resources in a better manner. In addition to the more narrowly logistical issues of conference servicing and documentation that we have to consider, it is also important to give some thought to the total structure of the organization, beginning from its conference, its intergovernmental mechanisms and the secretariat itself. On these very basic issues I do not wish to put before you any definitive proposals, but I do feel that it would be of use if I were to exchange some thoughts with you.

In regard to the Conference itself, we have had the practice of a major world conference occurring usually at four-yearly intervals. These world conferences have been seen by the international community to be major events. They have enjoyed a high degree of visibility among the public at large. There has been a great deal of expectation prior to the Conference, a high level of participation, and very large attendance. And yet, because of the great expectations raised, it has been observed that, perhaps without exception, each of the major sessions of UNCTAD has left behind a somewhat negative image of a failure to live up to expectations. Now, partly, this has been because the UNCTAD sessions have, without exception, tried to deal with the more difficult issues. The UNCTAD sessions have been concerned with what I call the "gut issues" facing relations between Member States in the international economic field. By their very nature, the issues have been difficult and the ability to come up with conclusions which would appear to be problem solving has been restricted. We ought to recognize that fact but I would not conclude from this that we should try to be more modest in regard to what the major conferences are trying to do and that we should shirk trying to flag major issues. But perhaps we ought to adopt a kind of procedure in which the results of a conference could be seen to be more definitive in the light of the inherent difficulties underlying the issues taken up. I have in particular two thoughts to put before you, perhaps three, which I would like you to consider. First, I was wondering whether it would not be possible, when a major conference convenes, for there to be some system whereby the proposals on which it is called upon to act could be prepared and presented in advance so that the governments could come to the conference with a full awareness of what it is they are asked to decide upon and agree to. As of today, despite the pre-conference preparations undertaken by the Groups, whether the Group of 77 or the OECD countries or the CMEA countries, although they come up in some cases with declarations and action programmes, they do not come up with proposals drafted as such. Often the drafting of the proposals themselves takes place once the Conference itself has convened. A glaring instance of what this involves occurred during UNCTAD V when the final resolution put up for action on item 8 of the agenda was presented in the last stages—I think on the Thursday—of a Conference scheduled to conclude on the Friday. This kind of procedure, I must confess, has a built-in guarantee of failure. If one really wants to get significant, meaningful decisions taken by the Conference on major issues, some mechanism ought to be devised whereby proposals, at least in draft form—which may of course be amended by the Conference, this is after all its task— could be presented in their totality to the Conference before the Conference convenes, allowing a sufficient amount of time for governments to know what these proposals are and how they propose to react to them when the Conference convenes. I think this is one issue to which some thought needs to be given.

A second suggestion—again this is not a definitive proposal, I am thinking aloud here—is whether it might not be beneficial to reverse the traditional procedure whereby ministers and high-level personalities are present at the commencement of the Conference and make statements in the general debate, and thereafter leave the work of the Conference—particularly the vital work of decision making—to the delegations which remain behind. Perhaps we are not making the best use of the presence of high-level policy makers and ministers by having a procedure in which they come at the commencement of the Conference and are not present when the real difficulties have emerged and the need is there for a process of negotiation. Would it be practical to have a procedure whereby the Conference begins at the level of senior officials in its first three weeks or so, with the senior ministers and other high-level personalities coming at the later stages when they could indeed make their general statements, but also be present when the final decision making takes place? This is a procedure which I noted is followed in other cases. Meetings of the non-aligned countries, for example, meetings of the OAU, and even meetings of the Group 77 at ministerial level, take this form of a first meeting of senior officials to be followed by a ministerial meeting in the concluding stages. I was wondering whether a procedure of that kind might not be more conducive to getting positive results out of a conference.

A third thought that occurred to me is whether there may not be some means of knitting together the results of a conference so that the decisions taken by the conference could be seen in their totality. Today it has struck me that the decisions of the conference take the form of a series of independent resolutions on various issues on the agenda. In some cases decisions have been taken by the conference, by consensus or by vote, in other cases no decisions have been taken, and in some other cases they have been referred to the Trade and Development Board. It is thus very difficult for the public at large, and even for governments, to really discern what has been the outcome of the conference. At UNCTAD I the Conference did end up with what was called a Final Act, and this Final Act put together in a single document all the resolutions and decisions taken by the Conference under its several headings. This Final Act, if I remember right, was even open for signature by the delegations. Again I am not making a proposal but this is something I would like to put before you for consideration, namely whether at the Conference itself we might not really work towards the adoption of a final act, a process which would be facilitated if the proposals themselves regarding what would go into the final act are drafted and made available in advance.

There is also the question of the permanent Committee of UNCTAD. I share the feeling which I have seen come out of the discussions of your group and the working groups, that in one way or another the permanent Committees of UNCTAD are perhaps not playing the role intended for them when they were established. After all, the Board itself and the Permanent Committees are part of the basic structure of UNCTAD and it is somehow not right that these permanent committees, and even the Board, should assume for themselves what is purely a management or housekeeping function. They were intended to be the focal points for substantive issues. We have to find some way in which this idea behind the role of the committees could be not only preserved but made more significant and real. I feel, of course, that there is much value in having a system of permanent committees, whether or not these merit regrouping, because the establishment or existence of a permanent committee is one way of recognizing the competence of UNCTAD as an organization in regard to the several subjects that are within its over-all mandate. The existence of an intergovernmental group involves an inherent and constant recognition on the part of governments that UNCTAD has a certain number of responsibilities within its mandate and that these subject areas are the concerns of permanent ongoing intergovernmental bodies of UNCTAD. In a world in which there is a great degree of pluralism in regard to the way in which the UN system functions, a great degree of duplication in regard to the work done by the different parts of that system, the existence of intergovernmental bodies is one element which adds a certain definitiveness to the role and mandate of UNCTAD.

I have no final thoughts about the possibility of regrouping these committees in order to reduce their number. In some of the documents that we have presented to you and to the Member Governments, even as early as UNCTAD IV, we did draw attention to the possiblity of a regrouping of the committees. But we should not exaggerate its importance and, in any event, in approaching this issue we should keep very much in the forefront of our minds the importance and relevance of the system of permanent committees so that in the process of regrouping we do not lose or diffuse the main rationale underlying the need for these committees.

There is one thought about the committees which I want to put to you. It has recently occurred to me that, even from the point of view of the secretariat, the present system of having the committees meet at intervals of one or two years spread throughout the calendar of UNCTAD does not really assist in giving a particular focus to the work of a committee. More often than not, and particularly in recent times, the main attention of UNCTAD as a secretariat has been on ongoing negotiations for which— rightly in my view—particular mechanisms have been set up, whether in the field of commodities, of the Common Fund, technology, restrictive business practices, multi-modal transport and so on. The main concern has been to make progress in these negotiations, and then when we find that a committee is scheduled to meet we see that with the negotiations already going on what the committee has to do is to address itself to a number of other issues, many of which are of a routine character. For that very reason it is very difficult for the secretariat itself to discern the priority which needs to be given to the meetings of a particular committee.

In this context, I was wondering whether there might not be some value in a new approach to the committees which might tend to bring them more sharply into focus and to give them more relevance in the work of UNCTAD. The thought I had in mind, and this is a rather radical thought, was whether it might not be a plausible idea to convene the meetings of the committees concurrently; whether we should not have one period of the year, an interval of three or four weeks, in which all the committees of UNCTAD would be meeting concurrently, so that we have during this one period a major event on which the secretariat and governments could focus. This concurrent meeting of committees could be preceded by a brief meeting of the Board and must certainly be succeeded by a regular meeting of the Board itself so that the committees themselves would be meeting as committees of the Board in an immediate and operational fashion in order to put before the latter issues for final decision. If we were able to do that it occurred to me that there are a number of advantages. For one thing it would make it possible for delegations to come from the capitals having in mind the whole gamut of UNCTAD issues at one point of time.

Secondly, it would also enable the secretariat—and the delegations—to see the interrelationship between the various issues coming up under the various committees, because these issues would then be the subject of action or decision making by the Board. It would also have the logistical advantage that having taken three or four weeks of the calendar for the meetings of the committees and the Board, the rest of the period—the other eleven months or so of the year—would be available for the organization and fulfilment of its more specific negotiating activities and for the execution of its work programme. In other words, the other eleven months would be clear for the meetings of the negotiating conferences, of preparatory meetings and so on. This period could be devoted to the implementation of work programmes without being cluttered up by the intervention of sporadic meetings of permanent committees. It seems to me that there is some attraction in this idea. I have not probed its implications to the full, but I thought that it was worth putting before you because if it does prove to be feasible and gain the acceptance of governments it might basically change the character of UNCTAD's work and give it more definition and more body.

Of course, one has to ask the question if the permanent committees and the Board were to meet in this fashion, how would it relate to the conference itself because it would have many of the facets of a conference now meeting every year. I feel that the answer needs to be explored, but it might pave the way for treating the conference itself in a different fashion, both affording an opportunity for the conference to focus on some major themes and thereby respond to the need for selectivity which has been expressed in many quarters at many times, and also enabling the conference to address itself to the major issues from the point of view of providing for the next period a new platform of thoughts and ideas which the permanent machinery could take up for development in the inter-conference period.

If we had this system we would be able to structure the conference itself in a different way and not have to respond to it simply because a conference is put into the calendar every four years so that some months prior to it we have to ask ourselves what issues should be put before the conference, what should be its agenda, and so on. The issue is one of the interrelationship between this new system of operation which I have been thinking about and the conference. I think it would lend itself to positive answers which would benefit both the conference and the functioning of the permanent machinery.

Once again, I do not want to say that these are firm proposals but I think it is the purpose of a meeting such as this to think aloud and to explore even boldly new ideas.

There is also the question of how the secretariat of UNCTAD should itself be adapted and geared to performing its tasks. I do appreciate two things that I have seen emerge from the work of your group. First, the understanding that the organization of the secretariat is essentially a matter for the Secretary-General himself; it is his prerogative and it is his responsibility. The responsibility for how the secretariat is able to deliver, how it can be organized, how it could be restructured cannot but be other than with the Secretary-General because he should not be in a position of having his responsibilities made the subject of decisions for which he is not responsible and of being able to take refuge, so to speak, behind these decisions. One has to be clear that the ultimate decisions on how the secretariat should be restructured, to respond to the demands of governments, is a responsibility of the Secretary-General himself.

But having said that, I would like to say very much that I do welcome helpful proposals and suggestions and ideas that might be made by groups or by Member Governments. After all, there are many delegations here who have a long association with UNCTAD's work, who have been able to see the secretariat's performance from the point of view of governments. Their reactions as to where we succeed, and where we fail, what our shortcomings are and how these might be put right, is something which would be of immense value to me. For that reason I welcome ideas and suggestions although the way in which the secretariat is organized must be the subject of decision making by the Secretary-General rather than governments themselves.

I have already been encouraged by a number of thoughts which have come out of your Committee. I was very much impressed by the attention that has been paid to the importance of long-term research. I think that it is right to draw attention to the need to strengthen this aspect of UNCTAD's work. Research has always been part of our concerns and our responsibilities but with the great preoccupation with negotiations and ongoing activities, the task of devoting attention to research has perhaps tended to decelerate in recent times. I believe that UNCTAD should be the source of new ideas, and that, even in recent times, UNCTAD has been generating new ideas. The whole concept of an integrated programme for commodities, the whole concept of a Common Fund, the ideas on the revision of the industrial property system, ideas relating to the brain drain, to the decommercialization of certain aspects of technology, ideas in the field of shipping—these have come out of UNCTAD in recent times. I do feel that we have not been absolutely remiss on this score. At the same time we could give even more attention than we have done to the analysis of long-term issues and long-term problems so that the scenario against which the activities of governments unfold could be better articulated, better defined. So on that score alone I welcome the ideas that you have put out. I also welcome the expression of desire on the part of delegations for closer contact with the secretariat, opportunities to make available the thinking of delegations to us and for us to make available our thinking to you. If we can find ways in which this process could be intensified, particularly in an informal way, this would be of great value and assistance.

I also very much appreciate the importance that you have given to the whole question of flexibility of operations. I have always been saying—and I have been saying this in New York as well as in Geneva—that there is a basic need for UNCTAD in terms of flexibility. The problem is that there is no set of rules or regulations in the UN system that deal with the requirements of a body like UNCTAD, which is not a specialized agency in the conventional sense and which is not at the same time a department of the United Nations secretariat in the sense that many of the departments of New York are. We are a secretariat which is servicing an intergovernmental organization, the Trade and Development Board, its permanent committees and all the subgroups that have been set up. We are in that sense a "quasi-agency", and it is one of the shortcomings of the present system that there is no body of rules to deal with the requirements of a "quasi-agency" which needs to have a certain degree of flexibility to respond to its functions, which cannot function on an absolute par with a department without the responsibilities of intergovernmental bodies, but which is not at the same time a specialized agency functioning in absolute autonomy on its own. This is one of the reasons why there have been so many problems in the search for flexibility for UNCTAD in its operation, whether it concerns personnel, budget or any other issue.

SELECTIVE INDEX

This index covers the majority of international meetings, institutions, countries, etc., referred to in the text. Terms are given, where appropriate, in both abbreviated form and in full so that the index also serves as a basic glossary. With a very few exceptions it does not refer to issues or technical terms which fall within UNCTAD's concerns or programme of activities. Nor are Santiago, Nairobi and Manila, as the sites of UNCTADs III, IV and V respectively, included.